*Epworth Com*

*General Editor*
Ivor H. Jones

# The Book of Genesis

# The Book of
# GENESIS

CLARE AMOS

EPWORTH

Extracts from the Revised English Bible are © 1989
by the Delegates of the Oxford University Press
and the Syndics of the Cambridge University Press
and are used by permission.

British Library Cataloguing in Publication data

A catalogue record of this book is available from
the British Library


0 7162 0584 X




First published in 2004
by Epworth Press
4 John Wesley Road
Werrington
Peterborough, PE4 7ZP

Typeset by Regent Typesetting, London
Printed and bound in Great Britain by
Biddles Ltd, *www.biddles.co.uk*

# CONTENTS

*Contents*

# GENERAL INTRODUCTION

The *Epworth Preacher's Commentaries* that Greville P. Lewis edited so successfully in the 1950s and 1960s having now served their turn, the Epworth Press has commissioned a team of distinguished academics who are also preachers and teachers to create a new series of commentaries that will serve readers into the twenty-first century. We have taken the opportunity offered by the publication in 1989 of the Revised English Bible to use this very readable and scholarly version as the basis of our commentaries, and we are grateful to the Oxford and Cambridge University Presses for the requisite licence and for granting our authors generous access. They will nevertheless be free to cite and discuss other translations wherever they think that these will illuminate the original text.

Just as the books that make up the Bible differ in their provenance and purpose, so our authors will necessarily differ in the structure and bearing of their commentaries. But they will all strive to get as close as possible to the intention of the original writers, expounding their texts in the light of the place, time, circumstances and culture that gave them birth, and showing why each work was received by Jews and Christians into their respective Canons of Holy Scripture. They will seek to make full use of the dramatic advance in biblical scholarship world-wide but at the same time to explain technical terms in the language of the common reader, and to suggest ways in which Scripture can help towards the living of a Christian life today. They will endeavour to produce commentaries that can be used with confidence in ecumenical, multiracial and multifaith situations, and not by scholars only but by preachers, teachers, students, church members and anyone who wants to improve his or her understanding of the Bible.

Ivor H. Jones

# PREFACE

It has been an enjoyable, though also challenging, experience to work on this commentary over the past few years. I would particularly like to thank Ivor Jones and the Epworth Committee for the confidence they showed in me in asking me to attempt it. I am also very aware of how much I owe to Cyril Rodd and Natalie Watson of Epworth Press for the assistance they have given. They both demonstrated exemplary care and interest, and gave support which went well beyond what one might justifiably expect from an editorial team. In particular I am grateful for Cyril Rodd's detailed scrutiny of the work as it progressed. His amazing eye for detail was invaluable.

I owe an immense debt of gratitude to the Ecole Biblique in Jerusalem where I did my postgraduate studies. Unlike many institutions of higher learning the Ecole Biblique was a place where one was encouraged first of all to look closely at the biblical text rather than books about it! My teachers there, especially Father Jerry Murphy O'Connor, were an inspiration for the way in which they held together scholarly wisdom and religious commitment.

I would like to thank Ted Todd, Verne Fletcher, John McCullough and Rupert Hoare for all having the courage at various times to appoint me to teaching situations in which I could discover how much I enjoyed communicating my love of the Bible. I also remember the many students in Jerusalem, Beirut, Cambridge, Kent and South London, from whom I have learned as much as I have shared.

In recent years I have had the privilege of working in the field of interfaith relations. This commitment and concern is apparent, I believe, in the commentary. I am grateful to colleagues such as Michael Ipgrave, David Marshall, Susanne Mitchell and Andrew Wingate, who have given me the confidence to believe that my exploration of the Bible could help to resource thinking about the Christian approach to other faiths.

If there is one thing I hope about this commentary, it is that it is not divorced from the experience of my whole life so far, including a significant number of years spent in the Middle East. My husband Alan was my companion through several of those years, and all the time since. It is in company with him, and more recently with our son Robin, that my theology has been worked out and wrestled over. Together with Alan I am still in process of discovering what may be the full meaning of Genesis 2.24.

Clare Amos
August 2004

# ABBREVIATIONS

| | |
|---|---|
| AV | Authorized Version |
| JSOTSS | Journal for the Study of the Old Testament: Supplement Series |
| LXX | The Septuagint Greek Translation of the Hebrew Bible |
| NRSV | New Revised Standard Version |
| REB | Revised English Bible |

# INTRODUCTION

One of the defining and most memorable moments of the history of the twentieth century was the day, a few months before Neil Armstrong set his 'small step' on the surface of the moon, when Apollo 8 circled the moon for the first time on Christmas Eve 1968. Television cameras on board the spaceship beamed back to earth awesome pictures of our planet as it appeared from the perspective of space, and a disembodied voice began to read from the Bible.

The passage that was chosen was not the account of the birth of Christ, nor even the Prologue of John's Gospel which sets Christ within a cosmic context. Instead the astronaut on that small spaceship, set in the skies by all the scientific skills and technical knowledge of the twentieth century AD, read the first chapter of a book that was more than 2000 years old, and came from what would normally be considered a pre-scientific culture. He read Genesis 1, a chapter which recounts in solemn cadences the story of the creation of those heavens and that earth.

I, like many others who heard those words being read to us from a quarter of a million miles away, was deeply moved. There was a rightness to the choice of the book of Genesis, not simply because Genesis 1 is a story of 'heavens and earth', but also because Genesis is an inheritance which belongs to humanity as a whole, even those who would not consider themselves to be overtly religious. There is a 'tingle factor' to Genesis that is wider than church or cult, which reaches beyond those whose faith is expressed within an institutional framework. For Genesis continues to point human beings towards the eternal dimension which underpins all human existence, to challenge us to ask the fundamental questions about the origin and meaning of life.

So it is a privilege and a responsibility to write a commentary on the book of Genesis precisely because it is a book of such potential (and actual) power. It can be a tool for good; it has also been dreadfully misused. It can kill faith as well help to create it. Those who teach or preach from the Book of Genesis need to be acutely aware of this.

Genesis begins with an ambiguity. Its title in the Hebrew Bible is *berĕ'shit* (the opening phrase of the book in Hebrew). But does that mean 'In the beginning', which is how it is normally read, or 'In the beginning of' which is how the NRSV takes it? Is the ambiguity significant? Perhaps it helps to remind us that Genesis was never simply a piece of writing about the remote past, about *the* beginning of things. It is always a living kerygma, a proclamation about God's redeeming activity. References back to creation are inspired by a concern to know the creator in the present: to know the way of God's working with humankind.

Genesis is a story which is continually reborn in every age. The existentialist movement has freed up our thinking, and allowed a new access to the Genesis stories. We are enabled to see that it is a telling of 'beginnings': of the forces of creation and renewal in the here and now.

Genesis speaks to us first of a Middle East, and then of a world, which is ridden with violence and radically unhealed. To address this violent world of reality, it holds up a number of powerful 'myths', the very telling of which is a way of singing hope into existence, of recalling humankind to remembrance of the overarching wings of the Creator God, and pointing us forward to the new possibilities and potentialities which derive from grace.

One of the ironies of Genesis is that this book of 'beginning' probably owes a great deal to times in Israel's history when the people's future existence was in question. Further comments on dates and sources can be found in the notes about 'Structure, sources, dates and contexts' on p. xviii, but the basic premise which undergirds this commentary is that the first impetus to gather together in a connected written form the traditions which now make up Genesis took place during the exilic period. The text was then edited and re-edited over a number of centuries, and may have assumed its *very* final form in another epoch of national threat, the Maccabean period. Genesis' re-telling of the 'beginning' at times when the 'end' seemed likely was a statement of hope for the future. It may be that Genesis has a message for our age too, a time when the relevance of tradition is called into question and when the Christian churches sometimes feel that they can do little more than carry on carrying 'Joseph's bones'.

## *The standpoint of this commentary*

1. I write as an Old Testament scholar working from within the Christian tradition and with an intended audience of those who broadly speaking also live and work within this context. There are two implications to be drawn from this statement.

    a. I regard it as a legitimate part of my remit to address the question of the relevance of Genesis within the life of the Church today. The story of the interpretation of Genesis in the Christian and Jewish communities over the last 2,000 years is a key part of the interpretative process. If Genesis was originally written 'from faith to faith' such an approach is truer to the spirit of its composition than a merely archaeological and historical survey of the book.

    b. I write as a Christian scholar of the Old Testament rather than a Jewish scholar of the 'Hebrew Bible'. This is not to say that I am unaware of Jewish interpretation of the Book of Genesis. At many points in this commentary it will be clear how much I am indebted to such interpretation. I firmly believe that Jews and Christians need to study what we Christians call the 'Old Testament' in an ongoing ecumenical dialogue with each other. At the same time I believe that studying Genesis as the first book of the Old Testament is a qualitatively different exercise from reflecting on it as the keystone of the Jewish Torah. The very terminology 'Old Testament' is a reminder that Christians read Genesis as part of a whole which includes for example, the Gospel of John and the Book of Revelation (both of which impact upon a reading of Genesis).

2. This commentary is not intended to compete with Westermann's *magnum opus*, the great three-volume commentary on the book of Genesis, nor even Westermann's cut down one-volume version! They are both superb works, and those who are encouraged by using the current book to explore Genesis further could not do better than to turn in Westermann's direction (see suggestions for further reading on p. xxiv).

    But the scope and purpose of this commentary is different. It is (along with the rest of the current Epworth series) a commentary on the REB translation of the book of Genesis. I have however where appropriate also referred to Hebrew words, expressions and phrases, partly because one of the fascinating features of the story of Genesis is the writer's delight in wordplay, punning on the meaning of a Hebrew word in a manner that is inevitably lost through translation. It is a particular characteristic of the Hebrew language to draw connections between words that share the same fundamental two or three consonants. If you look at the standard footnotes of the REB text you will find that some of these wordplays are actually noted in the footnotes, which helps to justify my decision to refer to them.

3. This commentary reflects some of the important developments in Old Testament and pentateuchal scholarship which have come about since Westermann's commentary first appeared in German in 1974. There has been an increased concern to look at the Bible and its individual books more holistically, exploring the story they are trying to tell us as a whole rather than engaging in the kind of 'excavative' scholarship which was overconcerned to break down the material into smaller units and spend time continually delving for sources.

As a part of the more holistic nature of biblical scholarship in the last 20 years a concern with the literary or story qualities of the material has become significant. I have found this an illuminating and refreshing approach and have tried to reflect this in the course of this commentary (though steering clear of the very technical vocabulary of some of the more modern literary critics). It is a challenge to any commentary writer to encourage, rather than impede, people in 'reading the story whole'. Reading the story is not simply an intellectual activity. Rather, the reader is caught up imaginatively by the story, and enters into the story and its world. The reader becomes a participant in its drama. By reading the story in this way, we assimilate the world of the story so that it becomes a world in which, progressively, we feel ourselves to be at home.

Alongside this recent interest, both academic and popular, in 'story' there have also developed particular hermeneutical concerns such as feminist perspectives on Genesis and the use of the book in liberation studies.

I certainly write as a woman, and I have been affected and stimulated by the work of scholars such as Phyllis Trible. I am sure that this commentary would read rather differently if I were a man. But I feel that it would be unhelpful and untrue to Genesis to segment out 'women's insights' or 'feminist perspectives' into a separate section, and so I have not done so. From the first chapter of the book we hear about 'male and female' together, and it is through the dynamic interaction of men and women that much of the story is carried along.

There is a tension here that it is important to acknowledge. Part of the re-birthing of Genesis in each age, must be that each age's concerns are and can be reflected. I have found that to be true in my own experience. My early adulthood was spent in the Middle East, both Jerusalem and Lebanon. It was a formative experience for me. I cannot now read the Old Testament without being reminded of modern Middle Eastern attitudes, practices and political concerns. When I say that Genesis is potentially a *dangerous* book, this is certainly part of what I have in mind. In the Middle East today real people really get killed in part because of beliefs some human beings may hold about the book of Genesis. I will never forget my incredulity at being told by a Palestinian friend of mine, an educated Christian woman from Ramallah, a town on the West Bank, how on a visit to Jerusalem she had had a conversation with a Western tourist. On discovering that she was a Christian living on the West Bank this person had informed her, quite categorically, that 'she couldn't be a real Christian, because if she were a real Christian she would of course have been willing to leave her hometown, since she would know that God had given the land to the descendants of Abraham, Isaac and Jacob'. One of the features of Genesis is the way in which it seeks to draw together universality and particularity: and the Middle East today is a region where the 'scandal of particularity' can feel truly scandalous.

The Middle Eastern context is in my bones and I make no apology for the way that it has impacted upon this commentary. But once again I have sought to explore this dimension as part of the whole picture rather than regarding it as a separate hermeneutical starting point.

If there is one overriding hermeneutical principle that undergirds this commentary, it is that our interpretation and understanding of Genesis must be linked in some way to the God who is *I AM that I am* (Exod. 3.14) who refuses to become a puppet for human beings yet from the beginning has been gracious in revelation. The mysteriousness and at times illogicality of God and of Genesis are not to be despaired of, but are there for wonder and for hope. In the questions themselves are the answers that the writers of Genesis have provided.

## Structure, sources, dates and contexts

It is an exciting time to be writing a commentary on Genesis. This is largely due to the fact that the source-critical theory about the origin of the Pentateuch associated with the names of Karl Heinrich Graf and Julius Wellhausen, which dominated Old Testament scholarship for more than a century, has, in the last couple of decades, come under serious challenge. The scholarly consensus has almost completely broken down. No longer is it appropriate for example, when producing work on Genesis, to assume the existence of a tenth century 'J' (Yahwist) source. Similarly there have been questions about the dates or existence of the other sources, 'E' (Elohist) and 'P' (Priestly). Indeed the issue of whether we can talk about sources at all, or whether we should rather think of one creative mind producing this great work, perhaps drawing on well-known tales and traditions, has been raised by a number of scholars, most notably R. N. Whybray in *The Making of the Pentateuch*.[1] The only thing that is certain is that we are in a time when certainties have disappeared.

The corollary of this however is that there has been considerable interest in the 'final form' of Genesis – as it appears in our Bibles. The format of this present commentary highlights the 'final form' and structure of the biblical book.

One of the features of Genesis is that the word *toledot* appears at ten key points in the narrative, and seems to be designed to mark where one section ends and another begins. This word *toledot*, which is variously translated as 'account', 'list', 'descendants', 'story', 'table' appears at 2.4; 5.1; 6.9; 10.1; 11.10; 11.27; 25.12; 25.19; 36.1 (repeated 36.9); 37.2. Of these ten instances of the word, five introduce a narrative section (often lengthy) and five a genealogy or genealogy with a short narrative. Five of them appear in 1.1—11.26, the part of Genesis often designated as the 'primeval story' and five in 11.27—50.26, the part of the book which focuses on the story of Israel's ancestors. Given the interest of Genesis in number patterns this is probably not accidental. The shape of the book is constructed for us by this word.

---

*Genesis at a glance*
(*In this table the word* toledot *is designated by the letter 'T'*)

PRIMEVAL STORY
**Section One: Creation and the antediluvian period**
Gen. 1.1—2.4 – Prologue
Gen. 2.4 T – introducing story (2.4—4.26)
Gen. 5.1 T – introducing genealogy and short narrative (5.1—6.8)
**Section Two: The flood and its aftermath**
Gen. 6.9 T – introducing story (6.9—9.29)
Gen. 10.1 T – introducing genealogy and short narrative (10.1—11.9)
Gen. 11.10 T – introducing genealogy (11.10–11.26)

STORY OF ISRAEL'S ANCESTORS
**Section Three: The story of Abraham (Terah's descendants)**
Gen. 11.27 T – introducing story (11.27—25.11)
Gen. 25.12 T – introducing genealogy (25.12–18)
**Section Four: The story of Jacob (Isaac's descendants)**
Gen. 25.19 T – introducing story (25.19—35.29)
Gen. 36.1 T (repeated 36.9) – introducing genealogy (36.1–43)
**Section Five: The story of Jacob's sons**
Gen. 37.2 T – introducing story (37.1—50.26)

---

By taking this pattern as our starting point for understanding Genesis we gain some important insights.

1. The English (and Greek) name of the book of Genesis is highly appropriate. Genesis literally means 'birth' and the word *toledot* comes from a Hebrew root which means to 'beget' or 'give birth to'. Genesis is a tale in which 'birth' will be important. The first instruction of God to humanity is *Be fruitful and increase* (1.28). Genesis tells the story of how this instruction, and God's blessing which accompanies it, operates in the story of creation and especially humanity. Life, of which birth is such a central part, will survive flood, divine curse, infertility and famine.

2. It is remarkable that several of the genealogies relate to a wider or different group than the leading characters featured in the narrative

material. 25.12–18 lists the descendants of Ishmael, and 36.1–43 those of Esau. 10.1–32 includes the descendants of Ham and Japheth as well as Shem. Genesis is interested in their destinies, as well as the fate of the offspring of Abraham, Isaac and Jacob. The very structure of Genesis therefore challenges any narrow focus on a chosen family or race. It is particularly striking that this point is made specifically through the use of genealogies, since genealogical status seems to have become a key marker for membership of the Jewish community during the post-exilic period. To employ a 'genealogical' device to structure the overall book in this way feels subversive. It raises important questions about inclusivism and exclusivism for both Judaism and Christianity.

3. If there are five examples of the word *toledot* in each of the primeval and ancestral parts of Genesis, it may well be that the *middle* example is particularly important in each case. Ancient narratives were often structured to direct their readers' attention to a mid point. In Genesis this certainly seems to be the case for specific sections of the book (See further on the Abraham story on p. 73 and Jacob on p. 160). It has been suggested that this feature also applies to the overall structure of Genesis, and therefore the story of the flood (in the primeval story) and that of Jacob (in the ancestral history) are both thrown into particular focus. Both sections may be particularly important therefore if we want to explore the impetus and context that brought Genesis to birth.

## The origins of Genesis: a working hypothesis

In spite of the work of scholars such as R. N. Whybray, it is likely that the book as a whole was composed over several centuries. The following is a possible description of the history of the book.

1. The kernel of the book originated among the Jewish community in Babylonia, during or slightly after the period of the exile (*c.*586–538 BC). Motifs such as the Garden of Eden and the flood have clear links to a Babylonian context, and may at times even show dependence on Babylonian or Mesopotamian literature. This could also have been the time when the figure of Abraham first became important as a 'national' figure – it is notable how little Abraham appears in those parts of the Old Testament which seem to be pre-exilic in origin. It is also clear that the adoption of Abraham as national ancestor was not universally popular (see Isa. 63.16), and may have

been due to the influence of a particular group among the exiles with links to Hebron, or the royal house. Stories about Jacob however seem to have been told widely as traditional tales over several centuries before the exile (see Hos. 12.3–4). They too are reworked at this time, so that the adventures of this ancestor increasingly reflect the fortunes of the nation whose name he was to take (32.28). The exile is a time when both 'flood' and the story of an ancestor who was forced to travel to Mesopotamia and travel back again would be very relevant.

2. The book continues to be developed during the Persian period (538–332 BC) and reflects some of the tensions and struggles of this time. In particular this was a period when the relationship between 'Israel' and the people of Edom was highly ambiguous, with an awareness on the one hand of the close affinity of the two peoples, but also intense hostility. Yet it was recognised that Yнwн himself was a deity with close links with Edom (Deut. 33.2; Judg. 5.4). The enmity with Edom was exacerbated as a result of ongoing Edomite control over southern Palestine and the increasing emphasis on Abraham's association with Hebron/Beersheba may be intended as a counterweight to this.

Even within the community of 'Israel' varied viewpoints were at play. It is far from certain that the primacy of Jerusalem and its temple was universally accepted at this period. Worship seems to have been offered to Yнwн at both Bethel and Shechem/Gerizim, and the importance given to these sites within Genesis may reflect the voice of 'priestly' groups who were not Jerusalem orientated. In particular the rigorous exclusivism that seems to have been practised at Jerusalem (e.g. Ezra) appears to have been gently challenged at various points in Genesis. Stories such as those of Abimelech (20.1–18; 21.22–34) or Dinah (34) are told with an awareness that 'Israel' needed to co-exist with other peoples of the land.

3. At some point the developing book was edited by an individual or group who moved it a long way towards its final form. This stage was also the time when further material was produced or incorporated into the existing narrative, for example 1.1—2.4; some of the genealogical material; parts of the flood story; 17.1–27; probably 23.1–20; 27.46—28.9; 35.9–15; and probably 46.1–27. The 'style' of these sections is distinctive, and would traditionally be described as 'priestly', though again their location was not necessarily Jerusalem. They may have been based in Babylon/Mesopotamia (see especially

27.46—28.9). This group may well have been responsible for the overall *toledot* structure of the book.

4. The extensive story of Joseph was added after most of the rest of the book was complete. This could have happened during the Hellenistic period, perhaps between 300 and 200 BC, a time when Palestine was ruled by the Ptolemies of Egypt. In adding this story an earlier briefer account of Jacob and his sons may have been displaced. (Traces of this earlier account may be found, for example in chapter 46.) The purpose of the additional material about Joseph was to explain how and why the family of Jacob came to be in Egypt and thus act as a bridge into the Book of Exodus.

5. Finally the chronological data (ages of the ancestors, etc.) in the form in which we now have them was added either in the late third century BC or, more likely, in the first half of the second century BC. The chronology of the patriarchs' ages is intricately worked out – apparently to a precise schema. Detailed analysis of the numbers and dates involved suggests a. that they may be linked to a calendar which was only introduced in Egypt by the decree of Canopus in 238 BC[2]; b. that the key dates of Genesis seem to form part of an elaborate time frame in which the Exodus happens in the year 2666 (after the creation of the world) and the year 4000 (the length of a 'great year' in ancient astronomy) would fall in 164 BC – the date when the temple was rededicated by the Maccabees and the Feast of Hanukkah was established.[3] It is unlikely that this is accidental – and the chronology of Genesis as we now have it seems designed to point to this event in the Maccabean period as the culmination of history. Some would also link the story of the adventures of Abraham in Gen. 14 to this time. It is however important to point out that the chronology in the Septuagint (Greek translation) and the Samaritan version of the Pentateuch both differ from that in the Masoretic text (the Hebrew version on which our English translations are based) and that the chronology as we now have it in Genesis may be a later revision of a previously existing earlier version.

In summary, the Book of Genesis came into existence during the exilic and post-exilic period and its content reflects concerns and challenges that were faced by the community during this time. It was written during a period when Judaism had spread beyond the boundaries of Palestine: the voices of the Jewish community in Babylonia, and perhaps also Jews who had close links with Egypt, are heard, as well as those living within Palestine itself. The story of post-exilic Judaism is echoed in its pages. Indeed part of its fascination lies in the fact that no other portion of the Bible addresses the tension between universality and particularity quite as compellingly as does Genesis.

# FURTHER READING

Among commentaries the following may be noted:

Claus Westermann's commentaries on Genesis have a 'classic' status and provide an essential point of reference, even if certain of the conclusions about dating and sources would now be challenged. His three-volume commentary on the Hebrew text: *Genesis 1–11*, Minneapolis, MN: Augsburg, 1984; *Genesis 12–36*, Minneapolis, MN: Augsburg, 1985; *Genesis 37–50*, Minneapolis, MN: Augsburg, 1986 is unrivalled, but is probably too detailed for those relying entirely on English translation. However the one-volume abridged version *Genesis* is accessible in paperback, published by T. & T. Clark (now part of the Continuum Group), 1988.

Gerhard von Rad, *Genesis*, London: SCM Press, 1961, revised edition 1972, is notable for the way in which it interweaves biblical scholarship and Lutheran theological reflection.

Similar in intent to von Rad, but more recent, is W. Brueggemann, *Genesis*, Atlanta: John Knox Press, 1982.

Not precisely a commentary, the two Sheffield Old Testament Guides on Genesis address a number of key issues in an accessible way: J. Rogerson, *Genesis 1–11*, Sheffield: Sheffield Academic Press, 1991, and R. W. L. Moberly, *Genesis 12–50*, Sheffield: Sheffield Academic Press, 1992. They are now also published as part of a composite volume, along with the Old Testament Guide on Exodus.

For those who wish to know more about the Pentateuch as a whole the following three books can be recommended:

Joseph Blenkinsopp, *The Pentateuch: An Introduction to the First Five Books of the Bible*, London: SCM Press, 1992.

David J. A. Clines, *The Theme of the Pentateuch*, Sheffield: Sheffield Academic Press, 1997 (2nd edition).

E. W. Nicholson, *The Pentateuch in the Twentieth Century*, Oxford: Clarendon Press, 1967.

Two translations that are particularly designed to help the English reader feel closer to the Hebrew idiom of Genesis:

Mary Phil Korsak, *At the Start . . . Genesis Made New*, Louvain: Leuvense Schrijversaktie, 1992, aims to provide a translation as literal as is possible in English.

Robert Alter, *Genesis*, New York: W. W. Norton & Company, 1996, is a translation with short commentary notes.

The following deal with particular parts of the book or themes raised within it:

M. G. Brett, *Genesis: Procreation and the Politics of Identity*, London and New York: Routledge, 2000, provides a 'reading' of Genesis which understands it as resistance literature against the ethnocentrism of the Persian period.

W. Lee Humphreys, *The Character of God in the Book of Genesis: A Narrative Appraisal*, Louisville: Westminster John Knox Press, 2001, considers how God functions as a character in the story of Genesis.

Trevor Dennis, *Looking God in the Eye: Encountering God in Genesis*, London: SPCK, 1998, contains very accessible reflections on the interrelationship between God and human beings at key points of Genesis.

Ellen Van Wolde, *Genesis 1–11 and Other Creation Stories*, London: SCM Press, 1996, looks at the creation stories, particularly aware of the interaction between human beings and the earth.

Karl-Josef Kuschel, *Abraham: A Symbol of Hope for Jews, Christians and Muslims*, London: SCM Press, 1995, offers a reflection on the various ways the figure of Abraham is used in the faiths that are often linked to his name.

Jon D. Levenson, *The Death and Resurrection of the Beloved Son: The Transformation of Child Sacrifice in Judaism and Christianity*, New Haven and London: Yale University Press, 1993, offers an exquisitely written and profound reflection on the motif of the actual or metaphorical sacrifice of a son as it appears in the biblical tradition, and especially in Genesis.

Thomas Mann, *Joseph and His Brothers*, London: Vintage, 1999, is a classic novel which elucidates the Jacob and Joseph stories in some unexpected ways. The details given are for the paperback edition.

# The Story of Beginnings
## 1.1—6.8

As we begin to read Gen. 1.1—6.4 we find ourselves listening to a song of creation. It is as though the writers of these chapters are part of a choir singing the song, standing in a line with others behind and in front of them. They borrow images and themes from other creation narratives in the ancient Middle East, in particular from the Babylonian geographical milieu. But even though Genesis transforms much of what is received, we are still allowed to hear echoes of earlier viewpoints, both Israelite and non-Israelite. Sometimes as in Gen. 1.1—2.4a these echoes are muted, at other points as with the cherubim of Gen. 3.22 or the strange story of the sons of the gods in Gen. 6.1–4 they can ring loudly or even discordantly on our ears.

So the early chapters of Genesis provide a model for those in every age who are prepared to deepen their own faith by listening to the sounds that other religious traditions can sing. The attitude they contain also acts as an implicit critique to those who would treat these pages as an absolute and unqualified statement of how the world scientifically came into being. For if you seek to read them flatly, on the one prosaic level, you are not really hearing the subtle orchestra of tones that empower them. Genesis will be a book in which the need for 'true' listening will be very important. These chapters offer us the overture.

### The song of the seven days
#### 1.1—2.4a

This magnificent chapter forms an awe-inspiring prologue to the Book of Genesis. It is also significant that it has come to introduce the Old Testament and the whole of the Bible. It is the intended starting point of the biblical story. It is deliberately placed before what is apparently an alternative account of creation in Gen. 2.4b—3.24.

1

Whoever wrote the measured and solemn 'liturgical' prose of
Gen. 1 was aware of what was to come next. They knew that the picture offered of the story of Eden in the next chapter was coloured very
differently. But they chose to give us first what we have received in
Gen. 1.

It is likely that Gen. 1.1—2.4a and 2.4b—3.24 stem from different
hands, possibly writing several centuries apart, and that this can help
explain the different style and feel of the two accounts. But the authors
of Gen. 1 knew full well what was to come next and deliberately gave
us this first chapter with its contrasting feel, not because they were
careless or unaware of surface inconsistencies.

The creation of the world and of human beings within it includes
paradox, and by setting Gen. 1 alongside Gen. 2 we are being reminded of this. We are both in the 'image of God' (whatever that may mean,
see pp. 11 and 40) and of 'the dust of the earth'. It is the glory and the
tragedy of the human condition that this is so. By beginning Genesis
with these two contrasting pictures, the authors of Genesis have set
out the vision that Ps. 8.4–5 expressed in a brief poetic couplet: *What is
a frail mortal, that you should be mindful of him . . . Yet you have made little
less than a god*.

When we read Gen. 1.1—2.4a it can feel as though we are standing in a
vast cathedral. Soaring above us are the heavens and their luminaries.
Around us the walls are coloured with pictures of the varieties of
plant and animal creation. There is an ethereal choir humming almost
wordlessly, and there is a voice which, as so often in a cathedral, you
cannot see, declaiming solemnly, chanting creation into being.

It is no accident that such a picture might spring to mind. The
authors of this passage inhabited a world in which cathedrals – or
rather temples, their ancient equivalent – were at the heart of religious, intellectual, cultural and economic life. It is possible that this
chapter was originally written for use in temple worship. It is prose
which stands on the borders of poetry and liturgy. We know that
other ancient creation stories were closely linked to worship. Such
stories told of the activities of the gods, and temple liturgies offered
the place and the time for human beings to come into contact with the
divine and be blessed.

Those who composed Gen. 1 probably knew the Babylonian creation story, *Enuma Elish*, which formed part of the temple liturgy in
Babylon, though they also offer a challenge to it. Creation stories,
such as *Enuma Elish*, were primarily interested in the past in order to

2

understand and sustain the present. 'Order' was what was desired: order over against the chaos and unpredictability of much of ancient life. People in the ancient Middle Eastern world were confronted with the turbulence of the annual floods of the Tigris-Euphrates rivers which could be both life-giving and death-dealing, with impotence in the face of most human illnesses, with the fragile veneer which constituted stable civilisation. Kings and temples had key roles in society to act as the guarantors of longed-for order. Reciting creation stories was also a way of bringing about stability, their telling reinforcing the 'order' of the present and dreaming hopes for the future into being.

So too those who authored Gen. 1 were concerned to portray or even help to create an ordered cosmos. We can debate their precise geographical and chronological context. Because of their connection with the world of priests they are often referred to as 'P'. Writing either in an exilic, or more likely post-exilic, context they were very aware of what a chaotic experience the exile had been: cherished theological and political traditions had been challenged, the people's very existence had been called into question. Some of the ways in which this concern for 'order' (and specifically the priestly view of 'order') is expressed in Gen. 1 include:

- A fascination with numbers and number patterns, linked to the way that numbers form part of the fabric of the regular pattern of human life and of the structure of the universe. The numbers 'ten' (ten fingers), 'seven' (the traditional seven planets), and 'three' were regarded as key elements of life. The number 'two' also had a particular importance, because it was the natural product of 'dividing'.
- A concern that different features of the universe should be 'separated' from each other. The very word 'separate' used in this chapter is characteristic of priestly vocabulary. It was a key task of priests to ensure that different elements with different qualities should be kept apart, e.g. the clean/unclean, the holy/common, and so God as creator is being described in priestly terms. The process of separation is good – creation proceeds by the recognition and naming of opposites, which in turn enables new forms of existence to take shape.
- The complementary patterning of the six days in which creation takes place, into two sets of three.
- The structuring of time and the narrative to emphasise the importance of the Sabbath day.

3

- The interest in genealogies hinted at in 2.4a and which runs through the book of Genesis will also be a symptom of these authors' quest for 'order'. Genealogies help to link people to their roots, particularly rootless people who have experienced exile, or are in diaspora. They can also help to ensure that only the right kind of people are chosen for a role: for example, priests needed to prove their fitness by tracing their ancestry. The time of Ezra and Nehemiah in the post-exilic period saw great interest in genealogies, in order to ensure ethnic purity.

And yet in spite of this desire for an 'ordered' world, both Gen. 1.1—2.4a itself, and the rest of Genesis, will help to subvert it. The neat patterns of numbers and words will almost work – but not quite; the outsiders, who one would not expect to be cherished if purity is paramount, will not only be allowed a place in the story, but become fundamental to it. Such is the God of Genesis, who will insist on being allowed to work in some surprising and unexpected ways.

1.1–2 *In the beginning*: There is no end to the beginning of Genesis. The book begins with a conundrum. How should we translate the first Hebrew phrase in this book, *bere'shit*, which does not actually include the word 'the' before 'beginning'? Some modern versions such as the NRSV seek to reflect this by making this first verse subordinate to vv. 2–3 rather than treating v. 1 as a separate sentence. But this translation in turn does not do justice to the full strength of the following word *created*. The REB has chosen therefore the traditional *In the beginning God created the heavens and the earth*.

Underlying this debate about language is an important theological issue. What is the grammar of creation? Is God here creating everything absolutely out of nothingness, *ex nihilo*, or is God's creation rather the bringing of form and order to an already existing chaotic morass? Was there already an earth, in the form of a vast waste, before God began the process of creation? The *Enuma Elish*, for example, speaks of creation in such a manner. The squelchy sea-monster Tiamat is torn apart to provide the raw material out of which the god Marduk fashions the world and its creatures. The *deep* (Hebrew: *tehom*) that is covered by darkness (1.2) may well be a word deliberately chosen to remind us of the Babylonian Tiamat, so are our writers of Genesis also thinking of creation in similar terms? Probably; but the particular attempts of translations such as the NRSV to emphasise this by link-

4

ing together vv. 1 and 2 fail to do complete justice to the power of this sentence at the beginning of the Bible's story.

One alternative way of understanding v. 1 is as a prologue summary to the rest of this chapter, rather as Gen. 1 is itself a prologue for the rest of the book. A careful reading of the REB translation of these verses allows for ambiguity. It is not necessary to suggest that v. 2 follows on sequentially from v. 1. We are metaphorically standing outside our world and its creation – looking at it from a distance, as did those Apollo 8 astronauts as they circumnavigated the moon in December 1968. But the telescope that we are peering through in this chapter collapses time as well as space. Can we properly speak of *the* beginning before time itself has begun ('time' will not be created until Days One and Four)? Perhaps that is the reason why 'the' is absent in the Hebrew text, though the limitations of English do not fully allow us to reflect this. And perhaps it is *a* rather than *the* beginning precisely because it is the start of a process that will be ongoing. We are being offered a perspective on the ultimate goal of creation – as well as its development. In the New Testament John 5.17 draws on this part of Genesis to reflect that creation is not yet complete – for the Father is working still.

It may well be that the *vast waste* and *deep* were believed to exist in some fashion before the word of God spoke to them and shaped them. And yet, did they ever really exist apart from God? For even before God spoke the *spirit of God* hovered over the chaos. The participle *hovered* somehow takes us out of time. The Hebrew word *ruah* can mean 'spirit', 'wind' and 'breath'. It expresses and sums up the force of life. It can be intensely personal spirit – or impersonal power. Yet even if we picture what is happening as a mighty wind swirling like a storm on the surface of the planet, it is still an intended sign that God is and always has been intimately involved with all that is, whether good or evil.

Perhaps those who composed this chapter wanted to begin their story with a mystery. There certainly will be others to come. The God we meet in the first verses of Genesis both transcends the created universe, and yet also eternally cherishes it, hovering over it like a mother bird (compare Deut. 32.11 – which uses the same word *hovers* to describe the Lord's care for his people). It is notable that the Hebrew word translated as *hovered* is expressed in a feminine form.

It is paradoxical but important both to say that God created *ex nihilo* and to acknowledge God as working with and through chaos. The one affirms that the nothing in the universe is outside the will

5

and power of God. The other is a reminder that God can bring good out of whatever mess humans beings and the created order find themselves in.

The language of the beginning of Genesis is echoed at various points in the New Testament. Most clearly in John 1.1–18, but also in Col. 1.15–20, and probably in the use of the word *beginning* in Mark 1.1 and the description of the *first* of Jesus' signs in John 2.11. When the word *beginning* occurs in several of these New Testament examples it is clear that what is meant is a process rather than a particular point in time. May not this be helpful as we reflect on that mysterious *beginning* at the start of Gen. 1.1? For all the emphasis of the words that will be used to describe the completion of creation (2.1–3) this account encourages us to look to the future rather than cast our eyes solely on the past.

*God created*: The world as we now know it owes its shape to God. *Create* (Hebrew: *bara'*) in the Old Testament is a word that is only ever used with God as its subject. It has been deliberately chosen by the author of this chapter to affirm God's absolute responsibility for the entire created universe, and it will appear a significant seven times in the narrative up to 2.4a. The word which is used for God, *Elohim*, itself reminds us of God's universality. This is a generic word for 'God' rather than the name of Israel's own special deity. In many creation stories in the ancient Middle East there was a focus on the author's own people or particular god. But that nationalistic element is largely missing from this account. So too is any real sense of struggle between God and other divine figures, which is remarkable when Gen. 1 is compared with other texts such as *Enuma Elish,* which link creation to a heavenly war. It is also suggestive that the word *Elohim* is formally plural, even though it normally appears in the Hebrew Bible accompanied by a singular verb. It teases us straight away to begin to reflect on God's unity – and God's plurality. Gen. 1 offers a majestic monotheistic vision, which shames us when so often our conception of God still seems unashamedly tribal. Yet there is also a plurality in unity of the divine which will be hinted at in 1.2 and 1.26 and act as a reminder that we cannot easily grasp this God (*Elohim*), either intellectually or as a convenient divine talisman.

*Vast waste.* This alliterative phrase is trying to preserve the sound play of the Hebrew words *tohu wabohu.* Probably a lifeless, dark and moonless desert is envisaged. In the next moment the picture of chaos switches to a vast *deep* or watery abyss. In the verses that follow this *vast waste* and *deep* and the *darkness* will not be consigned in their turn to non-existence or destruction: instead they will form part of God's new and emerging order. The *darkness* will be named as *night*, and help to structure the boundaries of time, the *deep* will become *seas*, eventually teeming with life.

1.3–5   *God said*: something that will happen a perfect ten times in the course of this creation account. God creates through his word. In Old Testament thinking words were powerful, had a concrete reality to them, and could effect what they spoke about. So the words of prophets were feared, precisely because if they predicted doom there was an inevitability about it happening. Yet like Isa. 44.26; 55.10–11, this chapter suggests that the proven power of God's words can be an effective source of hope. If God can speak and everything come into being then the corollary is that God's word is surely powerful enough to redeem and restore.

We too know God through his words, words are an essential part of self-communication, and tell us something about the real core of a person as John 1.1–18 will later remind us.

*Light* is the first thing to be created. This light is something apart from the sun and the moon, which still remain to be created on Day Four. This is a primal energy, a metaphor for the sense of consciousness that God has granted to the universe. Light will be used in the making of the later elements of creation, but not used up, even when the sun and moon have been formed.

As God *separated* the light from the darkness he implicitly created time, through the division between light and darkness. The emphasis on time will become more overt on Day Four. It is an indication of the importance of time in the world view of Genesis.

The phrase *God saw . . . was good* will recur seven times during creation. God is like an artist: it is only as an artist feels satisfaction with a painting or a sculpture that he or she is empowered to go on and create further. So with God: God's pleasure in each stage of the creative process will help the conception of the next stage. This affirmation of creation as *good* or beautiful is fundamental. The Old Testament is at its heart gloriously world-affirming and acts as a rebuttal to elements of the Christian tradition that have had an escapist or negative attitude to the world. If the world is created as *good* it is important that humanity continues to keep it so: concern for justice, peace and the integrity of creation ultimately stems from this chapter. In the New Testament we are reminded of God's intentions by Peter's words on the Mount of Transfiguration. *It is* good, *Lord to be here* (Mark

9.5) suggest that on that mountain for a brief moment creation was restored to its intended harmony.

1.6–13 Creation proceeds apace in the second and third days. Again it takes place through a process of separation. Notice that when the *vault* is created *God said* is reinforced by *God made*. The double way that God's creative activity is described helps to emphasise that what is made fits precisely into God's prior intention.

A traditional understanding of the cosmos is present here, with waters both beneath and above the vault that marks out heaven. The process of separating out the waters into their proper place is quite complicated and lengthy even for God (it takes two days before the dry land can appear!). Water is difficult to deal with: the ultimate chaotic element, as anyone who has experienced a Middle Eastern flash flood would know. The waters that are now being separated out are part of that primordial deep referred to in v. 2 and perhaps there is just a hint of their ambiguous status. Are they a force that stands over against God, or are they rather part of the 'good' of creation?

In many other Middle Eastern cultures the sea was personified as an evil god or goddess, who had to be defeated and killed by the power of divine order. That is a central motif in the *Enuma Elish*. It is remarkable how Genesis demythologises the ancient stories: the waters are no longer seen as having the characteristics of a person or god. Sea is here even specifically called *good* (1.10), even though there are other parts of the Bible which do come close to personifying seas and waters as an evil power that God has to defeat (e.g. Isa. 51.9–11; Rev. 21.1). *Who is this that wind and seas obey him?* mused Jesus' disciples as he stilled the storm (Mark 4.41). Throughout the Bible, reaching back into the folk memory of Israel the sea was viewed as a potentially hostile force, and, as here in Genesis, one of the supreme marks of divine power in the Bible was that God alone was able to control its waters.

It reads strangely to our modern eyes that plants should be produced by mother earth before sun and moon appear, since they would have had problems with photosynthesis. However from the perspective of the authors of Genesis the important distinction is that between creatures that move (created in Days Four to Six), and things that do not, which includes plants (created in Days One to Three). Plants are also (according to the thinking of Gen. 1) asexual: their reproduction did not depend on the merging of male and female. Rather they had the power of renewal within themselves, through their ability to propagate *each with its own kind of seed*. Plants form part of the milieu which will support the life to be created on Days Five and Six. The third day has been a particularly busy one, seeing both the appearance of the earth and this summons to the earth itself to produce plant life. If the *Enuma Elish* provided a pattern for the writers of Gen. 1, they needed to conflate what takes eight days to happen there into six days. This may be part of the reason for the increased activity on Days Three and Six.

| The Pattern of the Days | |
| --- | --- |
| *Non-moving creation* | *Moving creation* |
| Day 1   Light | Day 4   The moving lights (sun, moon, stars) |
| Day 2   Waters and the heavens | Day 5   Creatures that live in the waters and heavens |
| Day 3   Earth<br>Vegetation | Day 6   Earth creatures Humans (who are allotted vegetation to eat) |

1.14–25   With the creation of the sun and the moon we start the second set of three days of creation, which corresponds to the first set.

Yet the objects created by God are not named as sun and moon, but rather *two great lights*. In Mesopotamian culture the sun was venerated as a god, and sun worship also featured in Israel's own previous history (e.g. Ezek. 8.16–18). The guarded language of this chapter is intended to emphasise that these heavenly bodies are themselves merely a part of creation, with ironically one of their main functions being to ensure the proper worship of God.

This day, the fourth, is the mid point of the seven days, which have both begun and will end by God's shaping of time. Here too a focus on time is apparent: the heavenly bodies will serve as *signs both for festivals and for seasons and years*. This is a reflection of the 'priestly' concerns of the authors. It was important to ensure that religious festivals happen on the correct dates. In the post-exilic period there was bitter and ongoing debate over calendrical systems – whether the year should be organised on a solar or lunar calendar. This affected the writing of Genesis, indeed it may explain some of the chronological data in the book (see e.g. 5.22–24) The authors of Genesis believed that the calendar was built into the fabric of the universe.

Day Five corresponds to Day Two: the waters and the vault of the heavens are filled with their appropriate living beings. Once again the word 'create' is used, for the first time since 1.1, to mark the appearance of *living creatures* (1.21, Plants were not considered 'living creatures', see comment above on 1.11–12). 'Create' is a key word: a sign that what is happening now is a critical fresh stage in the orderly development of creation, and part of the deliberate intention of God.

It is remarkable that the *great sea-beasts* are mentioned first among the animal creation. We hear of Leviathan in Ps. 104.26, described almost as God's giant bath toy! Such semi-divine sea monsters appeared in the mythologies of Israel's neighbours. They summed up in animal form the terrifying and hostile nature of the sea. Yet in Genesis by contrast they are included in God's power and God's care. God's delight in the goodness of creation extends even to such as these.

God's act of blessing is also a sign of the new stage that has been reached. Sea creatures and air creatures are blessed. (It is interesting to speculate why land creatures are not blessed on the following day: probably the writer wanted to save up this important word to use it later that day of human beings.)

Blessing at its heart is connected with the love of and gift of life. Life has always been important in Old Testament and Jewish culture: preservation of life supersedes even the Sabbath. God's presence is to be desired precisely because in him is the fullness of life. Full life, however, in Old Testament thinking depended upon sufficient health and wealth to enjoy it, and the possibility of having the gift of life in oneself, exemplified by having descendants. Animals (unlike plants) need to be blessed to ensure their ability to reproduce and thus continue the chain of life. So here and in 1.28 blessing and the command to *Be fruitful* are closely connected. Throughout Genesis the author will repeatedly show us how this first command of God works itself out both in creation as a whole, and more especially in the world of human beings.

As we move into Day Six the parallel with Day Three becomes apparent. In both cases the earth 'brings forth' the plant and animal life that inhabits it – perhaps a dim reflection of the ancient belief in the earth as a kind of mother. And once again there is a great deal happening. Important though the creation of terrestrial animal life may be, it is slightly squeezed as we move on towards humanity, since the whole of creation needs to fit in to a seven day pattern.

1.26–31    Suddenly the chapter reaches a crescendo as the creation of human beings is reached. Gen. 1 makes it clear in several ways that this creation of humanity is a crowning moment. The plural *Let us*, draws sudden attention to the plurality in unity of God. In Christian tradition this has been understood as a moment when God deliberates within the Trinity before taking this step, while several parts of the Old Testament speak of a divine council surrounding God, made up of heavenly beings, 'sons of gods' or angels. In the book of Job their involvement with creation is majestically related: *Where were you when I laid the earth's foundations . . . while the morning stars sang in chorus and the sons of God all shouted for joy?* (Job 38.4, 7) demanded God of Job. In our author's eye, it is this divine council who is being invited to share in this particular moment of creation – perhaps because it may affect their own relationship with God.

For God states that human beings are to be created *in our image, after our likeness*. It was brave, even dangerous, language to use. For many who heard it the word *image* would have brought to mind statues and idols. Genesis takes a traditional concept and fills it out with a revolutionary meaning. It is no longer statues of wood or stone that best represent God, but living, breathing human beings. But how exactly are we human beings able to do this – represent God?

At the heart of the author's thinking seems to be the possibility of a relationship or partnership with God. Great emperors in the ancient world set up images of themselves in far-flung corners of their realms to remind their subjects that they still ruled even if they were not there in person, and to help reinforce the authority of the governor of the region. Similarly if human beings are in the image of God they are being offered the responsibility of being God's vice-regents over creation (e.g. 1.28).

Yet 'imaging God' also has consequences for how human beings relate to one another. There is an intrinsic connection between the plural verb used by God (*Let us make*), and the vocation of human beings to live as the *image* of God. God desires to exist in relationship rather than isolation. In so far as human beings then mirror or image God they too need to be in relationship, with God and with one another. It is human beings alone to whom God speaks directly as *you* in this chapter (1.29) – but it is in the plural that they are addressed. It is also notable that the other points in Genesis where God deliberates using the plural (3.22; 11.7) are both moments where the issue of human relationships – with God, and with one another – is to the fore.

One fundamental aspect of relationship is that of gender. Human beings are the only creatures that are described in chapter 1 as *male and female*. Partnership involves complementarity and there is no more basic form of complementarity than that which exists between male and female. If human beings are to fulfil their God-given task to *Be fruitful and increase* then both male and female are essential to this process. And both sexes are created in the image of God, in spite of later traditions reflected, for example, in 1 Cor. 11.7.

Could the writer be hinting that the 'plurality' of God in these verses is a plurality that transcends the normal boundaries of gender? Back in Gen. 1.2 the *spirit of God* which hovered over chaos was described in feminine terms. Throughout the rest of the chapter the God who speaks creation into being is grammatically male and singular. Is there a hint being offered at this moment of *Let us* that the creative working together of male and female human beings might image the working together of male and female within divinity?

1.27, the actual moment when God's plan to make this special creature is enacted, repeats the key word *created* three times, and is set out as poetry in the REB. Poetry in Genesis is reserved for significant moments in the story, and is particularly used to emphasise a relationship, for good or ill, between a 'pair' of individuals or groups. The form of Hebrew poetry facilitates this, with the structure of Hebrew poetic parallelism naturally inviting comparison and contrast between the two halves of a couplet. In 1.27 we have our attention drawn to two different sets of pairs: God and human beings form one pair; male and female the other (see further on image and creation on p. 40).

*God blessed them*: The fivefold form of blessing of human beings offered in 1.28 contains key concepts which reappear in other parts of Genesis, and provides themes which will recur throughout the story. One or more phrases from the blessing appear at critical moments in the story (see e.g. Gen. 9.1; 17.6). The various elements of the blessing seem to represent the opposite of the situation that early readers of Genesis must have experienced: they felt themselves to be few in number, 'barren' (see e.g. Isa. 54.1), subjugated and dominated by the great empires which had controlled the Middle East for hundreds of years. Was the author's vision written in the faith that God wanted to turn this situation around, and create a new creation in which all people would have their rightful place?

Gen. 1.28 contains forceful language. The word translated *subdue* is elsewhere used to describe the rape of a woman, and it is sometimes felt that texts such as this bear considerable responsibility for the lack of concern for the environment in parts of the Judaeo-Christian tradition throughout history. But the control of human beings over the rest of creation is actually restricted by these verses: the gift of plants for human food (1.30), implies that the eating of animals is off limits. The final verses of chapter 1 tie human beings firmly into the network of creation as a whole; God gives attention to the food of animals as well as human beings, and *all* creation, not simply humanity, is pronounced as *very good*.

2.1–4a    Human beings may be the crown of creation, but they are not also its goal. The creation story does not finish until the consecration of the seventh day. And when human beings begin to keep the Sabbath (Exod. 20.8–11) the very act of keeping this day holy will return ultimate control of the world to God. Note that the REB translation *on the sixth day* (beginning of 2.2) is an emendation based on the Septuagint. The Hebrew actually suggests that God brought everything to an end on the seventh day, but this implies that God himself worked on the Sabbath, a theological problem which John 5.17 also seems to be addressing.

Creation gets thoroughly finished off in these few verses! In Hebrew the verb translated *completed* and *brought to an end* is closely related to the word translated *everything* and *all*. The use of so many similar sounding words so close together at this point is for deliberate emphasis. What God has desired God has now brought to pass. All is completed.

Although the noun Sabbath is not used, no one could have read these verses without being reminded of it. In Hebrew the verb *finished* is *shabat* and the number *seventh* is *shebi'i*. They are similar in sound and also similar to the word 'Sabbath' (*shabbat* in Hebrew). By the time this chapter of Genesis was written the keeping of the Sabbath had become a distinctive mark of members of the Jewish community, both within Palestine and outside it (e.g. in Babylon or Egypt). To write the Sabbath into the very rhythm of the cosmos, as Gen. 2.1–4a does, was an extraordinary statement of self-confidence on the part of the writer. Since the Jewish community were the only people who kept the Sabbath, their existence must be as sure as creation. Even if the appearance of things at times looked very different, even if the people felt themselves to be few and getting fewer, in consecrating the seventh day God had acted to guarantee their present and their future.

The language describing how God *made . . . holy* the Sabbath is reminiscent of descriptions of temples being consecrated. Unlike the gods of pagan nations the God of Genesis had no absolute need of a temple – perhaps the very universe itself was his shrine. So instead of selecting a sacred space he has chosen for himself a sacred time to which all people can have access wherever on earth they are. And it will also offer liberation for all. Other ancient creation stories, such as *Enuma Elish*, often concluded with the gods taking a rest – after they had created human beings in order to do the work in their stead. By contrast the biblical tradition will suggest that God's rest on the seventh day provides a model of rest for his human creation – and a model which human beings are required to emulate as they too ensure that the humans and animals whose lives they control (Deut. 5.12–14) can also share in this privilege.

These few verses about the seventh day do not follow the ordered structural pattern of the previous six days. That is deliberate. Genesis will be a book in which patterns and order will be important. But it will be precisely the individuals and the events that flout the moulds which will be highlighted and give meaning to the whole. The seventh day is a foretaste of this. And this seventh day is a day without end.

*This is the story of the heavens and the earth after their creation*: The short sentence at the beginning of 2.4 is a kind of seam. It reiterates the phrase 'heavens and earth' and the concept of creation/created from Gen. 1.1 and was intended to round off this initial section of Genesis. At the same time it probably points forward to what is coming next. The *story* which it speaks of is a birth-story: elsewhere in Genesis this word often refers to a genealogical list of fathers and sons (see comments about the *toledot* in the introduction p. xviii). It might have jarred with those who first read this passage. It is an implicit reminder of how different this particular creation story is. Creation accounts normally began with the – generally unhappy – family history of the gods, and the world and its population resulted from their infighting in a haphazard fashion. By using the word *story* here the author draws attention to the very real difference in this account. We have not been given a pre-history or genealogy of the gods, but instead the created world has become the beloved 'child' of God (although see also comments on 2.4b below).

Gen. 1.1—2.4a has set the stories shortly to come – small and large – of struggling humanity within a cosmic and transcendent framework, and introduced a God whose ultimate sovereignty seems assured. It has presented us with an ideal (*very good*) that the other 49 chapters of this book (and the rest of the Bible!) will continually struggle to realise.

## *Fruits of the earth*
2.4b—3.24

As we turn to these chapters it is like putting our eye to a keyhole in the middle of creation. We are being given a snapshot enlargement that focuses on one aspect of the panorama which flashed before us through Gen. 1. As Gen. 1.1 can be described as a summary of the rest of that chapter, so in turn we can think of Gen. 1.26–31 as being unpacked in Gen. 2—3.

Of course this picture looks and feels very different from Gen. 1. The story of Gen. 2—3 is a traditional tale with ancient roots that must have been told and told again. Each time it was told the story grew, adapted and changed to fit new circumstances, yet at the same time conserved elements that had come to form an important part of the tale. The tale is rich with features such as wordplays and aetiologies, which aided this oral retelling. Most commentators also point to the anthropomorphic way in which God is pictured in these chapters: he 'forms' human beings like a potter working with clay (2.7) and then is prepared to walk with them in the garden (3.8). This God feels very different from the transcendent and all-powerful creator of Gen. 1, and he is named differently as well.

Until 20 (or so) years ago mainstream biblical scholars usually suggested that these chapters came at the beginning of what was called the 'J' or Yahwist section of the Pentateuch, a telling of Israel's history that was sometimes dated as early as 950 BC, the era of David or Solomon. However the Documentary Hypothesis (J, E, D, P) on which this identification was based is now being widely questioned, and in particular there is considerable discussion of the likely date of the parts of the Pentateuch traditionally credited to the Yahwist. For example, although it was frequently suggested that Gen. 2—3 implies a Palestinian geographical context, the themes and images in Gen. 2—3 actually seem to find their closest parallels in literature written in Mesopotamia, either found within the Old Testament or coming from extra-biblical sources. Ezek. 28.12–16 reminds us strongly of Gen. 3, while outside Gen. 2—3 the description 'Eden' as a name for paradise occurs mainly in the writings of Ezekiel and Isaiah 40—55 which seem to have a Babylonian context. Among extra-biblical writing the Epic of Gilgamesh and the Adapa myth (both from Mesopotamia) contain close thematic links to these two chapters of Genesis (see further p. 42). Does this imply that the story itself underwent substantial development and was perhaps first written down during the exile, even if it may have roots reaching back into pre-exilic Israel?

Those who incorporated these chapters within Genesis in their present position, who were probably the authors of Gen. 1.1—2.4a, wanted them to be read against that other account of creation for which they themselves were responsible. They acted as a counter-point to and expansion of Gen. 1.1—2.4a. Gen. 3.22 with its divine plural is purposefully reminiscent of God's deliberation in 1.22. We are thus challenged to look at Gen. 1—3 as a whole, puzzling over the irony and tension that is implicit in the relationship between human beings and God.

As against the measured stateliness of Gen. 1.1—2.4a, this section has an untidy and awkward feel to it both as a literary creation and as theological reflection. Does it all hang together? Has, for example, the mention of the 'tree of life' been dragged in to an account that origi-nally referred only to one tree, that of knowledge? And what about the theological ambiguities: a God who seems to want to keep his human creation in a kind of infantile ignorance to preserve his own standing?

As we read through Genesis we will find this feature recurring at key points: two literary strands set alongside each other, ordered genealogies and stately tableaux contrasting with messy stories which reflect real life. Together they make up what for Israel was the thread of faith; a certainty regarding God's purposes and his ability to fulfil them, and an awareness that doubt, ambiguity or paradox was the friend rather than foe of true faith.

One of the features of Genesis in which 2.4b—3.24 is particularly rich is a delight in wordplays. It is difficult to understand the story fully without being aware of these. This feature of the narrative is linked to the biblical belief in the effective power of words which sound similar even if they are not technically 'related' to each other.

2.4b–9 *When the* Lord *God . . .*: We are immediately confronted with the different way God is named in this section: Lord *God* rather than

*God* as in 1.1—2.4a. 'The LORD' represents the Hebrew YHWH, the personal name of Israel's own god. It is probable that it was pronounced Yahweh (with short vowels as in 'cat' and 'get'). Out of reverence and to avoid possibly taking God's name in vain, later Jews did not pronounce the name and substituted *Adonai* = 'the Lord' wherever it occurs, and this was followed by the Old Greek translation. REB adopts the traditional practice, reaching back to the AV, of printing LORD with small capitals when it represents the name YHWH. Throughout this section, with the exception of 3.1–7 (see below), it is YHWH God we meet.

The different namings of God were, for at least two centuries, one of the key reasons for the division of Genesis on the basis of sources. According to the classic Graf-Wellhausen version of the Documentary Hypothesis, the sections where God is called YHWH were identified as coming from the Yahwist. Yet here in Gen. 2—3 the deity is called not simply YHWH, but YHWH God. This particular designation occurs nowhere else in Genesis. So even if we argue on the basis of the presence of the name YHWH in 2—3, that the chapters come from the same source as, for example, 4.1–26; 11.1–9; 15.1–21, we need to explore why it is that in these two chapters we consistently have *Elohim* (God) written alongside YHWH. Perhaps this story originally used the name YHWH, but *Elohim* was added by the final editors who placed Gen. 1.1—2.4a before it. It was a device to help to weave the two different sections together and suggest that they needed to be read alongside each other to be properly understood.

But it may also be that a theological point is being expressed when God is named as *Elohim* or as YHWH or both together.

By the time Gen. 1 was produced the plural *Elohim* had become the generic word for 'God' in Israelite and Jewish theological writings. The plural helped to convey a sense both of the universality and transcendence of the only God of the whole world.

YHWH, the personal name of God, special to the people of Israel, reflected a sense of intimacy, and of close interaction between YHWH and human creation and human history. The word YHWH is closely related to the Hebrew verb for 'be' or 'become' (see Exod. 3.14). Is YHWH used to speak of God when in immanent relationship with that which he has brought into 'being', while *Elohim* reminds us at the same time that God cannot be bound and limited by creation, but also stands outside it, rather like an emperor ruling from afar? In chapters 2—3 the dual form YHWH *Elohim* reflects the tension between these two aspects of God, which perhaps lies at the heart of the story.[1]

*Made the earth and the heavens*: The order, the reverse of the way creation was described in 1.1—2.4a, is significant. What we are now going to read is a story that will be concerned mainly with life on earth, and even with the potential well-being of the earth itself.

Earth and its ground or soil form the foundation on which these chapters are based – quite literally. The introductory comment about the *story* in 2.4a may even contain a veiled hint that heaven and earth are in some way the progenitors of who and what is then made. The role of the human being is pre-ordained: it is to 'serve' (REB *till*) the ground (2.5). The destinies of humanity and ground are intertwined. When the human beings are punished for their eating of the forbidden fruit, it is the ground that suffers as much as they do themselves (3.17).

The rather long and ungainly sentence of vv. 4b–5 accurately mirrors the Hebrew, which is equally awkward. The geography of the scene is redolent of the Middle East. Water is precious – and one possible understanding of 2.5–6 is that throughout these early chapters of Genesis it does not rain. Rain will be a new phenomenon which arrives – with a vengeance – only when the great flood begins (7.5). Until then the fertility of the ground depends completely on primeval underground springs, such as the moisture referred to in 2.6. It is only when the ground is dampened by this moisture that God, the divine potter, gets to work – perhaps like all potters he needs wet rather than dry clay or earth to work with. Out of the earth God then forms a human being: the link between human and the earth is then reinforced by the deliberate punning between *'adam* ('human being', 'Adam') and *'adamah* ('ground'). It is difficult to reflect this pun in English although Robert Alter's human and humus is a good try![2] Other writers have sought to express the pun by calling the human being a 'groundling' or 'earthling'. Note that it is the human being who derives his name from the ground – rather than vice versa. This human creature is verbally as well as physically dust of the earth.

The intimacy of the mouth-to-mouth respiration with which God coaxes the human being into life is remarkable: never again in Genesis can a human being be as close to God. From now on, for better and for worse, human beings will have to work out their existence as separate beings from God. Separation can have its positive side – the whole of Gen. 1 has presented a series of separations which have resulted in a good creation. But it also has its flipside – and this biblical book will be an exploration of both its positive and negative implications. Life has originated in and come from God, how will it be sustained when humans and God travel their separate ways?

There is not a fully worked out Hebrew anthropology in these verses, but for a human being to become *a living creature* both the material *dust of the ground* and the God-given *breath of life* are essential. Human beings are not immortal souls temporarily imprisoned in material bodies. We are intrinsically bodily people, and the *'adam*/*'adamah* pun reminds us of this.

Next Eden is made: literally a garden of 'Delight' (the meaning of the word 'Eden') for human beings. It is *away to the east* – it is unlikely that the writer had any specific place in mind, but the east, the place of sunrise and also a region known for its wisdom (e.g. 1 Kgs 4.30), was the appropriate region to locate this garden of new beginning. Among all the trees of this garden two are singled out: *the tree of life*, and *the tree of the knowledge of good and evil* (see further on these two trees on p. 41).

Like all good storytellers the writer whets our appetite at this point – by telling us just a little before diverting into the luscious description of Eden's rivers. He will return to the subject of the tree of knowledge later on. The phrases *pleasing to the eye and good for food* with which the trees are described, seen as through God's eyes, anticipate the thoughts that the woman will have in 3.6. We are being prepared for what will shortly happen in the story.

A feature of 2.4–9 is the number of pairs mentioned: earth/ heavens, earth/ground, shrub/plant, tree of life/tree of knowledge, good/evil. At the moment of course there is only one human being, although perhaps the human being is to be paired with God. But the pairing of nature seems to act as an example for human life. There will shortly be two human beings, how will they relate? Constructive opposition can clearly be part of God's purposes, but will it be so in the case of humanity?

2.10–14 Our snapshot now opens out into a panorama. In case we felt that Eden was an insignificant far-away place of which we know nothing, the picture suddenly enlarges to encompass the whole earth. The four rivers of these verses between them 'skirt' the whole of the significant known world as it was known from the writer's perspective. The *Tigris* and *Euphrates* were the great rivers that made possible Mesopotamian civilisation. The *Pishon* may stand for the Nile, or may represent a smaller river in Mesopotamia. The *Gihon* has the same name as the spring at the foot of the hill on which

Jerusalem stood (see e.g. 1 Kgs 1.33). In spite of the link to the *land of Cush* (southern Egypt/Ethiopia) which might encourage us to think about the Nile, the original readers of this text would probably also have recalled that stream in Jerusalem, *the river whose streams bring joy to the city of God* (Ps. 46.4). What a compliment to such a small spring – to compare it with the Tigris and Euphrates! Yet this exaggeration is a reminder that this water was the lifeblood on which Jerusalem, the biblical holy city, depended. Biblical writers such as Ezekiel (47.1), Zechariah (14.8) and the author of Revelation (22.1) link to these images in Genesis to look forward to the days when a spring will gush so copiously from the heart of Jerusalem that it will make even the Dead Sea fresh.

2.15–25 *The* Lord *God . . . put him in the garden:* The story picks up again where it left off with 2.11, yet the repeated comment that God *put* the human being in the garden makes an important new point. For the word *put* is here (unlike 2.8) translating the Hebrew root *nuah* (from which Noah will take his name) which expresses the concept of 'rest'. God may have put the human being in the garden to *till* the ground, but it is certainly not the harsh back-breaking labour that human beings will later experience outside the garden. Several biblical texts which come from the time of the Babylonian exile speak longingly of entry/re-entry into Canaan as a time of 'rest' (e.g. Deut. 12.9). Perhaps the garden is being envisaged as a kind of long-lost promised land.

*You may eat . . . you are surely doomed to die:* Both eating and dying appear in the text using an emphatic Hebrew idiom. A death sentence is here being uttered if the human being contravenes Yhwh's command. It is paradoxical that so shortly after having discovered life, the human being is now threatened with death. Indeed, since he was not to eat of *the tree of the knowledge of good and evil* could he be expected to know what death meant?

What was *knowledge of good and evil*? Many different suggestions have been made: a key component seems to be that the knowledge of good and evil is something that comes with human maturity. Young children do not possess this knowledge (see Deut. 1.39). Such knowledge contains various elements: common sense, appropriate judgement, moral attentiveness and consciousness of human mortality. But it also seems to include sexual maturity and awareness.

It is no accident that Hebrew regularly uses the verb 'know' to describe sexual intercourse. This sexual dimension of the knowledge of good and evil will play a key part in Gen. 3: the story will not make sense without it.

Why is there this link made between human acquisition of sexual knowledge and human death? On the one hand, sexual maturity allows human beings to procreate, and allows for an increase in the human race. Without death, overpopulation would ensue, and even God's own position might be threatened (see 3.22). And from the human perspective the nature of sexual love inevitably has a bitter-sweet aspect to it: our feelings of love for another exacerbate the pain of loss. Song of Songs 8.6 eloquently reflects on this relationship between love and death. Those who love passionately long for the immortality of the loved one.

To eat of *the tree of the knowledge of good and evil* then is to acquire all the aspects of wisdom that human adulthood implies.

When God's command is uttered in 3.16 the solitary human being is in no position to'know good and evil' – precisely because he is solitary! So it is ironic that God then immediately sets about providing him with the companion that will facilitate the transgression. *It is not good for the man to be alone* is a significant statement when read in the light of the repeated pronouncement in Gen. 1 that all aspects of creation are 'good'.

God's first efforts don't exactly work out: though they do result in the creation and naming of the animals. The task of naming the animals is a sign of human control over them. But none of them is *a suitable partner* (2.20, compare 2.18) for the human being. Their very lack of human speech emphasises the loneliness of the human being. They are almost like toys with which the child-like human plays in God's garden.

*Suitable partner*: This is a very precise expression. The traditional translation 'help meet for him' does not bring out the equality of the two beings that stand before God. The woman is the counterpart of the man. Ancient commentators such as Philo and Ephraem the Syrian suggested that until the making of the woman in 2.22–23 the human being was in some sense androgynous. He had not been diversified by sexuality. That individuation now takes place, as the woman is made (literally 'built') out of the original human being by God, and man and woman greet each other. *At last* God gets it right: the words with which the man begins to speak perhaps suggest a degree of frustration with God's previous fumblings. And now the man's attention seems to be focused on the woman to an extent that must inevitably lead to him drifting away from God.

This is the first time the human being has used direct speech in Genesis. The ability to speak is what marks off human beings from the animals (and enables them to become close to God). It is appropriate that the first human speech relates to another human being.

The words are few but exquisitely measured, drawing attention to the way that the one has now become two. They are also poetry, and as above (see p. 12) the formal parallelism of Hebrew poetry draws attention to the interplay of one and two. The human being now speaks of himself as *'ish* (= man/male) rather than *'adam*, and with a pun that is fortuitously possible also in English addresses the *'ishshah* (= woman). Male and female are intertwined in the phrases 2.23. The REB has captured this well. The unity between the two is further reinforced by the writer's explanatory comment in 2.24.

Yet is this unity enough in the relationship of man and woman? It is only when we are aware of differences from others that a real partnership with them becomes possible. It is the difference as well as the similarity of man and woman that will make procreation possible. For the moment they play together childlike in Eden, as happily naked together as toddlers splashing in a paddling pool. But the final words of the chapter suggest that there is more to come, as the description *'arummim* (= naked) points us towards the *'arum* (= cunning) serpent whom we will meet so shortly. Is it not the very infantile innocence of the man and the woman which will leave them open to the wiles of the serpent?

3.1–7  We now meet a talking serpent. Although later reworkings of Gen. 3 personified this serpent as Satan, that is not how he is portrayed here. Wriggling 'Satan' into this passage has encouraged the reading of this story as a 'fall'. But snakes are sinister enough. They played an ambiguous role in Israel's religion, ranging from the plague of serpents in the wilderness (Num. 21.6–9), to the mysterious snake statue of Nehushtan that was kept in the Jerusalem temple for centuries until eventually expelled in Hezekiah's reform (2 Kgs 18.4). Snakes also have an ominous role in other Middle Eastern myths and legends: in the Epic of Gilgamesh a snake snatches the plant of eternal youth out of Gilgamesh's grasp – an intriguing parallel to the snake's role in the Garden of Eden.

Physical features of the snake help to explain its role in such stories. The snake renews its own skin, an apparent sign of its ability to recreate life. The skin looks naked – which would remind a Hebrew speaker of its *cunning* (see notes on 2.25 above). Its obvious resemblance to the male sexual organ facilitated its association with both life and sexuality, as in Gen. 3. And as one of the few poisonous creatures in the Middle Eastern world, it was most definitely feared.

The serpent engages the woman in conversation. Suddenly the name YHWH disappears: in 3.1–7 they speak only of God. The closeness and intimacy with YHWH God that had once been part of life in the garden has gone.

The conversation between the two parties has an opaqueness about it. Is the woman telling the truth when she tells the serpent that God told them not *even to touch* the fruit of the tree of knowledge? That was not precisely what was stated in 2.16. So is the woman being supercautious, or is it a lie which is the first stage of her determined journey to make her own decisions without reference to God? And as for the serpent, are his seductive words in 3.5 true or false? After eating the apple the man and woman do know good and evil, and they do not die – at least not immediately.

What happens is in large measure an allegory of the maturing of human beings both as individuals and as society (in Rom. 7.7–12 Paul seems also to suggest this). As the episode progresses the woman seems to be experiencing a sexual awakening. One by one the senses come into play, and the adjectives *pleasing* and *desirable* with which the fruit is described have a deliberately erotic quality to them. The serpent with its phallic shape is an appropriate instructor for this topic. It may also explain why the woman eats of the fruit before the man, since girls normally mature sexually at an earlier age than boys. And the desire of the woman and the man then to conceal their genitals is an understandable one for these now sexually mature adults, who are being constrained by the expectations of society.

There is of course a wider awakening. As suggested above sexual maturation is an important part of a wider development that takes place as humans reach adulthood. Human beings long to be wise . . . *the fruit . . . was . . . desirable for the knowledge it could give*. There was an extensive wisdom tradition in Israel linked to the name of Solomon that is reflected in the Old Testament. Wisdom sought to enable people to make sense of and control their lives, and the society in which they lived. Yet the Old Testament also reflects a somewhat uneasy attitude towards such wisdom. Did not wisdom seek to encourage human beings in their autonomy? Where was the place for God, and particularly the God of Israel in wisdom's scheme of things? Did not this quest for wisdom ultimately lead Solomon himself astray?

Can human beings really understand the deepest mysteries of their
existence, the problem of suffering, the issues of life and death or
does the fullest wisdom belong only to God (Job 28.12–24)? The book
of Job presents such dilemmas with which Israel's history sought to
wrestle.

Here in Gen. 3 a similar ambiguity about wisdom comes to the fore,
as the woman and the man gain knowledge only to become aware of
the nakedness and vulnerability of human wisdom. As human beings
grow up we learn about our mortality. We know enough to know that
we are going to die, but we do not know enough to prevent it. That is
both our glory and our tragedy.

3.8–19    *Where are you?* is the first question God asks in the Bible. He
has never needed to ask a question before. The question reflects the
increasing alienation between God and human beings. Yet at the
same time asking and answering questions is one of the best ways for
human beings to develop. The pathos of what is happening is emphasised by the way that YHWH God (the name is now back again for a few
more verses until the couple are sent out of Eden) is *walking about in the
garden* as he asks that question. It is the moment in Genesis when God
is depicted most anthropomophically, most like a human being himself. Human beings are so near to God – and yet soon so very far. The
sense of alienation develops as the man uses a repetitious sentence in
an attempt to blame both God and the woman for what has happened
. . . *It was the woman you gave to be with me who gave me fruit.* In turn the
woman's efforts to throw the blame on the serpent symbolise the lack
of solidarity between the animal world and humanity that will exist
from now on and which will form part of God's curse. The verbs in
3.10–14 are starkly singular (the 'I's contrasting with the earlier 'we'
used by the woman in 3.2–4). *Naked* ['arummim] *cunning* ['arum] . . .
and now *cursed* ['arur] (3.14, 17): the three words are linked by their
sound in Hebrew. A circuitous but perhaps inevitable journey has led
from one to the other.

In three brief poems one after another God confronts in turn the
serpent, woman and man. The parallelism of each poem helps in
each case to emphasise a once close pair now divided and disunited.
First the woman and the serpent, then the woman and the man, and
finally the man (here *'adam*) alienated from the earth (*'adamah*). Each
of the parties has a penalty to pay – and the penalty for each one
impinges upon others than themselves. Our actions always have
consequences which affect others. The serpent's penalty will lead to

danger for the woman and her brood, the woman's penalty will involve a change in the man's relationship with her, and the man's penalty will affect the earth or *'adamah*. The earth is the only party who had not taken part in what has just happened, yet the buck seems to stop with it!

Two of the poems allude to childbirth or descendants. That is appropriate in view of the new knowledge that the man and the woman have just gained.

Two of the poems speak of *labour* deliberately using the same Hebrew word. The woman's *labour* in childbirth is compared to the man's *labour* in the fields. Yet this equality of language does not reflect a future social equality between the sexes. The parity that was implied by 1.27 and 2.23 and by the expression *suitable partner* (2.20) has been profoundly dislocated. Now a hierarchy has developed and the man will be the *master*.

On the face of it the future looks bleak. These verses were certainly written in the knowledge of the harsh agricultural conditions that prevailed in much of the ancient Middle East, and in awareness of the dangers of childbirth for women (perhaps 50 per cent of adult women died through giving birth). But if the original blessing of Gen. 1.28 was to 'Be fruitful and multiply' is it a curse or a blessing that the man and the woman are now adult enough to begin to live out God's first hopes for humanity? The woman's childbearing pains may have been multiplied, but at least that meant that she could now multiply as God had wished!

3.20–24   When *the man named his wife Eve (hawwah) because she was the mother of all living (hay) things* did he do so ironically – in view of her responsibility for this new era in which difficulty and death would predominate? Or did he do so in truth, since it was only through the woman's initiative in eating the fruit that procreation had now become possible? Perhaps the writer wants us to keep both possibilities in mind.

And what of the gesture of YHWH in giving the couple animal skins for clothes? Was it a generous action, showing care for his human creation and enabling them to survive the rigours of life outside the garden? Or is it rather a making permanent of the situation that had been initiated by the couple themselves when they made themselves temporary clothing of leaves (3.7) and thus effectively segregated themselves from God? Once again the ambiguity may be deliberate. At any rate the verbal punning begun in 2.25 with the word 'naked' reaches its conclusion here with *skins* (*'or*) which sounds similar in Hebrew. We have travelled through naked . . . cunning . . . cursed . . . finally to land up with the human beings clothed yet also banished permanently from the garden where a naked innocence had been possible and human beings had nothing to conceal from God.

A defining moment is being reached. The divine plural of the statement *the man has become like one of us* recalls the moment of the original creation of humanity in 1.26–27 when God also spoke in the plural (see p. 11). There are other deliberate similarities between what God says now and what he said then. In both cases the likeness between human beings and God is referred to. Yet something strange has happened. Then it was at God's initiative and with God's blessing that human beings were created in God's image and likeness. Now YHWH God seems to be jealous of and threatened by such a similarity. Indeed YHWH God at this point resembles the gods of Greek and Babylonian myths who feel threatened and disturbed by the increase in the human population and decide to take vindictive action against humans. In now knowing good and evil humans beings have gained the ability to create/procreate which up till then has been a prerogative of the divine.

Procreativity and immortality added together would be a recipe for imminent overcrowding of the earth! So there is a logic in YHWH God's action, in sending forth the human beings from the one place where they would have been able to eat of the *tree of life* and defy the mortality that the Old Testament believed was intrinsic to human beings, and which is emphasised once again by the description of the man's role as *to till the ground from which he had been taken.*

But is it a total disaster for humanity? Translations load the situation with particular theological weight. We read that *the LORD God banished him,* but the Hebrew could equally be translated the Lord God 'sent him forth' which has a more neutral ring to it. Certainly there is no going back to Eden, since God had stationed the *cherubim,* fierce winged beasts whose statues traditionally guarded temples, to prevent their return. The man and the woman have indeed been driven out from YHWH God's presence, as Cain will be in 4.14. But perhaps the writer's comment at 2.24 can also stand as a reflection on what takes place in chapter 3. The man has now grown up and left his parent God, and cleaving to Eve his wife, the two together prepare to face the challenge of their new life.

## Brothers and sons
### 4.1—6.8

Gen. 4 is in many ways the continuation of Gen. 2—3 and deliberately spirals round to revisit some of the themes that were introduced in the garden of Eden. The verbal echoes of the earlier narrative remind us that our actions are influenced both by previous history and our environment. Correspondingly most of chapter 5 has a close affinity with 1.1—2.4. It also betrays a knowledge of the text now found in Gen. 4. There are some strange links between the two chapters themselves – note some names given in the genealogy of Cain in 4.17–24 which are similar or identical to the names given in the list of Seth's descendants in 5.1–26.

The two streams finally knit together in the announcement of the birth of Noah (5.28–32). They are complementary and together they are setting the parameters which will help us – and the later characters of Genesis – work out the meaning of our humanity once Eden has been left behind. There are also clear verbal connections between 5.29 and 6.5–8, verses which offer the first of two explanations for God's decision to bring the flood. Taken together the connections between the chapters encourage us to see the history of humanity from creation to flood as connected pieces within an overall pattern – albeit a largely pessimistic one.

4.1–16 The story of Cain and Abel conveys several messages, some explicit, others almost subliminal. It suggests that the hostility between the farmer and the shepherd, which has traditionally been a feature of Middle Eastern life, goes back to the beginning of human existence. The sharp differences in climate in a small area such as east of Jerusalem where the rainfall differential in a space of only ten miles is striking, accentuated this hostility, for it meant that groups with contrasting lifestyles lived in close proximity to one another. The antagonism of the biblical tradition to aspects of Canaanite agricultural and urban culture may also be reflected – Cain has connections with both agriculture and city-dwelling. There is a hint that sacrifice may not be totally desirable. But above all it is a story of two brothers, and as such could be said to act as an introduction to the rest of the book of Genesis, which spends chapters 12—50 digging deep into the meaning of brotherhood. The teasing out of the implications of the benefits and stresses of 'duality' to which we have been introduced in Gen. 1—3, is focused in this archetypal relationship.

4.1 dives in with the consequences of what has happened in Gen. 3. *The man lay with his wife Eve* – the older translations and the NRSV translate the Hebrew literally 'The man knew his wife Eve', drawing out that this is one important result of eating from the tree of knowledge. And the one named as the *mother of all living beings* in 3.20 starts to live out her role. She is very sure of herself *With the help of the* LORD *I have brought into being* (qaniti) *a male child*, punning on the name of Cain. She seems to be claiming a kind of equality with YHWH in the role of creation – indeed 'like the LORD' may more accurately convey the sense of the Hebrew here, though too daring for most translators. The expression *male child* is striking since the Hebrew word *'ish*, which it translates, normally refers to an adult male. It may deliberately recall the triumphal cry of 2.23, when YHWH God's making of *'ish* and *'ishshah* was celebrated. But Eve's exclamation seems almost designed to exclude her husband. Is it a symptom of the lack of harmony that has developed between the couple (3.16) and will such imbalances in creation that have resulted from the action of the man and the woman in Gen. 3 also have their effects on the next generation?

Cain, the first-born, seems to have everything going for him: the focus of his mother's attention. By contrast, Abel seems an afterthought. There is no obvious rejoicing in his birth and his very name Abel means 'nothingness'! (It is the word translated 'futility' or 'vanity' in the famous opening passage of Ecclesiastes.) Is this the reason that *the* LORD *regarded Abel and his offering* – because the God of the Bible does have a bias towards those whom the world regards of little account? Throughout Genesis we will discover a marked disposition in favour of younger sons. Perhaps it is significant also that Abel bought the *choicest* of his animals. But it is notable too that it is the sacrifice of the brother who worked the land (*'adamah*) and who offers its fruits which is rejected. Is this the 'curse' pronounced on the earth in the previous chapter working itself out?

This is the first time human beings have offered sacrifice. Sacrifice created communion with a deity: were Cain – and Abel – born outside Eden, intending by their actions to try and restore for themselves a closeness with YHWH that their parents had lost? Adam and Eve had 'grown up' and become independent of their parent God, but perhaps Adam and Eve's own children wanted to revert to being children before God once again. If so, then YHWH clearly needs to go on a parenting course! His way of dealing with the two brothers, and particularly with Cain, does not on the surface show him as the ideal father. The theme of sibling rivalry runs through the Bible, often provoked by a father's favouritism. Yнwн seems as inept a parent as Jacob and David are later to be (see e.g. Gen. 37.3; 2 Sam. 13—20), and the consequences are as dramatic as occurred among Jacob's and David's sons.

Yet maturity demands that we leave behind us jealousy of our brothers and sisters – perhaps what Yнwн is doing is forcing Cain to 'grow up' before he is ready or able to do so. Life *is* unfair but it is the mark of an adult to be able to accept this. Cain is an angry adolescent.

The metaphor of sight resonates through these verses. Yнwн *regarded* – literally 'looked upon' – Abel and his offering but did not regard Cain. In consequence Cain's face fell or *glowered*, so that he looked at neither Yнwн nor his brother Abel. He is sharply told to *hold [his] head up*, so that he can continue to look upon his brother. Instead he kills Abel, believing that he has thereby removed his rival from Yнwн's presence. But in doing so he ironically removes himself too, as he is forced to confess: *I must hide myself from your presence.* He discovers too late that if we want to look upon the face of God the route to do so is via the face of our brothers and sisters, who have been created in God's own image – a theme that will be revisited in the story of Jacob and Esau, Gen. 32—33. Alienation from our fellow human beings results inevitably in alienation from God, just as the separation from God in chapter 3 has led ultimately to this separation between the brothers. The first question of God, the *Where are you?* of 3.9 leads inevitably to the second question *Where is your brother Abel?* of 4.9.

There is another progression that climaxes in this chapter. In Gen. 1.18, 28 the destiny of human beings is to rule over the earth, in the same way as the sun and moon ruled over day and night. In Gen. 3.16 the man rules over the woman, a symptom of the new disordering of relationships. In 4.7 the expression is recapitulated once again as Cain is told *you will be mastered by* sin. Unless human beings can master themselves they cannot master their world!

The consequence of this is expressed in the other aspect of the punishment of Cain. Cain will be *banished from the very ground*, a stark fate for a child of Adam who had been created from the ground or *'adamah* (see 2.7), especially one whose life's work had been to tend it. The breach between Cain and the earth, a breach that leads on from the original fracture of 3.17, is described vividly and concretely. Then it had been the earth which was cursed, and now it is Cain. It is as though the earth (*'adamah*), polluted with the blood (*dam*) of Abel, cannot 'stomach' Cain anywhere near it. Our actions do not simply have repercussions upon our fellow human beings – they affect the environment in which we live.

Does the description of Cain as *a wanderer, a fugitive*, two words which alliterate in Hebrew (*na'*, *nad*), imply that he is being condemned to life as a nomad? Since Genesis is generally positive about the nomadic life, more probably we should think of the perpetual moving and shaking of the earth itself in an earthquake, along with the terror of those who try to flee it. Cain's eventual destination is the *land of Nod*: but even there he will not find rest, for 'Nod' is related to the word for *wanderer* and so means something like 'Land of the Restless Life'. He has lost his way, spiritually as well as physically. This land *to the east* would have reminded early readers of Genesis of Israel's own time and place of exile. Yet it is also a place where hope is possible. In this far-away land which was *out from the LORD's presence*, his writ still runs. His will to protect this murderer is a statement that his power extends beyond his 'home' territory. The *mark* of Cain is ambiguous: both blessing and curse. No one, not even the first murderer, stands outside God's grace. The special 'seven' makes its first reappearance since Gen. 1, with God's pledge of *sevenfold vengeance* on anybody who attacked Cain. Yet there must have been times when Cain wished his restless and guilt-ridden life could be ended by the release of death. Is it significant that Cain is one of the few male characters of Genesis whose death is not recorded?

4.17–26    The rest of this chapter will offer a pessimistic but realistic assessment of how the violence begun by Cain then multiplies by geometric progression – assisted by the development of human technologies. The ghosts of Cain have floated around the corridors of the Middle East ever since.

In the writer's mind Cain may have been associated with the Kenites – a tribe of metal workers who were associated with the Israelites in later history (see 4.22). Cain's is an untidy genealogy – contrasting with the much more ordered list in Gen. 5. The untidiness accentuates the sense of chaos that is a result of a lack of control among Cain's offspring.

Was it Cain or was it his son, Enoch, who built the first city? It is not clear but the link between cities and the family of Cain is notable. Cities were a development out of the agricultural mode of life, and the first great cities originated *to the east* (4.16) from Israel's geographical perspective. The Old Testament is ambiguous about the benefits and drawbacks of city or urban life. Cities could aid civilisation – but they could also become the locus of oppression, violence and even murder.

Back in 4.7 Cain's sin had been identified as a force of *desire* almost outside himself. Freud wrote of something similar which he identified as the 'id'. Without the 'id' of desire there would not be the energy for human progress or creative activities. Yet desire also needs to be controlled; otherwise it is ultimately destructive.

Cain's descendants witness to these characteristics of humanity. They discover new technology, they evolve the performing arts, all of which are important in the development of city life, but in the person of Lamech, the seventh generation from Adam, they give vent to unbridled violence. A city is a place of blessing if brothers and sisters dwell there together in unity – but perhaps it would be too much to expect the descendants of Cain to take to heart the meaning of brotherhood. The last words that are said about the family of Cain are ones of violence (4.23–24). The exaggeration of the number seven in Lamech's boastful speech threatening violence *seventy-sevenfold* jar when we remember what seven signified in Gen. 2.1–4a. Have we reached a dead end?

But God starts again – as happens often in this book. Another son is born to Eve, and once again she makes a play on his name. He is called Seth because YHWH had granted (Hebrew: *shat*) her a son. This time her jubilation is muted in comparison with the words used at the birth of Cain. Has Eve discovered that there is more to creating than merely giving birth? Cain, her first 'creation' had himself brought death rather than life. This time, God's, rather than Eve's own, role in the birth is emphasised. According to the REB she refers to *another son* but the literal meaning of the Hebrew here is 'other seed'. The term reminds us of the disaster in the garden and the fact that the serpent would strike at the seed (REB *brood*) of the woman (3.15), but also looks forward to the patriarchal narratives (e.g. 12.7; 15.18), where the term 'seed' will feature as a sign of hope in the promises to Abraham, although it is not apparent in the REB translation (where it is normally translated 'descendants'). Is there a wistfulness in Eve's use of the word 'God' (4.25) – a longing for the immanent YHWH who had walked with her in the garden, who has been replaced by the more distant 'God', creator of the universe? Human beings are gradually moving away from their original intimacy with YHWH, but they will shortly find a new way of relating to him.

*Seth too had a son, whom he named Enosh.* Enosh is an alternative

Hebrew word for 'human being', often used in contexts of weakness. In Enosh's time *people began to invoke the* LORD *by name*, a biblical idiom for worship. Is it the sense of human frailty reflected in the name Enosh which has led to a sense of dependence on God which needs now to be expressed in worship? It was a need that could only have been discovered by Seth's heirs, since Cain's descendants were so confident in their own strength. YHWH is now a god to be worshipped rather than a friend and sparring partner walked with in the garden. Yet the very name –YHWH – by which Enosh and humanity choose to worship suggests a God with them.

5.1–27   The clue to reading Gen. 5 is found in the first verse of the chapter. We are led back to 1.26–28 when human beings were created in God's likeness and blessed by him. The ten remarkably long-lived generations (once again a perfect number) of the genealogy in this chapter suggest that humans are living out this blessing by 'filling' the earth – although we will shortly hear that this 'filling' has a negative side to it as well (6.11).

The similarity between the names in this list and those of the descendants of Cain in chapter 4 may suggest that there was a common oral tradition which gave the names of people of 'ancient' days, or perhaps more likely, that the author of Gen. 5 has chosen to adapt the list of names found in the previous chapter as a means of emphasis that the responsibility for moral choices rests firmly with humanity – we cannot use biological difference as a justification for evil choices. The genealogy, introduced by a phrase including the strategic word *toledot* (*list . . . of descendants* 5.1) which last appeared in 2.4a, is one of the dividing points of Genesis, telling us that one part of the story is closing while another is soon to begin.

Although the lifespans given to these figures seem fantastic, there are Babylonian texts which give heroes living before the flood even longer lives such as 20,000+ years. Methuselah therefore is a mere stripling at only 969! The assignation of dates in Genesis has a logic to it – even if the numbers are unrealistic (see below on Enoch, Lamech and Noah).

*Adam . . . begot a son in his likeness and image, and named him Seth*. Since Adam was himself made in the divine likeness this means that Seth was also. (Genesis nowhere suggests that the divine image was lost to humankind as a result of the events of Gen. 3.) On the basis of this comment a wealth of traditions about Seth developed in later Judaism and early Christianity. Many of these were heretical in flavour: the name of Seth crops up frequently in the Gnostic writings discovered at Nag Hammadi in Egypt.

*Enoch walked with God, and then was seen no more, because God had taken him away:* Enoch is a mystery. He is the seventh, a sacred position, in the list from Adam with a far shorter lifespan than the other patriarchs: only 365 years – the link with the 365 days of the solar year is no accident. His name means something like 'Dedicated', and along with Noah he is the only person who *walked with God*. In Enoch's case the result of this was he did not die as did other humans (see e.g. Heb. 11.5–6) because God removed him. Against the stark backcloth of the repeated phrase *and then he died* applied to every other figure in this list, Enoch's alternative destiny is a reminder that God too lives in the tension between life and death.

There is an extensive literature in which the figure of Enoch is prominent. 1 Enoch is the most important example (the book seems to have been considered Scripture by early Christians, e.g. Jude 14–15), but the name of Enoch also crops up in Sir. 44.16; 49.14; and the Book of Jubilees. The strange story of Enoch clearly fascinated people. Not surprisingly he seems to have been a particular hero for those (like the writers of the Dead Sea Scrolls) who sought to follow a solar calendar rather than the lunar calendar employed by official Judaism in the post-exilic period.

It is likely that when Gen. 5.22–24 was written there were already stories and legends circulating about Enoch and these verses are the tip of an iceberg, most of which remains hidden from our eyes (although the stories would probably have been known to the first readers of Genesis, and would have helped them make sense of this curt and cryptic note). A similar situation applies to the strange story of the intermarriage between the *sons of the gods* and the *daughters of mortals* in 6.1–4. 5.22–24 and 6.1–4 seem to be in some way related, and both reflect the undercurrents of the tension between human knowledge and human immortality that is a central theme in Gen. 1—11.

*Methuselah . . . lived nine hundred and sixty-nine years, and then he died*: The lifetime of Methuselah, the longest lived of the patriarchs, has been nicely timed to ensure that he lived almost to the moment when the great flood began.

*Lamech lived seven hundred and seventy-seven years*: Lamech's lifespan, which is shorter than most of his ancestors, is explained by two factors. He needs to be dead before the flood starts (!), and there is an apparent cross-reference to 4.24 where another figure also called Lamech is associated with multiples of the number seven. But this

Lamech speaks with a piety (v. 29) which contrasts with his counter-part, and his age suggests completeness. Seven has been restored to its honoured place in God's schema.

5.28–32 *Noah . . . This boy will bring us relief from our work, from the labour that has come upon us because of the* LORD's *curse on the ground*: Verses 28–32 not only conclude the genealogy of Gen. 5, but also allude to the earlier story of Gen. 2—4, the curse that is referred to in 3.17 and the *labour* to which Eve and Adam are condemned in 3.16 and 17.

Noah is an exceptional person. He is the representative of the per-fect tenth generation, the first of the patriarchs to be born after Adam had died, and the first to be born in a new millennium. A new start is going to begin with him. He waits far longer than any of the other patriarchs (exactly half a millennium) before becoming a father. Like Enoch he *walked with God* (6.9, see notes below, p. 49).

There is an elaborate 'pun' on the name of Noah worked into 5.29 and 6.5–8. Noah is so called because he will *bring relief* (Hebrew: *naham*) (5.29). The two words sound similar, although they are not etymologically related. In fact Noah comes from a Hebrew root *nuah* meaning 'rest'. Words that come from this root 'rest' are used at key points in Gen. 1—11, although the English translations inevitably conceal this. The ark *grounded* (8.4) on Mount Ararat, Noah offered a *soothing* (8.21) sacrifice, while back in 2.15 the Lord God had *put* the man (again from this same verbal root) in the garden of Eden to till it. To be 'at rest' seems, in the eyes of the biblical writers, to be in a place where one rightly belongs, and where the earth will respond to the human beings who till it, without making them 'weary'. In 5.29 we are being given a hint of Noah's agricultural prowess which will come to the fore after the flood.

But the puns do not stop there. The sound-link made between *nuah* and *naham* allows for another set of connections. When God *bitterly regretted* (6.6) that he had made human beings one of the words used in this expression also comes from the same Hebrew root, *naham*, even though in English *regret* and *bring relief* do not seem to have much in common. A link is being drawn between the emotions of God and those of human beings: indeed the one results in the other, for an ironic consequence of the flood is that the earth will from now on be easier for human beings to work, because it will have regular rainfall, and regular seasons. Similarly, in another play on words, the *labour* from which Noah will relieve humankind (which was imposed on

Eve and Adam in 3.16 and 3.17) is also picked up in the Hebrew word that lies behind the *bitterly* of God's expressed regret for the creation of human beings (6.6). Teasingly Genesis is reminding us that God and human beings belong together, and their fates and emotions are interwoven – whether either party likes it or not!

6. 1–4    After the genealogy which has told us of the productivity of human beings comes the consequence: God's blessing of humanity, given in 1.26–28, is being fulfilled as *the human race began to increase*.

What comes next feels one of the strangest episodes in the whole of Genesis, and as suggested in the notes on 5.22–24, may well be the summary of a traditional legend already widely known to both the writer and his readers. There is a lot bubbling away under the surface of these few cryptic sentences, and quite possibly the narrator was embarrassed by their polytheistic undercurrent.

We are told of divine beings, members of YHWH's heavenly court *the sons of the gods* (see also Ps. 29.1; 89.5–7; Job 38.7 ) – who choose to intermarry with human women.Their offspring are half-divine and half-human and far larger than normal humans – in Num. 13.33 these *Nephilim* (6.4) are described as giants. Should this offspring count as mortal along with humans, or immortal, along with YHWH and his heavenly court? YHWH decrees that they will be mortal – with a life-span of *a hundred and twenty years*. Probably the original implication was that this is the normal lifespan for humans – although it will not explicitly fall to that limit until the final chapter of Genesis (50.26). An alternative view is that the *hundred and twenty years* refers to the time lag between these events and the coming of the flood – which will wash away this offspring altogether! The positioning of these verses, sandwiched here between an introduction to Noah and an explanation for the flood, suggests that as Genesis was edited connections were drawn to link this episode more closely to the following deluge.

The union of heavenly beings with human women is a common motif in both Greek and Mesopotamian mythology. There are also Mesopotamian stories which explain that the great flood was caused by the excess of number and noise of the human population, and this is perhaps being hinted at here too. The narrator seems to disapprove of what has been taking place, and to choose his words accordingly. Does *took for themselves such women as they chose* hint at unbridled lust? The reference to polygamy may be telling: marrying more than one wife seems to bring trouble and violence in its train as with Lamech

(4.19–24), Jacob, and possibly even Abraham. The story of these heavenly beings is further developed in the Enoch literature (see 1 Enoch 6—11) where a link is made between the fact that the sons of gods 'knew' human women sexually and that, rather like malevolent Prometheuses, they transmitted 'knowledge' of evil to human beings, leading to the flood. It is likely such legends were already in existence before Genesis reached its final form.

We have here a story about breaking boundaries set between humanity and divinity, and in that sense the story is parallel to Gen. 3. Both touch on the limited length of human life. In fact the expression *saw how beautiful . . . took* (6.2) employs the same Hebrew words chosen in 3.6 to describe the woman's perception and taking of the fruit. (The word translated in 6.2 as 'beautiful' is the same as that translated as 'good' [to eat] in 3.6.) And it is striking that on each occasion when the plurality of the divine is emphasised in Gen. 1—11 (Gen. 1.26; 3.22; 11.7 and here as *the sons of the gods* in 6.2) the issue at stake is the relationship between God and human beings, their closeness, but also the necessary distinction that God imposes. The descendants of this mingling of earth and heaven may be *people of renown* (literally 'of name', Hebrew: *shem*), but as we will discover later a 'name' is a gift from God rather than humanity's possession as of right.

Jewish writings from around the New Testament period tended to prefer to use stories based on Gen. 6.1–4 rather than Gen. 3 to explain the origin of evil in the world – it is perhaps more comforting to suggest that evil originates from outside human beings rather than from within!

6.5–8    It is a bleak picture of the state of humanity in these few verses. The naïve hopes for humanity with which the story of Gen. 2.4b began are turned on their head. There God had *formed* (*yatsar*) human beings, but now the *inclination* (*yetser*) that he had made was apparently only evil. God who in Gen. 1 had seen so much that was good, now sees only evil or *wickedness* (6.5).

The language used is intensive and emphatic – two words get used, in phrases such as *thought and inclination*, or *bitterly regretted*, when one would have done. The punning word-links (see comments on 5.29) draw together the human condition, the reaction of YHWH and the role of Noah as the person who will bring *relief* (*naham*) to human beings as well as becoming the agent through whom YHWH's 'regret' over the creation of humanity is tempered with his compassion. Relief, regret and compassion all come from the same Hebrew stem.

The ebb and flow of the different meanings somehow foreshadows the chaos that is shortly to befall the earth.

Then the confusion stops abruptly, as does this first section of Genesis, with the briefest sentence and verse in Genesis so far. *Noah* (from the Hebrew verb *nuah*) *had won the* LORD's *favour* (*hen*). This final (for the moment) pun on Noah's name both links us to what has gone before (e.g. 5.29) but also provides a much needed glimmer of hope for the future.

## Theological reflections

### 1. The One and the Two

The first word of Genesis in Hebrew is *bere'shit*. There are many stories told in Jewish tradition to explain why the story of the world's creation begins with the letter 'B', the second letter of the Hebrew alphabet. One response sometimes offered was that 'B' (Beth) was the letter which also begins the word for 'blessing' – *berakah*. And why not with an 'A' (Aleph)? Answer: Because that is the first letter of the Hebrew word for 'curse' (*'arur*). A more widespread tradition, however, drew attention to the fact that Beth as the second letter of the alphabet is also used to represent the number two. The tradition suggests that Beth was chosen for this honour precisely because duality permeates the created universe. That is certainly an insight that resonates through Genesis: creation in Gen. 1 is effected through a series of divisions or bifurcations; in Gen. 2 the animals are clearly 'paired' – contrasted with the human being whose aloneness is 'not good'; later the animals will enter the ark two by two. And then there will be the brothers whom we will meet – often in pairs – throughout most of Genesis.

Yet rabbinic tradition also held that behind this duality of creation lay the fundamental unity of God. The unifying aloneness of God is proclaimed through the Shema: *Hear, O Israel, the* LORD *our God, the* LORD *is one* (Deut. 6.4), in biblical passages such as Isa. 44.24, and in the great medieval Jewish hymn, 'Lord of the world, he reigned alone.'

These first few chapters of Genesis introduce us to the theme with which the entire book will be wrestling, both explicitly and implicitly. How can, or should, the 'one' and the 'two' relate to each other – so that neither dominates nor disappears? Both unity and duality are necessary. And human beings are required to live at the very heart of this conundrum – precisely because we are 'in the image of God'. The concept of image itself locates us somehow between the one and the two. An image is not identical to that which it 'images' – yet at the same time it can not be wholly apart from it. The task is to live properly in the world of duality – for that is the world in which God has set us – but at the same time to perceive and focus within ourselves the underlying unity of God. Commenting on the eating of the fruit of the tree of knowledge of good and evil Carol Ochs writes:

> The real problem represented by the tree is . . . that the serpent so focuses us on duality that we lose sight of the underlying unity. When we age, we need bifocal eye glasses. One sort of bifocal vision – seeing both duality and deeper unity at the same time – opens us to the context in which we have been set down and the awareness of the creator in and with the creation . . . our capacity to recognize both differences and underlying unity allows us to experience perspective and depth. We need both kinds of vision.[3]

A Talmudic 'number poem' about the commandments is also suggestive. It begins from the traditional Jewish statement that Moses received 613 commandments from God, and goes on: David reduced them to eleven (Ps. 15), Micah to three (Mic. 6.8), Isaiah to two (Isa. 56.1), and Amos to one (Amos 5.4). It then observes that Rabbi Akiva said that this one most important principle in the Law was *Love your neighbour as yourself: I am the* LORD (Lev. 19.18), but finally oberves that Rabbi Ben Azzai taught a greater principle even than this: 'When God created the human being, he created the human in the likeness of God' (Gen. 1.27). The rabbis were surely right that this 'greater principle' underlies all the commandments. It is because we 'image' God that we must honour other human beings who are also made in his 'image'. This will have important moral consequences, spelt out explicitly in Gen. 9.6 with its prohibition against murder. Elias Chacour's challenging comment (see p. 229) suggests what that this might mean in one of the most intractable hostilities of the modern age.

The Jewish philosopher Emmanuel Levinas has worked extensively to explore the concept of 'the other'. He comments:

> Men [sic] are not only and in their ultimate essence 'for self' but 'for others,' and this 'for others' must be probed deeply . . . Nothing is

more foreign to me than the other, nothing is more intimate to me than myself. Israel would teach that the greatest intimacy of me to myself consists in being at every moment responsible for others, the hostage of others.[4]

It is only when we acknowledge the radical otherness of the other, and yet our own responsibility towards that 'other', that we cease to make an idol of ourselves.

That is the challenge to which Genesis will keep on returning throughout its 50 chapters. Already in this first section it is met with in the relationship between man and woman, and between two brothers. The delineation of the relationship between man and woman is a key motif of Gen. 2—3. The natural world described in 2.4b—9 includes a number of 'pairs'. This is what is intended by the creator. So it is clearly *not good* for the human being, the crown of creation, to be *alone*. What life could he have if not life in community? His isolation is emphasised. When woman is created as a *suitable partner* the man rejoices. But the terms in which he speaks suggest over-identification. Before man and woman can properly become one flesh of each other they need to become completely themselves, and discover their identity in relation to God. The fourth century Syriac poet and theologian St Ephraem caught something of this in his remark, 'Adam was both one and two; one in that he was man (adam), two in that he was created male and female' (*Commentary on Genesis*).

Perhaps there is even a similar dynamic in the life of God for it is interesting that although the fundamental image of God in Genesis 1 is one of unity, the moment when human beings are created *male and female* is precisely the time when there is a hint of a plurality in God, *Let us* . . . Writing from the Christian perspective one can suggest that we are not far from the mystery of the Trinity, that doctrine which without compromising the unity of God holds that 'life in relationship' is an essential part of the nature of God.

The challenge of the 'other' also appears of course in the sibling rivalry between Cain and Abel, the first of a series of such struggles which will dominate this biblical book. The theme of 'brotherhood' is discussed in more detail on p. 157 and p. 226. But in relation to this specific story it is interesting to ponder whether the essence of Cain's sin was that he wanted God (Yhwh) for himself alone? The first act of religious worship led to the first murder. Yet he can only have God if he also has his brother. And the isolation to which he is condemned is a fitting punishment. Though he seeks to overcome this by building a city – he (and we) soon discover that there is no real community in a place where human beings have not learned what it is to be a brother or a sister.

## 2. *The image of God: being and becoming*

Though we have already touched upon the concept of 'image of God' in the previous paragraphs, the concept is so fundamental in Jewish and Christian theology that it deserves further exploration.

Quite literally the 'image' is remade in every age.

There are two closely related questions. What is it about human beings that means they are made in God's image? And, what are the consequences of this?

A prior issue is the relationship between the two words 'image' and 'likeness'. (1.26) Are they the same or not? Although there have been attempts, particularly in Catholic theology, to suggest a distinction, with 'image' referring to the natural image, and 'likeness' a supernatural characteristic, it is probable that as originally written the two terms were considered largely synonymous – and the use of both is for emphasis.

So what is it about human beings that mean we can be described as 'the image of God'? Answers have included:

- the physical appearance of God and human beings
- the spiritual qualities of human beings
- the human mind and ability to reason
- the capacity for human beings to have a relationship, with God, with one another and with creation.

This last, which perhaps includes elements of the two previous suggestions, is supported by Karl Barth and Claus Westermann, and has become influential in both doctrinal and Old Testament studies. That is broadly speaking the view that is taken in this commentary. Barth in fact explicitly draws out the connection with the creation of humanity as male and female. 'By the divine likeness of man [*sic*] in Genesis 1.27f. there is understood the fact that God created them male and female, corresponding to the fact that God himself exists in relationship and not in isolation.'[5] As Angela Tilby put it, 'The image of God is enfolded in our sexuality.'[6] Others would challenge this as too narrow, suggesting that the 'image of God' is to be found in the interrelatedness of a human being with others, regardless of whether that other is male or female. Certainly at a time of very considerable discussion about sexuality in the churches, it is a reminder that Genesis is a book still with power to impact on the present.

But if we are people of relationship, with God and with each other, a primary reason for this, as we reflect in the comments on Gen. 1.26–28, is to be God's representatives or vice-regents in creation. We noted that the language of image is probably partly drawn from the practice of setting up statues of an emperor throughout the length and breadth of his realm as reminders of his power. It has been suggested that Genesis 1.26–31 could be read as a liturgy for the 'enthronement' of human beings as rulers of creation. Ps. 8, where very similar ideas are stated, certainly uses the word 'crowning'. At a marriage service in the Eastern Orthodox tradition the bride and groom, representing the *male and female* of Gen. 1.27, wear crowns during the ceremony to express this concept.

However to speak of human beings as the 'image' in this way has a revolutionary feel to it. There is an attractive story told about the Rabbi Hillel that vividly illustrates this. Hillel used to go to bathe regularly, and when asked why he did so, he commented that since the images (statues) of the Caesars were washed so regularly he (Hillel) also needed to wash. Because he was made in the image of God he was greater even than a Caesar!

It was not only the people of Israel who reflected on the nature and role of humanity. Many peoples in the ancient Middle East did so and these chapters are imprinted with the richness of their reflections. Mythic images and symbols are used, particularly in Gen. 2—3, whose significance we cannot fully appreciate, perhaps because the Old Testament itself was always ambiguous about how far the mythology of other peoples should be offered space on its own pages.

So, for example, the serpent may have meant more to those readers of Genesis who had neighbours who worshipped a serpent god, while the guardian cherubim are close cousins to the Karibu who protected the entrances to the temples of Assyria. In particular the mysterious *tree of life* would have expanded its meaning in a culture where wooden tree-like figures were venerated as sources of life and perhaps even identified by many as a representation of Asherah, the female goddess. Similarly it is possible that the *tree of the knowledge of good and evil* may represent a parallel male principle to balance the tree of life's female one. The play and dynamics of the relationship of male and female is undoubtedly a theme in the story, but we cannot fully comprehend this because we are not conversant with the writer's code.

Even within the Old Testament itself there is a parallel passage which tells the human story and in which mythological elements seem to be given greater prominence than in Gen. 2—3. Ezek. 28.1–17 tells of a creature who arrogantly seeks to become a god but who is unceremoniously flung out of God's garden.

There are also at least two extra-biblical stories about humanity that can be helpfully read alongside the early chapters of Genesis. The Sumerian Adapa myth tells of Adapa, 'the man' who is bold enough to break the wing of the south wind and is summoned to the divine court to account for his actions. As he arrives in heaven he is offered the bread and water of life, but refuses them because he has been tricked by a god into believing that they are the food and drink of death. He catches a glimpse of heaven, but then is returned to his earthly and mortal existence.

In the Babylonian Epic of Gilgamesh, Gilgamesh, who is mourning his dead friend Enkidu, seeks eternal life. After a long quest he is directed by Utnapishtim (the Babylonian flood hero) to pick the precious plant of eternal life. He does so, but then it is snatched from his grasp by a serpent, and Gilgamesh like Enkidu before him is doomed to mortality.

What Genesis and these stories have in common is a recognition of the ambiguity of the human condition. In the image of God, greater than the animals, and *little less than a god* (Ps. 8.5) – but that little less is ultimately an unbridgeable gap. The story expresses wistfully the almosts and the might-have-beens. The interplay of human and divine wisdom adds poignancy to the ultimate acceptance that the human destiny is death. In Gen. 2—3 we can see a kind of arch: the link between the human being and the dust of the earth is categorically made clear both at the beginning and the end. But in the middle human hopes soar and for one brief moment we wonder if human beings can have it all, wisdom as well as eternal life. It is not to be. Yet it is not a 'fall' that human beings experience (although Ezek. 28 comes closer to suggesting this), but an over-abrupt rise, a too hasty transition from naïvety and innocence to maturity. Human beings are children who grew up too quickly.

We can never return to Eden, and the Old Testament is aware that the way forward for humanity should not be to try and keep one foot standing there. Nor are we to become gods, for there are boundaries between divinity and humanity which must not be transgressed. But Gen. 2—3 can only properly be understood if Gen. 1.26–27 is read first. Human beings *are* created in the image and likeness of God and for relationship with him, and nowhere in the Old Testament is it stated that we have lost this image (Gen. 9.6 makes this clear; Sir. 17.3–7 even links a comment about the image with a positive appreciation of humanity's acquisition of knowledge): if we are banned now from eating the tree of life in the garden we will need to discover a different way of reflecting God's image. God needs this no less than we, and the pages of Genesis will seek to work out this fraught but essential relationship.

This interpretation may come as a surprise to many readers, who, coming at Genesis wearing the Christian spectacles provided by Augustine of Hippo (with the help of St Paul) have been encouraged to view the beginning of Genesis as an account of the creation followed by a 'fall' of humanity. Careful analysis of Gen. 2—3 however throws this interpretation into question, and leads one to ask whether we are being presented with a story of the necessary maturing of the human race. Such a discovery has felt like a liberation to many and is a model of interpretation increasingly being explored.

Augustine's view of this story as a 'fall' was never the only (though it may have been the dominant) viewpoint in Christian history. The second-century theologian Irenaeus commented on Gen. 2—3 in a way that was probably far closer to the mind of the original writers. 'Being but recently made, they had no knowledge of procreation of children; they had to grow up first, then in this way to propagate themselves' (Adv. Haer. III, 32).

The language of image clearly has important implications for Christology. The New Testament explicitly describes Christ as the 'image' of God (e.g. 2 Cor. 4.4; Col.1.15; compare Heb. 1.3). A similar understanding is embedded in the discussion in John 1 of the revealing of God's glory through the Word become flesh. But the celebration of Christ as the 'image of God' does not imply its removal from the rest of humanity. Christ bears the image precisely because he is humanity's perfection. Our problem may not be that we are too human, but that we are not human enough. The task of humanity is to show God's 'glory', his visible presence 'imaged' in us. This image may be marred in us, but it is our potential birthright. The New Testament episodes of the ascension of Christ and his transfiguration on the mountain represent this birthright coming to fruition.

Within Christian tradition the Eastern Orthodox theology of iconography owes a great deal to the concept of image in Gen. 1.26–28; the very word 'icon' is simply the Greek translation of 'image'. As the material and visible icon enables the invisible and immaterial God to be sacramentally present on earth, so too human beings are his moving and breathing 'icons'. Irenaeus summed it up in a way that cannot be bettered, 'The glory of God is humanity alive, and the life of humanity is the vision of God.' Both halves of this statement are important, both belong together, and the story of Genesis takes us on a voyage of discovery to discover the potential of both.

For to speak of human beings as in the image of God, says something important about God as well as about human beings. One of the features of other Middle Eastern creation stories is that they normally begin with a complicated story of interaction between different gods well before the creation of the world ever gets started. Human beings appear in the story very much as an afterthought, and normally not in the most complimentary of terms! The *Enuma Elish* pictures human beings as being made from the blood of Kingu, one of the minions of the evil goddess Tiamat.

The monotheism of the Old Testament forced God into a different relationship with human beings when compared with these polytheistic stories: in spite of the sense of divine transcendence that runs through Gen. 1, God still needs human beings to form relations with – even as human beings need God!

# The Story of the Flood – and its Aftermath 6.9—11.26

What is it about the story of the flood that has made it probably the Old Testament story best known to children? On the surface a story about the almost total catastrophic destruction of the entire world hardly seems to be an appropriate tale for tender years – and yet for generations of children it has been a particular favourite. In part it must be the dramatic possibilities of the story which have been evident at least since the time of the medieval mystery plays. In part it must be because children (and others) can relate well to a story which focuses on the interaction between humans and animals.

The popularity of the flood story is not a modern phenomenon. The story of a great flood is the one of the most widespread of all folk tales or myths. Peoples from many parts of the world have told of the inundation of the earth by a deluge. It is likely that many of these stories grew up independently, reflecting the common human dread of uncontrolled and uncontrollable water. A feature they have in common is that they remind us in a pure form of the reason for myth: we tell the story precisely because we believe that by doing so we will prevent such a flood from coming again. This is a feature that is a part of the biblical flood story (see Gen. 9.9–16), which ends with a solemn promise on the part of God never again to visit flood on the earth.

And yet, of course, flooding would recur. The biblical flood story cannot be understood apart from the Mesopotamian accounts of the flood to which it owes several significant features, even though it also reworks the Mesopotamian tales to accommodate its own theological viewpoint. The geography and climate of Mesopotamia encouraged reflection on a 'flood': civilisation in Mesopotamia, the land between the great Tigris and Euphrates rivers, was only possible because of the annual flood of these rivers, swollen with waters brought down from the Taurus mountains. Without the annual flood the elaborate irrigation systems of the Mesopotamian cities would dry up: yet in years when there was an excess of water destruction and death would result. Water brought both death and life, and that tension is there also in the biblical story, where the destruction wrought by the flood is interwoven with the thread of new creation.

There are at least three Mesopotamian accounts of the flood. The best known is that set within the Epic of Gilgamesh. Gilgamesh in his quest for eternal life seeks out the survivor of the flood, Utnapishtim, who has been privileged to have been granted eternal life by the gods. Utnapishtim recounts to Gilgamesh the story of his experiences, and why it is that he was specially chosen. A much older story (on which the saga of Utnapishtim itself depends) was told by the Sumerians, whose civilisation in southern Mesopotamia flourished in the third millennium BC. The name of the hero in this account was Ziusadra. There is also a third version, which is in some ways the closest to the biblical tale. In this version the hero who escapes the flood is Atrahasis – 'the exceeding wise'.

There are also apparently two accounts of the flood in Genesis, in chapters 6—9. See the table below which refers to these. Unlike the creation stories of Gen. 1 and 2 we are not given two consecutive accounts, rather two versions are interwoven with each other

*The two versions of the flood story*

|  | A | B |
|---|---|---|
| Chronological information about Noah |  | 6.9–10; 7.11 |
| Reason for flood | 6.5–8 | 6.11–13 |
| Noah told to build Ark |  | 6.14–18a |
| Number of animals to take | 7.1–5 | 6.18b–22 |
| Entry into the Ark | 7.7–10 | 7.13–16a |
| YHWH closes the Ark | 7.16b |  |
| Description of flood | 7.22–23 | 7.18–21 |
| Length of rain/flood | 7.12, 17 | 7.24; 8.4–5; 8.13–14 |
| Flood stops | 8.2b–3a | 8.1–2a |
| Sending out of birds | 8.6–12 |  |
| Exit from Ark |  | 8.15–19 |
| Noah sacrifices/new relationship with God | 8.20–22 | 9.1–17 |

throughout, including, for example, two apparently different sets of instructions as to the number of animals to be taken onto the ark, two different chronologies for the period of the flood, and two different conclusions.

The material in column A has affinities with Gen. 2.4b—4.26 and that in column B with Gen. 1.1—2.4a and Gen. 5. This apparent doubling in the narrative complicates and challenges the assumptions of source criticism. On the one hand it *is* difficult to accept that one writer could be solely responsible for what appear to be two versions of the same story intertwined together; on the other hand it is not feasible that any final editor would weave together the two strands without noticing the kind of discrepancies that also perplex modern readers. So the question is: accepting the possibility that Gen. 6—9 features two different retellings of the traditional story of the Flood, what is the reasoning behind this apparently confused conflation of them in the final edition of Genesis? The setting of Gen. 1.1—2.4a alongside Gen. 2.4b—3.24 provided us with alternative and contrasting views about the nature of humanity: what does the intermingling of their counterpart narratives in Gen. 6—9 suggest to us?

We need to remember that the interaction between 'duality' and 'unity' is a focus throughout the whole of Genesis. The working together of 'one' and 'two' is presented as the ideal goal of creation. This is expressed perfectly by the ordered narrative of Gen. 1.1—2.4a in which number plays such an important part in the establishment of the 'good' creation. Conversely the 'breakdown' or dissolution of creation, which is how the flood is portrayed in Genesis, is aptly reflected in the numerical confusion in these chapters and the very fact that we have two narratives that are woven rather uncomfortably together. This jarring sense of de-creation is emphasised particularly through the contradictory references to time in the narrative. Since the establishment of time was such a central focus of Gen. 1.1—2.4a it is appropriate that 'creation undone' is marked by it ceasing to work properly. Yet for all these inconsistencies Gen. 6—9 does have an underlying structure – noted by Bernhard Anderson,[1] it is a chiastic or concentric form, in which the beginning corresponds to the end – and the narrator encourages us to work towards the middle, the most important moment. In this case that is Gen. 8.1, and the moment when *God took thought for Noah.* Similar chiastic structures mark out other sections of Genesis – the story of Abraham and that of Jacob.

We have included the 'post-flood' episode of the Tower of Babel, again reflecting a Mesopotamian geographical context, and the two genealogies which surround it, both introduced by the *toledot* formula, in this section. There is uncertainty as to where precisely they belong, and they seem to be used within the structure of Genesis both to conclude the primeval history and to open up the story of Abraham which follows. The focus on unity in the story of the Tower of Babel provides an intriguing contrast with the dualities which permeate the story of the flood.

Taken as a whole this section seems to 'replay' similar themes and motifs to those which were introduced in Gen. 1.1—6.8. The parallels have often been noted.

*Parallels in Gen. 1—11*

| 1.1—2.25 | 6.9—9.17 | Creation/uncreation/re-creation |
|----------|----------|---------------------------------|
| 3.1–24 | 9.20–21 | Problems with a fruit |
| 4.1–16 | 9.22–27 | Competition between brothers |
| 4.17—5.32 | 10.1–32; 11.10–26 | Genealogies |
| 6.1–4 | 11.1–9 | Breaking human/divine boundaries |
| 6.5–8 | 11.27–32 | Interlude introducing next section |

By 'replaying' the first section of Genesis in this way the materials in chapters 6 to 11 implicitly pose a key question about God's dealings with creation, and particularly humanity. The flood is God's statement that his first efforts had 'gone wrong' so drastically that he felt the need to start over again afresh. But when the new world that emerges from the deluge seems to have so many of the same problems as did the old, what will God do this time? Will he need to start over again – again – or is there another, and better, way forward?

## Washing the world clean
### 6.9—9.28

The introductory comments about the story of the flood which have been given above emphasise how this long narrative dominates the second section of Genesis.

**6.9–22**  *This is the story of Noah*: A new section of Genesis has begun – introduced by the key word *toledot* – which contains within itself the idea of 'birthing' or giving life. Yet this new section will start with so much death.

*Noah was a righteous man, the one blameless man of his time*: This is the first time in Genesis that anybody has been described as *righteous*, and it is a term that will be used very sparingly in the future. Abraham's bargain with God over the fate of Sodom, suggested that a few righteous men might be able to save a whole community (19.23–32). Noah's righteousness at least allowed him to save all his household (7.1) – and the future, even if not the present, of the world.

*Blameless*: This is an expression used frequently of 'perfect' sacrificial animals. Perhaps it is apposite, since Noah's muteness throughout the entire flood story is remarkable. He is no Abraham pleading for those who God has decided to destroy.

Like Enoch his great-grandfather before him Noah *walked with God*. Yet there will be an important difference. Enoch was mysteriously 'taken' by God and seems to have avoided death. A similar fate was met by the Mesopotamian flood hero Utnapishtim whom Gilgamesh consulted in his quest for eternal life. In spite of the correspondences that link Noah to both Enoch and Utnapishtim Noah will definitely die (9.29) albeit at 950 years.

Noah *had three sons: Shem, Ham, and Japheth*: These three sons tell us that a new era in humanity's history is about to begin (compare 11.26).

*God saw that the world was corrupt and full of violence*: This provides verbal reminders of Gen. 1. There God had told humanity to *fill* (1.28) the earth – and now he 'sees' just what they have chosen to fill it with. The word *corrupt* (*shahat*) occurs three times in two verses. The identical Hebrew verb, though translated as *destroy*, occurs as God pledges *I am about to destroy them*. It is like for like, quid pro quo.

One of the striking aspects of the judgement is the interplay it presupposes between human beings and the earth. It is acknowledged that human beings are responsible for the violence on the earth (6.13), but due to this the world itself *is corrupt*. Underlying this is a belief that blood shed violently (e.g. 4.10) physically polluted the earth. Such a contamination had also to be physically eradicated. The flood is when the earth is washed clean.

*Make yourself an ark*: The detailed description for the making of this ark is reminiscent of the even more elaborate instructions in Exod. 25—27 for the making of the Tabernacle. That is not accidental. The welfare of the entire human race will depend on both being properly built. The Hebrew word used for the ark (*tebah*) is rare: the only other time it is used in the Old Testament is in Exod. 2.3 where it describes the floating basket of reeds in which the baby Moses was kept safe. In both ark and basket the future of God's relationship with humanity is cradled with fragility.

*I am about to bring*: The tense of the Hebrew emphasises how soon the flood will come. The drops of rain are virtually starting to fall!

*The waters of the flood*: The 'flood' was the name given to the heavenly ocean on which God was enthroned (Ps. 29.10), divided from the earth by the vault (Gen. 1.6–7). So for this 'flood' to come *over the earth* was a mark of the dissolution of creation.

*Every human being that has the spirit of life.* It is deliberate that language so associated with humanity's creation (2.7) is re-spoken by God at this time of total obliteration.

*But with you I shall make my covenant*: At this precise moment when all is as dark as possible, the word 'covenant' is introduced into the Bible. Against all the odds there will be hope for the future. And it is a future that will involve a concrete relationship between God and human beings (see further on 'covenant' on p. 67).

*You are to bring living creatures of every kind. . . two of each kind*: The focus on pairs helps to reinforce the sense of duality which pervades this narrative.

*Noah carried out exactly all God had commanded him*: Now that the verb 'command' has been introduced into Genesis it will reappear twice within the next ten verses (7.5, 9). It will then disappear again. It is an appropriate verb to reflect the situation of the mute Noah and the lengthy monologue by God.

7.1–23 *The LORD said to Noah, 'Go into the ark'*: The instructions are repeated again, with some differences. Though these differences are probably due to the incorporation of material from two different sources, the repetition of the divine commands further emphasises Noah's obedience and God's determination.

*Take with you seven pairs . . . and one pair*: This is one of the most readily noted discrepancies between the two strands in the narrative. In 6.19–20 Noah had been told to save two of each kind of animal, now it is seven pairs for animals that are *ritually clean*. There is a logic to this larger number; it will allow for sacrifice, and for the fact that after the flood humanity is allowed to eat the flesh of 'clean' animals. 7.8–9 offers a still further variation.

*He was six hundred years old when the water of the flood came*: It is remarkable how many precise chronological notes there are in this story; for example, 7.10, 11, 24; 8.4, 5, 13, 14 (see further below, p. 52, comments on 8.13–14).

*The springs of the great deep burst out, the windows of the heavens were opened*: The flood is not simply caused by the rain referred to in 7.4, 12: rather the whole cosmos seems to break up as the work of the second day of creation is reversed. *The great deep* is the primeval ocean which as a result of God's creative activity had been confined beneath the dry earth. Underground springs were points at which it could still break through, and now these springs were surging up with overwhelming force. Water came from above as well. As in 6.17 we are reminded that the 'vault' of heaven had waters confined above it (compare 1.6): the opening of the windows in the vault threatened to release the destructive power of these waters too. This was no ordinary rain shower.

*The LORD closed the door on him*. The quaint, almost anthropomorphic, description reminds us of the deity who had once walked with Adam and Eve in Eden. It is an intimate gesture which suggests that in spite of God's determination to destroy almost everything, he was equally determined to ensure the safety of Noah and those entrusted to his care.

Coming at the end of a section (7.7–16) which habitually uses the word 'God' rather than 'LORD' these words have always been a problem for division of the flood narrative along traditional source-critical lines (see comments above). Perhaps the choice of the word 'God' or 'LORD' ( i.e.YHWH) to describe the deity may (at least in part) depend on the precise role God is playing in the story at any given point.

*They [the waters] increased over the earth*. Another reversing reminder of the creation story. Then humans had been commanded to 'increase' (1.28) – but now the 'increase' of the waters ensures a dramatic and almost total decrease in their numbers!

7.24—8.19 *God took thought for Noah*: God remembered Noah. This is the mid point of the story around which the waters of the flood may swirl but they cannot overwhelm. It is the tiny pin-prick of hope which will allow a new future to be inaugurated. Later on the same Hebrew verb *zakar* (elsewhere often translated 'remember') will often be linked to a covenant. So God will 'remember' how he is bound in covenant relationship with human beings and act accordingly (e.g. 9.15). But at this point in time there is no covenant yet inaugurated. God's 'taking thought' for Noah stems from the very nature of God.

*He caused a wind to blow*: The re-creation is beginning. 'Wind' or 'Spirit' – the same word *ruah* in Hebrew – had hovered over the deep in Gen. 1; so now it marks the beginning of God's new adventure with his world.

*The ark grounded . . . on Ararat*: The dramatic peaks of this mountain on the borders of present day Turkey/Armenia made it a suitable location for the grounding of the ark. Appropriately the verb *tanah* (*grounded*) used here comes from the same Hebrew root as Noah's own name.

*Noah . . . sent out a raven . . . a dove*: This is one of the points where there are very close links with the Mesopotamian versions of the flood story. In these a dove or a raven are also used as 'scouts'. Indeed the mention of the two birds perhaps suggests that more than one traditional source was in the writer's mind and there has been an attempt to collate them. The raven is rather redundant to the story as it now stands. The dove's first unsuccessful journey is curtailed because she *found no place where she could settle* (Hebrew: *manoah*) – yet another pun linked to Noah's name. Her later return with an olive branch in her mouth is the first time part of a tree has been mentioned since humanity was in the garden of Eden.

*On the first day of the first month of his six hundred and first year . . . By the twenty-seventh day of the second month*: The chronology of the flood plays an important part in the story. It is quite confusing but it seems likely that the author wants to suggest that the flood lasted exactly a year. It is probable that the two chronological references in vv. 13 and 14 are referring to the same day: in one case measuring it in terms of Noah's life, in the other in terms of the calendar. Back in 7.11 we had been told that the flood had been begun *on the seventeenth day of the second month,* so at first sight it looks as though the flood must have lasted a year and ten days. It has been plausibly suggested that this apparent discrepancy is due to the use of two different calendrical systems 'playing together' in this one text. During the post-exilic period there was fierce controversy about calendars. There is little contemporary evidence about the 'official' Jewish calendar, but 1 Enoch 72—82, Jubilees and Qumran show that in some circles two systems were known, a 'lunisolar' calendar with a year of 354 days (adding an extra month every 36 months), and a solar calendar with a year of 364 days (presumably with the addition of an extra month at intervals), though a 365 day year was also known. Perhaps the inter-weaving of the two calendrical systems in this one story reflects this debate and is an additional example of the 'confusion' of time which has symbolised the breakdown of creation throughout the flood.

But with the ending of the flood the 'right' time will be restored. The new beginning of the world on this day implicitly lays the foundation for the annual observance of New Year's Day, just as the creation of the world in Gen. 1.1—2.4a had laid a similar foundation for the keep-ing of the Sabbath.

*Bring out . . . let them spread . . . and be fruitful and increase.* Almost identical words had been spoken in blessing in 1.22 (to animals) and 1.28 (to humans). The flood had transparently undone the hope expressed in the earlier blessing – will humanity and the animal world fare any better this time?

8.20–22 *Noah built an altar . . . When the* LORD *smelt the soothing odour*: The version of the flood story in the Mesopotamian Epic of Gilgamesh tells us that Utnapishtim too offered sacrifice to mark the end of the flood and 'the gods smelled the sweet savour, they gathered like flies over the sacrifice'. However the choice of the word *soothing* (Hebrew: *nihoah*) to describe this particular sacrifice links it to the very reason for Noah's own existence. The linguistic connection between *nihoah* and Noah's own name, with its basic meaning of 'rest', is deliber-ate. Noah was celebrated as the one who *will bring us relief from our work, from the labour that has come upon us because of the* LORD's *curse on the ground* (5.29). And so with this sacrifice the wordplays on Noah's name which underpinned the flood narrative (see p. 34) come to their resolution: the promised rest to be brought by Noah is now actual-ised through this sacrifice, which 'rests' the anger of YHWH. The earth will no longer be cursed: its seasons and times will have a regular-ity which will allow it to be productive. Perhaps too productive . . . (see 9.20–21).

*Never again shall I put the earth under a curse*: It is God who has changed – not humankind. The *inclination* of human beings is still *evil* at the end of the flood, just as it had been at the beginning (6.5), when it had provoked God to take his devastating action. In this verse the entire relationship between God and his creation has shifted. God's very graciousness now means he forsakes his absolute power (see further, p. 63). The internal wrestling within the divine heart is emphasised by the way that YHWH spoke *within himself*.

*As long as the earth lasts*: The rhythms of this short verse aptly express the rhythms of the seasons which it is promising. The divisions of time, which had broken down so completely during the flood's uncreation, are now restored. This is the first of three short poems (9.6; 9.13—14) which highlight in turn the modus operandi to apply to the earth, to human beings and to God, in this brave new post-flood era.

9.1–17 *God blessed Noah and his sons*: Even more explicitly than in 8.17 the blessing of Noah recapitulates the original blessing offered to humanity in 1.28. Noah is presented as a 'second Adam' in this new creation. The fruitfulness of this tiny group of survivors will re-populate the earth. There are differences: human beings are no longer simply vegetarians. Animals, as well as plants, can now legitimately be consumed as food. Not surprisingly therefore the original trust between humanity and the animal creation pictured in Gen. 1—2 no longer exists. It is replaced by *fear and dread*.

But there are still prescribed limits to humanity's dominance of the animal creation. The eating of animals with their blood, where it was believed their life was concentrated, is prohibited. This is the foundation text for the Jewish (and indirectly the Muslim) food laws which prescribe a particular method of animal slaughter.

But it is to humanity itself that God then explicitly turns: with the punning in 9.6 between *dam* (blood) and *'adam* (human) strengthening his pronouncement. The phrase *the death of their fellows* (literally 'brother') immediately recalls Cain's killing of Abel, that primeval sin which had been multiplied by Lamech (4.23–24). This new creation is not to be marred by similar violent death.

Is this new creation to be an inclusive or exclusive one? Is it marked by diversity – or uniformity? It is striking how a connection is made between humanity's status *in the image of God* and respect for the sanctity of human life (9.6). Cain by his actions against his brother Abel had defaced the image of God in himself. The statement of Gen. 9.6 offers a remarkably wide-ranging vision of what it means to be human. The formulaic way in which it is set out implies that all human beings have a similar right to equality of protection. Pro-tection is owed to all descendants of Noah, which means everyone. There is no place for preferential treatment or discrimination over this fundamental human right. Any who wage war today, justifying their actions on the basis of the Judaeo-Christian tradition, do well to remember this. Western lives are not more valuable than those of the peoples of Africa or Asia.

The requirements laid upon humanity in this chapter underlie the later concept of the 'Noachide commandments', which rabbinic Judaism considered to be imposed on all humanity. According to this understanding Jews and Gentiles alike were required to abstain from murder, idolatry and sexual sins. The requirements laid upon Gentile converts in Acts 15.20 by the church in Jerusalem may also be linked to this.

Yet the inclusive vision does not stop there – for the covenant that is then granted by God is made not only with human beings, but *with every living creature* (9.10, 15, 16) and between God *and the earth* (9.13). After the flood, just as before it, human beings cannot separate themselves from the rest of creation of which they are a part.

*God said . . . I am now establishing my covenant*: Seven times the word 'covenant' occurs between vv. 8 and 17, a powerful echo of the days of creation and a symbolic reminder of completeness. Something fundamentally new – and creative – has entered the relationship between God and creation. The hidden commitment which God had made in 8.21 is now out in the open. The dualities which have dominated the flood narrative throughout finally come to their resolution in this one covenant made for all time and with all creatures. Unlike the Sinai covenant which is presented in conditional terms, and could be potentially terminated (Exod. 19.5) through human disobedience, the covenant offered by God in Gen. 9 establishes a relationship which God binds himself to – whatever the cost to himself, and however deep the intransigence of human beings. The reference to this covenant in Isaiah 54.9–10 captures perfectly the overwhelming grace of God contained within it: *my love will be immovable and never fail, and my covenant promising peace will not be shaken*. Through 9.1–17 Noah remains completely mute, accentuating the one-sided obligation which God is placing himself under (see further on 'covenant' on p. 67).

The choice of the rainbow as the sign of this covenant may owe something to Mesopotamian traditions, but it is also very apposite here. By placing his bow (with its seven colours!) in the sky God had put aside his weapon of war and was offering a covenant promising peace. Formed like an arc it mirrors the shape of the vault of heaven. It was a visible reminder that this barrier, so essential to the well-being of creation, would never be dissolved. God's 'remembering' which had initially sprung freely out of his own heart and on which the whole flood story had turned (8.1), is now linked irrevocably to the concept of covenant (9.15, 16).

At the end of the Mesopotamian flood stories the flood hero is removed from the rest of humanity and taken to live with the gods as an immortal. In this biblical equivalent Noah very definitely remains a man of the earth. Unlike Utnapishtim the 'life' that results from his experiences is not for him alone – his task rather is to be an agent of life for the entire world.

9.18–28   This final episode in the story of Noah feels, on the surface, rather like a comic contrast with the world-shattering events which have just taken place. But just as after Gen. 1—2 creation took some inopportune paths, so here too, the 'new creation' presents problems as well as possibilities. The actions of Noah recall Gen. 3. In both stories the eating of fruit has unforeseen consequences, and the theme of nakedness plays a part in each. There are also echoes of the fraternal rivalry of Gen. 4. Gen. 9.18–28 in fact has a key role in concluding the story of Noah and it may be no accident that the name of the son Ham, who is responsible for the outrage against his father, recalls the Hebrew word *hamas, violence,* mentioned in 6.11 as the primary cause of the flood.

The strange elliptic tale contains inconsistencies. Why is it implied at one point that Ham is the middle son of Noah, but elsewhere his youngest son (9.24)? Why is Canaan apparently unfairly cursed for his father Ham's actions? Perhaps there was a more extensive well-known tale of which this is a fragment. The story also points forward to what will transpire shortly: the comment that the descendants of Noah's three sons *spread over* the whole earth (9.19), prefigures the dispersal (same Hebrew verb) that occurs after the Tower of Babel (11.8, 9), though here, perhaps significantly, the verb does not appear to have the negative connotations with which it is often loaded in chapter 11.

With the curse now lifted from the ground Noah can become a productive *tiller of the soil*. Too successfully, as his imbibing of the wine from his vineyard leaves him in a pathetic drunken stupor. What exactly did his son Ham see – or do? Was it more than simply looking on his father's genitalia? Suggestions have included the possibility that he engaged in incest with him or even castrated him. But even 'looking' might well have offended social taboos, certainly in an Old Testament culture that disapproved profoundly of Canaanite fertility cults, in which drunkenness and sexual licence played a part. The specific mention of 'Canaan' as the object of Noah's curse may hint that this was partly what was in the writer's mind. However a glance

at Ham's descendants in the following genealogy (10.6–20) also suggests they represent nations that were feared either for their empires
or for their aggressive expansionism, just as Ham's misguided actions
had earlier seemed to give him inappropriate control over his father.
In the eyes of the writer of Genesis the curse of slavery would seem an
appropriate reversal.

His curse of Canaan, and blessing of Shem and Japheth, is the first
time that Noah has uttered a word throughout his entire story from
5.28 onwards. Back in 6.9 Noah had been described as *righteous* and
*blameless,* and he had mutely followed God's instructions all through
the lengthy narrative of the flood. But in this post-flood era righteousness needs to be more than that. God will begin to withdraw from
direct involvement in human society. It will not be enough for human
beings simply to relate to God, they need to discover how to relate to
each other in a way that fosters justice and peace between peoples,
rather than inappropriate competition. Noah, whose words were
used for centuries to justify the slavery of millions of Africans (the
putative descendants of Ham) may not be the hero we need for this
new time.

*He was nine hundred and fifty years old when he died*: This then is all
there is left therefore to say about Noah. He died at a great age, older even than Adam, and with a far longer lifespan than any of his
descendants. He lives – just – into the third millennium, but he will
have died by the time that the new era inaugurated by Abram has
begun (12.1).

## Peoples and languages
### 10.1—11.26

The two genealogies (10.1–32; 11.10–26) form an envelope around the
story of the Tower of Babel, and the whole section acts as a bridge between the primeval stories and the tales of the ancestors. Structurally
it is debatable where the primeval narrative ends and the ancestral
saga begins: some commentators regard 11.10–26 as belonging to the
Abram/Abraham saga which follows it. Others would suggest that
the primeval story ends with 9.29 and see the 'Table of Nations' (10.1–
32) as setting the scene for the call of Abram. The analysis of Genesis'
structure is affected by the theological presuppositions brought to it.
Certainly both genealogies and the story of the Tower of Babel look
forward in the overall tale of Genesis, as well as back.

10.1–32    The *toledot* formula reappears (10.1) to introduce what is often called 'the Table of Nations', which illustrates how quickly the blessing of 9.1 has come to fruition.

It is marked by its expansive diversity, setting out the entire 'family of the nations' as known to the writer of Genesis. One of its intriguing features is that it mentions three times (11.4, 20, 31) how each nation had its own language. Set, as it is, immediately before the story of the Tower of Babel, this feels a contradiction, but perhaps it is also a hint that we should not take the 'confusion of language' in the tale of Babel as negatively as is often done.

If one brackets out the reference to Nimrod which feels like an intrusion, designed perhaps to hint at the story of the Tower of Babel which comes next, the list contains exactly 70 names – a number which symbolically reflected completeness. It is not neat and tidy. Some names appear twice e.g. Havilah 10.7, 28. It includes the offspring of all three sons of Noah. Note that Ham, whose family is cursed as a result of his actions in 9.20–25, is still included in the list. However Ham's descendants do not have a particular ethnic profile. Genesis has no truck with an ethnic apartheid.

The use of the plural for some of the names (10.13–18) is a reminder that we have moved away from a focus only on individuals or a family, to human communities and civilisations. Though the saga of Abram/Abraham will revert to concentrating specifically on one small group – this table encourages us to set those doings of Abraham's family in a wider political and social context.

Some of the names are clearly identifiable with specific geographical localities, for example: Javan (Greece); Tarshish (Spain); Kittim (Cyprus); Rodanim (Rhodes); Cush (Ethiopia); Mizraim (Egypt); Put (Libya); Canaan; Seba and Havilah (areas of Southern Arabia); Asshur (Assyria); Lud (Lydia) ; Aram (Syria). In the case of others we can often guess the general area that is meant. Broadly speaking the family of Japheth is linked with regions north and west of Palestine, the family of Ham, Africa, and the family of Shem is located in Arabia and Mesopotamia.

But 'untidiness' creeps in. Why, for example, is Canaan, son of Ham – the eponymous ancestor of the land along the east Mediterranean coast to which Abram would journey – a 'brother' of those who are associated in this table with Africa? And why does Nimrod, son of Cush, migrate from Africa to Mesopotamia – and in the process overlap with a region and places (e.g. Assyria 10.11; Asshur 10.22) associated with the family of Shem?

Ellen Van Wolde[2] suggests that the divisions are not so much geographical as sociological. The descendants of Japheth were primarily coast-dwellers and seafarers, those of Ham primarily urban and sedentary, and those of Shem largely nomads. This may explain the emphasis clearly placed on 'Eber'. Although he was only the great-grandson of Shem he is mentioned alongside his great-grandfather in 10.21, where Shem is described as *the ancestor of all the sons of Eber*. Eber's name is related to the word for 'Hebrew', and comes from a word which means to 'pass by', 'travel' or 'cross over'. His name implies his nomadic lifestyle. It is from Eber that Abram will descend. Is being a 'wanderer' or 'migrant' therefore being 'written in' as a necessary characteristic of the branch of the family on which the story will soon focus?

Two references in the list linked to Ham hint at negative episodes that will shortly take place. Nimrod's kingdom includes Babel, in *the land of Shinar* (10.10) just where the Tower will be built. And we are very carefully told that Canaan's border included *Sodom and Gomorrah* (10.19, see 19.1–29).

Yet although the table of nations reflects the hostility between the different lifestyles of the ancient world, and in particular fear of the power of the great urban empires and kingdoms in Egypt, Mesopotamia and Canaan, the impression it creates is of a blessed diversity. And a question: where in all this is the nation Israel?

11.1–9   It is difficult to read the account of the building of the Tower without recalling modern skyscrapers, and particularly the Twin Towers of New York. Since September 2001 the analogy has often been pointed out. We have already had a hint that cities may not be the healthiest of locations – it was Cain or his son Enoch who built the first one (4.17). Other clues that something is amiss are found in the location, Shinar (where Nimrod's kingdom was), *in the east* (the direction in which Adam, Eve and later Cain settled). There are also verbal indicators that link this story with earlier episodes (3.1–24; 6.1–4) in which humanity had overreached itself and transgressed the boundaries between humanity and divinity.

Indeed it is remarkable that the builders set about their task with an exhortation in the first person plural *Come, let us make . . .* (11.4) that recalls God's own use of the first person plural when he created humanity (1.26). Equally telling – God's reaction, a few verses later *Come, let us go . . .* (11.7) both echoes the builders' own turn of phrase and also reclaims for God the majestic plurality used at that moment of creation. These people may think that they can 'make' something – and a *name* for themselves (11.4), but they completely fail to realise the awesome gap between themselves and the Lord of all creation, however high their tower might be.

Yet God's first instruction to humanity after their creation and repeated after the flood was to 'fill' the earth. That is precisely what these builders have forgotten. In their quest for unity and homogeneity focused on one small space of earth they have tried to obliterate God's creative vision of duality and diversity. To no avail – God's purposes will not be defeated. The ironic result of God's intervention is that they do receive a name – Babel/babble (11.9) – though presumably not the one they sought. And their 'scattering' (11.9) across the earth is not only a punishment but also the fulfilment of God's will in creation.

The story 'dances' with wordplays to reinforce its point: fittingly appropriate in a tale about language. As well as that between Babel and 'babble' (Hebrew: *balal*) which is apparent in English as well as Hebrew, the narrator plays with the words for 'build' (*banah*) 'brick' (*lebena*) and 'son' (*ben*) which sound similar in Hebrew. The Hebrew of 11.5 literally speaks of YHWH coming down to see what 'the sons of the human being had built', and this choice of words to describe the builders both hints at the puny competition they seek to offer YHWH ('What is the son of a human being that you should take notice of him?' (Ps. 8.4)) and reminds us of the original human challenge to the deity in Gen. 3. And it is surely not accidental, as Michael Fishbane suggests,[3] that with a subtle ironic twist, the 'babbling' or confusing of language which YHWH proposes in v. 7 (*nabelah*) inverts the same letters as the builders used in their bricks (*lebenah*).

But there is a further set of wordplays associated with 'name' (*shem*) which links the tale to what has immediately preceded it – and will shortly follow it. The basic pun is now between *shem* and *sham* (= 'there'), which is emphatically used on five occasions in these verses to designate the place where the tower was built. A 'name' is not made for oneself by doing something 'there', in 'that place'. Rather Shem, the son of Noah (with a name which means 'name'!), who will be mentioned again in the very next verse, shows us what a name is all about. It is associated with a nomadic life rather than city dwelling, and it will be given par excellence to Shem's descendant – Abram (12.3) as he sets off on a journey in obedience to YHWH's command.

11.10–26   Once again the *toledot* formula appears, this time to introduce a vertical genealogy of Shem's descendants. The list of ten names has a similar function at the end of this section of Genesis to the genealogy of 5.1–32 with its ten names at the end of the preceding section. It bridges the generations to take us speedily to the next important initiative in God's dealings with humanity.

Although the deaths of the ancestors are not specifically mentioned this time (unlike 5.1–32) their apparent lifespans are getting shorter. Shem in fact outlives all his descendants except Eber. Eber is the last ancestor to have a lifespan of more than 400 years: is the diminution after this due to the association of Peleg with the time when *the earth was divided* (10.25 – presumably a reference to the Tower of Babel)? Eber is the fourteenth ancestor (counting from Adam), a position that reinforces his symbolic significance (i.e. 7 × 2).

Though only one son is named for each ancestor the regular comment that they had *other sons and daughters* makes apparent the fruitfulness of humanity in response to the blessing of 9.1. It contrasts with Abram's lack of progeny, a theme which will shortly dominate the narrative of Genesis.

Finally we reach Terah – like Noah (5.32) he breaks the pattern by having three named sons, in his case *Abram, Nahor, and Haran*. And the fact that they were born when he was a 'perfect' 70 years old is another clue telling us that once again something important is going to take place.

## Theological reflections

### 1. The chaos of exile

The story of the flood is by far the longest episode in the 'primeval history' of Gen. 1—11 and it lies at the mid point of these chapters. This may mark its importance from the perspective of those whose own experience was formative in the writing of the book – those who were living through exile in Babylon. In these chapters we hear the echoes of their own story and their sense of being 'overwhelmed' by the chaos of exile. The Old Testament explicitly draws a comparison between flood and exile. In the exilic section of Isaiah, 40—55, Yнwн proclaims, *This to me is like the days of Noah* (Isa. 54.9). The exilic community felt acutely the sense of almost total loss that the flood narrative portrays, loss of land, identity, religious and social institutions, of hope and relationship with God. Everything had changed. All had apparently been swept away. The community had experienced too the 'violence' which had been the flood's precursor. The uncreation of which the flood story tells mirrored Israel's own.

Yet it was also as a result of the exile that they were able to discover the possibilities for new beginning. It was precisely the flood myths told and retold in Mesopotamia that provided the source for the Old Testament telling of the story of the flood – which did not ultimately end with destruction, but with new creation and the promise of God to sustain the future. To paraphrase T. S. Eliot's famous words the flood story was an acknowledgement that having faced 'the end' they were gifted a 'beginning' in which they might know themselves properly for the first time. Isa. 40—55 once again provides commentary, in its wrestling with both the reality of sin and the assurance of God's ultimate refusal to abandon the people. *When you pass through water I shall be with you* (Isa. 43.2). The relationship between God and his people is being hammered out afresh, and at a new depth:

> *In an upsurge of anger I hid my face from you for a moment;*
> *but now have I pitied you with never-failing love,*
> *says the* LORD, *your Redeemer. . ..*
> *as I swore that the waters of Noah's flood*
> *should never again pour over the earth,*
> *so now I swear to you*
> *never again to be angry with you or rebuke you.*
> *Though the mountains may move and the hills may shake,*
> *my love will be immoveable and never fail,*
> *and my covenant promising peace will not be shaken,*
> *says the* LORD *in his pity for you.* (Isa. 54.8–10)

Recent writers have pointed out how the motif of exile is one which speaks to our time in the early twenty-first century. Ralph Klein, in a thought-provoking monograph, *Israel in Exile*,[4] has argued that the literature that springs out of the 'exile' has a peculiar power to address us in these days when a spirit of alienation, change and rootlessness is widespread and the relevance of tradition is called into question. Along with the psalmist many of us might say, *I have come into deep water, and the flood sweeps me away* (Ps. 69.2).

Through the flood narrative Genesis recalls a violent humanity to remembrance of God's power to re-create. The story delivers us to resonances of hope which we desperately need.

## 2. The grieving of God

It is important to draw attention to the 'grace' which is written in to the story of the flood (see further the play on 'grace' and Noah's name p. 37) because at first sight the picture of God that this story offers is very dark indeed. Can we really worship a God who is prepared actively to wage total destruction on creation? Trevor Dennis comments that the only way he finds himself able to preach on the passage is by suggesting that the ocean on which the ark finds itself adrift is that of God's own tears.[5] He goes on however to suggest that that is not how Genesis itself presents it. But perhaps he does himself a disservice, perhaps the grief of God lies closer to the heart of the narrative of Genesis than we initially realise?

One of the features of the intricate wordplays in 5.29 and 6.6–8 (see p. 34) is that they bind together God and humanity with words of power and pathos. They thus contain a hint, albeit a tentative one, that God is not a stranger to human pain. This is accentuated by the double use in Hebrew of the word *leb* (which can be translated as 'heart') in 6.5–6 where a literal translation might be that the 'thought of the heart' of human beings was wicked (6.5) , and that God was 'pained to his heart' (6.6). As Walter Brueggemann puts it, 'this is indeed "heart to heart" between humankind and God'.[6] In these verses we are being presented with a deity who wishes to stand alongside his human creation rather than over against them in judgement. Yнwн is not detached from this decision. He is intimately caught up in it, as we all are when we take difficult and perhaps painful decisions which impact on those we love. Indeed the very word *regret* used twice in connection with Yнwн's intention to destroy comes from a Hebrew root (*naham*) that more usually means 'have compassion', 'console', 'pity'. It is used with that sense at the powerful opening of Isa. 40.1, *Comfort my people*. Even while we translate it here as 'regret', the word hints at Yнwн's ultimate 'compassion' for humanity, and the *relief* (5.29, a word from the same Hebrew root) which Noah will ultimately bring.

Admittedly 6.11–13 feels rather different. No longer is there the need for deliberation. God here is assured. *I am about to destroy them.* Yet it is important to note that the name of the deity has also switched here from Yнwн to *Elohim* (God), and this switch seems to reflect a different face of God. It is Yнwн that is used when the divine relationship to human beings is emphasised. And the placing of the two names, and two moments of decision together like this could even suggest a struggle in the very being of the divine, such as is expressed in Hos. 11.8–9 where God argues within himself about the fate of Israel, and even speaks of his *change of heart.*

But whatever we make of God before the flood, when we come to its aftermath we certainly discover a God who has changed. Not so human beings, the language used to describe their attitude after the flood is deliberately reflective of the words used to describe them beforehand. Once again we have the double use of *leb* to reflect the 'heart' of both God and humanity. The 'thought of the heart' of humanity is still evil (8.21, REB, *however evil their inclination may be*). Yet as YHWH 'speaks to his heart' once again (REB, *within himself*) this, his own heart, has moved from regret to compassion. The flood 'has effected an irreversible change in God, who now will approach his creation with an unlimited patience and forbearance'.[7] He will continue to grieve over human wickedness, but has pledged himself to show forbearance. And this means that the promise that God offers to Noah and all creation is one which will be of great cost to God and which will necessitate divine suffering. He will allow his love to be wounded – again and again. God will voluntarily limit his power, but in giving humanity this new freedom he will open up the possibility of a real relationship with them.

Back in Eden God had been fearful of allowing human beings to 'grow up' and make decisions for themselves. Their childish disobedience had been duly punished – for God had not yet realised that if he wants a real relationship with humanity it would inevitably involve confrontation. The flood is the moment when that original mode of relating reaches its climax – and God learns that it is not enough. In the world begun anew after the flood God will try another way, that will allow us to reflect back God's love. This is the paradox at the heart of Genesis: God has to allow human destructiveness to exist and take its course in order for there to be such a thing as divine love incarnate.

## 3. Our fragile globe

The corollary of this is that the responsibility for this world and its future now rests firmly with humanity. No longer can we 'merely' consider ourselves serfs who can blame a divine 'master' if things go wrong. God has limited his power to bequeath it to humanity. But the covenant in which he has done so is one that is deliberately couched in terms that remind humanity that the welfare of the entire creation depends upon them. The *'adam* (= 'human being') whose story we have been hearing in Gen. 1—11 is still to be responsible for the *'adamah* (= 'earth').

There was a tradition in apocalyptic writings that there would be another great cataclysm – but that this would be of fire, not water (see 2 Pet. 3.10). God had apparently pledged himself merely to refrain from bringing another flood (9.11,15).

As a folk song puts it, 'No more water, but fire next time.' But this is to misunderstand the climax of the story of the flood. If there is another world disaster, another cataclysm, it will probably be due to humanity, not God. The fact that often such feared disasters are described in language that is reminiscent of the flood or other early parts of Genesis emphasises their profundity and awfulness but also twists the knife of the irony. We cannot blame God – comforting though it might be to do so.

We cannot blame God for the nuclear holocaust of which Edith Sitwell writes in her startling poem, 'The Terrible Rain', an image which was echoed in the protest songs of the 1960s.

We may speak of Schindler's Ark when we hear about the activity of Oskar Schindler in saving hundreds of people from the Nazis – but we cannot blame God for the holocaust from which he was seeking to save them.

We cannot blame God for the violence that infests our world today, whether it be the direct violence of terrorism or the indirect violence which comes in the train of a certain kind of globalisation. We need to remember the words of Martin Luther King, 'It is no longer a choice between violence and nonviolence in this world; it's nonviolence or nonexistence.' But it is our choice – not God's.

And above all, we cannot blame God for potential and actual ecological disasters in our fragile world – for those who have seen an ecological significance in the 'rainbow covenant' that is offered in Gen. 9 have perceived something which is true to the heart of the story. Just as chapters 6—7 seem to suggest an 'Uncreation', so too does the following anonymous poem:

In the beginning was the earth.
And it was beautiful.
And man lived upon the earth. And man said:
'Let us build skyscrapers and expressways.'
And man covered the earth with steel and concrete.
And man said, 'It is good.'

On the second day,
man looked upon the clear blue waters of the earth.
And man said, 'Let us dump our sewage
and wastes into the waters.' And man did.
The waters became dark and murky.
And man said 'It is good.'

On the third day,
man gazed at the forests on the earth.
They were tall and green. And man said:
'Let us cut the trees and build things for ourselves.'
And man did. And the forests grew thin.
And man said 'It is good.'

On the fourth day,
man saw the animals leaping in the fields
and playing in the sun. And man said: 'Let us trap
the animals for money and shoot them for sport.'
And man did. And the animals became scarce.
And man said 'It is good.'

On the fifth day,
man felt the cool breeze in his nostrils.
And man said: 'Let us burn our refuse
and let the wind blow away the smoke and debris.'
And man did.
And the air became dense with smoke and carbon.
And man said 'It is good.'

On the sixth day,
man saw the many kinds of people on the earth –
different in race, colour and creed.
And man feared and said: 'Let us make bombs
and missiles in case misunderstandings arise.'
And man did. And missile sites and bomb dumps
checkered the landscape.
And man said 'It is good.'

On the seventh day, man rested.
And the earth was quiet and deathly still.
For man was no more.
And it was good! (Anon)[8]

God has offered us the freedom and privilege of a covenant with him. That is our blessing and our bane.

## 4. The challenge of covenant

What about the 'covenant' referred to above? In this section of Genesis the concept of 'covenant', so central to the entire Bible, is introduced for the first time. God has made a covenant with Noah and with 'all living creatures'. The motif of covenant will recur again in the coming chapters, most particularly of course in the account of God's making of a covenant with Abram (15.18; 17.1–14), but also in the agreements that will be made between Abraham and Abimelech (21.27–31), then between Isaac and Abimelech (26.28–31), and finally between Jacob and Laban (31.44–54). What is the essential meaning of this concept?

There has been a great deal written about 'covenant' in Old Testament scholarship over the past 40 years. Most of it however has focused on the Mosaic or Sinai covenant, and has drawn analogies with the international treaty system in the ancient Middle East, whether focusing on second millennium Hittite treaties, or first millennium Mesopotamian ones. But while such analogies *may* make sense of the Sinai covenant, presenting it as in effect a 'treaty' between YHWH and the people of Israel, they are far less satisfactory as an explanation of the covenants made between God and Noah or Abraham in Genesis. Unlike the Sinai covenant whose continuance apparently depended on Israel's willingness to keep the commandments, these two covenants seem to have an unconditional nature: God 'oaths' himself to Noah and his living creation without apparently making any corresponding demands upon them. The case of Abraham is slightly more complicated partly because of the two versions of the covenant; in Gen. 15 and Gen. 17 each has a slightly different emphasis. But even in Gen. 17, where a link is made between covenant and circumcision, it is likely that the covenant itself was perceived as eternal and irrevocable and that circumcision was effectively a sign of those who had agreed to identify themselves as partners in the covenant which God had established.

Studies of the actual Hebrew word for covenant, *berit*, have not been altogether fruitful, although there is a general consensus that there is a close relationship between a covenant and the pledge of an oath. Certainly an oath seems to be an intrinsic part of a covenant-making ceremony, and it is probably not accidental that the first and second covenants recounted in Genesis between two human parties both take place at Beersheba, a site apparently with the word 'oath' in its name.

A recent article by F. M. Cross, 'Kinship and Covenant in Ancient Israel' has however revived a view about the essential nature of a covenant which, while never completely forgotten, has often been overshadowed by the focus on the treaty analogy. Cross argues that we should understand a covenant as a

> legal means by which the duties and privileges of kinship may be extended to another individual or group . . . kinship relations defined the rights and obligations, the duties, status, and privileges of tribal members . . . kinship was conceived in terms of one blood flowing through the veins of the kinship group. If the blood of a kinsman was spilled, the blood of the kinship group, of each member, was spilled. Kindred were of one flesh, one bone.[9]

He also comments that marriage in ancient Israel should be understood in a similar way: the bride enters into a relationship of kinship with the family of the groom.

Cross's suggestion implies that when God makes a covenant with Noah and creation, or with Abraham and his descendants, he is, in effect 'adopting' the other party as kin, and agreeing to accept the mutual obligations inherent in kinship: 'He leads in battle, redeems from slavery, loves his family, shares the land of his heritage . . . provides and protects. He blesses those who bless his kindred, curses those who curse his kindred.'[10] He becomes 'the Divine Kinsman'. It is likely that such a concept of 'covenant' was initially applied to a specific national or tribal group (e.g. the descendants of Israel, or Abraham) and it was perhaps only during the exile that it was radically extended to relate to Noah and all creation. Given the link between kinship relations and marriage, it is telling that the analogy of the deserted, but now reinstated, wife of Isa. 54.1–8 appears immediately before the mention of a covenant with Noah in Isa. 54.9–11. Perhaps this was in fact one of the points where the biblical tradition said more than it realised, or even intended, in suggesting such a wide-ranging covenant, and we have been tasked with working out its meaning ever since.

For the corollary is that there is a family likeness in all humanity, a concept that perhaps may seem so obvious that it is redundant to state, until one remembers how the genocides of the twentieth century were facilitated by the belief that the 'other' was somehow sub-human. It is on this 'familial' assumption that the prohibition of murder in 9.6 is based. This is why it will be so important in the stories to come that brotherhood is 'got right' because ultimately it will be a pattern for relationships not simply between the descendants of Abraham, but also between the descendants of Noah – everyone.

## 5. Faith in the city

Cities do not, on the whole, get a good press in the Old Testament, or at least in Genesis. It was Cain, or perhaps his son, who built the first one (4.17). Our analysis of the 'Table of the Nations' (10.1–32) suggested that the great cities of the day were regarded as being inhabited by the family of Ham, again presumably a connection viewed negatively. And then there is the Tower of Babel, where not only a tower, but also a city, is built (11.4) – and destroyed. The French theologian Jacques Ellul has famously described the city as being a focus of evil throughout human history, an example of humanity's declaration of independence from God.[11]

Yet it is no accident that the Bible, which begins in a garden, will end in a city (Rev. 21.2—22.5). This is all the more striking since the 'tree of life', originally associated with the Garden of Eden, will end up being planted in the middle of this city (22.2). In the transference of the symbol there has been a deliberate shift from the garden to the city: the implication is that life can, or should, be found in the city. Even within the confines of the Old Testament itself the language with which the new Jerusalem is pictured, particularly in Isa. 56—66, offers us an alternative vision of the city as the place where God dwells. Cities are recognised as the places where human life can be lived with a particular fullness and intensity, for good or for ill.

So what are the dangers, and the possibilities, inherent in city life? One of the features of the city described in Rev. 21.25 is that, *The gates of the city shall never be shut by day, nor will there be any night there.* Is this significant? In the ancient Middle East what marked out a city over against, for example, a village, was the fact that it had walls. The primary image associated with a city, therefore, was defence, and possible warfare. And this sense of defensiveness is surely in the minds of the builders of Babel too, *Let us build . . . or we shall be dispersed* (11.4). Their first reaction to an apparent technological advance, the ability to make bricks, was a concern for self-defence.

Throughout human history there has frequently been a connection between the desire for security and the ordering of society along totalitarian models, in which difference is prohibited from being expressed. There are plenty of examples from the infamous 'evil empires' of the twentieth century. Most of these have now disappeared, but they have been replaced by the 'globalisation' of our world, which itself might be viewed as an ideology. Indeed since we are thinking about the Tower of Babel it is relevant to note that there is a strong link between the rapid spread of globalisation and the use of the English language. Whether intentional or not, this has privileged one language and culture over all others. In turn this has led this particular culture to a sense of defensiveness about itself. In view of the way that the events in America on September 11 2001 have been read alongside this biblical narrative, it is relevant to observe that there is an implicit arrogance in the title 'World Trade Center'. It begs the question, whose 'world' is it anyway? Who has the right to appropriate for themselves such a sweeping title?

Certainly our post 9/11 world does not seem to have considered that the way forward for the future is to find new ways to respect the 'The Dignity of Difference'. It is telling that Jonathan Sacks' book of that name, with its subtitle, 'How to avoid the clash of civilizations' has a sixteenth-century picture of the Tower of Babel on its cover. Sacks argues that the meaning of this biblical story is, at least in part, how God insists that people 'make space for difference. God may at times be found in the human other, the one not like us.'[12]

Since Christians often read the story of Pentecost (Acts 2.1–36) as an undoing of Babel, it is important to observe that the gift of the Spirit there does not make people identical – but facilitates their mutual understanding, while still preserving their differences. *All of us hear them telling in our own tongues the great things God has done* (Acts 2.11). As our churches have wrestled with the fact of globalisation and its significance, positively or negatively, for their mission, they have increasingly come to realise that their task may be to provide an alternative model which encourages inculturation and values difference.

The walls of the traditional city were a powerful symbol of the fear of the 'other'. Yet the story of Pentecost, which took place in the city of Jerusalem, itself showed how cities can be places where different cultures can meet and learn from each other in a way that would be impossible in rural or small town life. The last biblical word on the city, with its gates continually open (Rev. 21.25), asks us to find in the city a place of hospitality rather than defence.

# The Story of Abraham
## 11.27—25.18

With the journey of Abraham in Gen. 12 a 'New Start' begins: quite literally. It is the first significant event to happen in the third millennium
(2021) counting from the creation of the world, and just as Noah's
birth had announced a new beginning at the start of the second millennium, so Abraham's journey will also mark a new departure for
humanity. We are now entering an epoch and dealing with people
who have a basic familiarity about them: they will live lives comparatively close to the normal human lifespan, and the boundaries
between the divine and the human worlds will gradually be fixed in a
shape with which we are comfortable (though it will take till the story
of Joseph and his brothers to get this sorted out completely!).

The stories of the ancestors which fill the next chapters of Genesis
have a strange homeliness about them: they are the accounts of the
loves and hates of a family, with emotions such as jealousy, greed,
passion and longing all to the fore. They have been called 'The Forsyte
Saga' of the Bible! They remind us of some of the incidents in Gen.
1—11 (perhaps particularly the episode of Cain and Abel), but the
figures we are going to meet are no longer cardboard cut-outs from a
faraway time, but characters with whom we can begin to empathise,
in spite of their obvious differences of lifestyle and social mores.

Over the last half century a variety of approaches have been taken to
the ancestral stories linked to Abraham.

The 1950s and 1960s saw 'the quest for the historical Abraham'.
Working backwards from the later history of Israel, the time of the
patriarchs was hypothetically located in the eighteenth to the fif-
teenth centuries BC. The stories were then quarried for examples of
economic and social institutions which were regarded as particularly
characteristic of this period in the mid-second millennium BC. W. F.
Albright and others used their knowledge of extra-biblical Middle
Eastern cultures to provide parallels: one often quoted example is the

practice in the Hurrian city of Nuzi whereby a husband could adopt his wife as his sister, and thus also gain the status of her brother. This is linked by Albright with the occasions when both Abraham (twice) and Isaac (once) attempt to pass off their respective wives as their sisters (Gen. 12.11–13; 20.2, 12; 26.7). Another comparison frequently made between extra-biblical texts and Genesis is the use of a slave-girl by a barren wife to provide her husband with children (Gen.16.1–2; 30.1–4).

But during the last 25 years such an approach has been challenged: first by Tom Thompson in *The Historicity of the Patriarchal Narratives*[1] and shortly afterwards by John Van Seters, *Abraham in History and Tradition*.[2] Both writers have called into question the methodology used by Albright, which tended to over-emphasise similarities between Genesis and extra-biblical material and did not pay adequate attention to the context of these extra-biblical sources themselves. (Nuzi is actually far from the presumed trajectory of Abraham as he journeyed round the Fertile Crescent from Ur to Harran and thence to Canaan, while the Nuzi texts themselves stem from a period several centuries after the supposed 'patriarchal age'.) The views of Thompson and Van Seters have grown increasingly influential, and there would now be considerable scepticism about the validity of a 'quest for the historical Abraham', arguing that the stories reflect rather the social and religious context of the first millennium BC in which they were written down.

As with the primeval history of Gen. 1—11 these chapters have also been explored from a source-critical perspective. Source criticism has been employed to explain the number of apparent doublets in the chapters – the twice that Abraham attempts to pass off Sarah as his sister, and the fact that Abimelech, king of the Philistines, suffers the same gambit from Isaac as well as Abraham. In this part of Genesis too the differing ways that God is named were believed to provide a guide to distinguish the different sources.

However, the comments about recent developments in Pentateuchal studies made on p. xviii also apply here. Although it is almost certain that the final author(s) of this part of Genesis made use of earlier oral and written sources in compiling their work, it is now difficult to be confident as to the precise date and provenance of these earlier sources. In particular the apparent 'doublets' in the story may not reflect two parallel sources which have been combined, but have been developed as part of a storytelling device. And the rationale for the different names of God, which in this section of Genesis extends

beyond the words YHWH and *Elohim* met in Gen. 1—11 to include titles such as El Shaddai (e.g.17.1) and El Roi (16.13), may be primarily
due to the different modes with which God interacts with the variety
of characters in the tales.

A recent approach to the Abraham material, which owes a debt to
traditional Jewish scholarship, is to concentrate on the quality of the
narrative, and explore it from the perspective of literary criticism.
Apart from helping us to understand just why certain incidents in the
lives of the ancestors were apparently repeated, it allows us to make
sense of the stories as part of a greater whole. The core of this section
of Genesis is 12.1—22.19, which is begun and ended by two stories in
which God calls Abraham, in both cases using the unusual Hebrew
expression *lek leka* to do so. If we look at Gen. 12—22 in this way the
following structure seems to emerge.

*The literary structure of the story of Abraham*

    A1 12a The call (*lek leka*). Blessing promised
        B1 12b Abraham in Egypt. Wife-sister motif. 13 Controversy
        over livestock.
            C1 13–14 Lot in danger. Sodom.
                D1 15 Covenant
                    E 16 Hagar and Ishmael
                D2 17—18a Covenant
            C2 18b—19 Lot in danger. Sodom.
        B2 20 Abraham in Gerar. Wife-sister motif. 21b Controversy
        over livestock.
                 [21a Birth of Isaac/ Hagar and Ishmael.]
    A2 22 The call (*lek leka*). Blessing confirmed.

(adapted from an analysis by Jonathan Magonet)[3]

By omitting for the moment the stories of Isaac's birth and Ishmael's
expulsion in chapter 21, this provides us with a perfectly concentric
or chiastic pattern in which Gen. 12a is balanced by 22, 12b by 20,
moving steadily inwards until we reach the account of the flight of
Hagar and the birth of Ishmael in Gen. 16. This acts as the linchpin of
the structure. It is intriguing that the story of Hagar should have this
role in the narrative (see further on p. 91). It also helps to explain the
further story of Hagar and Ishmael in 21 which breaks the concentric
pattern. Chapter 21 *ought* structurally to be the ending of the literary

unit – the fact that it isn't increases our anticipation as we wait for chapter 22 (to which it is closely related, see p. 118).

Within this overall structure it seems that the two Hagar–Ishmael stories in chapters 16 and 21 form a further envelope surrounding the announcement of Isaac's birth in 17—18 and his actual birth at the beginning of 21. So the Hagar–Ishmael stories both provide the structural centre for the cycle, and also point away from Hagar–Ishmael ultimately to Isaac. This ambiguity reflects the place of Ishmael and his mother in these stories.

Although chapters 12.1—22.19 form the core of this section, they are in turn further framed by 11.27–32 and 22.20—25.18 which offer an introduction and conclusion to the saga of Abraham.

*Note*: Although we use the name 'Abraham' to describe the patriarch at points when we are considering his story as a whole, or looking back on his life from the perspective of his descendants, within the commentary below we have deliberately used the name 'Abram' to refer to him up till the point where his name is changed by God in 17.5.


## *The journey starts – and a detour*
### 11.27—13.18

The rest of Genesis will be dominated by a sense of 'travel'. So the motif is introduced at this key and opening point in the story of the ancestors. The description of Abram's movements in 12.8–9 deliberately uses words which draw upon the technical vocabulary of nomadic life. But we are reminded that there are various kinds of journeys, those like Terah's (11.31), which appear to stem from his own initiative, and those like Abram's in which divine initiative plays a leading role. We are also reminded that it is possible to take wrong paths, and potentially get lost: within the space of a chapter a major diversion will occur, which will require a speedy backtrack – and bring problems in its wake.

*11.27–32* Once again the word *toledot* (here translated 'descendants') appears, to mark out a new section of Genesis. Note that it is the *descendants of Terah*. Although the chapters that follow will focus on one particular descendant – Abram/Abraham – before the section finally concludes (25.18), other members of the family will have had their part to play in the story. Our appetite is being whetted.

Since the excavations of Leonard Woolley at Ur, on the banks of the Euphrates in Southern Iraq, *Ur of the Chaldees* has often been linked to this location. It is however perhaps more likely that a town in northern Mesopotamia was meant – perhaps modern Urfa (Edessa). *Harran* was an ancient city in what is now north-east Syria.

The overall impression created by these few verses is of death and sterility. Haran dies (11.28), Terah dies (11.32) and Sarai is barren (11.30). It is a negative picture with which to begin this section of Genesis, even if on a more domestic scale than the utter destruction of the human race with which the previous section of the book had begun. If there is to be the life and fruitfulness which creation had promised (1.28; 9.1) a new initiative is clearly going to be necessary.

12.1   *The LORD said to Abram, 'Leave your own country, your kin, and your father's house, and go to a country that I will show you.'*
The main part of Abraham's story begin with a summons and a peremptory one at that, particularly in the original Hebrew. The first of the two appearances of the alliterated expression *lek leka* (translated *Leave*) demands of Abram that he must sacrifice his entire past. (The second in Gen. 22.2 requires of him that he be willing to sacrifice his future.) And for what? *A country that I will show you* is an unbearably vague geographical expression, which calls straight away for an absolute trust in YHWH.

*I will show you* translates a Hebrew word that literally means 'I will make you see'. Sight, or the lack of it, is going to be a key motif in the Abraham cycle: from its beginnings here in Harran Abraham will journey to *the mountain of the LORD* (22.14) where he will eventually discover that there is vision.

The threefold list of what Abram is compelled to leave behind sharpens the sense of loss: it would not have been too great a burden for him to leave his country – after all, he was only a temporary and recent visitor to Harran. But *your kin* and then *your father's house* builds up the tension and increases the sense of isolation, particularly if we remember what we have been told only a few verses previously *Sarai was barren; she had no child* (11.30).

Abram is summoned by God speaking intimately as YHWH. YHWH will continue to use this name for his dealings with humans throughout most of the following chapters, though he will name himself as *God Almighty* in 17.1 at precisely the moment when Abram becomes Abraham (17.4). Names for humans and the divine are important in these chapters, though not necessarily as a marker for different sources.

12.2–3    In Gen. 1 God had spoken and called creation into being. The words now being spoken (particularly because of their close connection with blessing) recall that genesis and are equally as powerful. This is a new 'divine initiative in a world where human initiatives always lead to disaster, and are an affirmation of the primal divine intentions for humanity'.[4] God's promises to Abram are to be as sure as creation.

In line with the vagueness of YHWH's command the promises themselves have a lack of specificity about them – at least to begin with. They will be fleshed out as Abram's story continues.

To be a *great nation*, which means both numerically great, and politically significant, will require both offspring and land.

The promise that God will *make your name so great that it will be used in blessings* is written with one eye on the previous story of the Tower of Babel. The builders had set about their work in order to *make a name for ourselves* (11.4), now a great name is being freely offered to Abram by God. The secret is of course, as it is throughout Genesis, that when human beings seek to assert their own wills against God they are doomed to failure; when they acknowledge their dependence upon God they gain more than they would have ever dreamed possible. Abram, descendant of Shem (a word which means 'Name') is to fulfil the destiny to which Shem's very name points.

The promise moves from prose into poetry as what is meant by *I shall bless you* is elucidated. Abram is not merely himself the recipient of YHWH's blessing, but through his relationship with God is to become the source and means of blessing for others. This is a new initiative in God's relationship with humanity: once again a snippet of poetry marks out a milestone in God's adventure with the human race. As with other points when poetic forms appear (see p. 12), they help to emphasise a relationship, in this case between YHWH and Abram, and between Abram and *the peoples on earth*.

Resonances of the blessing offered to Abram surface again later in the stories of the ancestors, particularly at points of transition or difficulty (e.g. 22.18; 26.4). However even when no direct verbal links are expressed, many of the stories of the later patriarchs seem designed to show this blessing practically working itself out in action.

*Those who bless you, I shall bless*: God's promise of blessing will extend to those who support and work alongside Abram and his descendants, such as Laban the Aramean whose flocks multiplied while Jacob was working for him. The other side of the coin: *Those who curse you, I shall curse* is not clearly demonstrated in Genesis, but the language is echoed in Num. 24.9 when the Moabite opposition to the people of Israel after their escape from Egypt rebounds upon the Moabite king's own head.

*All the peoples on earth will wish to be blessed as you are blessed* : This is one way to make sense of an ambiguous piece of Hebrew. However, there is an alternative translation noted in the REB footnote: . . . *will be blessed because of you*. This, of course, makes more explicit how Abram becomes the channel of YHWH's blessing for others. Paul's New Testament theology of Abram (e.g. Gal. 3.8–9 and comments on p. 147) depends upon this alternative.

Gen. 12.2–3 are in essence the narrowing down of the blessing given at creation, and repeated to Noah. The blessing focuses now on one person, in order that it might eventually be shared by all humanity as had originally been intended. It is, of course, ironic that the outworking of a blessing which had insisted that human beings should *Be fruitful and increase* (1.28) should depend on this one, childless man.

12.4–9   Abram's age is mentioned at key points in his story, as here.

---

*Significant times in Abram/Abraham's story*

12.4 Abram is 75 years old when he leaves Harran.

16.3–4 Abram had been in Canaan for 10 years when Ishmael was conceived.

16.16 Abram is 86 years old when Ishmael is born.

17.1, 24 Abram is 99 years old when the covenant of circumcision is given.

21.5 Abraham was 100 years old when Isaac was born.

23.1 Sarai died aged 127. (Abraham would have been 137 years old.)

25.7 Abraham was 175 years old when he died.

This means that the life story of Abram from the moment when God called him spanned exactly 100 years.

---

If he was *seventy-five years old when he left Harran* then his father must have been alive when he did so, even though Terah's death has already been referred to (11.32). If Terah was still alive the command given in 12.1 to leave *your father's house* makes better sense.

Was it intended by YHWH that *Lot went with him?* On the surface it suggests that Abram was not fully obeying the instruction to leave *your kin*. Certainly Lot's presence on the journey and in Canaan creates problems and acts as a diversion and sub-plot before Abram's ultimate destiny is fulfilled. There is quite a lot of baggage which travels with Abram to Canaan: some, at least, of it will need to be stripped away before Abram is made ready to be the instrument of God's purpose.

Abram originally travelled to the major Canaanite sanctuary of Shechem, a key location in the story of the patriarchs, and throughout the later history of Israel (e.g. Josh. 24.1–32; 1 Kgs 12.1, 25). Magnificent trees such as terebinths (a form of oak) often marked out significant sanctuaries in Canaanite culture. They were a sign of abundant life, in a potentially arid land. Although worship *under every spreading tree* is condemned by prophets as syncretistic (Isa. 57.5; Jer. 3.6), the ancestral stories suggest that there were those who believed that it was not impossible for Canaanite religious practices to be 'baptised' into the faith of YHWH.

Once again YHWH speaks to Abram and what had been a vague location when he spoke in Harran now is made precise: one of the criteria for the fulfilment of YHWH's promise that Abram would become a great nation now becomes more explicit with the promise of land.

Shechem is an appropriate place for the ancestral story to begin: the same location implicitly ends the book of Genesis, for it is where Joseph's bones will eventually be buried (50.25–26; Josh. 24.32). First here at Shechem, then between the significant cities of Bethel and Ai Abram builds an altar, and standing in a line that goes back to Enosh, the grandson of Adam, calls upon YHWH by name (see 13.4, and notes on 4.26). In effect he thereby stakes out his and YHWH's claim to this land, although the comment *at that time the Canaanites lived in the land* helps to remind us that God's promise to Abram is still far from being fulfilled. (It also makes it clear that the narrator is telling the story from a perspective considerably later than the supposed era of Abram.)

*Abram journeyed by stages towards the Negeb*: We can assume that he is en route for the sanctuaries of Hebron (Mamre) and Beersheba to build altars there and to complete the 'claim' to the land. Shechem, Bethel/Ai, Hebron and Beersheba would mark out a very neat 'Promised Land'. But it doesn't work out like that, for something else intervenes.

12.10–20 *The land was stricken by a famine*: a frequent event in the hill country of Canaan where the variable and fragile annual rainfall pattern often meant that land used for agriculture one year became semi-desert the next. Where better to go than Egypt, a byword in the ancient world for food in abundance (Num. 11.5)?

But in the Old Testament people cannot go to Egypt without going *down* there – with all the negative connotations the word implies. To travel to Egypt is to undo the Exodus (Deut. 17.16) and that applies to Abram the forefather just as much as to kings who might rule Israel and Judah centuries later. There is a hint of lack of faith in Abram's decision to leave the land of promise and migrate Egypt-wards: it is certainly not a move sanctioned by YHWH.

Abram's next actions don't cover him with glory either. He is self-ishly far more concerned with his own safety (*they will kill me*) than with protecting his wife Sarai or preserving her dignity. Abram acknowledges that her life would never have been in danger: *they will let you live*. Sarai is treated merely as a chattel to be traded for Abram's own advantage. Perhaps it is fortunate that she is still barren, for otherwise (in the patriarchal culture of the day) YHWH's promises to Abram could go seriously askew, since the inference that Sarai had sexual relations with Pharaoh is clear. Does Sarai herself know about those promises that God made to her husband? There is no hint that she does – yet. Abram's hope *that all may go well with me* is reminiscent of the expression that God uses when people are blessed for keeping the commandments (see e.g. Deut. 6.18): it is ironic that Abram should use it of himself when he is where YHWH doesn't want him to be, and when he is doing what YHWH presumably doesn't want him to do!

Pharaoh on the other hand is presented reasonably positively. *He treated Abram well*. The gifts that he offers Abram are almost excessive. He is an innocent party, who is justifiably annoyed when YHWH, hitherto notably absent from these verses, has to step in and sort out the situation to prevent his promise to Abram from going adrift. There is a hint of the Exodus story around: *the LORD inflicted plagues on Pharaoh*. Pharaoh apparently has his wits about him and realises straight away the reason for the disaster (compare 20.3). But unlike the attitude shown by the Pharaoh of the Exodus towards Abram's descendants this Egyptian treats Abram with decency even when his deception is uncovered. It may be the first triumph over Egypt recorded in the Old Testament, but Abram has hardly as yet proved a blessing to the *peoples on earth* (12.3) – rather the opposite.

Yet he does quite satisfactorily out of his Egyptian adventure – he is allowed to keep all that Pharaoh had given him and has become very rich (a point reiterated in 13.2). Of course among the *male and female slaves, she-donkeys, and camels* that Abram took with him as he departed from Egypt we can assume that there was a female slave called Hagar, who will appear so prominently in Abram's later mis-adventures. In these ancestral stories one thing so often leads on to another.

13.1–9   The aftermath of the Egyptian escapade had other con-sequences too. It meant that Abram and Lot between them risked overloading the fragile land of promise. Too much cattle, too many possessions. The situation is exacerbated because other people are also around with their rights and their demands on the land. The com-ment first made in 12.6 is repeated: *The Canaanites and the Perizzites were then living in the land.*

Abram and Lot are still on their travels together, for due to their diversion into Egypt they haven't yet completed their stake-out of the land. It takes them some time even to get back to the spot between Bethel and Ai *where he had earlier pitched his tent, and where he had previ-ously set up an altar.* They then have to pick up the story again from the point where they left it before the detour to Egypt.

*Quarrels arose between Abram's herdsmen and Lot's*: The rancour hasn't yet infected the relationships between Abram and Lot themselves, which is fortunate for otherwise we could be retreating back to the story of Cain and Abel. But it risks doing so: *There must be no quarrel-ling between us.* The risk and reality of fraternal strife runs throughout Genesis. Even though Abram and Lot are uncle and nephew it can still infect them too: *we are close kinsmen* (the literal meaning of the Hebrew is 'we are brother people').

Opportunely Abram takes an initiative to ensure harmony. If YHWH's blessing of humanity is going to work brothers will have to learn to live in some kind of peace. It is up to Abram to start this process, even though he is going to make many mistakes before he is through. He generously suggests that Lot should settle in part of the land of promise, while he will choose another part for himself. *If you go north, I shall go south; if you go south, I shall go north.* But Lot chooses to go neither north nor south – but rather east, to the plain of Jordan. He removes himself from the promised land. (It is interesting how in Genesis going 'east' often means travelling in a direction that takes one away from God see 3.24; 4.16; 25.7.) In case we have not taken the hint from the direction in which Lot goes it is made clear. The place that Lot chooses was *like the land of Egypt.* And though it is here described as *well watered . . . like the Garden of Eden* – we know all too well that things can go wrong in Eden. The first readers of Genesis who were aware how barren was the landscape near Sodom must have appreciated the irony of the description.

Harmony has thus been secured at a cost – the exclusion of Lot from the promises. We were not sure if the reason that the childless Abram brought Lot with him from Harran in the first place was to take the role of his heir. But if so, what has now happened must rule it out. We are back to square one again, or even perhaps in minus territory, because the unspecified wickedness of Sodom, the place where Lot had chosen to settle, hints at menace and disaster to come. There would be another occasion when Lot would look *all the way to Zoar* (see 19.20–22). One thing certainly leads to another in the stories of the ancestors.

13.14–18    *After Lot and Abram had parted*: YHWH speaks to Abram again. It is as though YHWH couldn't really have a proper conversation while Lot was still around. Now we can really get down to the serious business of the promise. YHWH requests Abram politely (using the Hebrew particle *na* which will appear again in Gen. 22) to *Look around*. The relationship between YHWH and Abram is growing closer. YHWH does not command Abram to receive the promise; he invites him to.

The symbolism of seeing is a powerful motif throughout Gen.12—22. But when Abram is told to *Look around* there is something special to look at. In Gen. 22.13 he *looked around* and saw a ram which took the place of his son as a sacrifice.

It is a spectacular vista for him to glance at now. The Genesis Apocryphon (a reworking of part of Genesis that has been discovered among the Dead Sea Scrolls) suggests that Abram stood on top of Ramat Hazor, a magnificent hill near Bethel, from which even today you can see clearly as far as both the Mediterranean Sea and the Jordan Valley. This might well have been the very spot in the writer's mind. The land has been promised to Abram before (12.7) but not in such detail. He is instructed to complete the stake-out that he had begun before he had got diverted to Egypt. *Go through the length and breadth of the land*. He does so and finally, near Mamre, in the south of the country, near the ancient city of Hebron, he settled.

At this point in his story the working out of YHWH's promise to make Abram *a great nation* (12.2) takes another tentative step forward. The picture of the land which is to be granted to Abram is painted in with more detail. We also hear YHWH pledge to make Abram's

descendants *countless as the dust of the earth*: a paradoxical announcement to this childless man who was now effectively bereft even of his
nephew.

## The stranger in our midst
### 14.1–16.16

Although the three next chapters feel disparate, with their scope
ranging from the international to the domestic, and may well come
from different sources, as they now appear in Genesis they are linked
together through a series of wordplays and motifs, which encourage
us to read them alongside each other.

14.1–12   The tempo and the panorama changes. We are looking at
things on a completely different scale. Not the familial, but almost a
global perspective. The first four of the kings named here are not local
lords of small city states, but emperors of massive realms that created
the history of the ancient Middle East. Abram himself will be very
different too: no longer the cowering husband who hid behind Sarai's
skirts when he met Pharaoh, but a courageous war lord who refuses
to allow his *kinsman* (14.14 literally his 'brother') to be held prisoner
whatever the personal cost to himself. One might wish that Abram
had showed as much concern for Sarai as he now does for Lot.

Such differences have led some scholars to suggest that this chapter
was written by an entirely separate hand from the rest of Gen.12—
22. They believe that although it may contain early source material
it was appended to the rest of Genesis at a very late date, perhaps
even the Maccabean period. Others however have suggested that this
story of an encounter between Abram and Melchizedek may contain
traditions dating from the days of the monarchy designed to justify
the way in which aspects of Jerusalem's pre-Israelite and Canaanite
religious roots influenced the religious practices of the nation.

It is *four kings against five*. But the four emperors far outweigh
the petty princelings who are their opponents. They are the rulers of
Shinar (Babylon), Ellasar (possibly the kingdom of Larsa south-east of
Uruk), Elam (a powerful kingdom east of Babylon and to the north of
the Arabian Gulf) and Goyim (which means simply 'nations' but may
stand here for the kingdom of the Hittites). We cannot identify for sure
any of their names with known historical figures, though Amraphel
may refer to 'Hammurabi', the almost legendary ruler of Babylon,

and Tidal could be linked to Tudhalia which is known as the name of a Hittite king. There is an intrinsic unlikeliness to such a powerful group of emperors uniting in coalition to attack insignificant communities far from their home territory. Certainly there is no record of cities in the areas being *subject to Kedorlaomer*, the king of Elam.

Their opponents hardly deserve the title king in comparison: they rule the petty towns that are strung along the southern part of the Jordan Valley. Sodom and Gomorrah's eventual fate is well known from Gen. 19. Zoar was a nearby village that provided a temporary refuge for Lot as he escaped the destruction of Sodom; Admah and Zeboyim were also bywords for towns in the region of the Dead Sea destroyed by YHWH's wrath (Hos. 11.8).

The process that led to the war would have been a familiar one to the inhabitants of the small nations along the Mediterranean coast throughout much of the first millennium BC. Years resentfully spent paying tribute and, when it became too burdensome, a rash decision to throw off the imperial yoke – all too temporarily and inviting swift retribution. It was a pattern that dominated the history of Israel and Judah for centuries. The story which follows needs to be read in this light.

The battle is recounted using expressions of military vocabulary that are not found elsewhere in Genesis: *rebelled* (14.4); *laid waste* (14.7); *marched out* (14.8); *drew up* (14.8).

The list of those defeated in 14.5–7 includes some obscure names, but makes it clear that the four kings were being opposed by a much wider group than merely the rulers of cities in the Jordan Valley. The war seems to have spread to a wide area of southern Transjordan and the Negev, and may reflect authentic military scenarios in the region.

Then the story shifts back suddenly to focus on the Valley of Siddim, and Lot himself. Although this takes place before the destruction of Sodom and Gomorrah the *bitumen pits* into which the defenders fell seem to anticipate the later destruction. They hardly remind us of the *Garden of the LORD* (13.10) which was the vista that Lot had first seen. Although Lot had attempted to settle in Sodom, clearly he is not going to find there the security and riches for which he had craved.

14.13–17    Abram now returns suddenly to the story. He is introduced almost as though we have never met him before: *Abram the Hebrew*. This is the only time he is designated in this way. The term 'Hebrew' is used sparingly in the Old Testament, to describe the Israelites while slave labourers in Egypt (e.g. Exod. 1.22), or during the time of the wars with the Philistines (e.g. 1 Sam. 13.3). It is also used to refer to 'Hebrew slaves' – people who were forced through debt to sell themselves into temporary slavery (e.g. Deut. 15.12). The use of the term here seems to reflect the way the term Habiru (surely connected in some way to 'Hebrew'?) is used in a wide range of ancient Middle Eastern texts to refer to social groups of people who could be categorised as 'outsiders' or even 'outlaws'. So *Abram the Hebrew* is a kind of Robin Hood figure, leader of an armed resistance group who sticks up for the underdog against the powers that be. But in view of the fact that the Egyptian slavery of Abram's descendants will be mentioned in 15.13 the use of the description 'Hebrew' at this point may also act as a foreshadowing of what is to come. The biblical tradition also links the expression Hebrew to the name Eber, the descendant of Shem (10.21): so Gen. 14 may contain a veiled allusion to the supremacy of Abram, descendant of Shem and of Eber, over the inhabitants of Sodom and the other cities who were descendants of Canaan (9.25–27; 10.19).

Abram's companion Mamre has also changed – from being a place in 13.18 he is now somewhat unexpectedly a person. He and his brothers were *allies* (literally 'lords of the covenant') of Abram. This unusual description of them perhaps hints at the 'covenant' which will be the major focus of Gen. 15. It is one of a number of wordplays that link together Gen. 14 and 15.

The pursuit of the four kings and the rescue of Lot takes Abram beyond Dan. Not only does this allow for a pun on 'punish' (Hebrew: *dan*, see 15.14), but it is the traditional far northern boundary of the land of promise (see e.g. Deut. 34.1). Abram's control therefore extends over the entire land, even if only on a temporary basis.

**14.18–24** A tenth king now makes his appearance in the story – and this number is surely significant. Earlier on (14.9) the fact that there were nine kings had been emphasised, now this tenth king perfectly completes the story (as the number ten often does!).

He is very different from the others. They had brought war. He *brought food*. There is a pun on the two words, both of which in Hebrew contain the letters *lhm*.

The mysterious Melchizedek only appears in the Old Testament here and in Ps. 110.4. Since that psalm is very difficult to interpret, it simply increases the enigma. Based on these Old Testament texts the Epistle to the Hebrews devotes considerable attention to Melchizedek, further emphasising his strangeness: *He has no father,*

*no mother, no ancestors; his life has no beginning and no end* (Heb. 7.3).
An angelic figure called Melchizedek is also referred to in a Qumran
text (11Q Melch.) although it is not clear how much the Qumran text
owed to Gen. 14 and Ps. 110.

Melchizedek is both a king and a priest: that much is apparent both
here and in Ps. 110. Kings of the ancient world often had priestly,
sacral roles, acting as a channel for the divine among their people.
1 Samuel implies that Israel seems to have been hesitant about adopting the institution of kingship, probably partly because of its sacral,
religious overtones. But the accounts of David's capture of Jerusalem
in 2 Samuel suggest that after its capture such rituals were embraced
by the Davidic ruling house, perhaps based on the pre-existing royal
cult of Jerusalem (2 Sam. 6.17–19).

Melchizedek is *king of Salem*, which is probably to be identified
with Jerusalem. Perhaps it is here referred to as Salem to stress the
link with peace (*shalom*) and the contrast with the warlike activities
of the other kings. Names containing the Hebrew root *tsadaq* which
means 'righteous' often seem to have a close connection with Jerusalem (Adonizedek, Josh. 10.1, 3; Zadok, 1 Kgs 1.8; Zedekiah, 2 Kgs
24.18; note that 'ts' and 'z' are two different ways in English of writing
the same Hebrew letter).

Melchizedek blesses Abram by *God Most High* (*'el 'elyon*). The deity,
a manifestation of the chief Canaanite God El, creator of the world,
seems to have been worshipped particularly in Jerusalem (see e.g. Ps.
82.6; 87.5; Isa. 14.14). In Abram's response to the king of Sodom he
identifies this God with YHWH: *I . . . swear by the LORD, God Most High*.
The identification facilitated the process by which YHWH, originally
perhaps the tribal god of a small ethnic group, came to be viewed as
lord of creation.

The story is also an extraordinarily powerful portrayal of a non-
Israelite. For Abram, by allowing Melchizedek to bless him and by
offering him tithes, is effectively acknowledging him as a superior,
and accepting his legitimate authority as a priest of a major sanctuary
in Canaan.

We are also being prepared for what comes next: Melchizedek's
very name hints at righteousness (15.6); the oath that Abram swears
(14.22) prepares the way for the oath that YHWH proffers as he makes
a covenant, and even the unusual designation of Melchizedek's city
as Salem leads us towards this event, for covenants and peace (*shalom*)
often belong together (e.g. 26.31; Isa. 54.10); whether by chance or
design in 15.15 we have the first direct mention of *shalom* in the Bible.

By the end of this story Abram himself has changed. No longer is he the willing recipient of unethically gotten gains from a ruler (compare 12.16, 20). Now he refuses to accept gifts from the king of Sodom *not a thread or a sandal-thong*, but is therefore prepared for the *reward* YHWH is going to give him (15.1).

**15.1–5**   As with Gen. 14, so also with this chapter, widely disparate views have been expressed about the origin of the material it contains. Is this one of the earliest parts of Genesis, or one of the latest?

On the one hand the description of the covenant made in Gen. 15.9–20 with its features such as the cutting up of the animals and the sight of the flaming torch has a primitive quality to it. This has led some to suggest that there was an 'ancient' memory of a covenant between YHWH and Abram preserved at Hebron (possibly dating back to the second millennium) which may have been used as a model for the Davidic covenant tradition, and that this is reflected in the portrayal of the covenant made here in Gen. 15. The very name Hebron, in fact, suggests a connection with some group bound together in an 'alliance'.

Others however would suggest that the tradition of a covenant made between God and Abram probably depends on, rather than pre-dates, the concept of a covenant made between God and David. The description of the covenant offered in this chapter then comes from the time of the exile and addresses many of the same concerns as Isa. 40—55 for whom Abraham was an important figure of faith. (See e.g. Isa. 51.2.) There are apparent links in this chapter to the situation of the exiles in Babylon (15.13), as well as verbal allusions to the Sinai covenant tradition (e.g. 15.7, 17). It is significant that this chapter follows directly on Gen. 14, in which the king of Babylon (Shinar) is defeated, and, as we have already noted, contains wordplays that link it to the earlier chapter. The placing of these two chapters in proximity could help to provide a message of hope for Abram's exiled descendants. Broadly speaking this second view is the one adopted in this commentary.

A further issue is the relationship between vv. 1–5 and vv. 6–21. Possibly rather than reading them sequentially (as we do below) we should see them as alternative descriptions of the same event.

It is night. It must be if God is able to ask Abram to *count the stars*. It is also metaphorically dark. Abram is enduring a dark night of his soul.

He sounds now like a prophet *The word of the Lord came to Abram in a vision.* But like many a prophet he is afraid, doubts his vocation, and needs reassurance from YHWH (compare Jer. 1.6–8; 1 Kgs 19.1–18). This is the first time that Abram has spoken to YHWH. Previously the conversation had always been one way – the other way. Abram needs to be stripped, even vulnerable, before a real two-way conversation can start, and a proper relationship between God and this human being can begin.

God's words *I am your shield* (Hebrew: *magen)* straight away makes a punning connection with chapter 14, where in v. 20 Melchizedek had celebrated how God Most High had delivered (Hebrew: *miggen)* Abram from his enemies.

YHWH has promised Abram a *reward.* This is understood primarily as a promise of land, but as Abram immediately points out – land without descendants to share it is meaningless. It is a useless gift which will have no significance beyond Abram's own lifetime.

Note the way that Abram addresses God: *Lord GOD* (literally 'Sovereign YHWH'). It is repeated in 15.8 but it is not used elsewhere in Genesis. There is a movement in Abram's relationship with God. Previously he had been known as the comfortable, almost familial YHWH for whom Abram had built a series of altars (e.g. 12.7). Through his meeting with Melchizedek he has learned that this YHWH is also *God Most High, Creator of the heavens and the earth.* The terms on which he now speaks to YHWH suggest that his concept of God has deepened and become more aweful. In other places where the rare expression 'Sovereign YHWH' is used (e.g. Deut. 3.24; Isa. 30.15) it describes a powerful God in whom it is right to trust. Since Abram now understands YHWH to be *Creator of the heavens and the earth*, it is particularly appropriate that he should come to faith by being taken to look at the stars. Ps. 8 reads almost like a commentary on Abram's experience that night: the psalmist reflects on how he has become aware of the immeasurable power of God by looking at the stars in the heavens, and how it helps him to put human worries in their proper perspective. (The psalm, incidentally, also uses the designation 'Sovereign' to address God.) Isa. 40.26 also resonates with this story – there looking at the stars is an explicit reminder to the exiles in Babylon that YHWH is able to accomplish what seems to human beings to be impossible.

15.6–8  Day now dawns in the life of Abram, although night will come again shortly (15.12). There is a strange shift between night and day in this chapter, which seems to reflect the mood of the words.

*Abram put his faith in the* Lord, *who reckoned it to him as righteousness*: Abram's trust was hard won, but Yhwh didn't seem to mind. He is now considered by God as a righteous man. Noah had been described as *righteous* once (6.9); it seems to have come easier to him and without the struggle Abram has gone through. Noah was also called *blameless* (6.9) at the same moment in time. Abram will one day be exhorted to be *blameless* as well (17.1), but that is yet to come. God is learning something as Genesis goes on – that if you want human beings to have a relationship with you, you have to keep faith with them through all the mistakes they make and the wrong turnings on the journey to their land of promise.

*Put his faith in*: This expression comes from the Hebrew root *'aman* (from which 'Amen' comes). It is a root used most characteristically when the logical human response would be to do the opposite (see Isa. 7.9). But whether it was due to the stars, or the meeting with Melchizedek (who had 'righteousness' in his own name) Abram has made a breakthrough – at least for a moment.

The *righteousness* with which Abram is credited probably refers both to the right relationship with God he has now established, and to Abram's justness of character (which God discovers to his cost in Gen. 18, see p. 105). It may also hint at something else. In Isa. 51, a chapter in which the figure of Abraham appears, words from the root *tsadaq* are used five times. They have there an active sense, and can even be translated as 'victory' or 'deliverance'. Is it then possible that when Abram's faith is *reckoned . . . to him as righteousness*, we are hearing that Abram (and perhaps also his exiled descendants in Babylon) are being promised victory or deliverance?

*I am the* Lord *who brought you out from Ur of the Chaldees*: Yhwh does quite a lot of 'bringing out' in this chapter. First he brings Abram out of his tent in order to look at the stars (15.5), then there is this formula which is curiously reminiscent of the way God describes himself at the Exodus (*I am the* Lord *your God who brought you out of Egypt*, Exod. 20.2), and finally there is his role in the departure of Abram's descendants from Egypt (15.14). The 'bringings out' from the past, present and future belong together, and link too to the latter day exodus of Abram's later descendants from Babylon (which was, like Ur of the Chaldees, also a part of Mesopotamia).

*Lord* God, *how can I be sure that I shall occupy it?*: Is Abram's newfound faith dissipating so fast? Yet the *Lord* God of his address stills leaves him within the circle of trust.

15.9–21   An extraordinary scene now unfolds. It is Yʜᴡʜ's response to the uncertainties expressed by Abram. A selection of animals is dissected and set out by Abram. The cutting up of animals was often used to ratify a covenant or solemn agreement between two parties. By cutting up the animals the parties to the agreement were in effect binding themselves by an oath – if I break this covenant may I become like one of these cut up animals! When 15.18 reports *That day the Lᴏʀᴅ made a covenant with Abram* the literal meaning of the Hebrew verb is that 'the Lᴏʀᴅ cut a covenant' . . . Yʜᴡʜ is the clear initiator in this covenant, for Abram is actually asleep when the ritual is completed. The strange description of *a smoking brazier and a flaming torch which passed between the divided pieces* is a symbolic portrayal of Yʜᴡʜ himself, whose presence is often signified by flame (see e.g. Exod. 40.38). By passing through the dissected pieces in this way Yʜᴡʜ is binding himself by the oath of the covenant. He has promised to give this land to Abram irrevocably. The verbal promise uttered in 12.2–3 has now been incarnated in deed. For the first time Yʜᴡʜ uses the perfect tense of the verb in the Hebrew (15.18), 'I *have* given to your descendants this land' as he speaks to Abram, although this is not apparent in the REB translation. Previously it had always been a promise made in the future tense. Moreover the geographical detail of the map of promise is now sketched in. It is as though Yʜᴡʜ has drawn up a legal title deed. The borders given for the land, as also the list of the peoples whose territory it is, are reminiscent of similar lists and descriptions in Deuteronomy (see e.g. Deut. 7.1; 11.24). Unlike Deuteronomy however, it is not stated that Abram's right to possess will necessarily require the dispossession of these people, the land's original inhabitants. Indeed since the previous chapter demonstrated Abram's willingness to work with and for the people of this land, co-existence rather than confrontation seems to be hoped for.

But it isn't all good news. As darkness descended *Abram fell into a trance*, or a 'deep sleep' – the same Hebrew word used in 2.21 to describe the deep sleep into which Adam fell, when the first woman was drawn from him. As with Noah and the re-creation after the flood, this is a 'new beginning'. Abraham is almost a 'new Adam', being made ready to face the challenges which lie ahead. Here the trance emphasises the dark and fearsome history that awaits. The Egyptian experience of Abram's descendants has already been hinted at by Yʜᴡʜ's self-designation in v. 7: here it is made explicit *Know this for certain.*

The prediction is made that Abram's descendants will be *aliens* and *enslaved* in Egypt. This is the first use of the Hebrew noun *ger* (= alien) in Abram's story, although the related verb appeared in 12.10 (translated *live*). Both times so far the root has referred to a stay in Egypt. That corresponds to comments later in the Pentateuch (e.g. Exod. 22.21). Egypt was the place par excellence where Israel knew what it is to live life with the insecurity of a *ger*, and Israel's Egyptian experience is also used as the justification in the law codes to demand generous treatment of other people who lived with the status of *ger* among the Israelites in Canaan.

What was a *ger*? The word has been variously translated as 'resident alien', 'stranger', 'immigrant', 'migrant'. Older translations spoke of 'sojourner'. It is difficult to find an English equivalent which conveys the exact sense of the Hebrew word: unfortunately perhaps the REB's and NRSV's choice of 'alien' has been undermined by the extraterrestrial associations of the word in modern usage. A *ger* was a person who resided in a country or a town of which they were not a full native landowning citizen. They (or their forebears) might well have migrated to this country or a town from elsewhere.

Is there a reason why the alien status of Israel in Egypt is referred to here? Is it perhaps Hagar herself, an Egyptian, whom we are going to meet in the next chapter? Whatever the actual etymology of Hagar's name (and it may well be linked to a semitic word for 'flight' from which comes the Arabic and Muslim Hijra, the archetypal flight of Muhammad), to any Hebrew speaker it sounds curiously similar to *ha-ger* (= the alien). The shadow of the next chapter seems to be casting itself back to darken Abram's dream. Is there perhaps a connection between the way that Abram and Sarai will treat Hagar their Egyptian slave-girl, and the fact that their descendants too will one day know what it means to be a *ger* and enslaved in Egypt? This is made more likely when we look at the other comment made here on Israel's stay in Egypt: they will be *held in oppression* (*'innu*). The only other occasions when this particular verb occurs in Gen. 11.27—25.18 are in 16.6 and 16.9 where it describes how Sarai ill-treated Hagar. (The related noun is also used in 16.11.) Daringly, the writer hints at the reason for Israel's own later afflictions.

Yet ironically these threats are also words of hope – for if there are descendants to be enslaved, this must mean that one day Abram will be no longer childless. Adam's sleep had given birth to Eve, and the beginning of procreation between husband and wife. Does Abram's trance hint that the childlessness of Abram will soon be overcome as well?

16.1–6   With Gen. 16 we have reached the middle of the concentric circles into which Gen. 12—22 falls (see p. 73). Logically then we expect a kind of climax. And we are given one, but it is not quite the apparently intended solution. For we are now to meet Hagar, who has been described as 'the woman who complicated the history of salvation'.[5]

The central role of this chapter in the Abram/Abraham cycle is also hinted at by the use of the motif of sight: here and in Gen. 22 it assumes particular prominence.

*Abram's wife Sarai had borne him no children*: The hint of hope with which the previous chapter had concluded appears damned by the bleak sentence at the beginning of this one. But no, because in the very next line there is a *however*. *She had, however, an Egyptian slave-girl named Hagar*. Hagar must have been one of those slave-girls given to Abram by Pharaoh (12.16), so Abram's apparent deception in that escapade is going to have long-term consequences in his family life. As we have suggested above, names matter in Genesis and Hagar's name offers a clue to what lies ahead: whether linked by sound to the Hebrew word for 'alien', or related to a word for 'flight' (see comments above p. 90); by the end of her story here and in chapter 21 the name will seem almost unbearably appropriate.

Sarai suggests a solution to her own inability to bear a child – that her slave Hagar should act as a substitute wife. Ancient Mesopotamian parallels have been suggested for this practice but it is not clear how close these parallels actually are. (They seem particularly to relate to the situation of women who are priestesses.) The inference seems to be that any child born to a 'surrogate' slave-wife counted legally as the child of her mistress.

What are we supposed to think about this scheme of Sarai? Should we commend her altruism? She is offering her husband the opportunity to be delivered from the state of childlessness which so clearly grieved him (15.2), even though by doing so her own barrenness will become even more transparent. We wonder what Abram has yet shared with Sarai. Does she know about the promise of countless descendants that have been made to him? There is no sure indication that she does – and certainly it has not yet been made clear to the couple that the countless descendants of Abram will also be those of Sarai. And yet her use of language is striking: *perhaps through her I shall have a son*. Even in her despair she manages to produce a pun: the literal Hebrew meaning is 'perhaps I shall be built up through her', but the Hebrew words for 'build' and 'son' both contain the same letters,

*bn*. Is Sarai's role as the eventual matriarch being hinted at here? For
'building up' is something that happens par excellence to Israel as the
people of God. Does Sarai then know about those promises and is she
seeking by her own actions to participate in them? After all *When this
happened Abram had been in Canaan for ten years*. Sarai's agony of infertility had gone on a long time. Even God's promises may need human
machinations to chivvy them into fulfilment.

Whatever Sarai's motivation might be it is immediately made clear
that Yhwh does not sanction this scheme of Sarai, for Abram is now
about to play Adam to Sarai's Eve, as subtle textual connections are
made that link this narrative to what had happened in Eden.

There is the foreboding phrase: *Abram heeded what his wife said*. The
precise Hebrew expression translated *heeded* normally appears in the
Old Testament only when people heed God – if human beings heed
other human beings trouble usually lies ahead! Abram is heeding
Sarai, just as once Adam had 'heeded' Eve, his wife, and ate the fruit,
and later Jacob will 'heed' his mother Rebecca and deceive his father.

Our suspicions of a parallel are reinforced by the verbs of 16.3
which draw our memories back to the fateful actions of Eve. 'Sarai/
Eve took . . . and gave . . . to her husband' (compare 3.6). Can anything
good come out of this – or will it all go wrong once again? (The REB
translation of 16.3 slightly obscures the close parallel between the two
passages.)

At one level Sarai's efforts are successful – Hagar conceives
immediately. On another level it is disastrous for *when she* [Hagar]
*knew* [literally 'saw'] *that she was pregnant, she looked down on her mistress*. In offering her to Abram as a secondary wife, Sarai had elevated
Hagar's status – but this has not resulted, as she had hoped, in her
own elevation but rather her diminishment. Psychological tensions
surround surrogacy even today: whatever intentions may be, the
process of pregnancy alters relationships. With this verse the motif
of sight that runs through the story has now begun; corresponding to
the motif of hearing which first appeared with Abram's action in 16.2.

Neither Sarai nor Hagar come out of the situation particularly well.
Our instincts are perhaps first to side with Sarai (though see comments on p. 157). Strong words are now used to describe the breaking
of their relationship. Sarai is *wronged* by Hagar; in return she *ill-treated*
her. As we suggested (see above p. 90) that striking Hebrew root, used
three times in this chapter (*ill-treated*, 16.6; *submit to ill-treatment*, 16.9;
*ill-treatment*, 16.11) is the same word as appeared in 15.13 (there translated *held in oppression*) to describe the situation of the later Israelites

in Egypt. That is no accident. What is happening to Hagar is a sort of Exodus in reverse: she, an Egyptian, will flee from Israel's ancestors, into the wilderness, back in the direction of Egypt.

Abram has used Hagar, but after his use he washes his hands of her: his passive remark to Sarai *deal with her as you please* is identical to that with which Lot will offer his virgin daughters to a baying mob (19.8). The conflict of eyes that had begun with Hagar's pregnancy also continues: for his instruction to Sarai is literally 'do what is good in your eyes'. It is those hostile eyes, in that hostile face of Sarah, that Hagar now flees.

16.7–16   That it is a spring where the next scene takes place is a hopeful sign. For springs in the biblical idiom often speak of fertility and new life. Intriguingly the Hebrew word for spring (*'ayin*) is identical to that for 'eye', so the theme of sight still seems to be echoing through the story. A spring is *the* ideal place to see God! And a spring at *Shur* is even better since Shur can be linked to a Hebrew word meaning 'behold'.

This is the first time that a figure called *the angel of the* LORD has appeared to a human being in Genesis. As 16.13 makes clear, this is really God himself in human form. It is impressive that the first recipient of such an appearance should be a slave-woman, who is apparently not even a descendant of Shem, and who presently exists outside the land of promise.

There are other firsts associated with Hagar. She is the first woman to receive an annunciation in the Bible (the annunciation form is used, even though Hagar was already aware of her pregnancy). She is the first – and last – person to name God for herself, rather than simply calling upon him by name. No one else in the whole of Scripture has this privilege.

Hagar does seem to 'complicate the history of salvation'. What is YHWH doing, paying such attention to a woman whose son will not be included within the covenant (17.18–19)? Genesis exists in a sort of tension between particularity (God's special care for particular individuals and a particular people) and universality (God's involvement with all humanity). This tension is nowhere more visible than in the two stories of Hagar and Ishmael (16.1–16; 21.1–21). It is as though YHWH (as well as Abram!) cannot quite make up his mind what to do with her.

On the one hand he finds her *by a spring in the wilderness, the spring on the road to Shur*. Intriguingly, this is the precise location where the

Israelites will wander after the Exodus – though unlike Hagar they are not able to find water for themselves (Exod. 15.22). It sounds like one up for Hagar! On the other hand, she is then immediately told to return to Sarai and submit to the same *ill-treatment* from which she had fled in her 'Exodus'.

She is promised *I shall make your descendants too many to be counted* – almost identical words to those used to Abram (13.16; 15.5). Is this a hint that it will be via Hagar's offspring that the promise and blessing to Abram will come to fruition? Indeed the Hebrew phrase translated as *I shall make your descendants too many* is 'I will greatly multiply your seed', closely recalling the words spoken by God to the woman in 3.16, 'I will greatly multiply your pain'. Sarai may have sounded like Eve earlier in this chapter, but now it is Hagar's turn: and she seems to be reversing the curse – into blessing. Is it Hagar rather than Sarai, therefore, who is to be 'built up' as the matriarch of Israel? Although we know the answer, for the moment the story seems to be leaving the possibility wide open.

It seems even more likely when the angel comments *The LORD has heard of your ill-treatment,* and this is given as a reason that she is to call her son Ishmael (= 'God hears'). For that is exactly what happens when the Israelites are enslaved in Egypt (Exod. 3.7; Deut. 26.6–7). They are oppressed – and God hears. Surely any child with the name Ishmael must be a part of God's own people? But the trouble is, the 'hearing' in Ishmael's story did not begin with God, though it may end with him (21.17). Instead it started with Abram 'hearing' a desire of Sarai (16.2).

Ishmael stands so close: but his place in the story of the ancestors is ultimately delimited by another verse from the Exodus tradition: *You must not wrong or oppress an alien; you were yourselves aliens in Egypt . . . if . . . they appeal to me, be sure that I shall listen* (Exod. 22.21–22).

God has heard Hagar and Ishmael not because they are part of God's Israel, but because he cares for them as he cares for those who are *gerim* (aliens). Yet they will still impact on the ancestral story: they will be there in the background when Isaac is nearly sacrificed, when Joseph nearly dies, and when the Israelites suffer near extinction in Egypt. God's promise of protection for the *ger* (and for widows and orphans) is immediately followed by his threat of anger for those who fail them: the interplay between 15.13 and 16.6, 9, 11 suggests that we are not wrong to see Israel's own Egyptian servitude directly related to the treatment of this Egyptian servant.

However the description of Ishmael himself vividly evokes not servitude but the idealised freedom of Bedouin life. This *wild ass* of a child will know the freedom that Hagar lacks. *His hand will be against everyone*. (Contrast the way we were told that Hagar was *in* Sarai's *hands*.) *He will live at odds with all his kin*, although this apparent description of intra-family hostility may be more ambiguous than it appears at first sight (see theological reflections on p. 158).

A misguided sort of seeing had been where it had started to go wrong with Hagar's life: this episode concludes by returning to a truer vision. There is an aetiology here for a place name that will appear again in the ancestral stories (24.62), and (if we accept the REB reading of some problematic Hebrew words) a sense of wonder by Hagar that she is still alive after seeing God (compare Exod. 33.20). But the cryptic phrases of v. 13 remind us that seeing is two-way: Yнwн has 'seen to' Hagar (i.e. provided for her) as well as being the object of her sight. That same double sense of 'seeing' will surface in 22.14. For the moment Hagar drops completely out of view. We will see her again in chapter 21, and there too vision will have its part to play in her story.

No human being has spoken directly to Hagar throughout her story nor acknowledged her by name (nor will they do so when we meet her again in chapter 21). It is right that such a nameless one should have the particular power of giving God a name. That is her final moment of empowerment. For when Hagar returns to her servitude after her brief liberation, it is not she, but Abram, who actually gives the child his name. Even this power is now taken out of her hands.

## Abraham not Abram
### 17.1–27

Language, theology and ideology all link this chapter very closely to Gen. 1 and 9. It is one of the 'seams' with which earlier strands of material have been knit together. The fruitfulness which those earlier texts had seen as the destiny of humanity is now about to come to fruition with the establishment of this covenant with Abraham. The use of expressions like *for all time* (17.8), *everlasting* (17.7, 13) help to collapse time itself, and take us back to the very beginning of creation – as well as down to the writer's own era.

At the same time there are connections between this chapter and 15.1–20; 18.1–15. Many similar themes are repeated, albeit in a very different style. It is likely that 17 was composed deliberately using these other sections as sources, and then positioned at this key point in the Abraham cycle, complementing 15.1–20 as a frame for the story of Hagar.

17.1–22 is one of the few passages in the Abraham stories where the narrative context is lacking. We are not told where Abraham is, or what he is doing when this life-changing dialogue takes place. Should we perhaps imagine 17.1–22 as happening within the context of the story told in 18.1–33? Notice the curiously parallel way in which both passages end (17.22; 18.33).

17.1–8 *When Abram was ninety-nine years old*: By beginning the chapter in this way the passage of time is emphasised. The previous chapter had just concluded with Abram's age when Ishmael had been born. *Abram was eighty-six years old when she bore Ishmael.* Thirteen whole years have come and gone. Ishmael is now an adult by the standards of Jewish legal tradition. He is of the age when a Jewish youth would become 'Bar Mitzvah' – take upon himself the obligations of the covenant. In Gen. 15 we read a graphic description of a promise of an heir to Abram *Your heir will be a child of your own body* (15.4) and a covenant made not only with Abram but also his descendants (15.18). This was immediately followed by the birth of Ishmael. Surely after all this time, now that thirteen further years have passed, it must indeed be Ishmael who will be Abram's heir and the means of fulfilling the promises of the covenant?

The first few verses of chapter 17 do not discourage us from thinking this. Unless we already knew the story (which of course we do!) we could read 17.1–8 (or perhaps even to 17.14) assuming that Ishmael is going to be the means by which this covenant is going to come to fruition.

It is clear of course that something momentous is unfolding. *The LORD appeared to him* (Abram).

Although YHWH had appeared to Abram once previously (12.7), since Abram's misadventures in Egypt, which presented him in a less than *blameless* (17.1) light there had been no repetition of this inaugural appearance. (Gen. 15 comes close but the language used there seems to be deliberately mysterious and guarded: God spoke to Abram in a vision.)

Of course Hagar too has just seen God, even though in her case it is described as an appearance of *the angel of the LORD*. As with Hagar, Abram's theophany leads to the revelation of a new name for God. This time *I am God Almighty*.

We have arrived at a defining moment in Genesis. A new name, or at least title, for God is announced. *God Almighty* (*'el shaddai*) is a name particularly associated with the era of the patriarchs. Possibly linked to an archaic Hebrew word for 'mountain', it seems to be used in contexts which emphasise God's role in fertility, fruitfulness and blessing.[6] Such themes dominate this chapter: they apply to Abraham, (17.5–6), Sarah (17.16) and even Ishmael (17.20). The emphatic Hebrew expression, *me'od, me'od*, a repetition of the word for 'very', occurs three times (17.2, 6, 20). The first time that it occurs, in the phrase *and give you many descendants* (17.2) it helps to introduce the name change that Abram undergoes, from Abram to Abraham. In Hebrew there is only one letter difference between the two forms, the addition of the letter *he* (which English reads as 'h'). All five letters of Abram's new name are contained within the Hebrew words translated *and give you many descendants*. The point is further driven home by the words *father of many nations* (17.4), which also read like a deliberate pun on the name Abraham. Abraham can only truly be Abraham when he is enabled finally to be *'ab* ('father').

There is a solemn, 'priestly' feel to these verses. No longer do we meet the questioning Abram of chapter 15, but a stately figure who *bowed low* (17.17) in an attitude of worship (though see the comments on laughter p. 150). The demand on Abram that he should be *blameless* also echoes cultic ritual: the same word is used elsewhere to describe sacrificial animals (e.g. Exod. 12.5) though then it is usually translated 'without blemish'. The identical expression was employed to describe Noah (6.9), but there is an important difference between Noah and Abraham. Noah *walked with God* (as did Enoch), Abraham is told to *Live* ('Walk') *always in my presence*. The Hebrew verb is identical in both expressions: but the difference in the preposition helps to suggest that the exceptional nature of the ancient times when human beings could actually walk and talk with the deity is coming to an end. Abraham was a special person (he is sometimes referred to as 'the friend of God'), but he is an example for human beings to aspire to rather than a mythological figure who crossed the normal bounds separating humanity and divinity.

What is now said to Abraham goes beyond what he was told in 12.2 (that he would be made into a great nation) and perhaps beyond even the covenant of 15.18–20 which also seems to envisage one, albeit extensive, nation. The *many nations* suggest that he is to be father of a whole new humanity, almost on the scale of Noah.

*I shall make you exceedingly fruitful*: The language deliberately resonates with God's original words to humanity at creation in Gen.

1.28 and his restatement of it after the flood (9.1). There are also resonances of both the Noachic and the Davidic covenant traditions, especially the emphasis given to the fact that this is an *everlasting covenant* (compare 9.16; 2 Sam. 7.16; Ps. 89.29, 36, 37; Isa. 54.10; Isa. 55.3). Indeed Abraham is presented here as a royal figure, himself the ancestor of kings, and enjoying a name-change as kings of antiquity often did on their coronation.

There is of course a political dimension to the covenant with Abraham as those who told the story of Abraham in exilic or post-exilic times were undoubtedly aware. The particularity of the promise that the land of Canaan would be given as a *possession* to Abraham's descendants sits uncomfortably with the universality implicit in the *many nations*. But monarchs need their royal parks, and though Abraham's descendants may span the world, Canaan was to be a special land grant that effectively signified royal status.

The desire for possession of the land ran deep among those who were either landless exiles or seeking once again to get a toehold in the land of their ancestors. By now in the story we know all too well how vulnerable it is to be a *ger*, an alien (17.8), whether in Egypt, Canaan or Mesopotamia. Yet the covenant with Abraham cannot be used in a simplistic way to legitimate political and territorial aspirations. On the one hand there is the inconvenient fact that the covenant with Abraham gave him the privilege of being the ancestor of *many nations*, including some that the exilic and post-exilic Jewish community would have regarded with hostility. On the other hand the promise to Abraham which overshadows everything else is that *I shall be your God* (17.7, reiterated 17.8). These words are the first part of what is sometimes referred to as the 'covenant formula', which is normally completed by the corollary 'And you shall be my people'. God's promise to be Abraham's God, and that of his descendants, is a promise that goes beyond land, and can even be fulfilled among a people travelling in the wilderness (see e.g. Exod. 33.15–16) or, we might add, in exile or a diaspora.

17.9–14 Although the other half of the covenant formula is not explicitly verbalised, what it means is now set out. 'You will be my people.' The mark of circumcision will mark out precisely who are God's people.

*Circumcise yourselves, every male among you*: The practice of male circumcision was ancient and widespread in the Middle East. During the pre-exilic period most of Israel's neighbours performed this ritual on their boys or young men. The Philistines were one of the few exceptions. However by the time of the exile the practice was not normative in Mesopotamia. So from the time of the exile onwards circumcision became an important means of preserving the distinctiveness of the Jewish community and this seems to be reflected by the prominence given to it in this chapter.

Originally it is likely that circumcision was an initiation ritual performed on young men as they approached adulthood and in preparation for marriage. There are hints of this still in the mysterious passage Exod. 4.24–26. Interestingly, Ishmael, aged 13, would have been about the age at which youths had once been circumcised. We are not sure when the ritual was transferred to a boy's infancy. Perhaps the transfer is linked to the custom described in Exod. 22.29–30 which speaks of giving the first-born to God, apparently on the eighth day. But establishing infant circumcision is integral to the meaning of Abraham's story. Taking place *on the eighth day,* meant that it happened at the beginning of the second week of a boy's life – when it would be apparent whether or not he had survived the hazards of birth. It was symbolically the beginning of his 'new' creation, as a child of the covenant. It was a visual statement that God was intricately involved with the mysteries of creation, not only of the world but also of each human being. It was also an obvious reminder to each boy as he grew to adulthood and in his turn engaged in sexual intercourse that the blessings of sex and fertility were a gift from God, and that the fruit of them should belong to God as well.

It was therefore an appropriate visible mark for a covenant that promised the provision of an heir supernaturally to an old man and old woman well past the age of normal child-bearing. It is only once Abraham has been circumcised that his seed really belongs to God and God can work miracles with it. Isaac could not be born as the child of promise until this sign of the covenant had been inaugurated.

The relationship between what happens now and the covenant described in 15.6–20 is intriguing. The passages do seem to come from different sources, yet it is no accident that they are placed together as a frame around Gen. 16. They are complementary. Gen. 15 had vividly pictured the cutting of animals to inaugurate a covenant between God and a human being. Now the 'cutting' has to be internalised in the actual body of the human being before the covenant can come to fulfilment. Anyone who is not 'cut' in circumcision *will be cut off from the kin of his father* (see also comments about covenant on p. 68).

17.15–27   But what of Sarai? Up till now she has not been involved. It is far from certain that she knows anything about God's promise (see p. 91), and there has been nothing conclusive to say that it will be any son she bears rather than Ishmael who will be the child of the covenant. Perhaps in 17.9–14 there is a hint that the ideal child will be circumcised at eight days, in which case Ishmael has missed the boat since he is already 13 years old! But it is no more than a inkling.

If anything it is outweighed by Abraham's obvious focus on Ishmael. *If only Ishmael might enjoy your special favour*. Abraham does not think he needs another son now that he has Ishmael: the transparent pain of his words in 15.2 is replaced by a bout of surreptitious laughter (17.17). This is the first time in the story that the topic of laughter has surfaced and it will be a recurrent motif through the following chapters (see 17.17; 18.12, 13, 15; 19.14; 21.6, 9; 26.8. *Did not take him seriously* (19.14), *playing* (21.9) and *caressing* (26.8) are all translations of the Hebrew verb *tsahaq* 'to laugh'.) Isaac's very name itself means 'Laughter'. The link between laughter and fertility, both human and agricultural, runs deep in the Old Testament tradition (see e.g. Ps. 126). Words from the same root often refer to sexual 'play' (see e.g. Exod. 32.6). This first mention of laughter in the Old Testament paints an extraordinary picture of contrasts. Walter Gross comments that 'the Abraham prostrate in worship before God and yet laughing at the same time is one of the most inscrutable images in Holy Scripture'.[7] Perhaps such a picture tells us that faith can encompass even a laughing doubt of God.

God has not forgotten Sarai even if Abraham has. She too is given a new name – Sarah, which means 'princess' – appropriate for one who is to be *the mother of nations* (compare Gen. 12.2 *I will make you into a great nation*) and of kings. She is (as was Hagar in 16.10) mentioned specifically as the recipient of God's blessing in words that are redolent of the original blessing of Abram in Gen. 12. *I shall bless her and give you a son by her.* The link between blessing and Sarah's new role as birth-giver is important. In Eden Eve's curse included the pain of birth-giving: now in this time when God creates new relationships with humanity that curse is reversed into blessing.

And yet? Sarah is still apparently offstage while all this is going on. Her future is being discussed between her husband and his God. She is still effectively a passive bystander. Her only active intervention in the story so far led to the existence of Ishmael who complicated the 'history of salvation', and, one might add, Sarah's own life. God's final speech in this chapter, 17.19–21 is in a concentric or chiastic structure. At the centre of the chiasm in v. 20 are not words about Isaac, but words of promise for Ishmael *I have blessed him and I shall make him fruitful.* As father of 12 princes he will be Israel's parallel. Ishmael may not be able to 'live before God' (translated by REB *enjoy [God's] special favour* 17.18) in the way that Abraham himself does (17.1), but with a name like Ishmael ('God hears') he cannot be forgotten: God has *heard* Abraham as once he had also heard Hagar. Though the life of Abraham is moving convolutedly to its denouement, Ishmael's existence will continue to make its mark upon Genesis till almost the final chapter (see p. 271).

The final few verses of the chapter simply recount the carrying out of God's instructions about circumcision. Yet the detailed information about Abraham's and Ishmael's ages when the ceremony took place helps to reinforce a point. If *both Abraham and Ishmael were circumcised on the same day* this means that Ishmael cannot be fully a child of the covenant of circumcision even though he has been circumcised himself. Only one conceived after the moment when Abraham has been circumcised can fulfil that role, and we are shortly to hear of the strange circumstances in which his conception takes place.

## Entertaining angels unawares
### 18.1—19.38

Could the story in 18.1–15, which has a folk tale quality about it (there are loose parallels in both Greek and Middle Eastern mythology) be one of the ancient roots of the Abraham traditions? Set in Mamre, the location with which Abraham seems to have the closest links, it presents the pledge of offspring to Abraham in the course of a story. Westermann argued that this was the seed of the promise tradition developed elsewhere in the Abraham cycle: a seed dropped one day by the terebinths of Mamre.

18.1–15 God drops in. We can see it even if Abraham can't. Never before and never again in Genesis will God be quite so homely. The story reads rather like newspaper reports of the Queen dropping in for tea in a council flat. The difference is that most people would recognise the Queen if she called by. Abraham does not seem to realise who his visitor or visitors are, at least not until v. 10. In spite of the fact that he *saw three men* he doesn't really see who they are (as with chapters 16, 19, 21 and 22 the motif of sight is prominent).

There is both mystery and comedy here. Mystery because the description of who Abraham saw swerves backwards and forwards between the singular and plural. Is it one figure? Or is it three? Which one is YHWH? Or are they all? Are two of them simply angels? Is this a story born in other ancient cultures which were not monotheistic, and so it sits uncomfortably transposed into the monotheistic world of the Old Testament? Abraham addresses the men as *Sirs* – not aware of who he is speaking to, but ironically uttering the identical Hebrew word that later Israel was to use when people talked reverently about YHWH. It is not surprising that Christian tradition has viewed this passage as an Old Testament prefiguring of the Trinity, the Three-in-One or One-in-Three. There have been exquisite icons painted of this scene, as Christian artists have used the story to depict the life and work of the Trinity. The best known example is by Andre Rublev. The mutual hospitality which is at the heart of the life of the Holy Trinity is drawn forth by Abraham's readiness to show a welcome to three apparently unknown human beings.

Yet there is also comedy. The behaviour of Abraham is almost exaggerated. He is too polite with the courtly style of his greeting: *If I have deserved your favour, do not go past your servant without a visit.* He is too generous in his offering: it is not a *little food* he offers. *Three measures of flour* is an enormous quantity. He is too quick: how the calf is killed, prepared, cooked and ready within the space of one verse is a culinary miracle in the days before microwaves. He is not, of course, so polite to Sarah. His gabbled instructions to her, *Quick . . .*, distinctly lack the finesse of his greetings to the visitors. And after Sarah's Herculean efforts at baking there is no mention of the bread she produced along with the calf which Abraham and his servant offered. Once again she is sidelined. Is Abraham still the same fumbling figure that has seemed some times past to be so mismatched with the promises in store for him?

No, for as elsewhere in the Bible the sharing of food becomes the time of revelation. It is impossible to overstate how important hospitality is in the creation of divine and human relationships. Sharing food and drink seems to have been an integral part of establishing a covenant relationship (Gen. 26.30–31; Exod. 24.11). There is a hint that here too, the covenant between God and Abraham finally takes on a concrete reality only at this moment when Abraham shares food and drink with strangers. Abraham's mode of operations may have been clumsy, but at least they revealed the generosity of spirit for which God had been searching among humanity. Someone who offers hospitality to unknown strangers is indeed a person who is their 'brother's keeper'. It is significant to remember that this story is placed between several references to the fact that Abraham and his family were vulnerable *gerim* ('aliens', 17.8; 19.9; 20.1; 21.34) who had received the hospitality of the land of Canaan. It is only when Abraham eventually demonstrates an equal concern for others who are vulnerable that he and Sarah can take root in the land, via their descendants.

The exercise of hospitality has involved Sarah as much as Abraham. She may remain half-hidden behind the tent curtain, but it is only when she is involved, albeit indirectly, in the discussion that the promise of the heir which has so dominated several of the previous chapters can finally be fulfilled. 'Where is Sarah your wife' are the literal words used to Abraham in 18.9. They remind us of the question addressed to Adam (3.9) and even more that spoken to Cain (4.9). It is only when human beings are 'guardians' of each other, that the reversal of the ancient curses can proceed apace.

*This time next year*: Sarah will have the child for which she has waited so long. The Hebrew phrase translated *this time next year* in 18.10 and 18.14 is a rarely used expression: it means 'about the time of reviving'. It is probably a reference to the season of spring, but it perhaps includes a cryptic allusion to Sarah's and Abraham's situation. Old people, *Sarah being well past the age of childbearing* with only the winter of their lives to look forward to suddenly will experience a new spring, a moment of 'reviving'. She will become a new Eve (whose name also comes from this root).

There is a hint in the passage that it is not simply Sarah's post-menopausal condition which stands in the way of conception. Does Sarah's pointed remark *My husband is old* suggest that by now Abraham himself was impotent, or perhaps that sexual relations had ceased between the pair?

But nothing stands in the way of YHWH's desire to bless his people, or his ability to bring this about. *Is anything impossible for the LORD?* echoes the vocabulary used of the events at the Exodus, and when God's later acts of redemption for his people in Babylon are described.

First Abraham (17.17) and then Sarah had laughed at the ridiculous possibility of a son being born at their time of life. The last verse of the story hints at the uncertainties which still lie ahead. Eventually Sarah's laugh will ring out down the centuries like a shout of triumph, but for the moment it sounds like a cry in the dark. Yet YHWH himself has the last laugh when Isaac (= 'Laughter') is born!

18.16–33    God has made a covenant with Abraham, and it is going to have consequences for God as well as for Abraham and his family. If the relationship between Yнwн and Abraham is to be real, he must let Abraham into his plans. No longer can God act totally on his own terms – he must allow himself to be judged by the standard he has set down for others. If Abraham's family is charged *to conform to the way of the* Lord *and to do what is right and just,* the code of behaviour which is required by the covenant (see e.g. Mic. 6.8) then Yнwн too needs to conform to the same standard.

It is not accidental that the original promise to Abraham is hinted at in the language of these verses: *He will become a great and powerful nation, and all nations on earth will wish to be blessed as he is blessed* (compare Gen. 12.2–3). In the rest of this chapter we are going to discover what that means as Abraham intercedes for others, effectively seeking to become a means of blessing for them.

It is a decisive moment in the story of Genesis. Yнwн deliberates with himself: *The* Lord *had thought to himself, 'Shall I conceal from Abraham what I am about to do?'* There are only a few other points in Genesis when such divine deliberation is described (1.26; 3.22; 6.6–7; 8.21; 11.5–7). They are all moments of decision/crisis in God's dealing with humanity. All of them, except for this one, occur in the primeval history of Gen. 1—11. That is no accident, for there are hints in the story of Sodom and Gomorrah that it is a kind of 'replay' of the primeval history.

---

*Links between the primeval story and the story of Sodom and Gomorrah*

Gen. 13.10 The plain of Sodom like the Garden of Eden
Gen. 13.13 The wickedness of the people is monstrous (compare Gen. 6.5)
Gen. 19.5 Sexual misdeeds are referred to (compare Gen. 6.1-4)
Gen. 18.20–21 God descends and sees what is going on in Sodom (compare Gen. 11.5)
Gen. 18.12–13 Yнwн takes action to save one man and his family (compare Gen. 6.13–14)
Gen. 19.24 It rained (fire and brimstone) (compare Gen. 7.10)
Gen. 19.31 The daughters of Lot believe that there is no man left on the earth (compare Gen. 7.23)
Gen. 19.32–35 Lot gets drunk (compare Gen. 9.21)
Gen. 19.32–35 Incestuous sexual relations (compare Gen. 9.22?)

---

But this time, unlike in the primeval stories, a human being may, just may, affect the outcome, as he is made privy to those deliberations in the heart of God. It is striking that as two of the divine figures turn off towards Sodom *Abraham remained standing before the* LORD. It is as though he is blocking the way of this third and leading figure. At the very least Sodom cannot be destroyed before Abraham has had his say.

The modern Jewish writer Elie Wiesel describes Abraham's intervention: Abraham

did not hesitate for a moment to take God to task as he tried to save two condemned cities from destruction: How can You – who are justice – be unjust? He was the first who dared query God. And God listened and answered. For unlike Job, Abraham was protesting on behalf of others, not of himself. God forgave Abraham everything, including his questions.[8]

But, we may respond, did Abraham need to be forgiven? These verses are perhaps Abraham's greatest moment: the highpoint of his life and his relationship with God (greater even than his ambiguous willingness to sacrifice his sons, Gen. 21 and 22). A typical Middle Eastern barter scene unfolds, as God and Abraham bargain for the safety of the cities. *Suppose there are*: 50 innocent people . . . 45 . . . 40 . . . 30 . . . 20 . . . 10 . . .? Voltaire, the French eighteenth-century philosopher, poured scorn on Abraham's intervention – he regarded Abraham as a comic figure, an inveterate haggler who could not resist trying to cut a deal with God even at this moment. Yes, there are comic touches around, as there were earlier in this chapter when Abraham's effusive hospitality was painted, and there will be again when Abraham haggles once more, this time over a burial place for Sarah (Gen. 23). But Abraham's humanity, comic touches and all, is precisely what is going to be important. Because only a real human being will care enough for humanity to be a means of blessing for them, and in the process dare to try and teach God how God ought to behave.

Running through these verses are the keywords *tsaddiq* and *mishpat*, *right and just*. They appear together many times in the Old Testament as a summary of the behaviour required by God of Abraham and the people of Israel (see e.g. Isa. 5.7). Sometimes however *tsedeqah* (righteousness) is contrasted with *tse'aqah* (the cry of distress of an oppressed party). The pun is made clearly in Isa. 5.7, and perhaps also here as YHWH listens to *the outcry reaching* him (18.20). By contrast those who *do what is right* (18.19) must stand alongside the *innocent* (18.23, both words are linked to *tsaddiq*). Yᴇʜᴡʜ, as any good ruler or *judge of the earth*, needs to keep his side of the covenant by showing righteousness to those who are righteous/innocent and therefore in right relationship with him (see Ps. 72). That is the essence of justice. If Abraham is required to do *what is . . . just* (*mishpat*) so too must Yᴇʜᴡʜ, as Abraham points out to him. *Should not the judge of all the earth do what is just* (*mishpat*)?

Abraham's temerity is disguised by the English translation: the repeated *Far be it from you* literally means 'Profanation'. This is a word often used in connection with cultic worship, where it describes objects or people who are polluted and thus 'defile' or render invalid a holy place or ritual. In effect, Abraham is suggesting that if God allows the innocent to suffer along with the guilty not only is he not just, but he is also not holy, and thus not God! (Compare Ps. 82.1–8, where the 'gods' are demoted because they have 'judged unjustly'.)

Perhaps Abraham suddenly realises how far he has gone with his murmured apology and consciousness of his status as part of creation *I who am nothing but dust and ashes* (see also the comments he makes in vv. 30, 31, 32). But he shows an extraordinary boldness, possibly unique in the pages of the Old Testament. He also moves theology into a new dimension. Never before in the history of humanity has the possibility of vicarious salvation been raised. The righteous may have previously saved themselves (as in the case of Noah) but that is not what Abraham is asking for. He is requesting that they should be the means of saving not only themselves but also their compatriots. He begins with only a few, 50 is not many within the context of a city, and the numbers shrink still further *suppose ten can be found there*?

Why does he stop at ten? Later Judaism would argue that this is the quorum needed for a synagogue. It may also be that the number we are left with must be larger than the family of Lot. The lengthy encounter leaves some unanswered questions hanging over us: it has held us in suspense as we draw near to the moment when we shall arrive in Sodom. Will we find that Abraham been successful in saving this city after all his pleas?

*When the* Lᴏʀᴅ *had finished talking to Abraham, he went away*: Yᴇʜᴡʜ goes away and he will never again be seen so directly by Abraham. Perhaps such intimacy is too dangerous for Abraham, perhaps it is also too dangerous for Yᴇʜᴡʜ! *Abraham returned home.* The Hebrew words could be literally rendered, 'He returned to his place.' After this strange dialogue when God and a human being speak openly almost on equal terms it is now time for Abraham to 'know his place' and return to the normal status of a human being vis-à-vis the creator.

Yet something has changed. We will never again after this in Genesis read of internal deliberations in the heart of God. But perhaps we no longer need to, because the discussion between God and Abraham in this chapter has made it clear that human beings can know how God will behave. For now there is a covenant, and it binds God and humanity mutually together in righteousness.

19.1–11   Abraham had received the divine messengers with generous hospitality – how will they fare on their visit to Sodom?

The scene at the beginning of Gen. 19 deliberately echoes, and contrasts with, the picture of the previous chapter.

*Lot was sitting by the city gate*: Abraham had been sitting by the opening of his tent. It was *in the evening,* a time that hints at the sinister dangers that may lie ahead in Sodom, rather than the middle of the day when Abraham's visitors appeared. Lot bows low to the men and greets them with the same polite *sirs* that his uncle Abraham had used. As Abraham had done, Lot offers hospitality. But then subtle differences become apparent, his words are a little more curt, brooking no argument: he *was so insistent,* and the repast he prepared for them wasn't quite up to Abraham's standards. Does that *unleavened bread* hint at the speedy flight that will soon be necessary, as at the time of the Exodus?

It is as though we are re-reading the account of Abraham's hospitality once again, but in a way that is slightly off-key. Lot is doing his best, but he isn't quite Abraham, and he doesn't quite get it right. The previous chapter had ended with the phrase 'Abraham returned to his place' (18.33). In spite of the fact that Abraham is an alien (17.8) and still has some travelling around the land to do (20.1), he has a place where he fits in and which he can call his own. Lot, on the other hand, may look as though he is dwelling in Sodom, a proper city where people could live permanently (13.12; 14.12), but we are soon to discover that he doesn't really belong there. He may think he does – after all, he is settled by the city gate, where the city-elders normally met to conduct business and share in judging the affairs of the city. He may even call the inhabitants of Sodom *my friends* (literally 'my brothers'), but he soon discovers that he is a rank outsider with no place where he can feel safe. The men of Sodom put him straight: *This fellow has come and settled here as an alien . . . We will treat you worse than them.*

Perhaps he really knew that Sodom was no 'safe place' all along. Is that why he is so insistent that the strangers accompany him *into his house* when they are willing to *spend the night in the street*? Is that why the story emphasises how he goes out into the street to bargain with his fellow townsmen, carefully *closing the door behind him*? He is trying to preserve his house as an 'ark' of safety as hostility rages around him. But even his own personal space is no longer protected, as the men of Sodom *pressed close to break down the door*. Abraham is far more secure in a flimsy tent among wide open spaces than Lot is in a building in a walled city. It is only through the superhuman efforts of his guests that the safety of Lot, his house and his family is eventually guaranteed.

And what of the men of Sodom, *everyone without exception*, as it emphasises. What do they really want? The REB does not pull its punches. *Bring them out to us so that we may have intercourse with them.* They want to gang-rape Lot's guests. This may well be the meaning, but in fact the Hebrew is somewhat more ambiguous: they want to 'know' the men. Is what is being referred to here, a desire simply to 'know more about' these strangers, whether, perhaps, they were spies? Could it be that the basic problem in Sodom is not sexual perversion but xenophobia, the abuse of hospitality and fear of, or hostility towards, strangers. It is an intriguing suggestion.

On balance it seems most likely that the intention of those attacking Lot's house was to make a sexual assault on Lot's visitors. But it is unhelpful to regard the story as a normative description of homosexual practice (for example in the way that the term 'sodomy' which obviously derives from this incident has frequently been employed as a term for all genital homosexual activity). It is also mistaken to regard the sin for which the whole city of Sodom was soon to be destroyed as being primarily homosexual practice. The sins of Sodom are alluded to in a number of other places in the Old Testament: they include adultery, hypocrisy, lack of charity (e.g. Ezek. 16.49–50) but at no other point are they specifically stated to include homosexual activity. The sin of the city might best be summed up by the phrase to *do what you like with them*. Underlying these words, spoken by Lot to the men of the city as he offers them his virgin daughters, is the well-known Hebrew expression *everyone did what was right in his own eyes*. This phrase appears a number of times in the Old Testament (e.g. Judg. 21.25) to describe a situation of unbridled anarchy and violence, characteristic of times and places where relationships between human beings have broken down. Like Cain, the inhabitants of Sodom deny the demands of human 'brotherhood', explicitly to Lot, and implicitly to the strangers.

And what of Lot's offer of his daughters to the intruders? We are horrified by it today (though till very recently a number of male commentators on this passage were able to write as though it was to Lot's credit!). The silence of the storyteller is suspicious. Though it is not explicitly criticised, like other features of Lot's hospitality it seems distinctly off-key. Does Lot's willingness to see his daughters abused at this point pave the way for his own incest at the end of the chapter?

19.12–30   The end of chapter 18 had left the issue in suspense: will there be found ten righteous people in Sodom, in order to prevent its destruction? The answer seems to be a resounding 'No'. Lot and his immediate family are the only ones who could be possibly considered innocent, and they do not add up to ten. Abraham's intercession appears to be ultimately of no avail.

Yet Lot and his family are *spared*. Is it because of their own innocence, or is it rather because God *took thought for Abraham*? For several verses the question remains unanswered.

It is hard work to rescue this family, and eventually turns into a black comedy. The sons-in-law (which may mean the betrothed fiancés of Lot's unmarried daughters) do not get out at all. *They did not take him seriously* – a Hebrew word cognate to 'Laughter' appears in this sentence. It is the sound of unbelief. But the joke is on them at the end, as the tragedy unfolds.

As for Lot, his wife and daughters they *delayed*. The vividly onomatopoeic verb *yithmahmah* alludes to their hesitancy in leaving. In the Hebrew Bible this word is written with a rare Hebrew musical note called a *shalshelet* set above it. The *shalshelet* instructs a reader to modulate their voice up and down the musical scale three times before moving on to the next word. The word *shalshelet* itself means a 'chain' and it is as though Lot and his family remained 'chained' to Sodom which had been their home for so long. Perhaps his wife even more so than Lot: was she a native of Sodom with ties to the city that simply could not be broken? She was to remain there looking back to it for evermore.

The repeated word *Flee* (Hebrew: *himmalet*) then puns on the name of Lot. Perhaps it is fitting because once he eventually starts fleeing he goes all over the place: he cannot make his mind up where to settle. First he wants to go to a small *place* called Zoar ('small', Hebrew: *tso'ar*) in spite of the divine instructions to *flee to the hills*. He cannot leave city life behind entirely, at least not straight away. But as soon as he arrives there he is off again, this time to *a cave* in *the hill-country*. The story of Lot is the tale of a man who settles everywhere but cannot settle!

After Lot is finally sorted out the cities are destroyed, in a fashion that provided the raw material for later apocalyptic visions. What, if any, is the history behind the story of this destruction? It is probably a combination of geological observation, folk aetiology, and remembered traditions. There is no clear evidence of once large cities at the southern end of the Dead Sea (the presumed location of Sodom and Gomorrah). However earthquakes are prevalent in the region, as are sulphur springs (which may have provided components of the description). The almost lunar terrain of the area is dotted with weirdly shaped rocks, a wide selection, from which tourist guides choose their individually preferred 'Lot's wife'. Prehistoric archaeological remains do suggest that the climate of the area was once more equable and the terrain more fertile than it is today. It is even possible that the level of the Dead Sea altered suddenly and the tradition of that inundation further coloured the picture. Whatever the historical kernel it is intriguing that no other event in Genesis is referred to in the rest of the Old Testament as frequently as the destruction of Sodom and Gomorrah.

In the course of this chapter we seem to have deviated far from the story of Abraham. Indeed the destruction of Sodom reads more like a saga from the primeval history than part of the ongoing story of the ancestors. But now we return to Abraham who is exactly where we had met him last: *the place where he had stood in the presence of the* LORD. It was there that he had struggled to save Sodom, there now he sees the apparent failure of his efforts. Was it because there weren't enough innocent people in the city, or was it ultimately because God doesn't operate like that, saving the wicked because of the innocent? The question has hung over faith and history ever since.

Yet something has been accomplished, something won. Abraham had not asked for special treatment to save his nephew, but God had rescued him for Abraham's sake all the same. Abraham has begun to be a source of blessing for the nations – of which, as we shall shortly read, Lot is to be the father of two!

19.30–38   Our last sight of Lot reads like the final scene in a 'Rake's Progress'. The man who once had herdsmen, tents and so much livestock that the land could not support him alongside Abraham is now holed up in a cave with only his daughters. What happens next is perhaps just retribution for Lot's willingness to sacrifice these daughters sexually to his fellow dwellers of Sodom.

In a drunken stupor he engages in incest with them. He is presented not as evil but simply pathetic. *He did not know*, when his two daughters 'knew' him. From this performance are born the ancestors of the Moabites and Ammonites. With a punning wordplay the narrator hints that the ancestor of the Moabites was so called because he was born 'from our father' (Hebrew: *me'abenu*), and the ancestor of the Ammonites is called Ben-Ammi, because he is 'son of my familial people'. The actions of the daughters provide an aetiology for these two nations whose mutual antagonism to the Israelites and Judaeans was a constant factor in pre-exilic and post-exilic history. On the one hand, the story seems intended to disparage these ancient enemies: with a birth like that what can you expect! On the other hand, it does not let us forget that these peoples were close kin to Abraham's descendants, and deserve to be treated as such. (See e.g. Deut. 2.9, with its favourable comment on the Moabites as the 'children of Lot'.) As the story of Ruth will remind us, even King David had a Moabite woman among his ancestors (see also p. 241, the story of Tamar).

## The endangered future
### 20.1—22.24

Although the next three chapters appear diverse, they are subtly linked together. The stories concerning Abimelech are enveloped around the account of the birth of Isaac and the dismissal of Ishmael. In turn the eventual fate of Ishmael prepares the way for what may happen in the following chapter to Isaac. Running throughout the chapters is the topic of heirs – and their endangering. It is also conspicuous that God is rarely referred to as Yhwh in these chapters and the term *Elohim* (= God) seems to be preferred. Is this due to different sources being represented (see p. 17), or is there another reason intrinsically related to the story?

20.1–18 Abraham the 'alien' is on the move again. This time he travels south from Hebron to live *as an alien in Gerar*. The pun on the Hebrew word for alien (= *ger*) which contains the same letters as the name of this city to which Abraham has now moved, Gerar, suggests that Abraham's alien status is going to be particularly important in the immediate future. We have just seen in the story of Lot how insecure life as an 'alien' could be (19.9), even for people who had been settled in a particular place for a long time. Is Gerar going to be another Sodom? Perhaps this is why Abraham behaves as he does in the next few verses.

He is up to his old tricks! This time it is not the Egyptian Pharaoh to whom he seeks to pass Sarah off as his sister, but the king of Gerar (who is apparently a Philistine, see 21.34; 26.1). The repetition of this 'trick' by Abraham was once considered a significant reason for suggesting that Gen. 12.10–20 and Gen. 20.1–18 come from different sources. But it is not that simple. The very bare way that the writer of Gen. 20.2 introduces the incident: *He said of Sarah his wife that she was his sister,* implies that the writer (and the reader) knows the content of Gen. 12.10–20, where the explanation for such a deception is set out. The two incidents, with Pharaoh and with Abimelech, are complementary in their present form. Even if they did originate in different literary circles their 'doublet' presence in this part of Genesis is not mere repetition but designed for a narrative purpose.

We read of the incident with a heavy heart – it is really irritating that Abraham should try this one on again. Hasn't he learned anything over the past eight chapters? About trusting YHWH? About treating Sarah with respect? He had been 'getting there', but now it seems as though he is virtually back where he started. It is almost as though he is trying his hardest to jeopardise the promises that YHWH made to him. In 18.10 YHWH had promised that Sarah would have a child within a year. So by now she must either be pregnant (not the most appropriate state in which to join a harem!) or shortly to become so. And if she were to get pregnant in the next few weeks, nobody would know whether the child was Abraham's or Abimelech's. Some child of promise!

So God has to act quickly and authoritatively. In the earlier story Pharaoh probably did have sexual relations with Sarah, but this time God acts before Abimelech has a chance! Dreams are an effective way for God to communicate speedily with human beings, and will be used increasingly to do so as Genesis develops (see Jacob's dream 28.12–13). *God came to Abimelech in a dream by night and said, 'You shall die because of this woman whom you have taken; she is a married woman.'*

Not surprisingly Abimelech is put out! His (and Sarah's) continence is highlighted: *Abimelech . . . had not gone near her.*

Then in words that remind us of Abraham's conversation with YHWH in 18.16–33, he argues, *Lord, will you destroy people who are innocent?* Previously Abraham had acted almost as God's teacher, now it is to be this Gentile Abimelech. Words from the root *tsaddaq* are rare in Genesis outside Gen. 18, so the appearance of this root once again in the word translated *innocent* surely means that we are intended to see a connection with the last time it had been encountered in that dialogue about divine justice. There is therefore a contrast being drawn, between Abimelech and the inhabitants of Sodom. In Sodom no 'innocents' had been found, except from the family of Lot, Abraham's own kin. But lest Abraham (or Abraham's descendants, the first readers of Genesis) believe that no non-Israelite can be of *good faith* (literally, 'in the integrity of my heart') we have now been introduced to Abimelech, a righteous Gentile, whose responses should shame Abraham, and perhaps even call into question his own righteousness. *You have done to me something you ought never to have done,* says Abimelech to Abraham.

Abraham's responses hardly justify his actions. We are not even sure that he is telling the truth. Is Sarah really his half-sister, as he maintains? This is certainly the first we have heard of this, though it is not impossible, and it is perhaps significant that no ancestry is given for Sarah in 11.29. (Marriages between half-siblings with different mothers were considered acceptable at various times and places in the ancient Middle East.)

As for Abraham's professed belief that *There is no fear of God in this place* not only is it insulting, it is also clearly inaccurate. The story makes it clear that Abimelech does 'fear God' – his comments during the divine dream confirm that. And as for Abimelech's retainers *when he told them . . . the men were terrified.* There is plenty of fear around! Unlike what might have befallen him in Egypt (12.12), here in Gerar, absolutely nothing would have happened to Abraham if it had been known that Sarah was his wife.

The motif of 'fear of God' will appear again in Gen. 22, where it will be applied to Abraham himself. But it is paradoxical that the first time that this phrase *fear of God* should appear in the Bible it is effectively linked to a Gentile. The tension between universality and particularity that has pervaded the cycle of Abraham stories still continues. Perhaps that is also why the word God (*Elohim*) has been used (in the main) in this chapter rather than YHWH. The name YHWH seems to be reserved in the Abraham cycle for situations when God is dealing with or on behalf of those who will be his own people, or perhaps (as with Hagar in Gen. 16) in a situation of particular intimacy. In this encounter with Abimelech a 'Gentile' ruler the designation 'God'

113

is more apposite. The writers of Genesis seem to have believed that Gentiles could know God as God even if not as Yhwh.

Abraham evidently has one or two things to learn from Abimelech. Instead of 'fearing God' he seems distinctly grumpy about his divine call. *When God set me wandering from my father's house . . .* 'Wandering' frequently bears a pejorative sense: people in the Old Testament tend to 'wander' when they get lost physically or spiritually. Abraham seems for a moment almost to have lost the plot as well as his way! Is Abraham refuting the promise he was offered, or is he simply showing a certain amount of 'savvy'? Abimelech may not be too pleased to hear that his realm is intended as part of a promised land! The generosity of his recompense to Abraham in 20.15–16, offering not only money but the pledge that Abraham can *settle wherever you please*, may be something he might live to regret (see 26.16). Intriguingly, this is one of the few places where 'God' (*Elohim*) is linked to a plural verb. It is tempting to wonder whether Abraham is accommodating his form of speech to the Gentile Abimelech in this respect also.

Yet even though Abraham's flaws are all too apparent, God still has an important role for him, one that no Gentile could play. *He is a prophet and will intercede on your behalf* (20.7). This is the first time the word 'prophet' appears in the Bible. It will not appear again in Genesis. To refer to Abraham as a prophet is in one sense anachronistic. The writers of Genesis knew this well; the point they want to make here is not historical but theological. One key role of prophets was to intercede with Yhwh on behalf of people. This aspect of the prophetic vocation is referred to in Amos 7.2 and Jer. 15.1. It is what is being alluded to here. Earlier in Genesis, 15.1–4, language distinctive to prophecy has been associated with Abraham. At various points Abraham's story colours him not only as prophet, but also as priest and king. And when 20.7 describes Abraham as a prophet, it is not simply of him as an individual that it is speaking. The original promise of Abraham gave him and his heirs the responsibility of acting as a mediator of God's blessing to the Gentiles: *All the peoples on earth will be blessed because of you* (12.3, using reading as REB footnote). In Gen. 18 Abraham had interceded for the people of Sodom – ultimately to no avail. But in his prayer on behalf of Abimelech: *Then Abraham interceded with God, and he healed Abimelech* this vocation was beginning to come to fruition. For all God's willingness to deal with the Gentiles, and the recognition that they may have moral insights, the call and privilege of particularity was to be reserved for Abraham and his descendants.

114

And what of Sarah? Once again she has been silenced. Abraham does not even speak to her at all, which contrasts with Abimelech's gracious words to her in 20.16. Though is there a touch of pointed irony in his reference to *your brother*? Abraham speaks about the loyalty he has demanded from her (20.13) but he seems to have pushed this loyalty to the limit, and since the word *loyally* is vocabulary that is often used in relation to a covenant, we might wonder whether he is pushing divine loyalty to the limit too.

21.1–8   The sterility with which the previous chapter concluded (20.18) is swept away by fertility and new birth. A son is born who is 'a living and walking laugh'.[9] When people speak to or about Isaac they will speak 'Laughter'. Whenever Abraham and Sarah use his name they will remember how they had laughed in disbelief when his birth was announced to them (17.17; 18.12), and the proof that God can work miracles will be before their faces. *Sarah said, 'God has given me good reason to laugh, and everyone who hears will laugh with me.'* There is a delightful ambiguity about the last words of this sentence: *with me* could equally be translated 'at me'. Are we being invited to join in her joy, or laugh in amazement at this 90-year-old mother? Sarah is so happy that it doesn't matter any longer! It doesn't even concern her that Abraham did the naming of this child (21.3) even though mothers in the ancient Middle East often had this privilege reserved for them, and most other matriarchs of Israel assume this responsibility for their sons. After all, what better name than 'Isaac' could there be for this child who had been laughed into life? (The slightly awkward position of 21.6 in the text has led some commentators to suggest that in an earlier version of the story, Sarah actually did name the boy.)

What a hundredth birthday present for Abraham! *Abraham was a hundred years old when his son Isaac was born.* As always, in the Abraham cycle when dates are given momentous events are taking place. What has happened at this unique moment in Abraham's life must be very special indeed. It has been quite a year! The time reference encourages us to look back to the last point that Abraham's age was mentioned, chapter 17, a year ago, when he was 99. The link to that earlier passage is intensified by the precise reference to Isaac's circumcision when he *was eight days old . . . as decreed by God* (see 17.10–18). (Genesis does not refer to the specific moment when any of the later patriarchs were circumcised.)

Surely the story of Abraham has now reached its climax, as the covenant itself is being fulfilled in the birth and circumcision of Isaac (see 17.10–12, 21)? We can also turn our eyes further back to the original formulation of the promise in Genesis 12.1–3: there the word *great* had been repeated in God's pledge. Now that we learn that Isaac is weaned, and has survived the dangerous first two or three years of early infancy, we hear that word echoed, for Isaac, the first-fruits of this covenant, *grew* (literally 'became great'). The famine with which the story of Abraham had begun (12.10) is replaced by feasting, *a great feast*, barrenness by abundance. We have commented in the introduction on p. 73 how the concentric patterning of these chapters leads us to expect that we have now reached the conclusion.

21.8–13 Not so. It is not over yet. The laughter turns swiftly sour. Logically we anticipate that the blessing of greatness with which the Abraham cycle began is going to be confirmed. But we will have to wait the best part of two chapters for that (22.17–18), and they are not going to be easy stories to read.

The weaning feast of Isaac is not the story's closure, but the inauguration of further complications.

*Sarah saw the son whom Hagar the Egyptian had borne to Abraham playing with Isaac*: It is remarkable how the story cannot bring itself to mention Ishmael by name even once in these verses, as Sarah herself certainly is unwilling to do. (Although the REB prints the name Ishmael in 21.11, the Hebrew with a wonderfully subtle ambiguity states 'his son' at this point.)

What was Ishmael doing? Why was it so wrong for him to play with Isaac? The clue lies in that powerful root *tsahaq* which has threaded through the story of Isaac. Normally it has been translated 'laughter', now in a slightly different form it is means 'playing'. Was it that Ishmael was too rough in his play with his younger brother? In view of the possible sexual connotations of the word (see p. 100) was he even sexually abusing him? Was it rather (since the words 'with Isaac' do not appear in the Hebrew) that Ishmael was involved in sexual play with the young women of Abraham's household, a visible reminder to Sarah of how much older he was than her own son, and how great a threat he and his potential heirs might be to Sarah's line? Ishmael was, after all, the first-born, and in the natural way of things the first-born would inherit the greatest of his father's possessions. And with Abraham already so old . . . and Isaac so young? A recent creative suggestion[10] is that the word is a kind of double pun: Sarah objected because she saw Ishmael 'Isaacing', playing at being Isaac. There he is, the big brother, laughing and trying to be the centre of attention on what was supposed to be Isaac's big day! He still behaved as though he was the heir! How dare he pretend to be 'Laughter' when that should be reserved for Sarah's Isaac alone. If indeed this was the case (and it makes a lot of sense) then Ishmael's laughter is shortly to be turned into weeping (21.16).

Her language is fierce. *Drive out this slave-girl and her son.* As in Gen. 16 we have been taken fast-forward to Israel's own Exodus from Egypt once more. That harsh *drive out* was the action the Egyptian Pharaoh would take against the Israelites (Exod. 6.1; 12.39).

*This slave-girl . . . this slave's son*: Sarah's relationship with Hagar has altered from 16.2, 5 when she was *my slave-girl. This* can be a damningly distancing word, used, for example, when God disclaims any relationship with the Israelites (e.g. Exod. 32.9; Isa. 6.9). When God speaks about Hagar to Abraham in 21.12 he will call her Abraham's slave-girl, but she will never be Sarah's ever again. (In fact, the Hebrew word translated 'slave-girl' in this episode differs from that used in chapter 16. It may well be that the word used now implies a lower social status, so that the change further emphasises the diminishment of Hagar.)

It is striking that Abraham's *upset* is restricted to anxiety for his son, presumably Ishmael. God's next words to Abraham credit him with wider generosity of spirit than he actually seems to possess. *Do not be upset for the boy and your slave-girl.* But then comes the knife that will twist into Abraham's heart *Do as Sarah says* – superficially innocuous, though perhaps strange to listen to in a patriarchal culture. However the phrase contains the identical verb 'hear' and identical noun 'voice' that was used in 16.2 when *Abraham heeded what his wife said* and took Hagar as a concubine. As we suggested then (see p. 92) such an expression in the Hebrew Bible normally means that trouble lies ahead. The seeds that Abraham sowed then are now to be harvested: once he heeded Sarah and Ishmael was born, so now he must heed her again and the child has to be sent away. Since the same verb 'hear' appears in Ishmael's own name there is possibly another twist in God's words. Abraham 'heard' Sarah, even though he did not hear her use the name 'Ishmael'. So now this child of 'hearing' has to be silenced; will God hear him one day instead? The echo in 21.13 of the original promise in 12.2 offers Abraham only rueful consolation – were those glorious beginnings really supposed to work out like this?

*Early next morning*: We will hear this phrase again very soon (22.3) because once one gets in the habit of 'sacrificing' one son, one may find that one needs to sacrifice another. There are striking literary parallels between the dismissal of Ishmael and the near-sacrifice of Isaac. (See chart below.)

| Parallels between Gen. 21 and 22 | |
| --- | --- |
| Early next morning/in the morning | 21.14; 22.3 |
| Shoulder | 21.14; 22.6 |
| angel of God/LORD from heaven | 21.17; 22.11, 15 |
| He/she sent/raised (his hand) (Hebrew: *shalah*) | 21.14, 15; 22.10 |
| She saw/He saw | 21.19; 22.13 |
| Do not be afraid/A godfearing man | 21.17; 22.12 |
| Child/boy (Hebrew: *na'ar*) | 21.17; 22.5 |
| Bush/thicket | 21.15; 22.13 |
| (lit.) Heed the voice of … | 21.12, 17; 22.18 |

**21.14–21** *Abraham took some food and a full water-skin*: Literally, it is simply bread and water he offers and not very much of either. They may show Abraham's care, but they are a contrast with the *great feast* we have just celebrated for Isaac.

*He set the child on her shoulder*: a gesture that hints at a regretful tenderness – though some commentators would suggest that it was the bread and water, rather than the child, which is placed on Hagar's shoulders. The Hebrew syntax is convoluted here. One of the issues of course is the apparent age of Ishmael at this time. Practical maternal experience of the writer of this commentary suggests that carrying a child above the age of three or four upon one's shoulders is not feasible! But Ishmael would presumably be 15 or 16 at this time according to the chronology of the overall Abraham cycle (see 17.24; 21.8). However other features of this story (e.g. 21.15, 18) clearly picture Ishmael as a young child in this story. One is driven to suggest either that the editing of earlier oral or written material has been uneven, or that strict chronology has been deliberately overridden by a desire to emphasise the pathos of the situation.

*She wandered about in the wilderness of Beersheba*: What is significant about Hagar's banishment to this territory is that unlike Shur (to which she fled in chapter 16) it does not border her homeland of Egypt. It is exile to which she is banished, rather than flight to her homeland. The area is also (and presumably was in ancient times) a particularly waterless terrain. The rare word 'wander' appeared also in the previous chapter, when Abraham complained to Abimelech how God had made him *wander* from his father's house (20.13). It is ironic of course that in this present chapter Ishmael could have made the identical comment – if he is old enough to speak.

The water didn't last long. Such a water skin (I write from the experience of leading groups on walks in the Judaean and Negev wildernesses) would only contain enough water to keep two people alive for a couple of days. In normal circumstances anyone sending out a woman and child into the wilderness with just these supplies would be deliberately condemning them to a lingering and unpleasant death. Abraham presumably believed that he wasn't, because of what God had just told him. He is going to be required to show the same faith in the next chapter, when it comes to his other son, Isaac.

Ishmael is *the child*: not her child, not Hagar's. It is as though the narrator dare not let us get too emotionally close to him. He remains the child throughout the story according to the REB, although in fact the Hebrew switches from *yeled* to *na'ar* from the moment that the angel starts speaking to Hagar. *na'ar* normally refers to a slightly older child than does *yeled*, so it as if the angel is giving him a future by altering the way he is described. (It also emphasises the parallel with Gen. 22, where the angel refers to Isaac as *na'ar* in 22.5, 12, there translated 'boy'.)

Back in Gen. 16.4 Hagar had 'seen' (literal translation, REB translates as *knew*) that she was pregnant (see p. 92) and had then *looked down* upon Sarai. All that seeing then had eventually led to what has now befallen her: so it is appropriate that verbs of sight come to the fore once again at this crisis point in his life. *How can I watch the child die?* In that other story she had been looking at the quickening of Ishmael's life, now she fears to gaze upon the inertness of his death. Yet it will shortly be through seeing that her salvation will come.

But before sight first comes hearing. She *sat there, weeping bitterly*. It is fortunate for her that the child has been named Ishmael (= 'God has heard') since with yet another deliberate play on his name *God heard the child crying*. In case we did not get the pun it is repeated within the confines of the verse. God's response clearly echoes the language (the parallel is sharper in the Hebrew) used to Abraham (21.12 see above). At least we are now assured that if Abraham was then commanded to hear only Sarah, there will be another who will finally hear the child. Have those problematic and harsh instructions of God to Abraham had their sting drawn by the way in which God himself has done the listening to Hagar and Ishmael that he had forbidden to Abraham?

God may listen, but can Hagar still speak? The parallels between the present narrative and Hagar's earlier story (Gen.16.1–15) draw ironic attention to the differences. Both feature a water-source, in both there is a pun on the name of Ishmael, in both an angel speaks to Hagar. But this time it is the angel of God who simply *called from heaven*, rather than the intimate angel of the LORD whom she actually saw (16.13) on that previous occasion. She is become the passive recipient of a message, rather than one who speaks or names a deity. Once she had said *Have I seen God and still live?* Now her glance is restricted to a well of water – *God opened her eyes and she saw*, though that at least means that she and her son still live. The special dispensation that had been granted to her in that earlier revelation is now subtly withdrawn. Is this in fact why the text uses 'God' rather than YHWH in this story? She, like Abimelech, may be close to Abraham's family, but like him she is and will ultimately remain a Gentile. By contrast the narrator emphasises the closeness between Hagar and her son: *Go, lift the child and hold him in your arms*. The Hebrew words here literally read 'Hold him by your hand', another allusion to her earlier story. There that earlier angel had predicted how Ishmael's hand would be against all, and all against him, but now we see that at least does not include Hagar's hand. Though he may be alienated from the rest of his kin (16.12), he and his mother form a tight-knit unit together. Growing up in the *wilderness of Paran* (part of the Sinai desert) it will be logical for his mother to find him a wife from her own homeland of Egypt. Such an alliance distances him from the rest of Abraham's family and also prepares the ground for a later episode linked to Egypt in which Ishmael's descendants will have a part to play (37.25).

21.22–34   It is strange to meet Abimelech again at this point. He feels almost an intrusion between these powerful stories of the two brothers. Since this incident feels very much like the continuation of what happened in Gen. 20, we might ask why it has been separated from that earlier narrative. It is not unreasonable to suggest that the oaths of friendship which Abimelech demands from Abraham (21.23) are a corollary to the generosity he has previously shown in offering gifts and allowing Abraham to settle in his country (20.14–15). After all, Abraham's apparent deviousness has already seriously endangered Abimelech and his household (20.3–5). Appropriately, and perhaps pointedly, Abimelech uses the same Hebrew word *hesed* that Abraham had employed in his somewhat lame justification for his deception (20.13 translated 'loyally', 21.23 translated 'keep faith').

Abimelech seems to be rescuing this key biblical word from the dubious use to which Abraham had previously put it (see comments on p. 115). It is a word deeply rooted in Old Testament covenant traditions, expressing the mutual loyalty upon which the covenant relationship (or a marriage relationship) depends and which in turn the relationship should strengthen (e.g. Hos. 6.6, 'loyalty'). Abimelech was offering Abraham greater privileges than those that were his by right as a *ger* or 'alien'. Yet a powerful *ger* such as Abraham had become could well affect the political stability of the district where he lived, which appears to be on the geographical fringes of Abimelech's realm. It is no accident that now Abimelech is accompanied by *Phicol the commander of his army*, he felt that heavyweight support was necessary. Abimelech is reminding Abraham that with privilege comes responsibility. The vocabulary makes it clear that he is proposing a mutual covenant or *pact* with Abraham, and that is what transpires a few verses later (21.27).

However as the story now stands this *pact* is also linked to a specific incident in the ongoing saga of Abimelech's relationship with Abraham, a dispute about the ownership of a well, a matter of vital concern for a herder of animals such as Abraham. It may well be that this was originally told as an entirely separate story, for it fits uneasily with the previous verses. But when 21.22–24 was detached from 20.1–18, the incident of the well was incorporated here in order to give a rationale for the making of a covenant at this point.

The oath that formed a vital part of a covenant-making ceremony is particularly emphasised (21.24, 30, 31). It is used in 21.31 as an aetiology to explain the name Beersheba (= 'Well of the Oath'). A link is also made with the number 'Seven', a Hebrew word that sounds very similar. *Abraham set seven ewe lambs apart*, probably to be cut up in the covenant-making ceremony (see 15.10). There is a double-pun here, for the word 'oath' is itself connected to 'seven', and to 'swear' meant originally to 'seven oneself'. Because 'seven' was a sacred number it was used for this purpose in solemn ceremonies.

This is the only occasion that Abraham actually plants a tree (at other times he builds an altar next to an already existing terebinth or oak). The *tamarisk tree* is actually a large long-living evergreen shrub. Notable trees, particularly evergreens, have long been markers of holy places in the Middle East, their greenness acts as a sign of life and fertility amid the arid countryside. Perhaps it is only now, when Abraham has 'seed' (15.5; 17.9), that he can actually plant such a tree himself. It is no accident that he should invoke YHWH as *the Ever-*

*lasting God* (*'el 'olam*) at this point. Not only is there a connection between the 'everlasting' God and the 'evergreen' tamarisk. More significantly, *'olam*, everlasting, is a word that in Genesis is associated with covenant making (see Gen. 9.16; 17.7). Perhaps the only way for human beings to experience the 'everlasting' is through a covenant relationship that includes the divine. The almost throw-away remark of 21.34 that Abraham then *lived as an alien in the country of the Philistines for many years* reinforces this conclusion. It is only a covenant that makes long-lasting relationships possible, whether between God and humanity, or different groups of human beings.

This apparently intrusive story of Abraham's covenant with Abimelech has several functions within the overall Abraham cycle. It acts as a foil to the earlier occasion when problems had arisen for Abraham the herder in view of the scarce resources of the land (see Gen. 13.5–11). There in an incident which followed immediately on an occasion when Abraham had passed Sarah off as his sister, such controversy had led to division between Abraham and Lot. Now, by contrast, in another similar incident that also follows upon a wife-sister episode, the problem is resolved not by division but by the unity that is brought about through a covenant.

The reason for the displacement of this incident from its original setting directly after the events of Gen. 20 is probably twofold. First, it allows the threatened sterility of Abimelech's household (20.18) to be placed directly before the birth of Isaac and to contrast with it. Second, it also encourages us to compare Abraham's dealings with Abimelech and those with Hagar. Both stories are linked by the place name Beer-sheba and by a reference to a well, and remembering Hagar's name (see comments on p. 90) both seem to be linked to the motif of what it means to be, or treat others as, a *ger*. Is the covenant with Abimelech a better way forward for Abraham and his descendants to deal with non-Israelites? It is certainly a different way in which human beings deal maturely with each other allowing God to begin to retreat from centre-stage.

22.1–14   This is probably the best-known episode in the Abraham cycle, revisited by literature and theology many times in the more than two millennia since it assumed its current form. It is 'central to the nervous system of Judaism and Christianity'.[11] Its power is drawn from a variety of factors.

The austerity and restraint with which the story is told: it is remarkable how much is crafted in the short space of 14 verses (especially if one compares it with, for example, the lengthy retelling of the destruction of Sodom, or the betrothal of Isaac and Rebecca).

The narrative is at least as powerful for what is *not* said as for what is stated. One modern literary critic has described it as being 'fraught with background',[12] an element that encourages the readers to empathise emotionally with the story and to seek to interpret it for themselves.

It is constructed with an exquisitely painful precision: both literary structure and wordplays help to intensify its telling. 'Vision, the seeing that produces understanding, is a central theme in the story, but in the shadow of the all but unbearable beginning, Abraham is blind to it until the surprising end.'[13]

Its placement, near the end of the Abraham cycle, adds to its pathos and suspense; by now we have been through so much together with Abraham. Is it all going to end like this? Indeed the incident is retold in a fashion that seems deliberately to balance the opening of the cycle with the original call of Abraham back in Gen. 12 (see p. 75).

And of course there is the awful and awe-full subject-matter, which challenges our notions of theodicy today, as it did for readers in ancient times. The story could be (and has been) described as the Book of Job writ small, and like that other great example of Hebrew literature, it leaves those who read and engage with it profoundly disturbed, in spite of the apparently 'happy' ending.

*Some time later*: An innocuous beginning, although the Hebrew expression 'after these events' that lies behind these words suggests that we might read the story now to be told in relation to what has taken place most recently. This, of course, means Abraham's dealings with Abimelech, and perhaps even more so, the experiences of Hagar and Ishmael, Abraham's other son.

*God put Abraham to the test*: Does this statement relieve us? We know, though Abraham did not, that this is only a 'test', and therefore hopefully real life – with Isaac – will be able to proceed once the test is complete. Or does it make us angry, that God should behave in such a cat and mouse fashion with a human being?

This is the only time in the Pentateuch when an individual is tested by God, although it will happen to Israel as a whole on several occasions after the Exodus, and also during the entry into Canaan in the early chapters of Judges (Exod. 20.20; Deut. 8.2; Judg. 2.22). When God tested Israel, it seems to be an attempt to discover if the people are able to show a single-minded loyalty to God, perhaps even love (Deut. 13.3) for him, exemplified by their willingness to trust God to provide for them. It involves them in listening to his voice, showing appropriate 'fear' of him, walking in his way, and precisely obeying his commandments. Consistently, if they do this, they will prosper. All these elements of God's testing of Israel can be detected in the story of Abraham, either in this chapter, or in other passages that have a close affinity to it (Gen. 18.19; 26.5). The test is to discover whether Abraham trusts God enough to be single-minded, whether he has sufficient confidence to obey what God tells him to do. One could argue that he has been subject to this test once already – when he followed God's instructions and sent Ishmael and his mother away. But didn't we perhaps wonder then whether Abraham was using God as an excuse, a convenient way of sorting out a family quarrel? We can all hear God speaking to us when it is opportune to do so, and Abraham's loyalty to God has gone through so many twists and turns since we first met him in Gen. 12. Now, by contrast, the purity of Abraham's faith will be discovered as God demands of him the one thing that under no human circumstance would he ever have wished to relinquish.

It can help if we remember YHWH's conversation with Abraham in Gen. 18. There it is made clear that YHWH doesn't always know everything (18.21), so perhaps this too is now a genuine enquiry on God's part to discover Abraham's heart: he does not yet know how Abraham will respond. Perhaps this is not a cat-and-mouse god after all. And if we read this story having first listened to Gen. 18, we shall remember that 'the way of YHWH' involves righteousness and justice, and that the character of this God means that he does not glibly destroy the innocent. A small consolation, but one that will help us bear the terror of the story.

There is something else: normally in Genesis when the word *Elohim*, God, is used it appears without the definite article. But here, and in vv. 3 and 9 of the story, it appears prefixed with 'the'. It bequeaths upon the deity an intense solemnity as God addresses Abraham. However it is fascinating that most of the other occasions in Genesis when the word for God is given the definite article (e.g. Gen. 5.22, 24; 6.9; 17.18; 48.15) seem to be circumstances when a relationship of special intimacy with God is being portrayed. Is the inference that this test which Abraham is about to undergo is only possible because he is already so dear to God? For the very first time in the whole story cycle he is addressed by God simply as 'Abraham', as a man talks to his friend. This, it seems, is the context in which the 'test' should be read.

Abraham's reply *Here I am* is one of the defining structural features of the story. The single Hebrew word *hinneni* thus translated appears as a refrain twice more in the story (22.7 translated *What is it?* and 22.11 translated *Here I am*). This threefold *hinneni* powerfully builds up the drumbeat of the narrative.

*God said, 'Take*: The untranslated Hebrew particle *na*'added to the imperative verb adds a note of hesitancy or pleading. God is aware of the enormity of his request.

Reminiscences of Gen. 12 appear at several points. We note them in context.

As with that first call of Abraham the magnitude of what needs to be offered (country, kin, father's house) is gradually reinforced, *Your son, your one and only son Isaac whom you love*. The following comment found in the Midrash Bereshit Rabba, presented as a hypothetical dialogue between God and Abraham, perfectly captures this stepping up of God's request:

> Your son. He said to him, 'I have two sons'. He said to him, 'Your only one.' He said, 'This one is an only one to his mother and this one is an only one to his mother.' He said to him, 'Whom you love.' He said to him, 'I love both of them.' He said to him, 'Isaac'.

The vocabulary of the sentence is uniquely tender. *yahid*, translated *one and only son*, is the normal Hebrew word for an 'only child' but seems often to echo parental pain and passion. Like *hinneni* it will be repeated three times in the story (22.2, 12, 16), and through its pairing with the cognate word *yahdaw* (22.6, 8, 19) will carry much of the story's meaning. Some might object that Isaac wasn't Abraham's only son – for there was also Ishmael even if he was not a child of the covenant. But Ishmael had already been dismissed from Abraham's life, and at this point Abraham could not know for sure whether he had survived his ordeal in the wilderness. Isaac was the only son who now mattered.

And as for *love*, intriguingly this is the very first time the word has appeared in Genesis. After this story it will appear again in the book several times. It is fascinating that in Deut. 13.3 the words for 'test' and 'love' should also appear close together. (*The LORD your God is testing you to discover whether you love him with all your heart and soul.*) It is as though mutual love between human beings can only begin to flourish when we have first established that human beings can truly love God.

*Go . . .*': For the second time, we meet the unusual expression *lek leka* with which the story of Abraham had begun. Will he now need to sacrifice his future, as he had then been called to give up his past (compare 12.1)?

*The land of Moriah . . . on one of the heights*: This is the first of the wordplays around 'seeing' that will echo through the chapter. The name of this mountain is clearly related to the verb *ra'ah* = 'to see'. Moriah is 'the land of vision' (see chart of wordplays below). Since 2 Chr. 3.1 Moriah, the mountain of Abraham's sacrifice, has been identified with the temple mount in Jerusalem. Was this identification originally intended by the writer of Gen. 22? This has been frequently disputed, with suggested identifications for Moriah ranging from Moreh (see Gen. 12.6), Jeruel, a town in Judah (see 2 Chr. 20.16), Beer-lahai-roi (see Gen. 16.14) and Mount Gerizim (the Samaritan tradition). There may well have been various earlier 'editions' of this story in which one or other of these sites was intended. However by the time Genesis reached its final form Jerusalem was established as the pre-eminent cultic location of the people, it was the place one went to 'see' YHWH (e.g. Isa. 6.5). Since the ancestral stories of Genesis contain a number of aetiological stories explaining the origin of various Israelite and Judaean cultic sites (e.g. Bethel = 28.17–19, Mamre = 13.18, Beersheba = 21.33) it would be strange if there was no reference in Genesis to worship and sacrifice at Jerusalem, even if obliquely. It is likely therefore that one function of this story (though not the central one) was to act as an aetiology of the temple site in Jerusalem, and perhaps also to account for the fact that child sacrifice was not practised there. The shrine that is established after Abraham's sacrifice (22.14), where *The Lord will provide* is the *mountain of the Lord* (compare Isa. 2.2) in Jerusalem. The pun on 'seeing' that runs throughout the chapter strengthens this possibility: most of the verbs of seeing here begin with the form *yer* which inevitably encourages thought of *yerushaliyim* (= Jerusalem).

---

*Wordplays on sight in Gen. 22*

*Moriah* (place of seeing/vision) 22.2
*Abraham looked up and saw* 22.4
*God will provide* (lit. will see) 22.8
*godfearing man* 22.12 (The form of the Hebrew verb 'to fear' looks very similar to certain forms of the verb 'to see')
*Abraham looked round and saw* 22.13
*The Lord will provide* (lit. see) 22.14
*it was provided* (lit. was seen) 22. 14

---

*There you shall offer him as a sacrifice*: Several different kinds of sacrifice are referred to in the Old Testament: this one is to be a whole burnt offering, in which everything is given to the deity. The totality of what is demanded from Abraham is stressed.

*. . . on one of the heights which I shall show you*: This recalls the similar, apparently vague, language used at the beginning of the story of Abraham (*go to a country that I will show you*, 12.1). It is at least a reassurance that God will accompany him on this journey – as he had accompanied Abraham in the years since he had left Harran.

*Early in the morning*: This brings to mind the similar setting for the dismissal of Ishmael. (See the chart on p.118 with other parallels.)

*He set out for the place of which God had spoken*: This phrase, which is repeated in 22.9, makes it clear that Abraham is seeking to obey the instructions he has been given as precisely as possible. In terms of literary structure it opens a chiasm which leads us to the very heart of the story.

*The test of Abraham: analysis of its literary structure*

    A1  Abraham set out for the place of which God had spoken.

        B1  Abraham looked up and saw the shrine (literally 'place') in the distance.

            C1  Abraham took the wood . . . and put it on his son Isaac's shoulder.

                D1  The two of them went on together.

                    E  Isaac spoke. 'Father!' he said. Abraham answered, 'What is it, my son?' (Hebrew: *hinneni*). Isaac said, 'Here are the fire and the wood, but where is a sheep for a sacrifice?' Abraham answered, 'God will provide (lit. 'see for') himself with a sheep for a sacrifice, my son.'

                D2  The two of them went on together.

            C 2  Abraham. . . bound his son Isaac and laid him on the altar on top of the wood.

        B2  Abraham looked round, and there in a thicket he saw a ram.

    A2  Abraham named that shrine (literally 'place') 'The LORD will provide.'

*On the third day*: The third day is always a special day in biblical symbolism (e.g. Gen. 40.20; 42.18; Exod. 3.18; Hos. 6.2). Things happen on the third day; perhaps like death, and maybe even resurrection.

*We shall . . . come back to you*: Was Abraham really already confident that *both* of them would return, or was he seeking to allay any fears of Isaac and the attendants? The ambiguity is surely deliberate.

*Abraham . . . put [the wood] on his son Isaac's shoulder, while he himself carried the fire and the knife*: The story never misses an opportunity to stress the relationship between Abraham and Isaac: the repetition of *his son* intensifies the agony. Gerhard von Rad comments how Abraham makes sure that he himself carried the fire and the knife, which could be dangerous for the child[14] – ironic in view of the child's fate that lies ahead.

*The two of them went on together*. This is the first time that the word *yahdaw* (= together) appears. The identical phrase will be repeated in v. 8, which intensifies the emotional content. The punning between *yahdaw/yahid* has begun. Both expressions are connected to the Hebrew word for 'one'. When the father is prepared to offer his 'one' son, with the two of them intent on the action 'as one', the duality that has been a feature of human existence since Gen. 3 begins to be embedded in the divine unity. 'By showing his willingness to give up his only son, Abraham gets him back, and a much deepened togetherness begins, both between father and son, and between the Lord and his obedient follower.'[15]

*Isaac spoke, 'Father!' . . . Abraham answered, 'What is it, my son?'* Structurally vv. 7 and 8 form the chiastic heart of the story. Isaac's call to his father suggests the beginnings of his unease with the situation. (Is this why he doesn't mention the knife in his question?) Abraham's response to him is literally the identical *hinneni*, 'Here am I' with which he has already expressed his readiness to God (22.1). It is the response offering security that any parent might give to a frightened child when it calls out upon a dark night. But with bitter irony this father is apparently shortly to become the agent of his child's terror.

*Abraham answered, 'God will provide himself with a sheep for a sacrifice, my son.'*: Is this the exact moment when Abraham passes his test? When he shows this absolute trust in God's ability to provide (lit. 'see' – in the sense of 'see to') that God seeks from human beings? In terms of the wordplay that runs throughout this story, it is because he knows that God will 'see to' the offering for the sacrifice, that Abraham will be able to 'see' the sheep that has perhaps been there all along on that mountain named 'The Lᴏʀᴅ will see to it'. The literary structure of the chapter reinforces this conclusion: Abraham's verbal response at this point forms an exact parallel to his acted response of obedience when God addressed him in vv. 1–3. So does this mean that the ultimate 'test' is not so much whether Abraham is willing to sacrifice his son, but whether he is completely confident in God?

This may well be so, but the tension of the story is not allowed to dissipate immediately. We, the readers, are offered an excruciating choice: are the words *my son* simply a vocative, or are they intended to be in apposition to the expression *sheep for the sacrifice*, which has immediately preceded them? Is Abraham obliquely telling Isaac that he will be the sacrificial animal? The writer lets us make that decision for ourselves.

*The angel of the Lᴏʀᴅ called to him from heaven, 'Abraham, Abraham'*: This is an almost exact repetition of the divine words with which Abraham's ordeal began. But the doubled use of his name here somehow cancels out the original dreadful command to him: it may also indicate a note of haste – seeking to stop Abraham's action at the very last minute.

It is now *the angel of the Lᴏʀᴅ* speaking *from heaven*. Earlier it was God who spoke. The words *Elohim* (God) and Yʜᴡʜ (Lᴏʀᴅ) both appear exactly five times in this chapter – which certainly creates problems for assigning this chapter to a particular source on the basis of its use of the divine name! It may well be that the balance in the naming is deliberate, as the story shifts from the distant *Elohim* who instigated the dreadful command, to Yʜᴡʜ with whom Abraham has dealt intimately over the preceding chapters. There is a clear parallel to *the angel of God . . . from heaven* whom we met in the story of Ishmael (21.17); but Ishmael and his mother have now been excluded from the covenant, and because of that they can no longer know God by his familiar name, Yʜᴡʜ. On the other hand, in both stories the angel speaks *from heaven*. It would seem that Yʜᴡʜ is now withdrawing from Abraham's direct gaze as well. For now that Abraham has been directed to *look around* and see a sheep that God has 'seen', he no longer will be able to see the God who has appeared to him so directly up till this point! Among the many ironies of this story is the fact that from the time that Abraham reaches Moriah, the 'land of vision', he will never again see God in his lifetime. Sight is to be transmuted into fearing (*You are a godfearing man*, 22.12; see also notes on 13.14, p. 81, on *Look around*; and 20.11, p. 113, on *fear of God*).

129

*Then the angel of the LORD called from heaven a second time*: There had been no second call for Ishmael and his mother. The angel will speak in language that is reminiscent of the prophetic and Deuteronomic tradition but also remind us of the original and earlier formulations of the blessing of Abraham (12.1–3; 13.16; 15.5) and perhaps even take us back to the beginning of human history. Underlying the word *numerous* is a Hebrew expression that has also appeared in Gen. 16.10 (see comments p. 94) and Gen. 3.16 where it is used to speak of the greatness of the woman's suffering in child-bearing. One can wonder whether its reappearance here is intended to suggest that finally that ancient curse is undone, first through Sarah for whom childbirth had been a blessing (17.16), rather than curse, and now through the obedience of Abraham, which had superseded the disobedience of the garden.

That this possibility is likely is reinforced by the last words of the divine voice: *because you have been obedient to me*. Finally Abraham has got it right after listening to the voice of Sarah mistakenly (16.2) and of necessity (21.12; see comments on p. 117). But of course he wasn't the first man to 'listen to the voice' of someone other than God – that was Adam's responsibility (3.17). So Abraham is not only repairing his own mistakes but those of humanity before him.

*Your descendants will possess the cities of their enemies*: The divine oracle now looks forward as well as back. The words resonate with those pronounced over Rebecca as she left her homeland to marry Isaac (24.60). They also have a political and military content which looks forward to Israel's later history.

*Abraham then went back to his men*: The fact that Isaac is not specifically mentioned here generated considerable speculation among ancient and medieval exegetes. In fact, Isaac is almost certainly intended to be included within the final *together* of the story.

22.20–24 The Abraham cycle is 'tailed' by this brief genealogical notice, as it had been 'topped' by a similar report in 11.27–30: Abraham's brother Nahor features in both passages.

Two names stand out: *Uz*, which brings to mind the 'man from the land of Uz', Job, and his story so similar to that which we have just read. Yet in Job's experience there had been no substitutionary ram for his children. It is interesting to speculate whether the story of Job, well known by the time of the exile (see Ezek. 14.14) might have influenced the development of the Abraham cycle.

And besides the 12 sons (surely a significant number!) of Nahor, there is mention of one daughter, *Rebecca*. Isaac has emerged from his ordeal not as a boy, but as a man ready for marriage, and we are being prepared to meet his bride. But that's another story . . .

## A wedding and two funerals
### 23.1—25.18

Chapters 23—24 feel rather different in style to the earlier episodes involving Abraham. They are almost like an epilogue to the rest of the story, perhaps even squeezed in when most of it had already been composed. Their themes – burial and marriage – were pressing concerns to the post-exilic community, both in Palestine and in Babylon.

23.1–20   Jewish rabbinic tradition suggested that the reason for Sarah's death, announced so suddenly at the beginning of this chapter, was that she had heard a (false) rumour that Abraham had killed her son Isaac, and died of the shock. This is nowhere explicitly stated in the actual text but the jarring contrast between the style of Gen. 22 and 23 'shocks' the reader and makes such an interpretation feel entirely plausible. God, who has been so very present in the previous chapter, is almost entirely absent from this one. In the last chapter God had taken direct action to preserve one facet of the promises (offspring); now it will seem as though Abraham is on his own, at this crisis moment of his life, when his wife has died, and it will be up to him to acquire enough of the 'promised' land even to bury Sarah.

The mention of *the Hittites* is strange here; the great Hittite empire of the second millennium BC was centred on Anatolia (modern Turkey), but Hittite power extended into the coast and hill country of Canaan. However the term seems to be used to refer in a general way to the pre-Israelite inhabitants of the land.

*I am an alien and a settler among you*: Abraham's status as a *ger* is at the heart of this story. Normally an *alien* would not be able to own land outright. The term *settler* is paired with alien elsewhere in the Pentateuch (e.g. Lev. 25.23, translated 'tenant'). Since Lev. 25.23 strikingly claims the land as belonging to YHWH and maintains that the Israelites are still to be *aliens and tenants* – albeit now of YHWH rather than non-Israelites – one can wonder whether Abraham may here be hinting at more than the Hittites realise, or perhaps even more than he realises himself. The issue of ownership of the land is a major topic in this chapter. Should it belong to the Hittites? To Abraham? Or to YHWH?

*Make over to me some ground . . . for a burial-place*: Included in the expression *burial-place* is the Hebrew word *'ahuzzah* which means 'property'. It also appears in 23.9 (*take possession*) and 23.20 (*possession*). The word had first appeared in Gen. 17.8 when, during the making of the covenant, God promised that the land would be given *as a possession for all time*. The repetition of the word three times in this chapter is a verbal clue that the purchase of Sarah's tomb will be in effect a down-payment on that promise.

The Hittites are certainly aware of the significance of what Abraham is asking for. Their apparently kind offer to provide burial space for Sarah in one of their graves neatly sidesteps what Abraham is really asking for. Once he has been allowed to purchase land his political status will have been irrevocably altered.

But the Hittites' offer of shared space is not enough. Not least because the separation of Abraham's family from other peoples, which had been symbolised by the covenant of circumcision, would not be able to be properly fulfilled if in death his kin is intermingled with the Hittite dead. From the exile onwards members of the Jewish community sought to maintain their separate identity primarily via rituals celebrated in the family, associated with birth (circumcision, chapter 17), death (here), and, as we shall see in Gen. 24 and 28, marriage.

So Abraham asks respectfully (the elevated level of mutual politeness is one of the features of this chapter) to buy the cave of Machpelah belonging to Ephron the Hittite, *at the far end of his land*. The location is important: it would allow for access to the grave by Sarah's family without trespassing on Ephron's land. Sarah's welfare after death would partly depend on how well she was physically remembered and her grave was tended by her family.

But Abraham is offered more than he had asked for, in the bargaining scene which follows, with which those who have ever purchased goods in a Middle Eastern bazaar may be ruefully familiar. It all happens *at the city gate*, the place where trade and official business of a city was conducted. Everyone can see what is going on: this purchase is to be above board and completely legal.

Ephron offers to 'give' Abraham both the cave and the land where it was situated. The writer of the story must have chuckled as this verb is repeated in vv. 11 and 13. It is an expensive gift – for Abraham. As he is well aware the actual price will shortly be mentioned, in a throw-away fashion. Ephron has taken the opportunity to sell him his land as well as the actual cave. We can only estimate the value of the asking price *four hundred shekels of silver* but a comparison with the price paid by Omri for the whole site of the city of Samaria, 2 talents or 6,000 shekels (1 Kgs 16.24) suggests that it was fairly exorbitant.

By now, of course, Abraham cannot withdraw from the transaction without losing face. Not that he wants to. He *closed the bargain.* The distinctive idiom of legal vocabulary dominates vv. 16 to 18. We are being assured that this purchase will be unquestionably legal. Similar vocabulary is found in Jer. 32.6–15 when Jeremiah purchases a plot of land at Anathoth that had once belonged to his family. Jeremiah's action is a statement of confidence in the eventual future of his people in the land even on the eve of the Babylonian exile. Similarly here, Abraham's purchase of the tomb is both fulfilment and promise. For the patriarchs and matriarchs themselves it meant that the promise was coming to fruition, since in death at least they were 'no longer strangers', but really belonged in the land. For their descendants in Canaan, Palestine or exile it was a pledge, as Jeremiah eloquently puts it, that *houses, fields and vineyards will again be bought and sold in this land* (Jer. 32.15).

24.1–67  We are going on a long and dreamy journey. The tempo of this leisurely chapter reflects the swaying pace of the camel caravan with which Abraham's servant journeys to Aram-naharaim (literally Aram-between-the-rivers, i.e. Mesopotamia) to find a bride for his master's son.

This is the longest narrative in Gen. 12—36. Its style of narration, by which in vv. 34–49 the servant repeats to Rebecca's family virtually the whole of what we have already read in vv. 1–27, deliberately slows the story down. It is as though the writer is telling us that what is happening now is make-or-break time for God's promise to Abraham – if the right wife cannot be found for Isaac, everything could still ultimately fail. We need to be assured that Rebecca is the correct choice, and it is worth taking the time to do so, although we are kept in suspense until the story nears its conclusion.

It is Rebecca's story: she is exceptionally proactive (certainly for an ancient Middle Eastern girl!). By contrast, Isaac, her future husband, feels strangely passive in his own betrothal sequence. Note that he is not mentioned by name anywhere between vv. 4 and 62, he is simply referred to by the servant as *my master's son.* There may well be good reasons why Isaac should not go back himself to his father's earlier home to find his own bride, but this surrogate wooing for a man of

40 effectively prepares the way for the quiescent and almost supine Isaac we will meet again in Gen. 25.28; 27.1–46.

*Abraham was by now a very old man*: If there is to be a future it will be with a new generation. Sarah is already dead, but before she died we heard of the birth of another woman (22.23) who may be her substitute and successor as matriarch. That hint is now to become actuality.

*The* LORD *had blessed him*: During the course of this story we will discover that this includes economic prosperity (24.35), as well, of course, as the birth of the sons about which we knew already. God's blessing, as expressed by the theology of this chapter, does not involve clear and direct intervention by the divine, but is rather the undergirding by God of basic aspects of human life, nudging it in the direction of well-being. Similarly God is present in the actions of this story, but not as obviously as in Gen. 12—22. We are invited to regard the eventual success of the servant's mission as being due to the overarching providence of God, but are not forced to see it in these terms.

*Abraham said to the servant who . . . was in charge of all he owned*: The status of the servant is an indication of the importance of this mission. However it is remarkable that the servant remains anonymous throughout this lengthy narrative. (We perhaps assume he is to be identified with Eliezer of Damascus, 15.2, but this is nowhere stated.) The effect is to accentuate the role and guiding hand of Abraham himself in the journey and the negotiations which follow: the servant is not acting as an independent entity.

*The* LORD, *the God of heaven and earth*: The designation of God in the oath sworn by the servant to Abraham recalls the blessing formula used by Melchizedek (14.19). Abraham's vision of God is growing steadily wider: such a designation is appropriate for a deity who will accompany his servant on a journey that will take him far from the promised land. The assurance of the story that YHWH can be prayed to and worshipped (24.12, 26–27) in a foreign land contrasts with the picture given in 2 Kgs 5.17 where YHWH's presence seems to be linked to the very soil of the land of Israel.

*You must go to my own country and to my own kindred to find a wife for my son Isaac*: Abraham's anxiety over possible intermarriage between his family and native Canaanites undergirds the story. The same concern is raised in relation to Jacob (27.46—28.5). The situation of the Babylonian exiles (who would have lived not far from the hypothetical site of Aram-naharaim) and concerns about intermarriage in the early post-exilic period may be reflected here. Is the story implicitly criticising those who were prepared to intermarry with non-Israelites living in or near Canaan? (See also comments on Gen. 28 p. 179.)

The phrase used to describe the servant's destination is striking: *my own country . . . my own kindred*. Similar phrases are used at two further points in the story (24.38, 40). They are reminiscent of the expression used in Yhwh's original call of Abraham (12.1), and in case we fail to notice the parallel, Abraham conveniently repeats it in 24.7: *The Lord the God of heaven who took me from my father's house and the land of my birth*. For the woman whom the servant selects will need to make a similar leap of faith to that made once by Abraham himself, agreeing to travel with this anonymous servant to meet an unseen and apparently anonymous bridegroom in a land far from her own family. Yet only such a woman would be suitable for the role of matriarch of God's people.

*The Lord . . . will send his angel before you*: The angelic messenger has a different role in this story as compared, for example, with Gen. 16 or 22. There he spoke or was seen directly: here he is the personification of a more vague guiding presence who will accompany the servant on his journey. When the servant *bowed down and prostrated himself before the Lord* (24.26) it is presumably before the accompanying angel. It is however notable that the angel is not mentioned specifically again in the story, so is the eventual success of the mission due to angelic guidance, or human intuition, or is there a relationship between the two? A similar expression is used several times in the Exodus account of the wilderness wandering (Exod. 23.20). There too a divine presence watches over a difficult journey.

*You must not take my son back there*: This strong statement seems to be linked to God's promise of the land which Abraham has just reiterated (24.7). For Abraham or his descendants to return to Mesopotamia might undo this promise. And yet eventually one – Jacob – would have to. And what about Abraham's later descendants who had been taken to Mesopotamia as exiles? Had this invalidated the promise?

*The servant then put his hand under his master Abraham's thigh and swore that oath*: The intimate touching of Abraham's genitals that this implies reminds us of the connection between the servant's mission and the destiny of Abraham's progeny. The servant's own future is being vowed as well – if he breaks his oath he too will lack descendants.

*With all kinds of gifts, . . . [the servant] went to Aram-naharaim*: These helped to establish his credentials as the servant of a wealthy man, which might well make his mission easier to accomplish. They would also be used to pay the formal bride-price which was customary.

*To the town where Nahor lived*: Nahor, Abraham's brother, is suddenly mentioned in the story. We are aware of who Nahor is through the references to him in 11.26–29; 22.20.

*By the well*: So far in Genesis a well has been a place where God has been seen (16.7–14), where an angel has saved the lives of Hagar and Ishmael (21.19), where a covenant has been made (21.25–30) leading to the name of YHWH being invoked there. What will happen at this well? On the surface it is something much more secular – finding a bride – but will God be present at this well too?

For the first time in Genesis we listen to the actual words of a human being praying. Cain (4.13–14) and later Abram (15.2–3) perhaps called out to God in an agony of spirit, but these words and the later prayer of the servant in 24.27 are the first formal prayers in the Bible. In those earlier instances it may also be that God was regarded as being visibly present with the speaker, whereas now it is a petition to an unseen God. That prayer is an important part of the story is made clear by the way it is twice emphasised (24.42, 48) when the servant recounts his experiences to Rebecca's family. From now on prayer will be an important way for human beings to relate to God, it will bridge the gap between the earthly and divine worlds: 'Through prayer, this little part of worldly life is made into a part of the ongoing and providential purposes of God.'[16]

Although the condition the servant imposed upon himself (24.14) for selecting the 'right' bride might seem arbitrary, it actually shows a good deal of worldly wisdom. The test he has devised will reveal clearly whether the girl has generosity of spirit.

Rebecca is on the move! She suddenly appears in a hurry *before he had finished praying*, and throughout her story she moves and speaks fast and decisively (24.20, 28, 58). The swiftness of Rebecca seems like the ideal response to the servant's prayer. She has some obvious attributes (her beauty), which both we and the servant can see, and others (her virginity and genealogy) to which we alone are presumably privy. But what about her inner beauty? How will she fare in the servant's test?

Once before generous human hospitality had proved decisive in God's plans (Gen. 18), Rebecca's response reminds us of Abraham's on that earlier occasion. And, as then, there is a touch of comedy around. In both instances what is described as a little (18.5; 24.17) quickly becomes a lot! We fail to realise what a massive operation watering ten thirsty camels would have been, Rebecca must have been going up and down to the well like a yo-yo for an hour or more! No wonder she, and the story, pauses (24.19a) after the servant himself drinks, before she eventually makes the offer on which her future will, unbeknown to her, rest. It must have been a long pause – especially for the servant.

Robert Alter's work on 'type-scenes'[17] has made us aware of how certain typical literary scenarios can be repeated with subtle differences. One of these 'type-scenes' is the betrothal. In such stories a hero journeys to a foreign land, meets a young and beautiful maiden at a well, water is drawn, the hero meets the girl's family, and then she eventually becomes his bride. This 'type-scene' is reflected here, in Gen. 29.1–10; Exod. 2.15–20; Ruth 2.9; and even John 4.4–30, when Jesus meets the woman of Samaria at a well. It then becomes significant to note where a particular story deviates from the standard type. There are two points where Rebecca's does so. First Isaac, 'the hero' and potential bridegroom is absent, second it is often the man that does the water-drawing, particularly if it involves the large-scale watering of animals. Viewed in this light Rebecca's actions become even more remarkable. She will be a worthy daughter-in-law for Abraham.

*The man was watching quietly to see whether or not the* LORD *had made his journey successful*: YHWH clearly had done exactly this, but not by the kind of direct intervention we had seen earlier in the story of Abraham, but working through a human heart and mind. In fact YHWH helps the servant out on his mission even further. In his eagerness for his 'test', the servant had temporarily forgotten an important element of Abraham's original criteria, that the bride should be from his *own kindred* (24.4). And now the servant gives away weighty jewellery, presumably intended as part of the bride-price, without first enquiring who this girl is. It is somewhat forward on his part: it could even be disastrous!

It is indeed fortunate that the servant eventually discovers she is from the ideal family – there are no closer kin to Abraham. Is this mere coincidence, or does God's providence work like that? The servant's prayer in response gives us his view. In speaking of how YHWH's *faithfulness . . . has been constant and unfailing* he uses language that is rooted in Israel's covenant traditions: the words *hesed* (steadfast love) and *'emet* (truth), that are paired here, are also paired in God's own self-designation to Moses at Sinai (*The* LORD*, a God . . . ever faithful and true,* Exod. 34.6). So God is fulfilling his covenant with Abraham by using the common sense of the prudent servant to ensure that the right woman is discovered. It is more than chance.

*The girl ran to her mother's house*: Note that the subject of marriage has not yet been broached: it would be unthinkable to raise it directly with the girl herself, in an era of arranged marriages. Yet we already have a sense that Rebecca will be no passive object in the decisions of others. It is her *mother's house* to which she runs; an unusual expression. It fits with the way that her descent from a woman, Milcah, has been stressed (24.15, 24). By contrast her father Bethuel plays less of a role in the marriage discussions than might be expected (24.55): Laban, Rebecca's brother, plays a paternal role, perhaps a sign that it is time for the new generation to assume prominence.

*Rebecca had a brother named Laban*: Our first meeting with Laban raises our suspicions. On the surface he is exceedingly hospitable, but we cannot help wondering whether the warmth of his welcome has been coloured by the expensive jewellery that his sister has been given. Would he have *hurried out to the spring* unless he had first seen the nose-ring and bracelets? When we meet him again in his dealings with his nephew Jacob our original suspicions will be more than confirmed.

The servant *protested, 'I will not eat until I have delivered my message'*. The sharing of food helps to ratify relationships. It is only appropriate to delay eating until the business has been done. The speech of the servant recapitulates what we have already learned from the narrator, and by listening to the servant's conversation with Rebecca. But there are some subtle differences, which reinforce our impression that this servant is a man who is worldly wise. He emphasises the great wealth of Abraham (24.34) and the fact that Isaac is the heir to *all that he has*. It is from Abraham's *family* rather than simply his wider kindred (24.4) that the bride is to be found. The servant does not explicitly mention God's promise (24.7). Intriguingly, in his speech he changes the order of his dealings with Rebecca: now he states that he discovered that she was Bethuel's daughter before giving her the presents, whereas we know this discovery was only made afterwards. This alteration clears the servant from having made what would have been a social faux pas – it also helps to put the pressure on Rebecca's family to agree to the match! His final words veer somewhat towards moral blackmail: *tell me if you mean to deal loyally and faithfully with my master*. The servant repeats the same Hebrew words *hesed* and *'emet* with which he had thanked YHWH (24.27 see above). It reinforces the impression that the choice of Rebecca is providential, and that God has had a hand in it, working through the anonymous servant. His words have the desired effect.

Throughout the chapter the name Yhwh has been used both by the servant and by the members of Rebecca's family: sometimes it appears in association with God (*Elohim*). The choice of this 'particular' name for the deity helps to remind us that Rebecca's family are an intrinsic part of Abraham's kin. Although they reside far away, they are in effect closer to him than either Abimelech or Hagar, both of whom ultimately relate to God only as *Elohim*. The bride for Isaac has to come from a family where Yhwh is already known as Yhwh.

Were Rebecca's family having second thoughts by the next morning? We probably should not read a great deal into their delaying tactics: it is rather that the servant sounds abnormally anxious to depart. Now that his mission is accomplished, the pace of the story speeds up. But the exchange allows Rebecca a voice to participate in the decision about her future. We suggested above how it is important for the wider story of Genesis that a woman should make the same 'leap of faith' that once Abraham himself had made. But how is this to be made clear in this culture of arranged marriages where women, especially, had little choice over their potential marriage partners? In the earlier discussions with Rebecca's family she did not speak: she was simply an object to be passed over: *Here is Rebecca; take her and go.* Now she has the opportunity to imprint her own assent. Her stark response, *Yes, I will go* (one short word in Hebrew), reprises the verb with which Yhwh had commanded her future father-in-law to leave Harran 65 years before. Though God might be speaking to her through the promise of a new human relationship rather than the challenge of the totally unknown, she has proved herself a worthy matriarch of the family of faith. It is right that the blessing her family speak over her as she departs deliberately recalls the words of the blessing spoken to Abraham by the angel of the Lord after the near-sacrifice of Isaac.

It is intriguing that Isaac should have moved to Beer-lahai-roi, the very place to which Hagar, his father's concubine, fled while pregnant with his half-brother Ishmael. Does one detect in this a need on Isaac's part to distance himself now from Abraham, to find his own relationships and to discover his own future? The REB's translation *hoping to meet them* gives an impression of a reflective and perhaps solitary Isaac.

But what happens at this place of seeing is now very different from that which Hagar had experienced. Instead of divinity Isaac and Rebecca now catch sight of each other: and the loneliness of Isaac's existence after the death of his mother is apparently to be cured by their mutual love. This is only the second time the verb for love has been used in Genesis (compare 22.2), and the first time it has described the relationship between a man and a woman. Since Isaac and Rebecca are apparently the only absolutely life-long monogamous couple with a major role in Gen. 12—50, it is appropriate that it should be spoken of them. There are echoes of Gen. 2 around: for Isaac has now emotionally left his father and his mother (24.67) and attached himself to his wife. True there are differences: for the nakedness of the garden has been replaced by the reticence and veiling of Rebecca but the link is made again through the comment that Isaac was *consoled* by Rebecca. It is the same vocabulary as was used of Noah, who brought *relief* (consolation, 5.29) from the curse of the ground. The mutual love between this couple may help to unravel the breakdown of relationships into which Gen. 3 dissolved. Westermann puts it well: 'The story of love is also part of the history of God's dealing with his people.'[18] There are no parts of human experience outside the purposes of YHWH.

**25.1–11**  After the agonies of the intricate interrelationships between Abraham, Sarah and Hagar, Abraham's concluding years seem all so simple. He marries again, a wife whose name, Keturah, may link her to the 'incense trade' that originated from western Arabia. Some of their sons bear names (e.g. Midian) that link them geographically to the tribes that peopled north-west Arabia and southern Transjordan. The names of some of Midian's sons (e.g. Eldaah, Abida, Enoch) also seem to hint at the reputation of this region for wisdom (e.g. 1 Kgs 4.30).

In contrast with his indecisiveness in dealing with Hagar and Ishmael, Abraham takes firm action to ensure that these sons do not threaten the position of Isaac. He sends them away, though this time provided for, to a *land of the east*. As well as being far out of Isaac's way, the 'east' is also, in the theological geography of Genesis, out of YHWH's sight (e.g. 4.16; 11.2): they will not be sons of the promise, although the history of their descendants would interweave with that of Israel.

But it is not quite so simple as it first seems. What is the relationship between Ishmael and these other sons? Intriguingly, rabbinic tradition actually suggests that Keturah was another name for Hagar! And why does Ishmael suddenly reappear in the story (25.9), when he had been so conclusively dismissed by Abraham in Gen. 21. There also appears to be some overlap between the list of the sons of Keturah and those of Ishmael (25.13–15), although the names may be different, they are linked to the same geographical area. Similarly there is also an overlap between these genealogies and the genealogy of the descendants of Joktan given in 10.26–31.

It is probable that 25.1–11 was composed quite late in the development of Genesis and drew upon several different and sometimes conflicting earlier sources. But it is too simplistic to suggest that the writer was simply careless in his editorial work. On the one hand the presence of these various genealogical lists which have strong links with north-west Arabia help to reinforce the sense of close ethnic ties between Abraham's family and those whom later history would call the 'Arabs'. On the other hand, the apparent discrepancies provide a theological statement that the history of salvation is never neat and tidy, however much humans might like it to be so!

God fulfils his promises: Abraham died *at a great age, a full span of years* just as Yhwh had promised that he would (15.15). He is buried alongside Sarah, and the detail about his burial place clearly recalls the account of its purchase in Gen. 23, and reminds us that in his death he too becomes an actual inheritor of the promise of the land.

And yet those outside the covenant are not simply forgotten. Perhaps Ishmael logically shouldn't be there at his father's burial, but he is, acting in harmony with his brother Isaac.

25.12–18    The special *toledot* formula used to introduce a genealogy is now employed to list the descendants of Ishmael (see p. xx). As suggested above, there seem to be links between this list and that of the descendants of Abraham and Keturah. Again the names seem to be connected with north Arabia: the name of Nebaioth, the eldest son, may possibly be associated with the Nabateans; Massa is referred to in Prov. 30.1; Kedar is a location mentioned in Ps. 120.5 and Jer. 49.28. The specific mention of 12 sons is clearly intended as a fulfilment of the promise made in 17.20. Ishmael, like Isaac, will be fruitful (indeed, even more so!).

The concluding words about Ishmael remind us of the previous episodes in his life. Shur is mentioned, to which Hagar had fled while pregnant with him (16.7), so is Egypt, Hagar's own native land and the country from which Ishmael's wife had come (21.21). The REB translation of the final comment on Ishmael conceals the fact that it virtually mimics the language used about him in the angelic birth oracle (*he will live at odds with his kin*, 16.12). Although it is read by the REB as a geographical statement *he . . . had settled to the east of his brothers*, it may in fact be a statement of relationship – and just as when the words first appeared in 16.12, it was ambiguous as to whether hostility was implied, so too the ambiguity may linger here (see further Theological Reflections on p. 158).

With the genealogy of Ishmael the story of Abraham is finally completed. 25.19 will open the story of Jacob. To focus on the unfavoured son who is – just – outside the covenant is perhaps an unexpected way to conclude this great saga of promise, but it is deliberate. In a similar fashion the story of Jacob will conclude with the genealogy of his unfavoured brother, Esau. Both examples are salutary reminders that God will not be bound by any human desire for theological tidiness. Alongside 'the scandal of particularity', universality refuses to be forgotten.

## Theological reflections

### 1. Context and Promise

In his deceptively simple yet profoundly influential work *The Theme of the Pentateuch* David Clines has suggested that one reason that the Pentateuch still fascinates and challenges us today is because it is presented as a 'travel story'.[19] People in it are always on the move. That is of course especially true of Abraham. He starts in Ur, and travels via Harran in Upper Mesopotamia to Canaan. Even when he arrives in Canaan he doesn't stay in one place: in chapters 12—22 we have followed him down to Egypt (12.10), going through the length and breadth of the land (13.17), journeying to Mamre, Beersheba and then Moriah. The verbs chosen seem to emphasise his restlessness. And if he seems to settle somewhere it is made clear that this is only provisional – Abraham is always and everywhere a *ger*, and this fact dominates his story from beginning to end (e.g. 12.10; 20.1; 21.34; 23.4).

Who constructed this 'travel story' of Abraham and why did they do so? The short answer seems to be that it assumed its present structure, certainly with its distinctive focus on movement, close to the exilic or early post-exilic period, and that it did so because of spiritual, emotional, political and existential needs in the exilic community, either in Mesopotamia or during this community's partial return to Palestine.

It may well be that the figure of Abraham was celebrated in some circles prior to the seventh/sixth centuries BC, although intriguingly the name of Abraham (unlike that of Jacob or Isaac) does not crop up in the prophetic literature that can be clearly dated to the pre-exilic era. It is also fascinating that when references to Abraham do appear in prophetic literature they suggest that the figure of Abraham was not uncontroversial (see e.g. Ezek. 33.24–25; Isa. 63.16). One possibility is that Abraham may have originally been the founder (whether historical or legendary) of the sanctuary at Mamre near Hebron, and that the stories told about him there included a celebration of his overcoming infertility. Since the Davidic monarchy in Jerusalem had close and long-lasting links with the Hebron area they may have regarded him as a patron. This would help explain Abraham's eventual paramount position in the triad of patriarchs, Abraham, Isaac and Jacob, which is puzzling in view of the fact that the figure of Jacob in particular seems to have been much more widely known in the pre-exilic period. Abraham's name presumably facilitated this: *'ab* (= father), suggested that it was appropriate to consider him as the ultimate ancestor, the epitomy of the 'fathers' (Hebrew: *'abot*), a term which begins to be used in the Deuteronomic and prophetic literature in the late seventh century. *'ab* is also a royal title (see Isa. 9.6) since the king was considered the 'father' of his people, so between his name and his Davidic connections Abraham was well placed to become a powerful emblem of the nation during the exile.

He was particularly important to the leading groups of society, those who were actually transported to Babylon and some of whom later returned to Judah after the Persian conquest of Babylon. Indeed those who remained in Palestine seem to have objected to the way that Abraham was 'adopted' by these royal and priestly classes and used as a tool to reinforce their specific political and economic ends (as in Ezek. 33.24–25 and Isa. 63.16).

Yet those who took the raw tales of Abraham and constructed the narrative that we now have in this section of Genesis did so in a way that not only spoke profoundly to their own situation but has also carried on responding to the needs of generations since. Many even today have seen in Abraham their own longing for 'roots' and for a 'home', and with him have celebrated a promise that seems to go beyond hope.

It is possible that a connected story of Abraham's adventures was composed during the monarchy. Traditionally this has been linked to a figure referred to as the Yahwist, though many today would date this hypothetical Yahwist to the later monarchic period (during the time of Josiah *c.*625 BC) rather than, as was once popular, during the time of David and Solomon. Such a story would have been concerned to show how God's promises to Abraham were fulfilled, reflecting the anxiety of the immediate pre-exilic period when the tension between Josiah's expansionist hopes and the harsh reality of Mesopotamian imperial rule created insecurity. There are apparent connections with Deuteronomic theology (Gen. 18.19; 22.18) which argue for links at some point during the composition of the Abraham cycle. The concept of God's promise of the land given in Deuteronomy to those who had fled from Egypt was now transposed back into a greater antiquity to give it additional authority.

Others would suggest that this Yahwist was himself an exilic writer. What we can say with more certainty is that if there was such a 'first edition' of the Abraham cycle, it then provided the framework for an expansion of the story later in the exile. This expansion (which may have happened over several stages) probably drew in the story of the destruction of Sodom and led to the deliberate construction of a number of the 'doublet' stories. Further on still the Priestly writers added their distinctive touches (e.g. in Gen. 17) and the shape of the cycle took on its present form.

As it developed, the story of Abraham acted as both reassurance and challenge to the Jewish community living in the Babylonian diaspora. It is not now a tale of fulfilment so much as one of promise. Abraham is an example of a person who is called by God to journey from Ur of the Chaldees (an appropriate starting point if the story is directed towards those themselves living in Mesopotamia) to a land which he had been promised. His journey will not be problem-free, and he may not be able fully to possess the land to which he is journeying, but he will be bearing with him the threefold promise of God: a promise of progeny, a promise of relationship with God, and an eventual promise of land. So Abraham is being presented as an example for those were in Babylon to encourage them to return to their homeland and help remake their nation.

A major theological impetus during the exile was the use of the traditional motif of an Exodus from Egypt to anticipate the hope of a new exodus from Babylon (see e.g. Isa. 51.9–11; Ezek. 20.34–44). The Abraham cycle is itself drawn into this trajectory, so that the stories are presented as a kind of proleptic foreshadowing, an exodus before the Exodus. This is very clear in the account of Abraham's expulsion from Egypt (Gen. 12.10–20), the reference to the enslaving and oppression of Abraham's descendants (Gen. 15.13–14), and in the intricate interplay of the stories of Hagar the Egyptian, whose treatment at the hands of Abraham and Sarah is used as a hinted rationale for the later slavery of Israel. Similarly the experiences of Abraham anticipate the giving of the law at Sinai. Although Abraham lived before the giving of the law the behaviour demanded of him is analogous to that found in the law (see e.g. Gen. 18.19; 22.1, 18; 26.5, compare Deut. 4.1). The restlessness of Abraham points us forward to the Exodus, but beyond that to the conquest of Canaan. Yet this telescoping of the past is not simply an antiquarian exercise; it is concerned with the present and the future.

This is 'not only a narrative written in retrospect about an ancient "once upon a time." Where God . . . condescends to his people and promises himself to this people, we are not dealing with an aorist tense, but rather with a perfect, yes, even with a future perfect.'[20]

'The theme of the Pentateuch is entirely concerned with a future bound to a past out of which the present lives.'[21]

As Jürgen Moltmann has commented so eloquently in his *Theology of Hope*,[22] the nature of promise, a motif which is so dominant in the Abraham cycle, is that it binds human beings to the future.

Other specific issues that concerned the exilic community can be seen represented in these stories. There was the problem of justice with which the exilic literature wrestles (see e.g. Ezek. 18.1–32; Jer. 31.29; Isa. 40.2). What is the relationship between individuals and their community? Does God punish a righteous individual because of the corporate wickedness of their social group? Conversely, can a righteous person prevent punishment falling on the unjust? Gen. 18.23 addresses these questions which were a topic of lively debate among the exiles.

The extensive description of the destruction of Sodom and Gomorrah also reflects an issue that concerned those who lived through the destruction of Jerusalem. It is likely that the story of the downfall of Sodom and Gomorrah was a well-known 'myth' that circulated widely in Canaan in the pre-exilic period. But already in the writings of pre-exilic prophets parallels were drawn between the fate of these cities, and the destruction of Israel (Hos. 11.8) and later Jerusalem (see Isa. 1.10–17). According to Isaiah Jerusalem is to be punished because she is 'unrighteous', as was Sodom and Gomorrah. After the destruction of Jerusalem in 586 BC the parallels were drawn even more strongly (Ezek. 16.46–58). It is wearing these exilic spectacles that we need to read Gen. 19.

Similarly the account of the birth of Moab and Ammon in Gen. 19.33–38, reflects the tensions during the exile or perhaps in the period of resettlement afterwards. We know that the shift in the balance of power in Canaan/Transjordan when Jerusalem was destroyed allowed a surge in Moabite and Ammonite power, at least for a brief interval of time. This was bitterly resented by all Judaeans whether in exile or remaining in Judah. After the exile the ambiguity of the relationship between the Moabites, Ammonites and the Jews is a topic that is specifically highlighted in, for example, Ezra 9.1; Neh. 13.23–7. Either or both of these situations could be reflected in the account of the unorthodox birth of the eponymous founders of these nations. The story of Ishmael may similarly reflect the strains of Judaean relationships with the developing power of the Arabs and Nabateans (see below).

If there are features of the Abraham cycle that show a wariness towards foreign nations, there are also incidents that suggest a positive relationship is possible. The story of Abimelech stands out. So too does the third clause of the original blessing of Abraham in Gen.12.3, whatever its precise meaning (see p. 77). There are nuances here of the language of Isaiah 40—55, who of course used the figures of Abraham and Sarah (Isa. 41.8; 51.2). Along with the importance given to circumcision (Gen. 17.9–14) such examples reflect the situation of the diaspora Jewish community, faced with the tension of remaining distinctive and yet relating more immediately to the non-Jews amongst whom they were living.

The topic that dominates the Abraham cycle from beginning to end, that of the barrenness of Sarah, reflects a major social question for those living in Babylonia during the exilic and Persian periods. They were comparatively few in number and were surrounded by the seductive glamour and might of Babylonian culture and religion. They needed to know that they were not the last generation, that their faith would have children, despite all appearances. The traditions of Abraham and the poetry of Isaiah 40—55 (Isa. 54.1–3) laugh and sing their message of hope down the centuries, perhaps even to our own time when the alienation of children and young people from the churches seems to some to threaten a barren future. To all of us who want to have faith in the future, the stories of Abraham offer their challenge and consolation: 'Any one who knows of promise and ful-filment is responsible to a yesterday about which he has heard some-thing, and he walks toward a tomorrow.'[23]

## 2. *Abraham, the figure of faith*

One of the most attractive descriptions of Abraham occurs in Isa. 41.8. Abraham, says God, is *'My friend'*. This is alluded to in the New Testa-ment by James 2.23 in a discussion about faith and works. As well as mentioning that *Abraham put his faith in God, and that faith was counted to him as righteousness,* James goes on to mention *and he was called, 'God's friend'*. In Islam too the same description of Abraham is found: 'God took Abraham for a friend' (Qur'an, *Sūra* 4), and of all the titles that Muslim tradition could give him its preferred one is 'Khalil Al-lah' (= the friend of God). For Abraham is not only a figure of faith for the Old Testament, but also for the three great religions Judaism, Christianity and Islam, which have their roots in the Old Testament tradition, and which are often jointly called the 'Abrahamic faiths'. We have all claimed Abraham for ourselves, and sometimes we have demanded exclusive possession of him. And yet perhaps it is the rest-lessness of Abraham the *ger* that means he refuses to allow himself to be held captive by any one religion.

I write from within the Christian tradition, although appreciative of the wisdom of both Judaism and Islam. So I feel it appropriate to consider briefly the way Abraham is used in the New Testament, the foundation document of my faith.

The name of Abraham appears extensively in the New Testa-ment, beginning with the very first verse, where it helps to shape the genealogy of Jesus in Matthew's Gospel (Matt. 1.1–2). In Luke's Gos-pel Abraham appears as a father-figure of suffering (13.16), repent-ant (19.9), or even condemned (16.24) members of the Jewish nation. The figure of Abraham is used extensively in John 8.31–59, where the debate between Judaism and Christianity assumes a polemical form, as the author of John's Gospel challenges the claim of the Jewish com-munity of his day to call themselves Abraham's children. That debate is continued, though in a more positive spirit and without John's par-ticular 'edge', in the Pauline literature (Rom. 4.1–25; 9.6–9; 11.1; Gal. 3.6–29; 4.22—5.1). Here Paul is not so much denying the claim of con-temporary Jews to call themselves children of Abraham as claiming that right for Gentile Christians. He also wrestles at length with the question of what is meant by Abraham's righteousness: a key text for

147

him is Gen. 15.6. Paul's views on this have influenced the way that Abraham has been perceived in Christian tradition ever since. Then, of course, Abraham is the great hero of the galaxy of Old Testament saints in the Epistle to the Hebrews. His willingness to travel and then to offer Isaac in sacrifice seems to epitomise what this writer means by faith (Heb. 11.8–19).

Yet because he has been so appropriated by the New Testament as this figure of faith it is difficult sometimes for Christians to read the Old Testament account of Abraham without their New Testament spectacles filtering out the real humanity that is apparent in these Abraham stories. We have been so impressed with Abraham as a figure who is 'justified by faith' that we find it almost scandalous to contemplate him as a person who has 'warts and all'. It may be significant that the only New Testament writing which dares to describe Abraham with that exquisite yet humane phrase 'friend of God', is the Epistle of James, one of the most Jewish of New Testament books.

Commenting on Heb. 11 Gabriel Josipovici suggests that in spite of its 'rousing call' it still leaves anyone who has read the stories for themselves in the Old Testament a 'little uneasy'. 'As we read this chapter we inevitably ask ourselves whether it corresponds to our own memory of the text. Is this all there is to say about these people? We remember Sarah laughing when God tells Abraham in her hearing that she will bear a son, a scene important enough to be commemorated in the very name of the child, Yitzhak; we remember the early life of Moses; we remember the enormously complex and ambiguous relation of David to God – and we wonder: can all this be summed up under the single rubric of faith?' Quoting words of Mary Douglas, Josipovici goes on to suggest that our New Testament vision of Abraham is a little 'thin'.[24]

One of the benefits of a narrative approach to the Old Testament is that it enables us to see how Abraham develops through the 14 chapters under discussion. It allows us to admit that he isn't perfect, he is someone who makes mistakes, takes false trails, and that his dealings with both Sarah and Hagar leave something to be desired! Looking at the stories from a feminist perspective can be a refreshing and important tool in this exercise. There are important questions to be asked by feminist scholars: why is it, for example, that Abraham, so brave in the defence of Lot, is so cowardly when it comes to Sarah that he lies about their relationship and puts her at risk by his deceit? Some may respond that these are 'modern questions', but in fact they are posed by the text itself. (It is clear, for example, that the ancient commentaries on Genesis such as the Genesis Apocryphon feel a need to rewrite the story of Genesis at this point to present Abraham in a less unfavourable light!)

To point up the humanity of Abraham in this way does not lead to 'debunking' him, but rather can help us discover in him more easily a real rather than ideal model for our faith. Karl-Josef Kuschel whose book *Abraham: A Symbol of Hope for Jews, Christians and Muslims* makes clear the relevance of the figure of Abraham in interfaith issues, comments as follows:

> If we look closely at Abraham's way we discover that his faith is quite a complex one. There is no trace of blind readiness to follow, of an irrational act of the will, of the obedience of an automaton. Abraham's faith is tested by a long experience of life. And because this is the case, this faith is made up of quite different ingredients: there is a touch of doubt and a touch of cunning, a touch of anxiety and a touch of risk-taking with his God; a touch of wordless obedience and a touch of canny haggling. This faith includes humble sacrifice to this God and bold negotiations to spare innocent human beings. Here is a unique profile: faith as a process of setting out despite everything: despite all reservations, despite all gnashing of the teeth, despite all anxiety.[25]

At the heart of the Abraham story lies the man we meet in Gen. 18: the exuberant giver of hospitality who *entertained angels unawares* (Heb. 13.2). Even though he may be a bit 'over the top', even though he still leaves us with questions over his attitude to Sarah, he helps us in this encounter to discover God through his sheer humanity. It is therefore highly appropriate that this story of the hospitality of Abraham has provided the basis for the Orthodox Christian icons of the Holy Trinity. The hospitality that Abraham showed to these unexpected visitors reflects the mutual and overflowing hospitality that is at the heart of the life of the divine. A quotation from a twentieth-century Jewish source sums it up:

> Abraham's house was open to all the children of men,
> those going past and those returning,
> and day by day they came
> to eat and drink with Abraham.
> To those who were hungry he gave bread,
> and the guests ate and drank and were filled.

Those who came naked to his house
he clothed,
and helped them to experience God,
the creator of all things.[26]

Abraham is a man of contrasts. As we commented in 17.17, there is
something extraordinary in the scene when he lies prostrate before
God, laughing to himself. Is it an accident that laughter is such
a strong verbal motif in the Abraham cycle? Not if you believe the
following words of Harvey Cox:

> Laughter is hope's last weapon. Crowded on all sides with idiocy
> and ugliness, pushed to concede that the final apocalypse seems
> to be upon us, we seem nonetheless to nourish laughter as our
> only remaining defence. in the presence of disaster and death we
> laugh instead of crossing ourselves. Or perhaps better stated, our
> laughter is our way of crossing ourselves. It shows that despite the
> disappearance of any empirical basis for hope, we have not stopped
> hoping . . . It could conceivably disappear, and where laughter and
> hope have disappeared, man has ceased to be man.[27]

Abraham never ceases to be man.

## 3. The Aqedah

The story of the near-sacrifice of Isaac is often referred to in Jewish and
Christian theology as the *Aqedah* ('Binding'), which describes what
Abraham did to Isaac as he prepared for the sacrifice (22.9). It is of
course, as the writer to the Hebrews was aware (Heb. 11.17), a major
example of what we mean when we call Abraham a 'figure of faith',
but this episode in the life of Abraham has been so influential in later
religious history that it seems right to treat it separately. Søren Kierke-
gaard, for example, in his classic work *Fear and Trembling*, exploring
the story from a Lutheran perspective, believed that it expressed the
essence of what 'faith' means.

But is it really an example of Abraham's faith? What about Isaac,
the intended sacrificial victim? Although Genesis clearly presents the
story as a test of Abraham, the father, later Jewish tradition (and in a
different way, Christianity) developed it as the self-sacrifice of Isaac.

For a start, how old was Isaac supposed to be when he was so
nearly sacrificed? Our mental picture is probably of a young boy,

not more than six or seven: such a child is pictured in the depiction of the scene by the famous Beth Alpha synagogue mosaic (sixth century AD). But rabbinic commentaries on the passage measured Isaac's age quite variably – up even to 37 years old! (on the basis that the next incident referred to in Genesis is the death of Sarah, aged 127). Obviously a 37-year-old's perception of what is going on differs radically from that of a six-year-old. Isaac therefore becomes a willing participant in, rather than an unwitting victim of, the sacrifice. Indeed in several rabbinic texts Isaac actually sets in train the process that leads to the sacrifice, by offering himself to God during the course of a debate with his brother Ishmael. (In the process, of course, God is thereby let off the hook and declared innocent of any unreasonable divine demands!) If then this is a voluntary sacrifice of Isaac, it bestows upon him a particular merit. In turn this merit can be called upon by Isaac's own heirs, the Jewish community of a later period. There are many examples of this viewpoint; the following from the *Pesikta de-Rav Kahana* is particularly striking: 'By the merit of Isaac, who offered himself upon the altar, the Holy One (blessed be He) will in the future resurrect the dead.'[28]

Another development in the Jewish understanding of the offering of Isaac was to gradually link it to the sacrifice of the Passover lamb. It becomes a kind of prototype of the Passover sacrifice by the blood of which Isaac's descendants in Egypt escaped into freedom. This development has already taken place by the time the Book of Jubilees was written in the second century BC.

The link that was made between the sacrifice of Isaac and Passover was in turn to prepare the way for the Christian use of the Isaac tradition. For though Christians did on the one hand continue to see the sacrifice of Isaac as an example of the faith of Abraham, a more radical development of the *Aqedah* tradition quickly took root. Jesus Christ had died at Passover, possibly at the very time that the Passover lambs were being slain (John 19.14). The link between Passover and the *Aqedah* had already been made. Therefore, reflected Jesus' first followers, there must be a close connection between the near death of Isaac and the actual death of Christ. Christ was a 'new Isaac' and his death was the sacrifice that went one stage further than Abraham and Isaac had been required to go. The link was facilitated by parallels that could be drawn out of the respective stories of Jesus and Isaac. There was in both cases the 'wood' – of the cross, and on which Isaac had been bound. There was the close connection with the temple in Jerusalem, hinted at in Gen. 22.14, and which played a dominant role in the events leading to Jesus' crucifixion. And there was the terrible three-day journey that both Isaac and Jesus undertook.

It is clear that the link between Christ and the Isaac tradition was firmly established by the time Paul wrote his letters to the Galatians and Romans. Not only does he refer to Christ as Abraham's issue (Gal. 3.16), an epithet that originally belonged to Isaac, but in a meditation on the love of God in Rom. 8.32 he reflects how God *did not spare his own Son, but gave him up for us all.* The verb 'spare' here is based on a comparatively rare Greek word, which also appears in the Septuagint translation of Gen. 22.16 (*you have not withheld your son*).

Once this link was made, it influenced the development of New Testament Christology. It is likely that the description of Christ as the beloved son in the synoptic narratives of the baptism (Mark 1.11), the transfiguration (Mark 9.7) and the Parable of the Wicked Tenants (Mark 12.6) is owed partly to the description of Isaac as the beloved son. The association is still more pronounced in John's Gospel where the link with Isaac not only seems to underlie the description of Christ as God's 'only son' (John 1.14, 18), but also to be interwoven with the title 'Lamb of God' given him by John the Baptist (John 1.29, 36), and indeed with the language of God's love as it is expressed in John 3.16. There are those who would suggest that the Christian doctrine of atonement owes much in its formulation to the fact that the Jewish *Aqedah* tradition had already treated Isaac's suffering as atoning for the sins of his descendants. What is certainly true is that to speak thus of Christ is also to 'revision' God. For if Jesus represents Isaac then God must be Abraham, and the cost to God of the death of the beloved Son takes on a pathos that far removes it from the juridical language of the courthouse in which Christians have often verbalised their faith. Rather than omnipotent judge of innocent and guilty, God becomes the agonised and vulnerable father.

There is no doubt that the *Aqedah* tradition has enriched Jewish and Christian literature and theology down to the present time. It has been drawn on by Jewish writers trying to make theological sense of the non-sense of the Holocaust (Shoah). Israel itself is become Isaac, sacrificed now even to death. Among many possible examples, the following passage by Elie Wiesel (himself a former inmate of a concentration camp) stands out:

> We have known Jews who, like Abraham, witnessed the death of their children; who, like Isaac, lived the *Akeda* in their flesh; and some who went mad when they saw their father disappear on the

altar, with the altar, in a blazing fire whose flames reached into the highest of heavens . . .

Isaac survived; he had no choice. He had to make something of his memories, his experience in order to force us to hope. For our survival is bound up with his survival . . . Why was the most tragic of our ancestors named Isaac, a name which evokes and signifies laughter? Here is why. As the first survivor, he had to teach us, the future survivors of Jewish history, that it is possible to suffer and despair an entire lifetime and still not give up the art of laughter.

Isaac, of course, never freed himself from the traumatizing scenes that violated his youth; the holocaust had marked him and continued to haunt him forever. Yet he remained capable of laughter. And in spite of everything, he did laugh.[29]

And yet? In recent years there are those who would argue that the story of the sacrifice of Isaac has seduced us by the exquisite beauty of its telling, so that we have forgotten to ask the questions we should have demanded of it. Perhaps the remarkable poem by the British war poet Wilfred Owen was one of the first warnings of how dangerous a story it could be:

*Parable of the Old Man and the Young*
So Abram rose, and clave the wood, and went,
And took the fire with him, and a knife.
And as they sojourned both of them together,
Isaac the first-born spake and said, My Father,
Behold the preparations, fire and iron,
But where the lamb for this burnt offering?
Then Abram bound the youth with belts and straps,
And builded parapets and trenches there,
And stretchèd forth the knife to slay his son.
When lo! an angel called him out of heaven,
Saying, Lay not thy hand upon the lad,
Neither do anything to him. Behold,
A ram, caught in a thicket by its horns;
Offer the Ram of Pride instead of him.
But the old man would not so, but slew his son,
And half the seed of Europe, one by one.

A Jewish rabbi in Canada has dared to remark: 'Avraham failed the test. He chose God over his son. He chose being God's servant over being his son's father. He loved God more than he loved his own son, and he made the wrong choice.'[30] Feminist commentators on this story have pointed out how it reinforces a model of patriarchy in which a father has the power of life or death over his children. It begs some difficult questions: 'Why is the willingness to sacrifice the child at God's command the model of faith, rather than the passionate protection of the child? What would be the shape of our society had that been the model of faith?'[31]

And what of Sarah, so entirely absent from the story: her voice surely deserves to be heard. In the fourth century St Ephraem, the voice of Syriac-speaking Christianity, did explore the biblical story from Sarah's point of view, but by and large Sarah's silence has echoed down the centuries. Recently Phyllis Trible has reflected on Gen. 22 in an article entitled, 'The Sacrifice of Sarah',[32] a telling title in view of the way she has indeed been sacrificed in Bible and church tradition. But a meditation by Trevor Dennis entitled *The Other Women* (at the Cross) offers us the opportunity finally to listen to Sarah:

> Sarah was there also [at the cross]. Isaac had never come home. He had gone off one morning with his father, and she had never seen him again. Abraham had talked wild talk of a three-day journey, of fire and a knife and the building of an altar and the binding of her son, of how he had stopped and sacrificed a ram instead, and all she had asked was where Isaac was. He had not been able to tell her, so she had left and gone hunting for him. She had gone back to Ur, from where they had come originally, but Isaac was not there. She had gone down to Egypt, where once Abraham had so humiliated her, but they had heard nothing of her son. Christ had first discovered her among some tombs above the Sea of Galilee, where she had gone to see if Isaac's name was on any of the graves. Wild with grief, she had called Christ all the names under the sun and beaten his chest with her fists, and he had waited till she was done and could accept his embrace. She had kept him company ever since.
>
> So she came to Golgotha, and waited till he died. And when they came to take his body down, she sat on the ground and asked them to lay his body in her lap. And so they did, and she bent her face to his, and said over and over again, 'My son, my son, my son, my son.'[33]

## 4. Isaac and Ishmael: Palestine – the much promised land

Nobody today can read the stories of the Abraham cycle (or the stories of the other ancestors) without being aware of their impact on modern Middle Eastern politics. There is no tenser tinderbox in the Holy Land than the traditional site of the Cave of Machpelah in Hebron, bought by Abraham as a burial place for Sarah (Gen. 23), and where he, Isaac and Jacob, as well as Rebecca and Leah are supposedly buried. It, like Abraham, is claimed by both Judaism and Islam: often the claims have been made with violence. Ironically the Arabic name for the city of Hebron is 'Al Khalil' (= 'the friend'), recalling the title first given to Abraham.

It might be more comfortable for Christians if they could totally dismiss modern Israel as a completely secular state, with no relationship to a biblical past, or at least reject the territorial dimension of the promise to Abraham (*As a possession for all time I shall give you and your descendants after you the land*, Gen. 17.8) as a pledge which has been superseded by the coming of Christ. But it is not that easy. When I lived in Beirut in 1982 throughout the Israeli invasion of Lebanon and siege of that city, I might have laughed at the way the Israeli advance up the Lebanese coast was sometimes referred to on Israeli radio as the repossession of the territory of Asher and Naphtali – for, like Sarah, laughter in such a situation was the alternative to succumbing to terror. But intellectual integrity compelled me to acknowledge that within its own theological framework the ongoing doctrine of a promised land may well be a part of Judaism. It was not a theoretical question for me: as it certainly was not either for the Palestinian Christian students in Beirut to whom I taught Old Testament. Naim Ateek, a Palestinian Christian theologian puts it thus:

In Israel-Palestine today, the Bible is being quoted to given the primary claim over the land to Jews. In the mind of many religious Jews and fundamentalist Christians the solution to the conflict lies in Palestinian recognition that God has given the Jews the land of Palestine forever. Palestinians are asked to accept this as a basic truth . . . Palestinian Christians must tackle the land from a biblical perspective, not because I believe that the religious argument over the land is of the *bene esse* of the conflict, but because we are driven to it as a result of the religious-political abuse of biblical interpretation.[34]

What can we say about this question, on the basis of our exploration so far of the stories of Abraham? There are three points I would like to offer for reflection:

1. The first is that made by David Clines in his study of the theme of the Pentateuch[35] that the promises in the Pentateuch exist in a tension between expectation and fulfilment. They were offered in a historical context when they could not immediately become fully operative. The promises therefore accompany Israel through its historical development and struggle as goals to be aimed for; sometimes these goals seem an unrealistic burden, a mirage; sometimes challenging and attainable. But is their physical attainment perhaps to destroy the nature of the promise itself? Like the ancestors themselves there is the need to live today in the interval between yesterday's promise and tomorrow's redemption.

2. In an interesting study entitled *The Land is Mine*, Norman Habel has drawn attention to the fact that the land-theology of the Old Testament is not monolithic. Several different ideologies are given space. Habel suggests that the ideology of the ancestral stories speaks of 'land as host country' and he explores how in the Abraham cycle the land is offered and received within stories of mutual hospitality, between Abraham the *ger* and the inhabitants of Canaan.[36] In other words we can argue that unless land is lived in and shared in a hospitable spirit, the promises to Abraham cannot be used as sanction for ownership of such land. Such a viewpoint would have clear implications for any who choose to claim land as 'promised'.

3. The crucial role that Hagar and Ishmael play in the Abraham cycle is also relevant. Did their stories originate and first circulate among the Arab and proto-Nabatean tribes of the Negev and southern Transjordan, before they were adopted by those who composed the Abraham cycle and incorporated them into their larger framework? The vividness of the language suggests that they may originally have been told among those who venerated Ishmael as their ancestor, or Hagar as the Madonna of a desert shrine at Beer-lahai-roi. Certainly both figures were later to have a life outside the pages of Genesis in the foundation stories of Islam. Hagar's name may be included in the Syriac word *Mahgraye* and the Arabic *muhajirun* by which the earliest followers of Muhammad were known.[37] The name referred to the flight or *Hijra* that took them from Mecca to Medina, marking

the beginning of the Muslim era, and for which the flight and banishment of Hagar (Gen. 16; 21) provided a sort of prototype. Ishmael was viewed among early Muslims as the favoured son of Abraham, and stories told in Genesis of Isaac are then recounted of him: it is Ishmael who was nearly sacrificed by his father at a shrine at Mecca, visited by those who go to the city on pilgrimage.

If Jews count Isaac as their ancestor in the faith, then Arabs reserve that honour for his brother Ishmael. Is it possible to use the stories of Genesis that deal with Hagar and Ishmael to suggest a model of coexistence that can be emulated by their descendants? I believe that read sensitively the stories can be used to challenge any who seek to use the promises to Abraham to sustain a glib particularity.

In the comments on Gen. 16 we noted that 'Hagar is the woman who complicated the history of salvation.' We also suggested that many of us find it easier to identify with Sarah than with Hagar. But that reflects the bias of white First World commentators – Elsa Tamez observes how women from the Third World would naturally identify with Hagar. The analysis that we have suggested for the Abraham cycle, with the story of the birth of Ishmael taking centre place in the cycle, leads us to ask whether this identification with Hagar is what the writers of Genesis actually intended all along, so that particularity is not allowed totally to displace universality, and so that Ishmael retains a place in the continuing story along with his brother Isaac. The comments made on Gen.15—16 (see p. 90 and p. 92) suggested that a hint was being offered that the very reason for the later slavery of Abraham's descendants in Egypt is the mistreatment that was once meted out to a woman of Egypt at the hands of Israel's founding father and mother. Somehow a demand for justice and compassion for all 'aliens', of whom Hagar is being presented as an archetype, is being written into the very fabric of the covenant.[38]

The implication is being made that the healthy continuance of this covenant relationship depends at least in part on the willingness of Abraham and his family to offer justice to others and that the eventual destiny of Isaac's descendants is affected by how Ishmael and his mother are treated. Certainly his role is completely different to the other half-brothers, who are born to Abraham after the death of Sarah (Gen. 25.1–6). Alongside his brother Isaac, Ishmael alone shares in burying their father at Hebron, the two brothers standing alongside each other in a way that would be unthinkable to many of their present-day descendants. There are, as we commented on p. 118, also remarkable parallels between the trials both Ishmael and Isaac suffer – in each case almost to death. In the birth oracle of Ishmael (16.12) the angel had predicted to Hagar that Ishmael would *live at odds with all his kin*. That is one possible translation and it is the one adopted by the REB. But in fact the Hebrew words are more ambiguous and may not include a sense of hostility at all: some other versions tell us that Ishmael will live 'alongside his brothers'. The destiny of the Holy Land perhaps lies held between these two possibilities. There is a powerful poem by the Israeli poet Shin Shalom included in the liturgy for the New Year Festival in Reform synagogues in the United Kingdom. It expresses just how much Isaac and Ishmael, and their respective descendants, still need each other. If there is to be a future it will – and must – include them both.

> Ishmael, my brother,
> How long shall we fight each other?
>
> My brother from times bygone,
> My brother, Hagar's son,
> My brother, the wandering one.
> One angel was sent to us both,
> One angel watched over our growth –
> There in the wilderness, death threatening through thirst,
> I a sacrifice on the altar, Sarah's first.
>
> Ishmael, my brother, hear my plea:
> It was the angel who tied thee to me. . .
>
> Time is running out, put hatred to sleep.
> Shoulder to shoulder, let's water our sheep. (Shin Shalom)[39]

# The Story of Jacob
## 25.19—36.43

By titling this section 'The story of Jacob' it immediately begs the question: what about Isaac, where is his story? In fact there really is no separate 'Isaac' cycle in Genesis: such episodes as feature him are woven into the one of the two major sequences of stories about Abraham and Jacob. Isaac figures almost as a tool to knit together the episodes relating to the other two patriarchs. It is interesting to note the effect created by the placing of the references to Isaac. Locating the only chapter in which Isaac is the major figure (26) after the account of the birth of the next generation helps to suggests that past, present and future depend upon and inform each other. (See further comments on Gen. 26, p. 165.)

The Abraham cycle began in spectacular and optimistic mode: 'a New Start', a divine command and very shortly afterwards a divine appearance (12.7). By contrast the Jacob cycle commences in a much more gritty fashion: a difficult conception, a dangerous pregnancy, and two brothers who squabble from birth. It is not another 'new start' but God continuing to work with and through the raw human material that is available. The opening of the cycle prepares us for what lies ahead: these will be stories in which the horizontal (human–human) relationships will assume as much prominence as vertical (divine–human) ones. God will appear in these stories, in spectacular and numinous form. But God will not appear so often – and he will not assume the role of *deus ex machina*, which he seemed to play on occasion during the life of Abraham. God will also increasingly use dreams as a means of communicating with humanity, and will encourage human beings to work out their own salvation among themselves, albeit with fear and trembling.

The Jacob cycle seems, like the Abraham cycle, to fall into a concentric or chiastic pattern – not perhaps as tightly knit, but still effective.

*The literary structure of the story of Jacob*

    A1  Birth of Jacob. Struggle of Esau and Jacob
        B1  Isaac and Abimelech (Relations with non-Israelites)
            C1  Theft of Esau's blessing
                D1  Jacob meets God at Bethel
                    E1  Jacob and the well-stone
                        F1  Laban tricks Jacob (about his bride)
                            G  Birth of Jacob's sons (culminating
                                in birth of Joseph)
                        F2  Jacob tricks Laban (over his herds)
                    E2  Jacob and the stones of the covenant with
                        Laban
                D2  Jacob meets God at Penuel
            C2  Offer of restitution of Esau's blessing
        B2  The rape of Dinah, and destruction of Shechem
           (Relations with non-Israelites)
    A2  Birth of Benjamin, Death of Rachel and Isaac. Joint burial
        of Isaac by Esau and Jacob

This means that the birth of the next generation lies at the heart of the story. 'Genesis' lives up to its name.

*Double trouble*
  25.19–34

As we suggested above, placing this introduction to Jacob's sons, which takes them in a few verses from conception to active adult protagonists in the story, before the incidents in which their father appears, will encourage us to read chapter 26 as a kind of interlude, almost a byway, in the ongoing narrative.

25.19–26 *This is an account of the descendants of Abraham's son Isaac:* The language in Hebrew is exactly and deliberately parallel to that with which Ishmael's genealogy had been introduced (25.12). But what follows is entirely different. Not a simple list, but a complicated story, in which once again the very existence of these descendants is only possible because of Yhwh's direct intervention.

    Note how Isaac is referred to: he is *Abraham's son.* The information is then immediately repeated. *Isaac's father was Abraham.* Throughout most of the events of his life, particularly in Gen. 26, that is how Isaac will appear. He will be presented as a reflection of his father, rather than as a fully independent agent.

*Isaac . . . married Rebecca . . . from Paddan-aram*: The reference back to Isaac's marriage provides a perspective from which to view the episode of Rebecca's childlessness. Twenty years pass before the children are eventually born (25.20, 26), a bitterly long time: yet in contrast with the childlessness of Sarah the years are subsumed in only a few verses. It is an indication that in the life story of Isaac and Jacob the topic of progeny, so prominent in the Abraham cycle, will yield to that of the possession and use of the land and the meaning of nationhood. But nonetheless the fragility of the family of promise is emphasised by the positioning of this episode after the account of the death of Abraham. According to the chronology Rebecca's childlessness must have been resolved before Abraham died (Isaac was 60 when Esau and Jacob were born, 75 at the death of his father). To locate the issue here reinforces the sense that once again the future hangs by a thread, and that YHWH will need to intervene directly in the lives of his chosen instruments.

*Paddan-aram* is an alternative name for Aram-naharaim (24.10) and is the term preferred in this section. 'Paddan' is probably a word loaned from Aramaic (the language used in northern Mesopotamia). It is likely to mean something like 'Field of Aram'. It may indicate the Mesopotamian background of those who were responsible for creating the consecutive narrative of Jacob out of a number of diverse threads.

*Isaac appealed to the LORD*: The technical vocabulary of prayer and worship is employed here, as also when Rebecca *went to seek guidance of the LORD*. Relationships between humanity and divinity are still possible, but they begin to assume a formality that is qualitatively different from the unfettered conversation between YHWH and Abraham.

[*YHWH*] *said to her*: Remarkably Rebecca alone is the recipient of this oracle, and there is no suggestion that she shared the information with Isaac. It grounds her preference for Jacob (25.28) in God's purposes: by contrast Isaac's predilection for Esau is linked to his own stomach! Partly on the basis of her role here it has been suggested that Rebecca (rather than Isaac) is the key ancestor of this generation.

*Two nations . . .*: The binary thrust and repeated sense of doubling which runs through the entire story of Jacob and Esau is grounded in this key poetic oracle which both introduces it and seems to control the later narrative. Although there are other pairs of brothers in

161

Genesis who are contrasted with each other, especially Cain and Abel, who provide perhaps the closest parallel to Jacob and Esau, nowhere else is the contrast taken back to the moment of birth – or even into the womb – and nowhere else is it delineated in such a wholehearted fashion, incorporating physical appearance, moral attributes and the love of their parents.

The table below sets out how the brothers are contrasted:

*A comparison between two brothers*

| Jacob | Esau |
|---|---|
| Stronger | Weaker |
| Younger | Elder |
| Master | Servant |
| Smooth | Hairy |
| Stayed in tents | Outdoor man |
| Loved by Rebecca | Loved by Isaac |
| Cooks vegetables | Hunts and prepares meat |
| Lives for the future | Lives for the present |
| Scheming | Sensual |
| 'Female' | 'Male' |
| Israel | Edom |

As we move into the story of Jacob it becomes increasingly clear that we are travelling into the story of two nations, Israel and Edom. In the development of the story the individuals eventually become their eponymous peoples, in a fashion that goes well beyond anything in the earlier story of Abraham. This crucial oracle alerts us to what lies ahead and how we should read what is, on the surface, simply an account of bitter family rivalry.

*There were . . . twins in her womb*: The relationship between Jacob and Esau is thus as close as is biologically possible. This reflects an awareness that there was a close ethnic (and possibly religious) re-lationship between the Edomites and Israelites, of a different order to that between Israelites and other nations. Texts such as Deut. 23.7, for example, treat Edomites as a 'special case'. This did not rule out intense hostility between the Edomites and Israelites/Judaeans which had ancient roots. The Edomites resented the vassal status to which they were consigned by David and Solomon (1 Kgs 11.14–25); in turn they took the opportunity provided by the Babylonian conquest of Judah to invade Judaean territory, an action regarded by several Old Testament prophets as 'back-stabbing'. In the early post-exilic period Edomite control spread over much of the Negev. It is no accident that the description of how the twins *pressed on each other* in Rebecca's womb employs a verb that could equally be translated 'oppressed'. The Old Testament prophetic oracles about Edom are particularly vitriolic, but the hatred contained in them seems partly due to the supposed relationship between the nations – Edom should have behaved differently, precisely because it was Jacob's brother (see Mal. 1.2; Obad. 10).

There is some evidence that the roots of Yahwism are linked with the region of Edom. The original homeland of the god Yhwh may have been Mount Seir (Judg. 5.4; Isa. 63.1) before the worship of Yhwh was adopted by the Israelites. This would accentuate Israelite closeness to the Edomites – but also explain the bitter rivalry for birthright and blessing that is the central motif of the Jacob story. In reality, once upon a time, Esau's descendants may have been the primeval people of Yhwh, and it was not a position that they would willingly concede.

From the Israelite perspective the words of the oracle that describe Esau as Jacob's *servant* are both reminiscence and aspiration – there was a time when this might have been true, but by the time the final form of Genesis was written it was far from the case.

*The first to come out was reddish and covered with hairs*: The initial description of Esau makes clear his links with Edom. The name 'Edom' is related to the word for 'red' or *reddish* (Hebrew: *'adom* or *'admoni*) – because of the remarkably red sandstone rocks of the region, most famously at Petra, that 'rose-red city – half as old as Time'. *Hairs* (*se'ar*) alludes to Seir, the mountainous heartland of the country. The writer allows us to make the connection for ourselves rather than spelling it out at this point – saving up his punch line for 25.30, when the birthright is sold off so cheaply.

*His brother was born with his hand grasping Esau's heel*: Jacob's name is transparently related to the word for 'heel' (Hebrew: *'aqeb*). It not only pictured his action during his actual birth, but also his behaviour throughout his life: he was a 'heel' or fraudster – a description that is as disparaging in Hebrew as it is in English! The punning will continue in 27.36 where we will discover how Jacob *supplanted* (a word from the linked Hebrew root '*aqab*) his brother.

It is extraordinary how the Old Testament is so willing to be ruthlessly honest about the moral nature of the figure who became the eponymous ancestor of Israel. Nor is this honesty restricted to Genesis. Besides the reference to Jacob in Hos. 12.3, the identical pun on 'supplant' occurs in Jer. 9.4 , while in Mal. 3.6–9 a similar sounding, though unrelated, verb meaning 'to defraud' (Hebrew root: *qaba'*) is used several times in a way that suggests it is being connected to the name of Jacob.

25.27–34  *Jacob lived quietly among the tents*: The tents were the province of the women – he is definitely a 'mummy's boy'! The REB's *quietly* contrasts with the unrestrained and violent temperament needed by hunters like Esau. However, it is a slightly unexpected translation for the Hebrew word *tam*, which normally means something like 'wholesome', or 'morally innocent'. A closely related word appears in 20.5 where it forms part of an expression translated *in good faith*. It is tempting to wonder if its use here for Jacob is ironic.

*Isaac favoured Esau . . . Rebecca favoured Jacob*: In both cases the word translated 'favoured' is the normal Hebrew word for 'love'. Now that love has been let loose in the world (see comments on 22.2) it is a dangerous and powerful phenomenon and must not be abused – or cheapened. By not telling us the rationale for Rebecca's fondness for Jacob, the writer encourages us to connect it to the providential oracle she received earlier. By contrast the stated reason for Isaac's partiality for Esau, *he kept him supplied with game*, hardly portrays either father or son in a good light.

*One day Jacob was preparing broth*: The flair of the writer of this story is evident in his choice of words. He has deliberately used a verb that hints that what Jacob 'cooked up' was not only a pot, but a plot!

The brief description of Esau's actions is also a brilliant character sketch! *Give me a helping of that red broth*. In reality Esau can't even remember the name of the food: he is so anxious to stuff himself that he actually calls it 'that red, red . . .!' (Hebrew: *'adom*) It is now, significantly, that the writer makes explicit the connection with Edom. *This is why he was called Edom*. For our mental picture of Edom is thus coloured (literally!) not so much by Esau's physical circumstances at birth but rather by his adult behaviour: Edom comes across as a greedy, inarticulate nation with no interest in the higher aspects of life. (A slander, incidentally, upon the Edomites, who were well known for their expertise in 'wisdom' e.g. Jer. 49.7.) The rapid-fire series of verbs with which Esau leaves the scene, *he ate and drank and went his way*, reinforces this portrayal of an almost animal being, who lives only for the present.

Jacob, by contrast, plans for the future! Perhaps that is what the bearer of the promise needs to do. The birthright of the eldest was a very concrete package. Deut. 21.15–17 makes it clear that he inherited the lion's share of his father's property. Ancient law codes are even more specific than this. Esau presumably assumed that this positive bias in the inheritance was what he was relinquishing. We know, and we may wonder whether Jacob was aware, that the birthright in this case means much more and it included inheriting the covenantal promises made to Abraham. In this episode of word plays one final one is left hanging over – by spurning the *bekorah* (birthright) in this private conversation with his brother, Esau effectively sets in train the process that will lead him shortly to be deprived of the *berakah* (blessing).

## His father's son
### 26.1–35

*There is nothing new under the sun* (Eccles. 1.9). It is striking how, with the possible exception of the sowing of seed in 26.12–13, all the incidents in Gen. 26.1–33 mirror or allude to previous events in the life of Isaac's father Abraham. The chapter has been constructed by a writer who was aware of the content of Gen. 12—22, and clearly drew upon it, at the same time making subtle but important changes.

Why are these incidents related at this juncture in Genesis? What we have reads like an interruption in the story of Jacob and Esau, which has just begun and which is going to continue so explosively in the following chapter. Yet it also feels 'out of time' because of the continual harking back to parallel events in the life of Abraham. It both breaks into the future and reminds us of a mixed bag of incidents from the past. That is exactly the point.

The perceived repetitions begin to create a sense of design to what otherwise might be considered random, indeed rambling stories. Each generation, at least to some extent, relives the plot of its predecessor. The larger story of the family is not simply linear, but frequently coils around to pick up bits of the past – failures as well as successes. Every generation essentially provides the same kind of 'stuff' from which God is to build a 'great nation'.[1]

It is striking that the most lengthy parallel is the attempt by Isaac to pass off Rebecca as his sister. For this shows him in precisely the same unsavoury light as the earlier examples of the genre/incident did his father. It is as if all the hopes for a 'new start' that we have invested in Isaac, the long-awaited child of the promise, are being brought down to earth. He is made of the same old all-too-human stuff as Abraham. And by locating this chapter after the rivalry between Jacob and Esau has been made apparent, the broad hint is being offered that future generations of this family will not be problem-free either.

And yet . . . this is not a replay of Gen. 1—5, when the story of humanity went so far downhill that it ended in cataclysm. This time God will stick with these people, instead of bitterly regretting (see 6.6) his choice to deal with them. It will be a choice that will prove costly to God, even before the end of the story of Jacob (32.26).

26.1–5  The undercurrent of famine pervades the whole chapter. It also takes us straight back to Abraham's story with its reference to the famine that had taken Abraham down to Egypt (12.10–20). That had been a false step in Abraham's life and so many complications had resulted from it. Isaac must not make the same mistake *Do not go down to Egypt.* Unlike his father Abraham, Isaac is not summoned by Yhwh to go anywhere, but rather to stay. It is in living in this country, Canaan, as an alien, that blessing will be found.

The words Yhwh addresses to Isaac allude both to the original command of Yhwh to Abraham in Gen. 12.1–3, and also quite strongly to the words spoken after the near-sacrifice of Isaac. The motif of obedience in particular connects it to Gen. 22.18. The whole story of Abraham seems to float before our eyes as we listen to these words: *because Abraham obeyed me.* Underlying this translation are the words 'Heard my voice'. We might ruefully reflect that eventually Abraham did, with the willingness to sacrifice his son being the supreme example, but it took a long time, and that first he listened to Sarah.

Note how everything that is offered to Isaac is grounded in God's relationship with Abraham: *fulfilling the oath which I swore to your father Abraham.* In Gen. 22 we saw how Abraham and Isaac became 'one' – this is the theological consequence. Effectively God relates to

Isaac through and because of Abraham: this will not be the case with Isaac's own son, Jacob, whose relationship with God will be intensely personal and travel as yet untrodden paths. The one crucial additional promise that God makes to Isaac is *I shall be with you* (26.3; cf. 26.24). It is strange that these words, central to God's self-revelation throughout the Bible, were never precisely said to Abraham. Perhaps because God was with Abraham so often, it didn't really need to be stated. But their explicit statement now is an assurance that even if God withdraws from such overt contact with human beings as Abraham experienced, humanity will not be abandoned. God has become Immanuel.

On the whole Isaac is a conservator, an inheritor rather than an innovator. His role in the story includes reopening *the wells which were dug in the lifetime of his father Abraham* (26.18), and that feels like a metaphorical symbol for his life, as well as comment on a specific action. But does this mean that Isaac can use the point Abraham reached in the journey of faith as his starting-point – so that we don't have to work through the chapters of mistakes to get there?

26.6–11   Or do we? Isaac may not have gone down to Egypt, but he immediately makes a similar false move to his father – attempting to pass off his wife as his sister. It is striking how this third example of the wife-sister motif in Genesis draws from, and needs to be read in the light of, both the previous two examples of the genre. (Instead of supporting the hypothesis of separate Yahwist and Elohist sources a careful scrutiny of these three incidents undermines it.)

We already know from the previous incident that Abimelech is a godfearing king and Gerar is a godfearing place, so Isaac's deception is totally unnecessary. Although chronologically one might wonder whether the person named Abimelech in Gen. 26 could be the person of the same name in Gen. 20 it seems clear we are intended to identify them. Isaac's deception is also incompetently executed – this time the king does not need either divinely sent plagues or a dream to discover the truth; he can use the evidence of his own eyes, since Isaac cannot sustain his hoax. He fully lives up to his name: Isaac is discovered 'Isaacing' – or *caressing* (Hebrew: *metsaheq*) his wife. Note the pun once again (see p. 100). Is Isaac a person gripped by sensual pleasures – sexual and of the gullet? By contrast Rebecca's role in the trickery seems completely passive, even more so than Sarah in the earlier incidents: a striking feature in view of her proactive role in other episodes. Perhaps it encourages our sympathy for her and our sense that when, in the next chapter, she in turn conspires to deceive Isaac, it is no more than his due!

26.12–18 *Isaac sowed seed . . . and the same year he reaped a hundred-fold*: Given that this was during a time of famine (26.1) the miraculous fertility of the land is a clear sign of Yʜwʜ's blessing. There is no indication that Abraham planted crops: he was a pastoralist. So Isaac's actions constitute an important development – gradually the patriarchs are becoming rooted in the land where they are residing as aliens (see 26.2–3). God's blessing is steadily coming to fruition. Isaac's agricultural success is carefully linked to the original blessing of Abraham by the threefold repetition of the word for 'great' which is present in 26.13 (though concealed by the English translation), recalling its appearance in the original blessing of Abraham (12.2). A literal translation of 26.13 might be, 'The man became great, and went on growing great until he was very great.' The connection is also hinted at by the verb 'sow' itself (Hebrew: *zaraʻ*). As we pointed out on the comments on 4.25 (see p. 31), one of the features of many modern translations, including the REB, is that they choose not to preserve the fact that when the ancestors are promised *descendants*, the Hebrew word used (*zeraʻ*) is one that can also be translated 'seed'. Isaac's success with seeds in the ground acts as a sign that the 'seed' of Abraham and his family will be equally fruitful.

Isaac's blessing is dependent on that which had been promised previously to Abraham. It is symptomatic that when he re-opened those wells of his father that had been stopped up *He called them by the names which his father had given them.*

26.19–33 The quarrel with the Philistines also reflects an earlier story, that of Abraham's dealing with Abimelech (21.25–34), but it takes on a different hue. Then the relationship between Philistines and Abraham's people had been resolved without major confrontation. Now however the quarrel over the meagre resources that the land can provide assumes a bitterness that both reflects Israel's long-term hostility to the Philistines as well as foreshadowing the breakdown of relationships that will be the theme of the next chapter and will dog the whole story of Jacob. Eventually the conciliatory attitude of Isaac helps to mend the breach. So too does Yʜwʜ's transparent blessing of Isaac, and Abimelech's refreshing willingness to acknowledge this. He eventually shows the same open spirit as he had displayed when he encountered Abraham.

This only transpires after disputes over specific wells – whose names are intended to reflect their role in the conflict ('Difficulty', 'Enmity', see REB footnotes). It is no accident that the conflicts cease once Isaac has dug the well at Rehovoth ('Roominess'): its very name evokes the promises to Abraham: when Abraham was told *to go through the length and breadth of the land* (13.17) that instruction included a word linked to Rehovoth. This name Rehovoth seems to register an awareness that all too easily one people's promised land can become another people's dispossession, and hint that this is not God's intended way forward. There can be room for all: only then will the final clause of the Abrahamic blessing be fulfilled (12.3). It is therefore appropriate that at this point God appears directly to renew once again the promise and blessing to Isaac. But even now this is for *the sake of my servant Abraham.* Isaac remains overshadowed by his father.

The final episode of the dealings between Isaac and Abimelech clearly reflects the earlier account of the covenant made between Abraham and Abimelech, and makes the same pun on the name Beer-sheba (see comments on Gen. 21.22–34 p. 121). As he had done previously with Abraham, Abimelech acknowledges that *the LORD is with you*, so God's promise to Isaac (*I am with you*) of a few verses earlier is already being visibly fulfilled. However Abimelech's retinue has now increased in size – this time with the addition of *Ahuzzath his friend.* The name Ahuzzath means 'Possession'; it is identical to the Hebrew word used in 17.8 and 23.9 to refer to Abraham's possession of the land. What are we to make of this? Is the involvement of a person of this name in this covenant made with Isaac a visible symbol that God's promise of possession (17.8) is coming to fruition? Or is it rather that Abimelech is determined to hold on to possession of his lands in the face of the threat posed by Isaac? Perhaps the ambiguity is deliberate. There is clearly tension around: the very rationale for the covenant is expressed negatively rather than positively. There is also self-interest on Abimelech's part, but this is appropriate given that the original words to Abraham spoke of blessing those who blessed him and cursed those who cursed. It is in Abimelech's vested interests to discover a *modus vivendi* with this disturbing *ger*. It is a *modus vivendi*, not more: after the covenant Isaac and Abimelech part company. They have found a way of living nearby each other, although not together. Genesis is realistic in its expectations. This model of breach and rapprochement offered by this chapter is a pattern for a similar exploration in the coming story of Jacob and

Esau, though there the story will unfold with greater passion given that it is a quarrel between brothers.

*We have found water*: These are the last words addressed to Isaac in this chapter. Isaac's adventures here began with famine, but end with a life-giving discovery. To this day the scarcity of water resources is a major underlying cause of conflict in the Middle East. Isaac may be (literally) a laughable figure, but the laughter associated with him can perhaps, as in Ps.126, be linked to the discovery of water in the arid Negev desert (Ps.126.4), and become a source for the renewal of life.

26.34–35  *When Esau was forty years old*: The same age as Isaac was when he married Rebecca (25.20). Is Esau thereby hoping that he will please his father? Is he going to be a chip off the old block in his turn? If so he goes about it the wrong way. The verses introduce the topic of marriage/intermarriage, which will be a major concern throughout the Jacob story. The Hittites are the same people elsewhere referred to as Canaanites (see notes on Gen. 23.3, p. 131). At one level these verses feel misplaced and as though they should be located at the beginning of Gen. 28. However their placement at this point seems deliberate. Esau's actions provide an apparent justification for the actions of Rebecca and Jacob in Gen. 27.

In fact Esau's choice of brides must have been *a source of bitter grief* indeed. One of his new fathers-in-law was named *Beeri* (which means 'My well'): not a tactful choice in view of the dissension over wells that has dominated the second half of this chapter!

## *The stolen blessing*
### 27.1—28.9

Now we will discover how the hasty and private transaction over the birthright (Hebrew: *bekorah*) between Jacob and Esau in Gen. 25.33 is to result in an objective and semi-public consequence: not only the *bekorah* but also the *berakah* (blessing) is passed to the younger brother. Note the pun on the two words in 27.36. But does Jacob ultimately receive this blessing because of his own deviousness, both then and now, or because throughout Genesis God chooses younger sons? The question remains tantalisingly open.

The structure of the story emphasises how Jacob's blessing is almost 'torn' out of Isaac, for whom Esau is the favourite son: willy-nilly he is forced to reverse Esau's position and bless the son who deceives him.

In 27.1–4 he expresses his intention to bless Esau, but the sequence concludes in 28.1– 4 with him blessing Jacob yet one more time.

It is telling that nowhere in this episode do Jacob and Esau appear 'on stage' together: a narrative demonstration that their relationship has already been fractured – by Jacob's acquisition of the birthright, or perhaps even from the time of their prenatal quarrels.

At the heart of the story are the two poems in 27.28–29 and 27.39–40, which like poetry elsewhere in Genesis (see p. 12) help to set the prose narrative in which they appear within the context of God's grand design.

**27.1–4**   Once before in his life Isaac had heard the reply *Here I am* (Hebrew: *hinneni*) in response to his exclamation (22.7, *hinneni* is there translated in the REB as *What is it?*). Back then he had called out, 'My father': here he cries out *My son*. Is this a hint that we need to read this story, set in the twilight of Isaac's life, in the context of that earlier experience? In both cases he seems to be ignorant, even deceived. At Mount Moriah Abraham, his father, had come to a new insight, literally and symbolically (note the play on 'seeing' throughout Gen. 22. p. 126). Abraham seems to have been a person of vision throughout his life. Yet now when we meet his son Isaac *his eyes had become so dim that he could not see*. Does Isaac's blindness epitomise his blinkered view, skewed by his attachment to sensual pleasures? Or, as in the case of Oedipus in the Greek dramas, does this physical blindness now facilitate spiritual sight? After all if Isaac had now been able to see, Jacob would never have been blessed, and Yʜᴡʜ's oracle to Rebecca (25.23) would never have been fulfilled.

The physical senses will play an important role in this story. Again and again Isaac is guided – and misled – by his senses of taste, touch and smell (27.4, 9, 12, 14, 21, 22, 26, 27). It is because he *likes* the taste of Esau's *savoury dish* that Esau is his favoured son (25.28). Three times Isaac's liking for this dish is stressed (27.4, 9, 14), a sign of its importance to the storyteller. In fact the verb 'like' here is the same Hebrew word elsewhere translated 'love'. Somehow 'love' has been cheapened by this use for the word. Love had only entered human history when it was employed to emphasise the exquisite pain that Abraham experienced when summoned to sacrifice his son (22.2). It had then been used appropriately to describe the love of Isaac for Rebecca, a man for a woman (24.67), yoking them together to become bearers of God's promise, and afterwards for the parents' love for the two children of that union (25.28). But now to employ it of mere food: it seems almost promiscuous! From the moment that love has been let loose in the world we will discover that it can be dangerous (37.3). It must not be abused, yet that is exactly what Isaac now appears to be doing.

Perhaps it is not Isaac's fault. Has he been irreparably scarred by that experience of his youth, which will echo again in this story (27.18)? Is it easier simply to restrict oneself to the practical and overtly physical? If we care too much for someone or something will it eventually be taken from us?

Robert Alter also suggests a connection between Gen. 22 and this scene. Isaac is 'the most passive of the patriarchs. We have already seen him as a bound victim for whose life a ram is substituted; later as a father, he will prefer the son who can go out to the field and bring him back provender, and his one extended scene will be lying in bed, weak and blind, while others act on him.'[2]

27.5–17   If Isaac is controlled by his senses of taste, touch and smell, Rebecca, by contrast, is someone for whom hearing is central. *Rebecca had been listening* (27.5) . . . *I have just overheard your father say* (27.6) . . . *Listen now* (27.8) . . . *Do as I say* (lit. 'Listen to my voice') (27.13) . . . *Now, my son, listen to me* (27.43).

She, of course, was the one who had originally heard the oracle of YHWH regarding the eventual destiny of the sons in her womb. She already knows the importance to the divine schema of being willing to listen. As the story of Genesis develops hearing becomes a key physical sense. Even now at key moments in the story women, in particular, have listened (e.g. Eve, Hagar, Sarah) and helped to change the course of history. Rebecca's listening to Isaac's conversation with Esau, stands in the tradition of Sarah who listened behind the tent-flaps, and it is equally momentous.

Yet who you listen to is critical. When women themselves are heard – complications invariably seem to ensue. Once again (see comments on Gen. 16.2, p. 92) the dangerous phrase 'Listen to the voice of . . .' makes its appearance. Although concealed by the English translation it comes three times in this story (27.8, 13, 43) as Rebecca demands that Jacob should listen to her. What will happen to Jacob as a result of his willingness to listen to his mother's plan may ultimately be part of God's intentions, but it will involve pain, exile and separation (as did the story of Hagar and Sarah). When Jacob is forced from home as a result of their mutual deviousness, Rebecca will apparently never see this beloved son again.

*Bring me some game . . . that I may bless you in the presence of the* LORD *before I die*: In retelling the words of Isaac to Jacob, Rebecca subtly embroiders them. There had been no mention of YHWH's involvement in Isaac's actual speech. What he had been proposing was perhaps simply a familial rite of inheritance for the eldest son: how interested was Isaac really in YHWH's 'big picture'?

Rebecca however knows that the consequences of her family history reach well beyond the interests of this unit of four people. It embraces the destiny of nations, and perhaps even of humanity. *In the presence of the* LORD was a phrase used to describe the way Abraham himself was called to live (17.1; 24.40): significantly it was a phrase that Abraham had begged for Ishmael but which was withheld from him (17.18, same idiom in Hebrew, though REB translates *Might live before you*). Rebecca knew, perhaps more than Isaac himself realised, that to be *in the presence of the* LORD was the foundation of her family's role in YHWH's promises.

*Go to the flock and pick me out two fine young kids*: This will not be the only time that goats assist with deception in the story of Jacob – and his sons (see 37.31; 38.17).

*Esau is a hairy man . . . my [Jacob's] skin is smooth*: The connection with Mount Seir in Edom that had been made at Esau's birth is reinforced (see p. 163). Jacob's contrasting smoothness extends to more than his skin! In Hebrew, as in English, the word 'smooth' has a wider negative ring such as 'smooth-talker' (see e.g. Ps.12.2–3; Prov. 26.28).

*Suppose my father touches me; he will know that I am playing a trick on him and I shall bring a curse instead of a blessing on myself*: There is irony in Jacob's words, even if he doesn't realise it. Literally the words are 'I shall be in his eyes as one playing a trick', yet he knows full well that those eyes cannot see anything. As Jacob worries about being cursed rather than blessed, our thoughts are taken back to the original blessing of Abraham which mentioned both possibilities (12.3). Those words of 12.3 will shortly be explicitly repeated for the first time when Isaac does bless Jacob (27.29). But for all Rebecca's protestations we may wonder whether Jacob does bring a curse upon himself – as well as the blessing – and perhaps upon his mother too. The aftermath of their deception will be bitter for them both.

*Rebecca then took her elder son's clothes, Esau's best clothes which she had by her in the house, and put them on Jacob*: From the beginning of human history clothes have been used to conceal reality (3.7). As the story of Genesis continues they will increasingly be used as instruments of deception (e.g. 37.31–33; 38.14; 39.15). *In the house* is a reminder that the lifestyle of Isaac's family has become more sedentary than that of his father who lived in tents (18.1).

**27.18-29** *He went in to his father and said, 'Father!' Isaac answered, 'Yes, my son'*: In Hebrew the first word of Jacob in this scene and the first word of Isaac's response are identical to the words which Isaac and his father spoke as they travelled to Moriah (22.7). In both cases the exchange is followed by a sentence through which Isaac is deceived – in the past by Abraham about the identity of the proposed sacrifice, now by Jacob about his own identity. The parallel intensifies the sense of Isaac's passivity and vulnerability here. There is something almost obscene about this trick played here upon a helpless old man. However, in the previous chapter Isaac falsified his own identity (26.7), so perhaps it is little more than he deserves. Those who deceive, will be deceived in their turn, as Jacob will, in the future, discover to his cost.

And yet, that parallel with the journey to Moriah somehow helps to relieve the guilt of Jacob's deception. If we were willing to forgive Abraham's earlier misleading answer to Isaac, because we believed it to be part of God's plan, should we not do the same for Abraham's grandson, since the primacy he is now seeking has been so clearly proclaimed even before his birth (25.23)?

Jacob's answer is clearly false – he is not Esau: yet there is more truth about it than appears at first sight. For here the adjective *elder* (Hebrew: *bekor*) that he claims is a word closely related to that for 'birthright' (*bekorah*) and that he has purchased from Esau. The link is reinforced by Jacob's request for the blessing (*berakah*) in the same verse.

However his response to his father's query about the speed with which the dish has been prepared is breathtaking in its cynicism. *The LORD your God put it in my way.* Whatever 'taking the name of the LORD in vain' (Exod. 20.7) may have originally meant, to use the divine name to reinforce such deception surely comes close to it! It is of a piece with Rebecca's deliberate addition of YHWH's name (27.7) when she retells the conversation between Isaac and Esau.

It is no accident that Jacob speaks of *the LORD your God*. YHWH is Isaac's God, but not so far Jacob's! Even when the longed-for blessing is bestowed on Jacob in 27.28 it is given in the name of God (*Elohim*) rather than that of the more particular and relational YHWH. Jacob will not begin to know YHWH as his own God until his vision at Bethel (28.13), but even then something of the closeness that is associated with knowing God as Yʜwʜ will elude him (32.29): the rejected Leah will use this name more readily (29.32–35) than Jacob himself will do.

Isaac's suspicions are clear and are hinted at several times throughout the sequence. From his initial question, *Which are you?* (27.18), through his concern about apparent speed (27.20), his puzzlement over Jacob's voice (27.22), his repeated query about identity (27.24), and even his request to be kissed (27.26), which allows him to smell his son, one senses that Isaac is aware that something is not right. Is it possible that Isaac deliberately allowed himself to be deceived? It would have been the easiest way of allowing his natural inclination for Esau to be overruled by what he had perceived to be the intention of Yʜwʜ.

Yet the writer nowhere suggests that this is what happened. Rather, a contrast is made between his sense of hearing, which, like his wife Rebecca, Isaac should have trusted, *The voice is Jacob's voice*, and his other senses, on which he erringly depends. Rebecca has done her work well: it might have seemed unnecessary to dress up Jacob in Esau's clothes since Isaac will not be able to see them, but it is the smell of these clothes that finally convinces the father. Perhaps a father who makes the bestowal of his blessing contingent upon his sense of taste *Bring me some of the game to eat, my son, so that I may give you my blessing* deserves no less than to be misled by his sense of smell.

For the first time we meet the word *recognize* (27.23). It is a link word that draws together what is now taking place with Rachel's deception of her father Laban (31.32), the robe of Joseph dipped in goat's blood to deceive Jacob himself (37.32), Tamar's deception of Judah (38.25), and eventually Joseph's own unrevealed recognition of his brothers (42.7–8). Each time it is used it is with a twist which points up discrepancy between what is being recognised and the underlying or present reality. As the first of this long list, it suggests that the consequences of Isaac's lack of recognition will be far reaching.

When Isaac speaks of blessing his son (27.25) he literally says that it is his *nephesh* which will transmit the blessing. *nephesh*, the same Hebrew word used when Yʜwʜ first made humanity in 2.7 emphasises the way the total personality of Isaac is bound up with this action. Karen Armstrong puts it like this:

> When clerics bless their congregation today, it can be a rather impersonal gesture . . . This is very different from the biblical notion of blessing. [Isaac] was communicating his life essence to his son, breathing his very soul into the other. To do this, he had to get close

to Jacob. He asked him to approach, kissed him, felt his body, and smelled his clothes. Blessing involved the body as well as the spirit. Only when this degree of intimacy had been created could he pass the power to his son.[3]

Equally a blessing should be appropriate for the person to whom it was delivered. So in this instance the 'smell' of Esau's clothes reminds Isaac of *the smell of open country*, which epitomises Esau who was an *outdoor man* (25.27, same Hebrew word). In turn this dictates the content of the first part of the blessing, which seems ironically more appropriate for Esau for whom it was intended than Jacob to whom it was actually given. The agricultural prosperity, *corn and new wine in plenty*, alluded to hints at the changes that have taken place in the lifestyle of Abraham's family since he first travelled to Canaan as a pastoralist with herds.

Then the blessing moves onto a different plane, reminiscent of the earlier oracle to Rebecca (25.23). Is the reference to *mother's sons* (27.29) intended to draw our attention to this link? Now it is not so much Jacob, or Esau, the individual who is being addressed, but the relative destinies of the nations of which they will become the progenitors.

The poetic form of the blessing helps to make clear its fundamental character: it is one of the defining moments of Genesis. Blessings can never be withdrawn, even if they are bestowed upon the wrong person. But words spoken as poetry have greater significance still – for in these moments the human beings that speak them tap in to the very structure of creation.

> *A curse on those who curse you,*
> *but a blessing on those who bless you!*

The explicit verbal link between these lines and the original blessing of Abraham (12.3) is striking. But their irony is also powerful. Isaac believes that he is cursing the enemies of Esau, though it is actually Jacob, Esau's 'enemy' who hears them spoken. So are they for Jacob blessing or curse? Perhaps they are both: as the next chapters of Jacob's story makes clear, to steal the blessing brings difficulties and dangers in its train.

27.30–40 There is a farcical quality to what happens next – beginning even with Esau's entrance. The analogy is appropriate. One could imagine a dramatisation of the story with Jacob going off stage left just as Esau enters stage right!

The dialogue between Esau and Isaac reflects the earlier exchange between Isaac and Jacob. But subtle differences emphasise the closer relationship between Isaac and Esau. Throughout the whole episode it is notable that Isaac has nowhere called Jacob *my son* except when he believes that he is Esau.

*Your brother came full of deceit*: Significantly the Hebrew word translated 'deceit', used of Jacob's actions, reminds us of the adjective 'cunning', which described the serpent in Gen. 3.1. Jacob has been a real 'snake in the grass' in this family, and like Adam and Eve before him, Isaac has allowed his senses to control him – with unwanted results.

*'He is not called Jacob for nothing,' said Esau. 'This is the second time he has supplanted me. He took away my right as the firstborn, and now he has taken away my blessing.'*: The puns both on the name of Jacob, and on first-born (*bekorah*) and blessing (*berakah*) are here revisited. The concrete nature of the Hebrew language means that the verb 'supplant' (Hebrew: '*aqab*) derives from the noun 'heel' (Hebrew: '*aqeb*) – with the literal sense of 'coming up on one's heel' i.e. overtaking someone. Jacob has really lived up to his epithet of heel! A similar link between Jacob's name and his action of supplanting is made in Jer. 9.4 and Hos. 12.3 (see also comments on p. 163).

*Esau wept bitterly*: Esau comes over as pathetic in his despair. Three times he beseeches his father for any 'left over' blessing (27.34, 36, 38). It is a dangerous request, for when Isaac finally responds to it he does so with words that sound more like curse than blessing, but which, because they have now been uttered will inevitably come to pass.

It is the mirror image of Jacob's blessing. Servitude rather than lordship, and aridity rather than plenty. Once again the destiny of a nation is referred to: both in terms of Edom's status as vassal of Israel, from the time of David and throughout much of the monarchy, and also in terms of its geographical situation in southern Transjordan eking out an existence in terrain that is often indistinguishable from desert. Those who wrote this story knew of the perennial conflict between the desert and the sown which has so dominated the history of the region.

> *But the time will come when you grow restive*
> *and break his yoke from your neck.*

The one meagre hope offered to Esau is that one day this servitude will be ended, a presumed reference to the time of the Babylonian destruction of Jerusalem when the Edomites took the opportunity not only to throw off any remnants of Judaean/Israelite lordship, but also participated in looting Jerusalem and southern Judaean towns.

**27.41–45** *Esau harboured a grudge*: We fear a rerun of the saga of Cain and Abel: that it is avoided seems to be due to Rebecca's adroitness.

*The time of mourning for my father will soon be here*: As it turns out Isaac lasts at least another 20 years – all of the period of Jacob's 'exile' in Mesopotamia. He is still alive when Jacob returns (35.27). Our awareness of this length of time he spends in a supine state reinforces how passive this patriarch is.

*Rebecca called Jacob . . . Now, my son, listen to me*: Unlike Isaac, Rebecca knowingly addresses Jacob as *my son*. The expression *listen to me* repeats the same Hebrew words as were used in vv. 8 and 13. Because Jacob listened to his mother on that earlier occasion and participated in the deception of his father he must now listen to her again and accept a future of exile. (A similar pattern occurred in the Abraham cycle, see p. 117.)

*I will send and fetch you back*: In fact after this chapter Rebecca completely disappears from the story. She never sees her son Jacob again. The banishment forced upon Jacob because of the imminent expectation of his father's death is ultimately unnecessary, but results in permanent separation between a mother and her beloved son. Is a moral price being paid for their mutual plotting? As a result of listening in, Rebecca has secured the blessing for Jacob: now she listens in again (27.42) and believes that she is securing his life – but this time the listening ultimately proved unnecessary. She has listened once too often.

The story of Abraham climaxed with the near death of his beloved son, now the story of Rebecca and Isaac comes to an end with a different kind of 'death' for her much loved child. Will it also be a pattern repeated in the next generation?

**27.46—28.9** At first sight these verses tell a very different story to that portrayed in the previous family quarrel. The rationale for Jacob's journey to Mesopotamia is now to avoid intermarriage, and preserve the purity of his family lineage. The verses come from a different hand to that of the original author of 27.1–45. But this new reason for Jacob's departure is clearly composed in awareness of the earlier story, with 27.46 as a seam which joins the two. The narrative appears to come from a period in Jewish history when the issue of intermarriage was particularly pressing, with opposing views being expressed by different sections of the Jewish community (see also comments on Gen. 24, p. 134).

*Rebecca said to Isaac, 'I am weary to death of Hittite women!'*: Rebecca is determined to keep Jacob safe, but needs to get Isaac on her side to permit him to travel to Mesopotamia, particularly in view of the fact that Isaac before his marriage had been prevented by his father from travelling there. She skilfully uses this ruse of the need to avoid contact with the local 'Hittite' women. The verse should be read alongside 26.34–35, which at one time it may have directly followed, where Esau's marriage to such women has been reported. As an additional bonus Rebecca now cleverly manages to damn Esau without even mentioning him by name!

The final editor of this section of Genesis has been as adroit as Rebecca: two different reasons for Jacob's departure have been seamed together!

To describe Canaanite women as 'Hittite' suggests that these verses come from the same hand as the author of Gen. 23.

*So Isaac called Jacob, and after blessing him . . .*: This additional blessing for Jacob reinforces the sense of exclusion for Esau. It seems that Isaac did have more than one blessing to give, but they are both for Jacob!

*Go now to the home of Bethuel . . . in Paddan-aram*: Although there are connections between the account of Jacob's journey to meet his Mesopotamian kin and the earlier journey there of Abraham's servant, the two episodes seem to originate from different hands. One clue is the different name for their destination: in Gen. 24.10 Aram-naharaim, here Paddan-aram (see comments on 25.20, p. 161).

*May God Almighty bless you; may he make you fruitful*: This is only the second time that the title God Almighty (*'el shaddai*) has been used in Genesis. The first occurrence was in 17.1. As there, it appears now alongside a promise of fruitfulness and fertility and is also linked to possession of the land (see notes on 17.1 p. 97). Here it is remarkable how the promise of the land is made to Jacob just as he is forced to leave it. Promise therefore assumes the character of reassurance.

The blessing both builds on, yet also corrects the impression given by the account of Isaac's marriage in Gen. 24. As in that earlier story the land of Mesopotamia is viewed positively: it is a place that facilitates the preservation of the purity of genealogical lineage. But Gen. 24 was adamant that Abraham's descendant must not himself return there: did this damn therefore those from Judah and Jerusalem who had been taken to Babylon by force? So now a later descendant of

Abraham does go there himself, and will discover that God does not abandon him through his years of servitude.

*Esau went to Ishmael, and . . . married Mahalath . . . daughter of Abraham's son Ishmael*: Even now Esau can't quite get it right. In attempting to please his parents he ends up reinforcing his status as an outsider. In linking himself with Ishmael through marriage to his daughter he seems to be edged out one stage further from the blessing, promise and covenant. The geographical territory of the Edomites and that of Ishmael's Arab descendants overlapped. So the apparent familial connection probably reflects a recognised historical reality.

## *Visions of the night*
### 28.10–22

Jacob's numinous experience at Bethel is one of the two major theological pillars in the construction of the Jacob cycle. It seams together the stories of Jacob and Esau and those of Jacob and Laban. It resonates against the other seam and pillar, Gen. 32.22–32: the two episodes complement each other.

28.10–15  *Jacob set out from Beersheba and journeyed towards Harran*: He is beginning Abraham's journey in reverse: it is appropriate that this is the moment when the voice that once spoke to Abraham will finally speak to him. Up till now God has never related to him directly: as he had rightly said to his father Yнwн was *the* Lord *your God* (27.20) not Jacob's own. Perhaps Jacob even hoped to leave Yнwн behind in Canaan, along with all his family troubles. All that will now change, as for the first time Yнwн confirms to Jacob that he is indeed the bearer of the promise, even if it was apparently gained by trickery.

*He came to a certain shrine*: This translation presupposes that there was already a sanctuary at Bethel before Jacob's visit. However, whatever the actuality, the story seems to suggest that Bethel became a sacred site precisely because of Jacob's experiences there.

*Because the sun had gone down, he stopped for the night*: We will not read of the sun rising again until after Jacob's fight at Penuel on his return to the land (32.31). A powerful symbolic darkness pervades the whole period of time Jacob spends in a strange land.

*He took one of the stones there*: Stones feature significantly from now on in Jacob's story (28.18, 22; 29.10; 31.45–47; 35.14). They reflect his changed situation – no longer is he a 'mummy's boy' but becomes capable of Herculean feats of strength, hard himself, like stone. The last time that 'stone' was mentioned in Genesis was when people attempted to use bricks for stone to build the Tower of Babel: the falsity of this action reflecting their false move. Jacob's vision at Bethel is now presented as a contrast with that earlier attempt to link heaven and earth.

*In a dream*: This is the first time a member of Abraham's own family has explicitly encountered God by this method. Previously the relationship had been more informal. Jacob's experience at Bethel has a numinous quality that probably exceeds anything we have encountered up till now (Gen. 15.17 may be the exception): but the corollary of this will be that interchange between human and divine will never be so 'normal' or easy again. Dreams will be increasingly used by God to communicate with human beings – perhaps a reflection of increasing distance between the two worlds.

*He saw a ladder*: We are probably intended to think of this as a kind of ramped tower, like a Babylonian ziggurat, which symbolically connected earth and heaven. *With its top reaching to heaven* closely parallels the description of the Tower of Babel, *with its top in the heavens* (11.4). The difference is that this structure is clearly sanctioned by God, reaching down from heaven to earth, rather than that vain attempt of the human builders to reach up from earth to heaven.

*Angels of God were going up and down on it*: The heavenly traffic indicates that this place is a 'boundary' on Jacob's journey away from Canaan. Is one way that God can be present with people when they are away from this land via an angel (compare Gen. 24.7; 31.11; cf. Exod. 23.23)? The angels may be descending to earth in order to accompany Jacob on his journey, although they will then be invisible (see further on New Testament links to this passage on p. 222).

*The LORD was standing beside him saying, 'I am the LORD'*: God finally reveals himself as YHWH to Jacob, as he had previously done to Abraham, and more ambiguously to Isaac. The relationship between YHWH and Jacob has at last been established, although it will never be a totally easy one, and for long years Jacob will apparently have to survive by his wits, rather than by YHWH's ready intervention.

*The God of your father Abraham and the God of Isaac*: The language recalls the earlier oracle to Isaac (26.4–5, 24–25) and before that the promises to Abraham (13.14–16; 17.7–8; 22.17–18). The continuity is itself a form of reassurance in view of Jacob's desperate plight. But the words to Jacob go beyond even the extravagance of these earlier assurances. *You will spread far and wide.* Is the implication that the 'spread' of Jacob's descendants will extend even further than the land of Canaan, to include the diaspora? That would be appropriate in view of Jacob's intended destination, and would resonate with any early readers of this passage who happened to be in Babylon. It would suggest that even there they were not outside the limits of God's promise. The verb *spread* sounds similar (though is not related) to the word *dispersed* which described God's response to the builders of the Tower of Babel (11.8). It is a positive echo of that earlier action: to be spread is now clearly stated to be a means of blessing, rather than a form of punishment.

*I shall be with you to protect you wherever you go*: Although YHWH had previously promised to be *with* Isaac (26.3, 24), these words assume an even deeper significance here, as Jacob prepares to depart from YHWH's own land. Other Old Testament texts hint at the perplexity people felt as they wrestled with the issue of whether YHWH's presence could be effective away from Canaan (2 Kgs 5.17–18; Ps. 137). Yet as Exod. 33.16 makes clear, if people were without God's assurance of presence any promise that YHWH was their God and that they were YHWH's people was ultimately meaningless. During Jacob's stay with Laban, God will not feature frequently: but Jacob seems to be confident that despite contrary appearances God is with him (31.5).

*I shall bring you back to this land*: Abraham's journey required him to turn his back on the past and his homeland. Not so, this time with Jacob. That is important: otherwise the future that began with Abraham would be soon aborted.

But the words also bear another significance. Unlike Abraham where wrong paths that have been trodden seem to be simply banished from the story, in the story of Jacob mistakes have to be revisited and redeemed. In the time of Abraham Hagar and Ishmael were expelled; but for Jacob one day peace and reconciliation in *this land* will have to be sought from his brother Esau.

28.16–22 *Truly the* LORD *is in this place, and I did not know it . . . This is . . . the house of God . . . the gateway to heaven*: In the ancient world what gave a sacred building its meaning was the belief that a god was present there. A temple was the dwelling place or 'house' of the deity. Among other purposes, the episode therefore seeks to explain why the important Israelite sanctuary of Bethel gained its special character. The very name Bethel (= 'House of God') that Jacob now gives to the place is a pun on the function that it will have (see 28.17, 19, 22).

In view of the extremely negative portrayal of Bethel in several parts of the Old Testament (e.g. 1 Kgs 12.28—13.34) it is striking that Bethel should be presented so positively here, with its name suggesting that it was the archetypal temple, or house of God (see comments on p. 222).

Temples were regarded as locations where heaven and earth could meet: hence Jacob's words *a gateway to heaven*. But there may be an additional reason for the choice of this phrase. The real meaning of the name Bab-el (Babylon) is 'gate of God' although in 11.9 the name is deliberately misconstrued as 'babble'. Could the writer of Genesis 28 be challenging Babylon's claim to this epithet by claiming it for this site in Canaan? The other resonances between 11.1–9 and 28.10–19 make this feasible.

*He was awestruck and said, 'How awesome is this place!'*: Jacob has learned 'fear' of God, a quality for which Abraham was praised at the time of his great test (22.12). He is already a different personality from the son who uses Yʜwʜ's name to deceive his father (27.20).

*He took the stone . . . and set it up as a sacred pillar*: Stone pillars or *matsebot* are common features of Canaanite sanctuaries and can be seen today at many archaeological sites in the Holy Land. Originally they may have symbolised a 'male' deity, but, gradually, as here, they came simply to represent the divine. The hostility of certain parts of the Old Testament to such cult symbols is quite marked (e.g. 2 Kgs 23.14): perhaps the careful way in which the writer here links the *pillar* with the ladder which *rested* (28.12) on the ground and Yʜwʜ *standing* by it (28.13) (all three words are connected, in Hebrew, to the root *natsab*) is due to the need he felt to justify Jacob's setting up of this object. It is also remarkable how intricately Jacob himself is linked with the divine message: the wordplays associate his own head (28.11), the head of the ladder (28.12), and the head of the stone (28.18). Perhaps at the end of the day Jacob has become part of this open portal to heaven (see further on p. 223).

*Pouring oil over it* (lit. 'over its head'): Anointing with oil was the normal way an object (or person) was 'consecrated' for divine service.

*Jacob made this vow: 'If God will be with me . . .'*: Jacob's words remind us of his desperate plight. In spite of two extravagant blessings from his father, which promised *the richness of the earth* (27.28), he had arrived at Bethel uncertain even of the basics of food and clothing. God had come to him when he was at his lowest ebb. And for the first time in his life he wants to give something rather than take it! But the words also remind us that Jacob was a perennial bargainer: with Esau, (25.31), Laban (29.18; 30.31–33) and here even with God!

*Tricksters tricked*
29.1—31.55

At first sight what we now have is a 'pastoral symphony' – an interlude with plenty of folklore and comic touches, to encourage readers
to laugh at their ancient enemies the Aramaeans. But the experience
of Jacob during his stay with Laban is deliberately placed at the heart
of the Jacob cycle: the 'trickery' that is a motif dominating these three
chapters acting as a counterpoint to Jacob's earlier deception of his
father and his brother. Within the chapters the account of the birth of
Jacob's children forms an inner core, highlighted by the wordplays
that greet their birth. Born away from the land of promise they may
be, but their existence and their number constitutes the guarantee that
God's extravagant promise of 28.14 was not an empty word.

29.1–14 *Jacob, continuing his journey*: The literal meaning of the
Hebrew words that underlie this translation is 'Jacob lifted up his feet
and went'. This unusual expression suggests that after his dream at
Bethel there is now a new spring in Jacob's step!
   *The land of the eastern tribes*: First Adam and Eve, then Cain and later
Ishmael had all settled in the east. People who live in the east appear
to be on the edge of God's purposes.
   *There he saw a well*: Momentous events have previously transpired
at wells. Our appetite is whetted: what is going to happen this time?
   *Over its mouth was a huge stone*: A good omen? Jacob's last encounter
with a stone provided salvation.
   *All the herdsmen used to gather*: Words derived from the Hebrew verb
*'asap* will run like a thread through the story. Here *gather*; 29.7 *penned*;
29.8 *assembled*; 29.22 *brought . . . together*. Finally in 30.23 the identical
verb (translated there as *take away*) will be used to explain the name of
Joseph, Jacob and Rachel's son. It is as though we are being alerted in
advance to the climax of these chapters, the birth of offspring to this
shepherdess (29.9) and this super-shepherd (29.7; 30.29).
   *Where are you from, my friends?*: Literally 'my brothers'. Before
now Jacob's appreciation of the requirements of brotherhood has
been singularly lacking. Is this story going to provide him with an
opportunity to redeem his understanding of brotherhood?
   *Laban the grandson of Nahor*: This description of Laban as Nahor's
grandson, rather than Bethuel's son, helps take us back to the time of

Abraham, and sets what is to follow within the wider framework of the whole story of Abraham's descendants.

*There is . . . Rachel coming with the flock*: Rachel's name means 'Ewe', a pointed link both to her own profession and to her later role as a matriarch of Israel, YHWH's own 'flock' that he has promised to watch over (28.15; 49.24).

*It is still broad daylight . . . Water the flocks and then go and let them graze*: In contrast to the shepherds, apparently lazy and not wanting to exert themselves with the heavy stone, Jacob is now prepared to give lessons in basic husbandry! His skill at shepherding seems to have developed considerably since the days when he lived *among the tents* (25.27).

*Immediately Jacob saw Rachel . . . he went forward, rolled the stone off the mouth of the well and watered Laban's sheep*: The contrast now is not only with the indolent shepherds, but also with Jacob's own father Isaac, whose vicarious wooing of Jacob's mother, Rebecca, these actions now recall.

A generation ago another well nearby was the scene for the meeting of Abraham's servant with Rebecca. Now this 'type scene' which leads us to expect matrimony is repeated. Once again a 'hero' from a foreign land meets a virgin by a well. But unlike Isaac Jacob does his own wooing – he needs no substitute – and this time the water is drawn by the man for the woman after performing a super-human feat of single-handedly removing the stone over the mouth of the well. Jacob's virility here compares with the passivity with which Isaac is portrayed. For Isaac it was so easy: the bride was his simply for the servant's asking. It seems that it may be as simple for Jacob: before the next verse is through *he kissed Rachel*, a brazen gesture that scandalised Calvin when he commented on this passage! But in fact the stone that Jacob needed to remove symbolises the obstacles that will be put in his way before he is able to consummate this relationship with Rachel.

*He was her father's kinsman*: As elsewhere, the Hebrew word underlying kinsman is *'ah*, literally 'brother', which is often employed to describe a blood relationship that is more distant than sibling. But its use here encourages us to read the story of Jacob's dealings with Laban in the light of his earlier exchange with Esau, his actual brother. Will Laban be any better 'brother' to Jacob than Jacob had been to Esau?

*Laban . . . hurried to meet him . . . and welcomed him to his home*: On the surface Laban's actions signal generous hospitality, but we cannot forget that we first met Laban when Rebecca was wooed – and then he seemed far too interested in the apparent wealth of the visitor who came from the west (24.30). Will Laban be disappointed when he discovers that this visitor has arrived as a fugitive rather than with a camel train of jewels? He certainly sets Jacob to work very quickly, and gets a *whole month*'s free labour out of him.

*Jacob told Laban all that had happened, and Laban said, 'Yes, you are my own flesh and blood.'*: What was it that Jacob confessed to Laban – how he had stolen what had belonged to his brother? If so, there is irony in Laban's response. At first reading it sounds as though Laban's exclamation is returning us to Eden: for his literal words 'You are my bone and my flesh' echo Adam's cry of joy there at meeting Eve. Has Jacob truly found a 'brother', is Cain's conflict with Abel undone and paradise restored? That must have been what Jacob was longing for! And yet Laban's answer can also suggest that he was recognising in Jacob a kindred spirit, a fellow trickster – on whom the tables will soon be turned.

29.15–28   At first Laban seems more than reasonable. *Why should you work for me for nothing simply because you are my kinsman [brother]?* It is only when we look a little closer that we discover that Jacob has already been labouring for Laban for a 'month of days', presumably without payment, and it is only when we read on that we discover that, because of Laban's later trick, Jacob will in reality labour for Laban *for nothing* for seven whole years!

*Now Laban had two daughters*: The last time the word 'two' appeared it described the prenatal hostility between Jacob and Esau. Trouble surely lies ahead, especially as the two sisters are then contrasted, as were Jacob and Esau in 25.23.

*Rachel was beautiful in both face and figure*: The identical description is given of Rachel's son, Joseph, in 39.6. Beauty, as we already discovered in 12.14 can cause problems!

*Jacob had fallen in love with her*: Three times Jacob's love for Rachel is mentioned (29.18, 20, 30): it is a powerful force. But as with the love of Isaac and Rebecca, each for their favoured son, love is dangerous and can cause strife.

*Jacob . . . worked seven years for Rachel, and they seemed like a few days*: A 'few days' was literally the expression Rebecca used in 27.44 (translated there as *for a while*) when she encouraged Jacob's 'temporary' departure. Those few days have become years of exile. But it is symptomatic that finally Jacob has to remind Laban that his time is up.

*Laban . . . held a wedding feast*: There would have been lots of wine to drink. Was it a drunken Jacob on whom Laban passed off the deception, and his elder daughter?

*When morning came, there was Leah*: Jacob's come-uppance is well and truly executed! As the darkness of his father's blindness had helped his own deception of his father Isaac, so in turn the darkness of night facilitates Laban's deception of himself.

*Jacob said to Laban . . . 'Why have you played this trick upon me?'*: The screws of nemesis are further tightened as Jacob refers to this *trick* of Laban? Did he not know that his own trickery was described by the cognate word *deceit* when he cheated his brother out of their father's blessing? (Both words come from the Hebrew root *ramah*.) There is a snake in the grass in Paddan-aram, just as there was in Canaan, and as there had once been in Eden (see notes on 27.35, p. 177).

*Laban answered, 'It is against the custom of our country to marry off the younger sister before the elder.'*: The slap in the face for Jacob is brutally ironic. His own trick had involved a younger sibling taking the rightful place of the elder. Now Laban's trick on him has resulted in an elder sister taking the place intended for the younger. The words are carefully chosen: *elder* is the feminine form of the word *firstborn* (elder) that had been used to describe Esau, and is closely linked to birthright. Laban's self-justification acts as a clear rebuke to Jacob for the way he had seized the place that belonged to his elder!

*Then Laban gave Jacob his daughter Rachel to be his wife*: On the surface it looks as though the deception is quickly resolved in a way that meets the needs of everybody: certainly with far less grief than Jacob's deception of Esau. But appearances are themselves deceptive: the emotions that have been stirred by these actions will have consequences that will reverberate throughout the rest of Genesis.

29.29–35  *When the LORD saw that Leah was unloved, he granted her a child*. The translation is euphemistic. Leah is positively 'hated', partly because of her complicity in her father's deception of Jacob. However the language also recalls the law code of Deut. 21.15–17 which reads almost like a commentary on the later story of Jacob and his sons:

> *When a man has two wives, one loved and the other unloved, if they both bear him sons, and the son of the unloved wife is the elder, then, when the day comes for him to divide his property among his sons, he must not treat the son of the loved wife as his firstborn in preference to his true firstborn . . .*

If only Jacob had adhered strictly to this law, how much less grief would there have been later on!

God's bias towards the unfavoured is evident here in the story, in the law code, and in the rest of Genesis. It is fascinating that the naming of at least one of Leah's sons, Simeon, recalls the name given to Hagar's son Ishmael, as does the rationale for the giving of that name (see 16.11). And when Leah speaks of her *humiliation* as her first son is born she uses the same word (*'oni*) that the angel applied to Hagar, there translated *ill-treatment* (16.11). It seems that Hagars can exist within the community of promise as well as outside it. That same word *'oni* will also be used when the last son of Jacob is born, Benjamin, whom Rachel sought to name Ben-oni as she died giving birth to him. Leah had the fertility, and Rachel the love. Is the story suggesting that one without the other is dangerous and can be the cause of humiliation and grief?

*Leah conceived and gave birth to a son*: In apparently rapid succession Leah has four sons. She names each, explaining her choice of name, with an explanation linked to it by sound.

In each case Leah associates Yhwh with the giving of the son. The names of the first three all reflect her despair, as well her desire to be loved by Jacob. But with the fourth son, Judah, she apparently manages to overcome her pain, and his birth is an occasion of fulfilment: *Now I shall praise the* Lord.

Does this reflect Judah's special place among Leah's children, both in terms of the story (he figures prominently in the story of Joseph) and as the eponymous ancestor of the tribe and kingdom of Judah? In a book, Genesis, in which younger sons assume particular prominence, Judah, the youngest among this initial quartet of Leah's sons, may be specially marked out by God, particularly because his eldest brother Reuben appears to lose his birthright (35.22; 49.4), and the next brothers Simeon and Levi are condemned by their father for their violence (34.30; 49.5).

30.1–24 *Give me sons, or I shall die!* This is actually the first time we have heard Rachel speak, and these impetuous words seem to define her character. She even makes it clear both now, and after Joseph is born, that she is not content with one son. Does her outburst paradoxically presage her early death, while giving birth to Benjamin?

*Jacob said angrily to Rachel, 'Can I take the place of God?'*: Robert Alter has pointed out[4] how often the biblical narrative responds to the situation of a barren but favoured wife by offering an 'annunciation' in which the woman prays to God, and the deity promises the wife a child. But in the case of Rachel we have to wait till 30.22 for this to happen. Quite literally Rachel seeks to make Jacob *take the place of God* – and it is telling that the name YHWH does not appear again in the story until Joseph is eventually born.

*Here is my slave-girl Bilhah*: We seem to have returned to the story of Abraham and Sarah, as Rachel offers her slave-girl as a substitute wife. She even uses the same phrase, punning on the sound link between 'build' (*banah*) and 'son' (*ben*) as did Sarai: *Through her I too may build up a family*. Rachel almost seems to be playing Sarai to Bilhah's Hagar! And as with Sarai the apparent successful outcome will really be no solution.

*She may bear sons to be laid upon my knees*: The placing of the newborn child of her slave-girl upon Rachel's knees was a recognised gesture of adoption.

*Jacob lay with [Bilhah] and she conceived*: It is notable that the naming of the two sons of Bilhah does not bring YHWH into the frame.

The rivalry between the two sisters now begins to take on the character of a bedroom farce as Leah, not to be outdone, offers her slave-girl Zilpah as a surrogate for Jacob. Although Leah has no problem with fertility, she seems to be denied sexual access to her husband. YHWH is being further and further excluded from these human machinations: note that in the case of these sons, Gad and Asher, neither God nor YHWH is associated with their naming. Indeed both these names may well be linked to the titles of pagan gods.

*Reuben . . . found some mandrakes*: These plants, with oddly shaped roots, which are native to Palestine and neighbouring countries, were long held to have magical properties, both as an aphrodisiac and as an aid to fertility. Leah apparently could do with assistance in one respect, and Rachel in the other! But the Old Testament is consistently hostile to such magical attempts to manipulate God. Is it accidental then that though it is Rachel who makes use of the mandrakes, having 'hired' them off Leah, it should be Leah rather than Rachel who then bears another son? God (not mandrakes!) is the giver of new life: the next son is born because *God heard Leah's prayer*.

*Leah said, 'God has rewarded me . . .'*: At first sight the sequence seems confused. Shortly after Leah sleeps with her husband, having hired (Hebrew: *sakar*) him by giving the mandrakes to Rachel, she bears a son named Issachar (Hebrew: *yissakar*). However she links this name not with the episode of the mandrakes, but to the fact that she had previously 'hired out' her slave-girl to Jacob. Perhaps the narrator is trying to establish that employing mandrakes or other magical means is absolutely not God's way: even the use of a surrogate is preferable!

*Later she bore a daughter whom she named Dinah*: Dinah is quite literally an afterthought! Apparently not even her name merits attention, or a pun. The sad story of her life (see Gen. 34) is being foreshadowed.

*Then God took thought for Rachel; he heard her prayer and gave her a child*: Finally the longed for child is born; not via mandrakes, nor a substitute slave-girl, nor even Rachel's desperate cry to Jacob. The child is born through God's initiative, and because of God's relationship with this woman. For the first time since 29.35 the name of YHWH now appears in the story: *She named him Joseph, saying, 'May the* LORD *add another son to me!'*

Two completely different reasons are given for the naming of Joseph. Not only is it linked to the root *yasap* (= add), but in the previous verse it has been connected to *'asap* (= take away). It is strange to link this one child to two words that have almost opposite meanings. Is it a signal that Joseph was supposed to achieve in his life a balancing of opposites – a kind of equilibrium that might bring harmony to this unruly family?

Note how the link with *'asap* 'catches up' and reiterates a word which was used several times as the story of Jacob and Rachel opened (see p. 184). It perhaps hints that the purpose of Jacob's time in Laban's land is now drawing to its close.

30.25–43 *Jacob said to Laban, 'Send me on my way'*: Certainly that is Jacob's view. It is time to return to Canaan – and not empty-handed! *Is it not time for me to make provision for my family?*

At the beginning of the negotiations Jacob and Laban agree on one salient factor. Laban states: *the* LORD *has blessed me through you*. Jacob agrees: *wherever I went, the* LORD *brought you blessings*.

In spite of the apparent secularity, and some unsavoury features, of Jacob's interlude in Paddan-aram, YHWH has been working through him, to bless others. The promise that Abraham and his descendants would be a channel of blessing for others is being fulfilled; and this blessing of YHWH extends to the area of everyday life and economic prosperity.

The REB translation *I have become prosperous* (30. 27) is questionable. NRSV's 'I have learned by divination' is closer to the meaning of the Hebrew at this point. Not only does this better preserve a link to a theme that will become important in the story of Joseph (44.5), but in the context of chapter 30 it offers a reminder that YHWH's power to bless is apparent even to those, such as Laban, whose religious practice (i.e. divination, presumably linked with foreign deities, see 31.19) locates them outside the immediate community of faith.

The negotiations between Jacob and Laban begin politely, in a way that is reminiscent of the occasion when Abraham bargained over a tomb for Sarah. But two consummate bargainers and tricksters are at work here, each flexing their skills against the other. And as with Abraham and Ephron even if little is being ostensibly requested, much is in reality being demanded – by both parties.

It is not in fact clear whether Laban is prepared to let Jacob go at all. Is the offer of *wages I owe you* a device to persuade him to stay? In his opening remarks to Laban, Jacob had reiterated the word *service*. It is a loaded word, used also of the later Israelite slavery in Egypt. There too people had come as guests, and eventually found that they had become slaves and were unable to leave. Is that what is transpiring here? One reading of 31.41 might suggest that between the time of these negotiations and Jacob's eventual departure, six whole years elapse.

At any rate by v. 31 Jacob agrees to *be in charge* [*of Laban's flocks*] *as before*, and makes the seemingly generous proposal that for his wages he should receive *nothing at all*. But as with Ephron's apparent generosity in the earlier negotiations with Abraham he is actually asking for quite a lot. He requests the unusually marked sheep and goats from Laban's flock for himself.

Although Laban ostensibly agrees to the suggestion he then immediately takes steps to ensure that the sheep and goats in this category will be as few as possible. At one level it is appropriate that Laban should specifically remove *all* [*the goats*] *that had any white on them*, for they have an intrinsic connection to his very name, Laban, which means 'white'. But the assumption that Laban is also making is that by removing animals in this category, any offspring produced among Jacob's flock will not be the sort which Jacob can claim. Was Jacob expecting this trick? It seems likely, since he then has one of his own up his sleeve.

Behind Jacob's actions seems to be the traditional belief, popular in the days before the science of genetics, that the sight of a particular object at the moment of conception influenced the appearance of what was conceived. In other words, animals seeing stripy rods, produced stripy offspring. In describing Jacob's actions the narrator includes another subtle pun on Laban's name – for the word for the *poplar* tree (*libne*) also comes from the Hebrew root *laban* ( = white), and we are further reminded of this through Jacob's action in *expos-ing the white of the rods*. With a chuckle we are being told how Jacob is managing to out-Laban Laban! Last time there was a discussion about wages (29.15–28), Laban had outmanoeuvred Jacob, but now the tables are turned. Scientifically (and perhaps morally) dubious all this may be: but like both his forebears Abraham (24.1) and Isaac (26.13), Jacob simply cannot help prospering: *so Jacob's wealth increased more and more*, a clear clue that God's blessing is with him as much as it was with his perhaps more conventional ancestors.

31.1–18    However just as one deceit leads to another, once ill-feeling has set in, it spawns further bad relationships. Jacob's outwitting of Laban's attempts literally to 'fleece' him, simply exacerbate the ten-sion with Laban and his family. *He noticed . . . that Laban was not so well disposed to him as he had once been*. In the concrete and vivid idiom of the Hebrew language the words here are 'Jacob saw Laban's face, and be-hold it was not with him . . .' Over the next two chapters the language of 'face' will become a central motif as Jacob journeys back to Canaan to encounter Esau once more. The appearance of the word just at this point, as Jacob receives YHWH's command to begin the journey, is a foreshadowing of what is to come.

*The LORD said to Jacob, 'Go back to the land of your fathers and to your kindred'*: The vocabulary deliberately echoes the original command to Abraham. Once again a patriarch is directed in the direction of Canaan: but this time it is to return to his kindred, rather than to leave them. Yet in view of the hostility surrounding Jacob as he left his home 20 years ago, to return may be for him the more difficult option.

*I shall be with you*: The identical phrase spoken by God at Bethel had pointed Jacob into exile. As Jacob is shortly to affirm to his wives (31.5) it had been amply fulfilled. Now the phrase points him home again. In 28.15 a promise of protection was explicitly added: here it is included implicitly.

*Jacob sent word to Rachel and Leah to come out to where his flocks were in the country*: This instruction suggests that Jacob is aware that his projected return is rapidly turning into a flight. He needs to have a conversation with his wives without the danger of being overheard.

The repetition of the comment about Laban in 31.5, first made in 31.2, intensifies the focus on 'face' (see comment above).

*He . . . has changed my wages ten times over*: The number 'ten' here probably means 'a lot': it does not need to be understood literally. However Jacob's further complaint (31.8) suggests that the wheeling and dealing between him and Laban was even more complicated than it appeared in 30.32–42.

*It is God who has taken away your father's livestock and given them to me*: Jacob seems to suggest to Rachel and Leah that his success in out-manoeuvring Laban is due to God's direct intervention. This is the first we had heard of that; in 30.37–40 it seems to be simply a question of Jacob's own native cunning! The reference to God's role in this, as well as the detailed description of Jacob's divine dream, seem designed to help persuade Rachel and Leah to take the momentous step that Jacob is asking of them. He succeeds!

*He has sold us, and used the money paid for us*: Normally the bride-price, which a bridegroom offered for his wife, would be channelled by her family at least in part to the married woman. Rachel and Leah complain that Laban has appropriated their bride-prices (namely Jacob's seven years of labour for each of them) solely for his own benefit.

*All the wealth . . . is surely ours and our children's*: Gradually Jacob's departure from Laban is taking on the hues of the later Exodus of Jacob's descendants from Egypt. And as that escape included plundering the wealth of the Egyptians (Exod. 12.36), Laban's wealth (and even his household gods) is now apparently the booty of Jacob and his wives (see also comments on 12.16, 20).

*To go to his father Isaac in Canaan*: This is the first indication we have that Isaac might still be alive, 20 years after we last met him on his apparent deathbed!

**31.19–55** *Rachel stole the household gods belonging to her father*: The household gods were small terracotta figurines, which, in pagan culture, represented the gods responsible for the well-being of a family or household. Their loss would have been felt keenly. What was the motivation for this theft? Perhaps Rachel was concerned lest they might bequeath Laban power over the fugitives, or perhaps she was unable to leave her past behind as she fled into an unknown future.

The hill country of Gilead, east of the Jordan, where Laban caught up with Jacob, was frontier territory for the later Israelite tribes. It marked a boundary with the Aramaeans of Damascus. The description here of Laban as *the Aramaean*, hints at this later political division, and also distances Laban from the intimate family of Jacob.

*Be careful to say nothing . . . not a word*: This phrase, apparently spoken to Laban by God in a dream, and repeated as Laban recounts the dream in 31.29, includes similar words (in Hebrew) to those used by Laban and Bethuel as they permit Rebecca's departure in 24.50. It suggests that the departure of Laban's daughters, Rachel and Leah, is following the pattern established first by Laban's sister, Rebecca, which was clearly intentioned by God.

*You have deceived me and carried off my daughters as though they were captives taken in war*: Laban's words of complaint to Jacob accentuate the motif of 'plunder'. The 'carrying off' of his daughters is described in terms that suggest the 'driving off' of cattle seized as war booty. The Hebrew root *ganab* resonates throughout 31.19–30. With its underlying meaning of 'steal' it is used to describe both Rachel's theft of the teraphim (31.19, 30, 32) and Jacob's duping of Laban with his surreptitious departure (31.20, 26, 27).

*Why did you steal my gods?* At the end of a lengthy tirade in which Laban's remarks are either unbelievable (can we really believe that he would have thrown a party to celebrate Jacob's departure?) or unjustifiable (as in his description of his daughters being herded like cattle, although they had gone of their own free will), his final complaint of theft has validity.

*Whoever is found in possession of your gods shall die for it*: Rachel, the thief of her father's gods, is not in fact found – as a result of her own 'trick'. She hides the figurines under where she is sitting, and announces that she is menstruating (31–35), which means that both she and her seat are made 'unclean', and Laban is thus prevented from a close search. Menstruation, the visible sign of her difficulties in bearing a child, now becomes the means of her successful deception of her father. But do Jacob's words unintentionally condemn Rachel to the early death that she will suffer when later she bears her second son in Canaan? Perhaps they seem to hint at this. Throughout the story of Jacob trick has been piled upon trick, first Jacob, then Laban, now Rachel. In fact this trick of Rachel mirrored the 'trick' of Jacob with which Jacob's story had opened: both, younger siblings, deceive their father in order to obtain a blessing, Jacob from Isaac's lips, Rachel via the household gods which were believed to bless those who possessed them. Does all this deceit finally somehow have to be brought to an end and Rachel pay the ultimate price for them with her own life?

There is, of course, another issue. The veneration of household gods was a pagan practice – clearly Rachel in spite of her marriage to Jacob had not fully understood what it meant to be a worshipper of Yhwh. Will her desire to hold on to the ancient religious practices of her ancestral home ultimately disqualify her from participation in the community of Israel? At the very least Rachel's actions suggest that she is no Rebecca willing to set out in blind faith for a strange land.

*Identify anything I have that is yours*: As the theme of trickery draws to a close, another motif has begun to be explored. Rightful and wrongful identification or recognition of people or objects will dominate the story of Jacob's sons. The Hebrew word *nakar* meaning 'identify' or 'recognise' that appears in this verse has already been used when Isaac failed to recognise Jacob because he was dressed up in Esau's clothes. But soon Jacob himself will be on the receiving end of the verb! (See comments on 27.23.)

*Jacob heatedly took Laban to task*: Jacob's pent-up anger, which festered under the surface during his 20 years of near servitude, suddenly explodes with a verbal violence using language that is reminiscent of the law court. He throws a series of accusations at Laban, which are intended to make it clear that he had acted above and beyond the normal call of duties of a shepherd. He rounds off the speech with another legal idiom: *last night* [*God*] *delivered his verdict*, presumably via the dream that Laban had experienced.

During the speech Jacob refers to the help he had received from *the God of my father, the God of Abraham and the Fear of Isaac.* One suggested way of looking at the relationship between Jacob and Laban (at least from 30.25 onwards) is to view it as a 'contest' between the gods of both parties: YHWH on the one hand, and the household gods of Laban on the other. If so, it is no contest! The power of YHWH, who can impose his will upon opponents (e.g. Laban, via the dream) is contrasted with the impotence of Laban's gods who have to be protected – by an unclean woman! The same kind of contrast is made in literature from the exilic period (e.g. Isa. 46.1–4, and Ps. 96). The Exodus events are also presented in a similar fashion, as a contest between YHWH and Pharaoh (e.g. Exod. 7.8–25). It is interesting therefore how Jacob notes *God saw my labour and my hardships*, a description that parallels God's observation of the suffering of his people in Egypt (Exod. 3.7). (See also the comments on '*oni* on p. 188.)

The unusual title of *the Fear of Isaac* given to the God of Jacob occurs only here and in v. 53. The meaning of the Hebrew has been disputed: an alternative translation of 'Kinsman of Isaac' has been proposed, which would emphasise the close relationship between God and Jacob's family. However the REB translation may well be correct: God has been fearsome in the life of Isaac (Gen. 22) and he will soon be fearsome in the life of Isaac's son. In fact, does the introduction of the title here and in v. 53 suggest that Jacob's psyche is beginning to anticipate the dangers that lie ahead and the anxiety that he has about his homecoming, and meeting with Esau once more? However the title probably also includes the sense of 'the Fearsome one who protects Isaac', with the incident in Gen. 35.5 almost acting as a commentary on this meaning. Similar epithets suggesting protection are linked to the other patriarchs: Shield of Abraham (15.1) and Strong One (Bull) of Jacob (49.24). In both cases, as also here, the titles appear at crisis moments in the ancestral story (see also comments on 'covenant' on p. 68).

The juridical nature of Jacob's complaints is appropriately addressed by the making of a pact or covenant, which itself has a legal status.

As with the earlier pact that Isaac made it is the other party (26.28) who proposes making the agreement and who thus implicitly acknowledges the power of YHWH: *May the LORD watch between you and me when we are absent from one another*. The traditional features of a covenant-making ceremony, the oath (31.53) and the feast (31.54) are represented in both covenants. But unique to this pact is its visible reminder, the setting up of a stone pillar (31.45, 51) and a stone cairn (31.46, 51–52). Once again stones figure prominently at key moments of Jacob's life, indeed the *sacred pillar* here recalls the stone pillar Jacob had erected 20 years previously at Bethel (28.18), which was also highlighted in a dream (31.13) as a symbol of God's protection. In this case the stones also function as a boundary marker, designating a political division, between the territory belonging to Jacob's descendants (the Israelites) and that belonging to the descendants of Laban (the Aramaeans). For as the story of Jacob unfolds, the individual person is gradually taking on the features of a nation. The international character of what is transpiring is emphasised by one of the names given to the site of the covenant: *Laban called it Jegar-sahadutha and Jacob called it Gal-ed*. The two names have an identical meaning, 'Cairn of Witness', but Laban has used Aramaic, the 'international' language of the ancient Middle East, which originated with his putative descendants, the Aramaeans, while Jacob has employed Hebrew.

The previous pacts in the Old Testament made between human beings, between Abraham and Abimelech (21.27) and Isaac and Abimelech (26.31) were both made with people that were unrelated by blood to the patriarchs. They created a reasonably civilised relationship where none had previously existed. By contrast Laban is Jacob's uncle, cousin and father-in-law! The family links are emphasised in his words: *The daughters are my daughters, the children are my children.*

Yet the effect of covenant making on this occasion is to create a formality and a distance, emotional as well as physical, so that Laban's position becomes parallel to that of Abimelech, a person with whom Jacob's descendants might have civilised and non-aggressive dealings, but no longer part of the family. Too much mutual hostility has happened to expect more than that. In making the covenant, Laban is, as he acknowledges, giving up the rights of control over his daughters and their children.

Does the reference in Laban's final words to *the God of Abraham and the God of Nahor,* the grandfathers respectively of Jacob and Laban, indicate for one final time that Laban is striving for a parity between their gods and reminding Jacob of their relationship? And if so, is Jacob's oath taken only in the name of *the Fear of Isaac* a deliberate omission: a refusal to grant equal status to a foreign deity? Or does the title hint once more at what lies ahead: for the next chapter contains possibly the most numinous episode in the entire Book of Genesis?

Laban's final actions, which mirror his opening gestures (29.13), signify the closure of this long section as well as his role within the story. His name will not appear again: not even in a genealogy.

## *Touching God*
32.1—33.20

One can meet God in a variety of ways, but the two different means by which Jacob will now meet God approach the profoundest insights of biblical spirituality. These chapters have the quality, and the mystery, of some of the resurrection stories of Jesus. Indeed we are about to read a story of death and resurrection: in which symbolically Jacob dies and Israel is reborn. They are not comfortable chapters, indeed that is their power. We, like Jacob, need to wrestle through them. But, as Jacob himself ultimately discovered, it is only by struggle that the blessing comes, and the people of God is brought to birth.

Intriguingly these chapters fall about as far from the end of the book of Genesis as the mysterious encounters of Abraham with God in Gen. 18 do from the beginning of the book. There too the interweaving of the vertical and horizontal dimension of faith was prominent, there too the ambiguities of the relationship between God and humanity was explored. It may be more comfortable to meet God in the noonday of a lunch-party, as Abraham did, than in the dark night by a lonely river, but there is a sense that Jacob's experience is the one that many of us can identify with and make our own.

One of the particular features of this section is the extensive use of wordplay. Indeed 'wordplay' seems a superficial term for what is happening here.

> It seems . . . to be an attempt to bed down the meaning of the story, right into the roots of the words actually used to tell the story. [The writer] is not tinkering with the narrative to produce a clever effect, but is deeply structuring his writings to create a climate for the acceptance of particular theological concepts.[5]

**32.1–8** The angels of God at Bethel had bidden Jacob farewell for his journey to Mesopotamia; now angels, almost like divine border guards, greet him on his return to the land of promise. An easy symmetry – but a deceptive one. For in these chapters it is God's turn to play the trickster, and the true parallel with Jacob's experience at Bethel will not be these welcoming angels, but the mysterious antagonist that still lurks for him near the fords of Jabbok. In the depths of Jacob's despair at Bethel God had lifted him up. Now he is returning, replete with family and possessions: flushed with his victory over Laban. Jan Fokkelman has commented that when Jacob leaves Laban, 'As God's protege, [he] goes away a victor; he is unassailable, and he knows it.'[6] But the God who lifts up the broken in spirit, is the same as the one who brings low the proud; theology and theodicy demand that Jacob does not have it too easy on the road ahead. Before God is through with him the unassailable must be made vulnerable.

Punning on his meeting with the divine 'company' Jacob names the place Mahanaim (= Two Companies). The duality explicit in this name will quickly write itself into the story. *Jacob . . . divided the people with him, as well as the sheep, cattle and camels, into two companies* (32.7, see also 32.8). Duality has been a striking feature of the Jacob stories so far: two brothers who were twins (see comments on p. 161), two sisters, two locations, home and exile, even the division of the flocks that Jacob was guarding for Laban into two distinct sections. Now this sense of duality comes to dominate the narrative, giving everything that happens its own mysterious undercurrent or consequence. Though it even threatens to overwhelm Jacob, tearing him apart to the core of his very being, it is, as he discovers, ultimately cathartic, giving him the integration, at least for a short space of time, for which he had yearned for so many years.

*Jacob sent messengers*: These are, of course, human messengers but
the Hebrew word used is identical to that translated 'angels' i.e. messengers of God in 32.1. The encounter with the divine messengers
seems to have prompted Jacob to take the initiative in seeking a way
forward in his relationship with his brother Esau.

*To his brother Esau to the district of Seir in Edomite territory*: We last
met Esau at the family home in Beersheba, but while Jacob has been
staying (literally 'lingering') with his uncle Laban Esau has migrated
to Edom and already become the kingdom that was associated with
him from birth. Jacob has a lot of catching up to do!

*My lord, your servant Jacob sends this message*: The language used is
courtly and deferential, such as a vassal might use in correspondence
with his overlord. Is this the way that one brother should greet another? It is ironic that Jacob has to adopt this tone: for it inverts the
vocabulary used in his blessing and Esau's anti-blessing, which spoke
specifically of Jacob as lord (27.29) and Esau as servant (27.40). That
stolen blessing is haunting the story and demanding its retribution.

*I have acquired*: Jacob is superficially self-confident. His omission of
any direct offering of a gift is striking, but does the reference to his
desire to *win your favour* (a word that is picked up and explored more
extensively in 33.5–11) suggest that he is attempting to restore the
fruits of the stolen blessing? Though they are worlds apart in meaning, and in the English language, the consonants used in the words for
*company* (*mahaneh*) and *favour* (*hen*) are very similar in Hebrew. Is the
link intended to suggest that it is the appearance of this *company* sent
by God (32.2) that has prompted Jacob to seek Esau's *favour*? Grace
received leads on to grace offered (see further on 33.5-11 p. 207).

*Esau . . . with four hundred men*: The number suggests a reasonably
sized raiding party: potentially made even more terrifying in view of
the promise given to Esau in 27.40 that *by your sword you will live*.

32.9–12 *Jacob prayed*: Jacob's shattered confidence leads him swiftly to prayer. This is the longest formal prayer in Genesis. It alludes
both to Yʜwʜ's command to Jacob to return to the land (31.3), and to
the earlier encounter Jacob had with God at Bethel (28.13–15). But it
reaches back beyond both of these experiences of Jacob to link with
God's original call to Abraham. As in 31.3 the language used deliberately recalls Abraham's summons of 12.1–3. We are also pointed in
that direction by Jacob's expansive opening *God of my father Abraham,
God of my father Isaac*. In the later pages of the Old Testament there
would be other occasions when people would ground their prayers

in the assurance of God's love for Abraham and the other patriarchs (e.g. Deut. 26.5–11). Jacob is the first of many, and his words implicitly suggest that by facilitating his own homecoming God is also bringing his ancestor Abraham 'home' at last.

*I am not worthy of all the true and steadfast love*: True enough, yet is Jacob aware, as the first readers of Genesis certainly were, that the God of the Bible is one who almost extravagantly expresses a bias towards the 'unworthy'? And with the vivid concreteness of Hebrew idiom Jacob is actually saying, 'I am too small', using a verb from the identical root as the adjective 'younger' which has been used twice before to describe him vis-à-vis Esau. We know that the God of Genesis consistently seems to display partiality towards younger brothers: is Jacob, even in his fear and contrition, subtly reminding God of this?

*True and steadfast love*: If any words can sum up God's 'character profile' in the Bible it is these. *True* conveys God's quality of reliability, *steadfast love* God's constancy, particularly linked with covenant promises and relationship. They appear again translated as *ever faithful and true* when Yhwh introduces himself to Moses on Mount Sinai, after the episode of the golden calf (Exod. 34.6).

*The last time I crossed the Jordan*: The Jordan marked the eastern boundary of the land of promise (Deut. 3.27) and to cross it was to leave or enter the land. The reference apparently contradicts Jacob's presumed actual location, near the River Jabbok. It may suggest some Deuteronomic editing of this passage (see further on *Jabbok* below).

*Save me, I pray, from my brother Esau*: This is the heart of the prayer, to which Jacob has been building up.

*You said, 'I shall make you prosper'*: This phrase, which virtually repeats the expression *who promised me prosperity* used in 32.9, may be an example of Jacob gilding the lily. Although 28.14–15 does refer to Jacob being blessed, the explicit promise God makes there is to be with Jacob, rather than to make him prosper. Is the inveterate bargainer of the previous chapters still up to his old tricks?

The prayer of Jacob clearly marks a significant shift in Jacob's relationship with God, with his brother Esau, and with himself. But even as it is prayed – heartfelt though it may be – it still leaves questions in the reader's mind. Is the link between Jacob's self-interest and his new found religiosity too close? Back in Gen. 21 we wondered whether Abraham was using God a bit too conveniently to sort out domestic difficulties. But he was then confronted by a trial of faith (Gen. 22), which cut to the quick of his being; will a similar trial await this patriarch?

**32.13–21** *Jacob chose a gift*: The sound-plays of vv. 1–8 still seem to continue with the deliberate choice of the word *minhah* for 'gift'. It too contains the letters *hn* (albeit in a different order). The 'company' (*mahaneh*) of angels has encouraged Jacob to seek Esau's favour (*hen*) by offering him a gift (*minhah*). However *minhah* is used especially to describe either an offering made to a god or tribute given to a political superior. Both the word itself as well as the size of Jacob's gift reinforce the sense of Esau's powerful superiority.

We may well wonder however whether the complicated organisation of the gift is a device to mislead Esau into believing that Jacob is more powerful than he actually is.

*Your servant Jacob . . . my lord Esau*: As with 32.4 the terminology inverts the language used in Isaac's blessing of Jacob.

*He himself is coming behind us*: Jacob has always been a 'behind' (*'ahar*) or 'afterwards' person, from the very moment of his birth (25.26). He had *stayed* (32.4) for a long time with Laban, a verb which is related to the preposition *'ahar*. The preposition itself is repeated twice in 32.20. To understand the role of the concept in this story it helps to realise that it is probably linked to a word for the physical 'back' or 'hinder parts' of a human being or animal. (In the same way as the preposition 'before' derives from the word for 'face', see below.) *Behind* acutely defines Jacob the 'heel' who came up upon people from the rear and overtook/supplanted them (27.36). Very shortly Jacob himself is forcibly going to be turned right round, and compelled to look others in the face!

*I shall appease him with the gift that I have sent on ahead, and afterwards, when we come face to face, perhaps he will receive me kindly*: There is an extraordinary quality to the story here, which can only be conveyed by giving a very literal translation of the Hebrew: 'I shall appease his face with the gift going to my face, and afterwards I may see his face. Perhaps he will lift up my face!'

The words themselves begin to sing the story, as the concept of 'face' (Hebrew: *panim*) which will interpret Jacob's next two encounters: with God (32.30–31) and with his brother Esau (33.10), is now introduced almost as a chorus. (See comment above on the link between 'before' and 'face'.) Jacob has never found it easy to look his brother in the face. It is remarkable how the lengthy episode in which Jacob steals Esau's blessing keeps the two brothers apart, so that they are never in each other's presence, and Jacob steals Esau's blessing from behind his back (see e.g. 27.30). He needs this gift to act as a precursor, before he can attempt a face to face meeting.

*Appease*: This suggests both Jacob's awe of Esau and his sense of guilt. It too is a technical word from the vocabulary of sacrifice, used particularly to describe an offering to an angry deity. Its connection with sin and atonement indicates that Jacob has a guilty conscience for what he has previously done to his brother.

*He . . . stayed that night at Mahaneh*: Although understood by the REB as a proper name, *mahaneh* probably simply means 'the camp'. It continues the verbal jousting which has been prominent in this chapter so far.

32.22–32  Literary critics have tried to analyse what makes this brief (less than 200 words) narrative so compelling. There seem to be two complementary features.

First, it is a story in which layer is built imperceptibly on layer. There is a hint that this was originally a tale about a river demon, who controlled a ford, whose power was only operative at night and who could not tolerate the daylight: a sort of ancient Middle Eastern 'Billy Goats Gruff'. On top of this was etched an ancient traditional story of how the Israelite patriarch Jacob wrestled with an angel, which dates back at least to the time of the prophet Hosea (see Hos.12.3–4). It may be that during the exile was added another layer, which drew upon a reflection in Jer. 30.5–17, in which Jacob comes to personify the exiles, as hope is expressed for their return to the land. Finally those who drew the account into the wider story of creation and the ancestral history created a new layer, with cross-references to the extended story. Gerhard von Rad's comment cannot be bettered:

> [The narrative] contains experiences of faith that extend from the most ancient period down to the time of the narrator; there is charged to it something of the entire divine history into which Israel was drawn. This event did not simply occur at a definite biographical point in Jacob's life, but as it is now related it is clearly transparent as a type of that which Israel experienced from time to time with God. Israel has here presented its entire history with God almost prophetically as such a struggle until the breaking of the day. The narrative itself makes this extended interpretation probable by equating the names Jacob and Israel.[7]

Another aspect of the story, which has been illuminated by an influential essay by the French structuralist critic Roland Barthes,[8] helps to explain its peculiar frisson. Barthes noted that traditional (folk) tales like this one normally operate on a standard format. There is a Hero, who is sent on a Quest by an Originator, and who, before the Quest can be fulfilled has to confront and defeat an Opponent. The story of Jacob at the Jabbok contains all these features. Jacob is the Hero (albeit a dubious one!) who is sent on a Quest (to return to the land) by an Originator (God). But then dramatically the form is subverted as at its denouement we realise that God the Originator is also the Opponent. The ordered world of the folk tale has been turned upside down – and that can be terrifying, for the reader who reflects on the story as much as for the Hero who participates in it.

*During the night*: 'Night' here is not simply a chronological reference, but as in John's Gospel (e.g. John 3.1; 13.30) it vividly intensifies the precariousness and uncertainties of the situation. In the dark night Jacob – and we – cannot easily see whether his antagonist is God or Esau.

*He sent . . . his eleven sons*: It is interesting that among the family sent across the ford there is no mention of Jacob's daughter Dinah: a telling omission.

*The ford of Jabbok . . . a man wrestled with him*: The name 'Jabbok' sounds very similar to the verb *wrestled* (Hebrew: *'abaq*), which appears in both vv. 25 and 26. A wordplay is clearly intended. The name 'Jacob' also contains the identical letters (in a different order) as 'Jabbok', a point of which the storyteller was well aware. The double wordplay helps to reinforce the sense that this is Jacob's defining moment: his destiny from the moment he was named was to arrive at this place and consummate there the 'wrestling' that had been part of him ever since he was in the womb.

This may lie behind a puzzling feature of the story. A careful plotting of the place names given in the course of Jacob's journey from Paddan-aram (i.e. Gilead, Mizpah and Mahanaim) reveals that at this point Jacob was apparently south of the river Jabbok, and that he had just sent his family across the river from south to north (which might suggest that he was sending them out of Esau's power). In that case the man who wrestled with him was preventing Jacob himself from retreating to the safety he sought, a safety that would mean refusing God's command to return to the land of promise. However normally the story is read rather differently, with the struggle to cross the river in some way marking Jacob's entry to Canaan. It is just possible that at some point in the story's history, it was the Jordan, rather than the river Jabbok that was the scene of the contest (see 32.10), and that the location was later transferred to the Jabbok (perhaps by those who were not personally acquainted with the geography of the region) because of the close bond the name expressed both with the name of Jacob and the action of wrestling.

Rembrandt painted a picture of the scene. In it Jacob is held by the wrestler in such a way that his head is gradually being forced round so that he is compelled to look his opponent in the face. He will not be allowed to avoid confronting his past, his present and his future.

*He struck him . . . so that Jacob's hip was dislocated*: Jacob was called Jacob because of the link made to the word 'heel' (25.26) but if one delves deeper in the Hebrew language, the word 'heel' itself may derive from a root that means 'curved' or 'not straight'. Is that what is happening here? In dislocating Jacob's hip, is the night wrestler making visible what Jacob really always has been – crooked, rather than straight?

Touch had been the primary means by which Jacob had deceived his father Isaac. So it is appropriate that his wounding comes by this stranger's touch.

*'I will not let you go unless you bless me.'*: The night wrestler's anxiety to disappear before daybreak is the point where this story comes closest to the world of fairy tales. It is reminiscent of the traditional troll who will be changed into stone by sunlight. Jacob's response reminds us how his desire to be blessed had governed his whole life. But unlike the blessing which he had obtained from Isaac by trickery, this blessing will be legitimately won by arduous struggle. But before the blessing can be bestowed there is a question . . .

*'What is your name?' 'Jacob,' he answered*: As with other significant narratives in Genesis the episode appears to be structured so that it pulls the reader into its centre, in other words, to this question and answer and the night wrestler's further response. The whole of Jacob's past life has been leading up to this question – once before, years ago, he had been asked a very similar one by his father Isaac, and he had given a fraudulent response, claiming to be his brother Esau (27.18–19). The last 20 years of his life have been shadowed by that lie. This time the truth is dragged out of him. As Fokkelman points out, in acknowledging that he is called Jacob, he is effectively making a confession of guilt, for he has named himself as 'Fraud', the intrinsic meaning of the word Jacob (27.36).[9] It is only when this has been publicly stated, that his healing and blessing can begin.

*Your name shall no longer be Jacob but Israel*: Like Abraham Jacob's name is to be changed as a sign of his new relationship with God. But this name change means both more – and less – than the earlier one.

It is more because the new name, and the circumstances in which it came about, somehow describe not only an individual, but a whole people, and the history of their struggling relationship with God. It is less because Jacob cannot entirely leave his old name behind: both in the later chapters of Genesis and in the history of the people for whom he will be the eponymous ancestor, this name Jacob will continue to be used alongside that of Israel. As Paul was to observe centuries later, the 'old man' can never be wholly vanquished (Rom. 7.15–20).

The name 'Israel' is interpreted by the text itself as meaning 'the one who strives (Hebrew: *sarah*) with God (*'el'*), although originally the name probably meant rather 'God strives'. Perhaps there is a deliberate ambiguity: for the story suggests that now the destinies of God and his people are inextricably interwoven.

Is this renaming the blessing that Jacob has sought? This may be what we are supposed to assume. For the content of the bald statement *he gave him his blessing there* is not otherwise spelt out. To become Israel rather than Jacob is a blessing, albeit a hazardous one. It means that Jacob is now expressing in his very name, God's promise 'I will be with you', but, as he has just discovered, that too can be a dangerous promise. The moment of his life when God is most with him is this wounding and lengthy struggle.

*Why do you ask my name?*: Ultimately the relationship between Jacob and the divine wrestler is not and cannot be a completely equal one, in spite of Jacob's prodigious strength. The divine wrestler preserves a difference and distinction: Jacob does not learn the name of his opponent in spite of being forced to reveal his own. God will not be revealed as Yhwh, until he himself chooses to make that revelation (Exod. 3.14) (see further comments in Theological Reflections on p. 225).

*I have seen God face to face*: Jacob's exclamation echoes the earlier relief of Hagar (16.13). A few others in Israel's later history will 'see' God, but they will always be aware it is a dangerous favour (Exod. 33.20; Judg. 13.22; Isa. 6.5). The 'seeing' that had once seemed so natural to Abraham will become an exceptional privilege, until it is re-gifted in the pages of the New Testament (John 1.14, 18). It is no accident that when God is seen by a Moses or Isaiah he is closely associated with fire. 'God has a terrible double aspect, a sea of grace is met by a seething lake of fire.'[10] Jacob is the first person in biblical spirituality to discover God as a 'fearful yet fascinating mystery'.

*My life is spared*: Earlier in the chapter (32.11) Jacob had prayed, *Save me*. The storyteller suggests that now his prayer has been answered.

But this has happened by his willingness to participate in a dangerous struggle with God, for the word *spared* comes from the same Hebrew verb that was earlier translated as 'save'. The struggle had spared – and saved – him.

*The sun rose as Jacob passed through Penuel, limping because of his hip*: The sun that set upon Jacob all those years before at Bethel as he journeyed towards exile has now finally risen upon him again as he becomes a new person, with a new name and a new life. With his limp he now walks 'crookedly', but is able to look his brother Esau straight in the eye as he meets him at last.

*The Israelites do not eat the sinew that is on the hollow of the thigh*: This is one of the few occasions when the author of Genesis steps back from the story to address his readers directly, here linking a common practice to these shattering events at Penuel. It is also the first time *Israelites* have ever been mentioned, an appropriate point to introduce them just after their eponymous ancestor has himself been named Israel.

**33.1–11** *Jacob looked up and there was Esau*: Whenever the Hebrew expression underlying 'looked up' has been used before the sight to be seen has always been important, sometimes miraculous, or at least directly prompted by God (e.g. 13.14; 22.13; 31.10). No less is true here. Jacob had not seen his brother for two decades, but now he was going to be enabled to see him in a new light.

*He divided the children*: By placing Joseph and Rachel at the rear he was offering them the place of greatest safety. The favouritism which will divide his family during the story of Joseph is being foreshadowed.

*He himself went on ahead ... bowing low to the ground seven times*: Having seen the 'face of God' Jacob has ceased to be a 'behind' person (see comments on p. 201). He now goes *ahead* or 'before' to greet Esau. In the blessing that had been stolen from Esau, Jacob had been promised that his *mother's sons would bow down* to him. That he himself, as well as his descendants (33.6, 7), should now bow down to Esau not once, but seven times, is ironic retribution being exacted from him.

*Esau ran to meet him*: The spontaneity of Esau's generous welcome still contrasts with Jacob's more formal responses. Throughout the episode it is Esau alone who addresses Jacob as *my brother* (33.9). That intimate endearment is never reciprocated by Jacob, who insists, even after their reconciliation, on addressing Esau as *my lord*. The depiction of Esau's generosity is reminiscent of the father's welcome to the younger son in the Parable of the Prodigal Son (Luke 15.20). This is hardly surprising for the Parable itself seems to draw on the story of Jacob and Esau for its colouring. But in terms of that parable Esau is playing a double role – he is both the elder brother and the father. Jacob's words in 33.10 will express this 'dual' significance of Esau's position.

After the violent wrestling of the previous incident, as well as the 'sparring match' Jacob and Esau have experienced since their shared days in the womb, this loving, rather than brutal, embrace is all the more unexpected.

The verbal playing on the Hebrew letters *hn* that dominated the previous chapter now suddenly sparkles into life again, almost like a firework display.

It includes:

> *The children who God has graciously [hanan] given* (v. 5)
> *That company (mahaneh) of yours* (v. 8)
> *It was meant to win favour (hen)* (v. 8)
> *If I have won your favour (hen)* (v. 10)
> *Accept, I pray, this gift (minhah)* (v. 10)
> *God has been gracious to me (hanan)* (v. 11)

A clear connection is being made between the graciousness Jacob now perceives he has received from God's hand, and his desire to show graciousness to and receive it from Esau.

*I come into your presence as into that of a god*: The connection is made even more explicit as the writer digs deep into the word *panim* once more, to express the profound climax of these two chapters. Once again a literal translation is helpful: 'for I have seen your face like seeing the face of God'. Now we glimpse another meaning of that dangerous divine encounter: there was indeed a connection between that strange wrestler and Esau. There are rabbinic legends that suggest the wrestler was the guardian angel of Esau, and those legends are not so far off the mark. At the very least Jacob's experience has changed the way that he looks at Esau, perhaps he has even begun to understand the truth that it is only by loving our brothers and sisters that we can begin to see and love God (1 John 4.12). In overcoming, for a brief moment, the duality between God and humanity, the division between human beings themselves is also overcome. And in becoming one with his brother, perhaps at last Jacob has become whole. Has he finally earned the epithet *tam* with which he was credited in 25.27 (see p. 164)?

*Accept this gift which I bring*: The REB, like other English translations, inevitably has to conceal the way Jacob's vocabulary has shifted. Up till now the word 'gift' has been translating *minhah*, which as we suggested (see notes on 32.13, p. 201) conveys the notion of tribute, or an offering for a god. It is an appropriate present therefore for Jacob to proffer as he comes *into [Esau's] presence as into that of a god*. But when *gift* reappears in 33.11 it is now translating *berakah*, more usually translated as 'blessing', that word which Jacob stole from Esau 20 years ago (27.35). Its use at this point seems to suggest that at last Jacob is restoring the cheated blessing to his brother. He now had no need of it, for he now possessed another blessing that he had won for himself by struggle rather than deceit. Yet by this time we have known Jacob too long not to wonder even here at possible duplicity. To shift from *minhah* to *berakah* is also to shift the power relations, for the one is offered by inferior to superior, the other by superior to inferior. No longer is Jacob's language awestruck by terror of Esau: if he can stand as equal with God, he can stand at least as equal with this brother who has received him in God's own way. And though he may offer to return the blessing to Esau, it is noticeable that he never explicitly restores the birthright.

33.12–20 *Esau said . . . but Jacob answered*: The brief moment of complete unity soon passes, even though a real reconciliation has been accomplished. It is clear that Jacob never intended to follow Esau to Seir, his destination was always going to be the land of promise. Was the reason for his polite dissembling to preserve face for Esau, or was he still afraid of him and the military escort that his brother was proposing? There is quite a lot of the 'behind' Jacob still around in his suggestion! And as Robert Alter points out,[11] in Hebrew, the very last word Jacob addresses to his brother is *my lord*!

*That day*: The phrase is employed to suggest a key moment in the history of God's dealing with his people. It is a time when Esau makes his choice – and so does Jacob.

At Succoth Jacob *built himself a house and made shelters for his cattle*. This is a signal that the long period of wandering for Jacob, and his ancestors before him, has come to an end. God's promise of permanence is finally coming to fruition. This is the first time one of the patriarchs explicitly builds a house (though see 27.15). Now even the cattle get *shelters* (Hebrew: *sukkot*) constructed for them!

*Jacob arrived safely at the town of Shechem in Canaan*: The comment sits uneasily with what has just gone before it. It suggests that having built his house at Succoth, Jacob immediately ups sticks and travels to Shechem. Of course in doing so, he crosses the important theological boundary of the River Jordan; Succoth is to the east of the river, Shechem to the west. So his purchase of land here for the price of a *hundred sheep* is another important signal (compare Gen. 23) that he and his family are now being rooted in the land of promise. But in view of what will shortly happen, for how long?

*Jacob arrived safely*: The word translated *safely* comes from the same Hebrew root as *shalom*. Its use here suggests that this arrival fulfils the promise made in 28.21. Ironically however it is also related to a word that will appear in 34.21. *These men are friendly (shelemim)*. As it turns out that will be far from the case!

*He erected an altar there and called it El-elohey-israel*: The name of this altar 'God, the god of Israel' sums up both Jacob's own experience at Penuel, and the destiny that his father and grandfather have been moving towards.

## A troublesome brood
34.1–31

With Gen. 34 we have reached an uncomfortable chapter, both theologically and in terms of its position within Genesis. The young children who need protection in Gen. 32—33 have suddenly grown up and start taking the law into their own hands. Is Gen. 34 a later addition to the body of the book, perhaps partly prompted by the need to explain Jacob's words to Simeon and Levi in 49.5? On the other hand, it does seem to reflect ancient traditions about Shechem, which consistently portray the city both as a key location for the establishment of Israel as a political and national entity (Josh. 24) and also as the site of attempts by groups of Israelites and Canaanites to unite together in marriage and in covenant (see Josh. 24; Judg. 9).

It is however also worth noting that the issue of intermarriage between Jews and others also arose in the region of Shechem during the post-exilic period, and is one factor behind the rise of the Samaritans. It is intriguing that the writer of Ben Sira refers to *the senseless folk that live at Shechem* (Sir. 50.26), since foolishness is a motif that runs through Gen. 34. Jewish attitudes to the Samaritans may be reflected in this story.

It is notable that God does not appear in this chapter at all, in spite of the brothers' apparent concern for the religious nicety of circumcision (34.14).

34.1–12  *Dinah, the daughter whom Leah had borne to Jacob*: In this description Dinah is not only separated from Jacob by eight words, but also by an emotional gulf. She is the daughter of his less favoured wife, whose name had no explanation attached to it at birth, and who didn't count when the family crossed the river (32.22). She had apparently received no paternal concern up till now, and she will receive none in this story.

*Shechem, son of Hamor the Hivite, the local prince, saw her*: The use of the name Shechem, identical to the name of the city, at this point, is a clue that we have here a tale that is as much about the political and social relationships between two peoples as it is about Jacob's own family. From the point when Jacob is named Israel (32.28) the story of Genesis begins to shift its focus towards the national history of the people Israel, as tribes and as a nation.

As for Shechem's father, his name Hamor means 'ass' or 'donkey' and it was as uncomplimentary a label then as it is now. As the episode develops it is clear that he is a bit of one!

*Hivite*: One of the terms used to describe the original Canaanite inhabitants of the land (see Gen. 10.17).

*He took her*: Apparently he then raped her, although the Hebrew is more ambiguous than the translation suggests. But it is immediately made clear that he had a real affection for Dinah: *deeply attached* recalls the language used of husband and wife in 2.24, *loved* had previously described the relationship between Isaac and Rebecca.

The verb translated *violated* is actually *'anah*, which is elsewhere used when, for example, Sarah ill-treated Hagar 16.6. Clearly it does have a wider range of meaning than 'rape'. Lyn Bechtel in a thought-provoking article, 'What if Dinah is not raped?'[12] argues that in 34.2 it should be translated 'humiliated', not necessary implying that she was forced to have a sexual relationship with Shechem, but that by choosing to have such a relationship with someone outside her clan/family she was humiliated and defiled in the eyes of her brothers. I well remember a railway journey in 1979 along the banks of the river Euphrates in Syria. Travelling with my husband (an Anglican priest) we met and started talking to an Assyrian Christian from north-east Syria. On discovering that we were fellow Christians he started confiding his family problems to us. Apparently he had had a sister who had chosen to marry a Muslim. In the eyes of her birth family this had brought shame upon her and her kin. So, our travelling companion proudly informed us, he himself took a gun and shot both his sister and her husband dead. For this double murder he was put in prison, but fortunately (from his perspective) his religious community considered that he had performed an honourable deed so they paid money and he was soon released. The story of Dinah sprang to mind as he related this. Certainly Dinah's tale focuses more on her family's sense of defilement than it does upon Dinah's individual feelings.

*Jacob . . . held his peace*: Clearly inertia had its advantages, in view of Jacob's precarious situation with his sons away from home, but his lack of concern for his daughter is hardly impressive. It is notable that Jacob does not speak at all throughout the episode until 34.30.

*Jacob's sons . . . were distressed*: Jacob's response contrasts with that of his sons. The same verb was used in 6.6 to picture God's distress and grief before the flood. Something cataclysmic may happen here too!

*Shechem had done what the Israelites hold to be an intolerable outrage*: Here the narrator is clearly stepping back and giving us a later perspective on the story. The fact that the words echo those used by Tamar, daughter of David, as she is raped by her brother Amnon (2 Sam. 13.12) may suggest a literary link between the two incidents.

*Let us ally ourselves in marriage*: The eagerness of both Hamor and Shechem to resolve the issue with appropriate decorum is emphasised as well as Shechem's continuing affection for Dinah. On the face of it the suggestion is very conciliatory, and advantageous to Jacob's family. An opportunity is being offered to this group of semi-nomadic travellers to become part of a settled society, with the economic and security advantages that would bring. Is this even perhaps the way that God's promise of land to Jacob can be fulfilled? The only problem is that Deut. 7.3–6 forcefully prohibits exactly what Hamor suggests!

34.13–31    *Jacob's sons replied to Shechem . . . deceitfully*: Like father, like sons. The identical word was used to describe Jacob's own earlier deception of Isaac. Like him these sons are now going to act a bit like snakes in the grass! (see comments on 27.35, p. 177).

*We cannot give our sister to a man who is uncircumcised*: Although no direct reference is made to the command to Abraham in 17.10–14, the assumption that circumcision is the sign of God's covenant with Abraham's descendants seems to underlie the brothers' demand. If the Shechemites agree to be circumcised *and become one people* with Jacob's descendants, effectively becoming one religious as well as ethnic community, then God's promises of land and descendants will no longer be threatened. The situation presupposed by Deut. 7 would no longer apply. Awareness that circumcision was originally a ritual of puberty and marriage (rather than infancy) seems to be indicated here.

*The young man, who was held in respect*: The good qualities of Shechem are emphasised at several points in the story.

*These men are friendly to us*: How far can one be deceived! The sentence reuses a Hebrew root *shalam*, here translated *friendly* which appeared earlier when Jacob arrived *safely* at Shechem (33.18). A related word was employed to describe how Jacob's father Isaac lived peaceably (26.29, 31) with other non-Israelites. So up till now the stories of the patriarchs have stressed how they sought to live in harmony with the peoples of the land: Hamor's confidence is not unreasonable, even if naïve. In 'selling' the potentially uncomfortable proposal to their people Hamor and Shechem inevitably emphasise the eventual benefit *all their chattels will then be ours.* That does not speak of an equal future between the two parties. Perhaps neither side in this discussion is being totally honest.

The attack which follows, instigated by Simeon and Levi, is portrayed in terms that accentuate its treachery and totality. Hoped for ethnic unity swiftly becomes the Bible's first example of ethnic cleansing. It is also the first time in Genesis that the prohibition of murder after the flood (9.6) has been contravened.

*Jacob said to Simeon and Levi, 'You have brought trouble on me.'*: Finally Jacob speaks, but words that smack of cowardice and self-interest. This is a break between two epochs, not simply two generations. During this episode the balance of power has shifted: Jacob is no longer pictured as devious son, clever nephew, wily brother, fought over husband, but as a father, and a not very competent one at that! The time of patriarchal coexistence is drawing to a close, the days of nationalist conquest are dawning.

This story has been frustrating to read because the narrator never quite allows us to decide where our sympathies should lie, yet this moral ambiguity is also its strength. The story goes out of its way to elicit some understanding for Shechem in spite of the apparent brutal action with which he set events in motion. It allows us to feel that Simeon and Levi's response is disproportionate, even if, at first sight, it tallies with the viewpoint regarding non-Israelites enjoined by Deut. 7. Surely, shouldn't the willingness of Hamor and his family to undergo circumcision have counted for something, so that the demands of Deuteronomy no longer apply to the situation? And as for Jacob, is he to be praised for his seeming desire for moderation, or damned for his uncaring insouciance regarding his daughter? Dinah, alone, is unambiguously a victim, a voiceless one, and after this story she will undoubtedly remain alone for the rest of her life. The family honour may have been restored by her brothers' action but her defilement – like a *common whore* – will endure in the eyes of her family.

## Deaths and births
### 35.1—36.43

35.1–29  We now move into a series of short episodes, probably originating from a variety of hands, which seem to be drawn together to round off the story of Jacob. They remind us of the transitoriness of human life and death, set against the eternal nature of the promises of God.

*God said to Jacob, 'Go up now to Bethel'*: The comparative importance of Bethel as Jacob's religious goal is indicated by the expression *Go up*, which we see frequently in the Bible in relation to Jerusalem. These verses allude back at several points to God's earlier appearance to Jacob at Bethel (28.10–22) and Jacob's actions are an acknowledgement that God had carried out the promises he made then.

To mark this important religious moment a ritual of purification is introduced. The motif of purification in these verses contrasts with the theme of defilement which had pervaded the previous chapter. There are two aspects to this purification *put on fresh clothes* – the change of garments is a ritual used in several religions to suggest a decisive break with the past and to mark a new beginning (e.g. primitive Christian baptismal practice) – and *get rid of the foreign gods*. The idols referred to would presumably include the household gods brought by Rachel from her father's house, as well perhaps as the gods of the Shechemites which Jacob's family might have been attracted to during their stay there. Earrings were also buried: shaped as small figures of the gods. Josh. 24.14 also associates the site of Shechem with a decisive rejection of other gods. It is a symbolic statement that the family of Jacob are in the land, but not of it. Such ritual actions prepare the way for the new stage (with a new name) that is going to be offered at Bethel.

What has happened in the last chapter and now here reads almost like a commentary on Deut. 7.21–26.

*There he built an altar*: This is the first time that a patriarch has built an altar in response to a direct demand from God (35.1). Does God's next appearance to Jacob depend on the fact that he has followed this instruction?

*Rebecca's nurse Deborah died*: It is strange to learn of the death of a person whose name we previously did not know. It is also strange that Rebecca's nurse was travelling with Jacob! Probably Deborah's grave was a well-known site near Bethel, and the mention of Bethel has prompted this notice. However by referring to her burial the writer has framed the remaining incidents in this chapter within an awareness of human mortality: they begin with the death of Deborah and end with the death of Isaac.

In view of the desperate struggle through which Jacob acquired the name Israel in 32.22–32 it is strange and rather jarring to read in vv. 9–15 a repetition of the granting of this name, reported seemingly without any awareness of the previous occasion. These verses seem to conflate Jacob's earlier experiences at both Bethel (28.10–19) and Penuel (32.22–32). Presumably different literary sources play a part: but the presence of divergent accounts within Genesis reinforces the ambiguity of what it means to be Israel; it is both struggle (32.22–32) yet also, as here, freely given gift. It may also remind us, after Jacob's less than impressive performance at Shechem, that Israel needs to be reborn as Israel, again and again!

In spite of its not particularly dramatic context the oracle that follows delineates a key juncture in the structural progression of Genesis. Its language of fruitfulness marks it out as one of a sequence of oracles or blessings that reach back to creation (1.28), and the new world after the deluge (9.1). Its closest affinity is with the promise given when God's covenant is made with Abraham (17.6). It finally fulfils the hopes expressed when Isaac blessed Jacob in 28.1–5, echoing the language found there: *God Almighty* (28.3), fruitfulness (28.3), a host of nations (28.3), the gift of land (28.4), as well as the reference to Paddan-aram (28.5). It is telling that Isaac himself may have been blessed, but he did not directly receive a blessing by God named as God Almighty. Such a privilege is given only to the patriarchs who themselves have just been renamed (35.10; 17.5) and each time it marks a distinctive stage in God's relationship with this family. As with Abraham, the blessing of Jacob promises kingly offspring, and also extends the promise of the land beyond Jacob into the future time of his descendants. It is against these words that we need to measure the rest of this chapter.

*Jacob raised a sacred pillar of stone*: The detailed description of Jacob's cultic actions makes it clear that he is seeking to carry out scrupulously the promises he made at Bethel more than 20 years before (28.20–22).

Over the course of this chapter the relationship between God and humanity has subtly shifted. We are not told the context in which Abraham received the blessing of God Almighty, unless perhaps it was a lunch party (see comments on 17.1–22). But Jacob's blessing had apparently happened at a place already sacred, and after he and his family had undertaken a ritual act of purification. In Israel's future, holy places and holy things will increasingly become the channel for divine–human association.

*Rachel went into labour*: The midwife's words during this labour, *this is another son for you* echo Rachel's own earlier hopes when Joseph was born (30.24). But with ironic tragedy the birth also recalls Rachel's angry cry from the time of her infertility: *Give me sons, or I shall die!* (30.1) At last she has indeed been given sons by Jacob, but it is also the last moment of her life. Rachel, who could not bear to leave her ancient gods behind in Mesopotamia, is herself buried, just after these gods have been buried by Jacob in order to begin his new life in Canaan.

So, Benjamin is born in pain and grief, and from that originates the name Ben-oni, 'Son of My Grief', that Rachel sought to give him. Intriguingly years earlier her sister Leah had used the same word '*oni*, there translated 'humiliation', when she celebrated the birth of her first son, Reuben: *The LORD has seen my humiliation* (29.32). The births of Jacob's children, of Israel, are encircled by pain and suffering: an apparent foreshadowing, for the word '*oni* will be used many times during their slavery in Egypt.

*But his father called him Benjamin*: For all his love for Rachel Jacob would not fulfil her dying wish. To do so would have condemned this youngest child to an 'unlucky' future. He tried to avert this by renaming the boy. *yamin* means 'right (hand)', and as in many cultures, the 'right' is associated with prosperity. But it also suggested the special place Benjamin held in his father's affections: he was his 'right-hand boy'!

*Rachel died and was buried by the side of the road to Ephrathah, that is Bethlehem*: There is geographical confusion apparent. Ephrathah was a small town in the territory later linked with the tribe of Benjamin, a few miles north of Jerusalem, not far from Bethel and Ramah. According to 1 Sam. 10.2 this was where Rachel's tomb was to be found. However, possibly under Judaean pressure, a competing site for Rachel's tomb, near Bethlehem, grew up (multiple and competing sites for 'holy places' is a feature not restricted to the modern Holy Land!), and at some point a gloss associating Bethlehem and Ephrathah was added to the text.

Originally and appropriately it seems that Benjamin was born and Rachel died in the territory of the tribe of Benjamin. In Israelite history Benjaminite territory was to be the buffer between the northern tribes and Judah, and therefore perhaps the 'heart' of Israel.

And in view of its place within Christian tradition as the birthplace of Jesus Christ it is also telling that the first time Bethlehem is mentioned in the Bible it is as a place of birth – and death.

*Reuben lay with his father's concubine*: This is an action that is explicitly prohibited by Deut. 22.30. As a result of it Reuben lost the prerogatives of the first-born (49.3–4). Why did Reuben do this? Was it the birth of Benjamin, named as his father's 'right-hand' boy, a position that Reuben as the eldest would have considered his by right, that finally provoked him to take revenge for the humiliation his mother Leah had suffered over decades? Or perhaps it is an attempt to seize power in the family from his ageing father: in the story of David the seizure of power by Absalom is accompanied by his expropriation of his father's concubines (2 Sam. 16.20–22).

*The sons of Jacob were twelve*: The 'fruitfulness' promised in 35.11 is now becoming an actuality, after two generations in which family survival seemed tenuous. The tradition preserved in these verses (which come from the same hand as 35.9–12) seems to conflict with 35.16–18 by suggesting that Benjamin too was born in Paddan-aram.

*Jacob came to his father Isaac at Mamre*: Finally Jacob has come home to his *father's house* as he had prayed to do in 28.21.

*Isaac . . . died . . . and his sons Esau and Jacob buried him*: Isaac's age when he died as the oldest of the patriarchs suggests the blessed equilibrium that marked out his life. That his burial was organised by his two sons acting as one, reinforces a sense of peace and reconciliation. Esau is even listed first: a sign that in spite of Jacob's purchase of Esau's first-born rights, Esau still had a valued place in the family.

36.1–43 *This is an account of the descendants of Esau, that is Edom*: The impression given by 35.29 is reinforced by this whole chapter. Introduced by the ninth example in Genesis of the *toledot* formula (36.1, repeated 36.9), it is the longest unbroken section containing genealogical information in the entire book.

There are four distinct sections:

1. A list of Esau's wives and sons, to which is appended a notice about Esau's migration to Seir (36.1–8).
2. A list giving details about the families of Esau's sons, in two parallel forms (36.10–14, 15–19).
3. A list giving the genealogy of Seir the Horite *the original inhabitants of the land*. i.e. before Esau moved there (36.20–30).
4. An ancient king-list of Edom, which shows an awareness that the institution of kingship developed in Edom centuries before it arose among the Israelites (36.31– 43).

Taken as a whole they suggest considerable interest by the writers of Genesis in the situation of the Edomites, as well as a willingness to make use of Edomite sources, which must have helped in garnering at least some of the information. The 'untidiness' of the lists is suggestive of authenticity. At points there are discrepancies, for example the names and parentage of Esau's wives, and overlap with the family of Ishmael. A number of names are listed that appear elsewhere in the Old Testament, for example there is an Eliphaz who is a friend of Job (Job 2.11) and a Reuel who is described as the father-in-law of Moses (Exod. 2.18). Though we cannot be sure that Gen. 36 is identifying the two sons of Esau mentioned in 36.10 with these figures, the commonality of names reminds us that there were a number of different tribes and nations (e.g. Edomites, Midianites, Ishmaelites, etc.), broadly speaking all linked to the geographical area of north-west Arabia, who seem to have overlapped in the Old Testament retelling of history.

In 36.12 *Amalek* is almost certainly intended to be seen as the eponymous ancestor of the Amalekites. The Old Testament reserves a special vitriol for the Amalekites (e.g. 1 Sam. 15.18).

*Seir the Horite* (36.20): Horite probably means 'cave-dweller'. A careful reading of the lists indicates that this family, the indigenous people of Edom, intermarried at several points with Esau's descendants.

The particular information that *Anah . . . found hot springs in the wilderness* (36.24), reminds us how important water resources were in a region as arid as Edom.

Taken as a whole the lists of names suggest an awareness of an ongoing relationship between the Edomites and the descendants of Jacob throughout different epochs of history. At times there was rapprochement, at other moments, vicious hostility. In part this would have been dictated by the political currents that eddied round the ancient Middle East, and also by internal power politics in the Judaean capital of Jerusalem or Edomite capital of Diban.

Esau's departure from Jacob and migration to Edom is, in this chapter, portrayed in terms that are amicable. The brothers may not be able to live close together, but this is because of their mutual prosperity, and they finally part fraternally on good terms. The Old Testament is aware that there is a 'special relationship' with Edom: *Do not regard an Edomite as an abomination, for he is your own kin* (Deut. 23.7).

That there were kings in Edom *before there were kings in Israel* (36.31) is perhaps a sharp reminder that, blessing or no blessing, the family of Esau has prospered more speedily than the family of his brother Jacob. But the fact that, in this chapter, Esau has so clearly become the nation Edom, prepares us for 37—50, during which the sons of Jacob will overtly become the nation Israel.

# Theological reflections

## 1. The setting

If the Abraham cycle appears to have its geographical centre in the south of Canaan, around Hebron and Mamre, the Jacob stories seem to originate in the north, with their focus on Bethel and Shechem. Unlike the figure of Abraham, who does not figure prominently in texts that are clearly pre-exilic, the name of Jacob appears in prophetic materials that stem from the time of the monarchy. A particularly interesting example comes in Hos. 12.2–4, which suggests that several of the tales about Jacob circulated widely for some centuries before they evolved into the connected narrative we find in Gen. 25—35. A tradition about Jacob also surfaces in Jer. 9.4, while Jer. 31.15 apparently knows of a tragic event associated with Rachel. There are also texts from pre-exilic (as well as later) times that seem to be fully aware of Jacob's traditional hostility with Esau (e.g. Obadiah). In these passages the name 'Jacob' is sometimes used to refer to the patriarch himself, and sometimes to the people and nation Israel. For example, 'Jacob' appears frequently in poetic texts in parallelism to 'Israel' (e.g. Jer. 31.7; Isa. 43.1). The two different usages inform and explicate each other, so that the people called 'Jacob' are frequently painted with the character traits of their ancestor, while the stories of the ancestor clearly reflect the historical experience the nation Jacob/Israel is going through. Israelites in exile, as well as more recent readers, could readily identify with Jacob, whose exile and restoration mirrored their own. It is what gives these stories their particular compelling quality: however unattractive Jacob may be as a person, we can discover through him what it means for us too to wrestle with God and to rediscover our brothers and sisters with new eyes.

The northern geographical references in these stories suggest that the figure of Jacob was particularly associated with the northern kingdom during the period of the divided monarchy. This fits with the reality that 'Israel' was primarily a designation adopted by the northern kingdom. The major shrine of the northern kingdom was Bethel (1 Kgs 12.32), while Penuel (1 Kgs 12.25) and Shechem (1 Kgs 12.25) both had strategic roles in the history of this kingdom. All three sites figure prominently in the stories of Jacob. After the fall of the northern kingdom in 722BC, it is likely that the Jacob traditions became the common heritage of the community centred on Jerusalem, which regarded itself as the heir of 'Israel'.

The positive role allotted in Genesis to these northern locations, particularly Bethel, contrasts with its consistently negative presentation in 1–2 Kings, and various prophetic texts. Perhaps it suggests that although the Jacob cycle has reached us via post-exilic Judaean spectacles, the traditional tales of Jacob, firmly rooted in oral tradition over several centuries, had for so long associated his name with Bethel that not to link Jacob's experience with this particular sanctuary was unthinkable.

It may also be that in spite of the destruction of the sanctuary at Bethel by King Josiah of Judah (2 Kgs 23.15–18), Bethel remained more important in the post-exilic period than the traditional 'history' of Israel allowed for and actually continued as an important religious site for several further centuries. This tallies with the current re-analysis of the history of the region. Certainly though Genesis in its final form is a post-exilic production it is less dominated by a pro-Jerusalem bias than some other parts of the Old Testament.

## 2. An immoral God?

One of the striking, and refreshing, features of the Old Testament tradition is the willingness of 'Israel' to identify itself with an ancestor whose morality seems, to our eyes at least, distinctly dubious. Those, prophets and others, who spoke to the Israel of their day had no illusions about the human frailties of their audience. Even though they regarded Israel/Jacob as having a particular role to play within God's purposes, it was a task that had to be undertaken by fallible human beings (see e.g. Isa. 42.19). For such a 'chosen people' Jacob was the ideal chosen ancestor. Jacob's devious character was an inheritance for his descendants, just as much as the blessing he had been granted by God (e.g. Mal. 3.6–7).

Clearly it would be inappropriate to try and use (as some Christian traditions are inclined to attempt) Jacob as a moral exemplar. This stricture applies to all the patriarchs. They are not role models for behaviour in the twenty-first century. But at the same time the Jacob stories do raise, in a different form from that of the Book of Job, the question of the morality or immorality of God. Does God reward trickery and deception? Is this how God wants his people to operate – 'smoothly', just as Jacob did?

One of the valuable aspects of the Jacob cycle is the way it subtly addresses questions about morality without labouring the point. Jacob's deception of his father, and claim of the right that belonged to the first-born, is confronted by a similar deception that he himself experiences at the hands of Laban, when Laban insists on the rights of his first-born daughter. It is a form of just retribution. Indeed in the section that explores the relationship of Jacob and Laban, one trick is piled on top of another – until finally Jacob unwittingly invokes a death sentence on the then unknown thief of Laban's household gods – and Rachel's premature death seems to be an exacting of the penalty, in part vicariously, for the whole cycle of deception into which she has been caught up. The irony of the stories is a powerful moral tool: we feel a sense of satisfaction that Jacob who, as a result of the theft of the blessing, has been promised that his brother would 'bow down' (27.29) to him, should before his story is through end up bowing low to his brother – not once but seven times! (33.3).

This intricate and sometimes humorous interweaving that melds the cycle together creates the impression that wrongdoing does not remain unpunished. Justice may be slow, but its day will come. But conversely, God continues to work with and through imperfect human beings and imperfection is not a pre-emptive disqualification for having a starring role in the working out of God's purposes. Such a message was, of course, critically important to those in Babylonian exile, battered by the condemnations issued by the pre-exilic prophets, and having come to understand their exile as divine punishment. God could still work with them, as he had worked with their ancestor Jacob, and their ongoing struggle for life and faith in the middle of adversity is not only retribution but also an opportunity for growth, since in the struggle is also the blessing (32.29).

## 3. An elusive God-with-us

Just as interaction on the human plane between Jacob, Esau and Laban helps to foster a process of moral development in Gen. 25—36, so also the relationship between human beings and God is matured.

God does not appear or speak directly in every chapter. But new ways for relating to him begin to be explored. A family plagued by infertility can *seek guidance* of him through an oracle (25.22); God speaks in dreams to both Jacob and Laban (31.11, 24); God can be accessed via religious and ritual actions, such as tithing (28.22), anointing (28.18; 35.14), formal prayer (32.9–12), the erection of sacred pillars (28.22; 35.14) and an offering (35.14). There is the beginning of formality in relating to God. One might say that God spoke with Abraham as a man to his friend. That does not quite happen in the stories of Jacob. Was it on Mount Moriah that fear first became a necessary element of the divine–human relationship (22.12)? If so, Jacob lives at a time when God's gracious friendship with the family of Abraham has begun to be tinged with an element of fear.

It is interesting to notice how reticent the Jacob stories are about using the name 'Yhwh', which has previously expressed an intimacy between God and human beings. In fact the final time it appears in this cycle is in Jacob's prayer in 32.9, when Yhwh seems to be linked specifically with the land of Canaan and with the command to Jacob to return to it. The refusal of the night wrestler to disclose his name (32.29) seems to deny Jacob the right to use the name Yhwh during the rest of his life. In fact before Jacob dies in 49.33 the word Yhwh will only pass his lips once more, in his final blessing of his sons (49.18). And even here, it expresses future hope as much as a present relationship. Jacob's wives, particularly Leah, will use the name more freely in naming their sons. Perhaps this reflects a powerful link between Yhwh and creativity. Jacob's own preferred description for God seems to be 'the God of my father'. Does this title bring God near, within 'the family' or distance him – at one generation, so to speak? The ambiguity remains.

However the Jacob cycle also speaks of two major encounters with the divine, at Bethel and at Penuel, and these two passages, which stand like two matching structural pillars, holding together the stories of Jacob, have had an immense impact in developing our comprehension of God, both within the biblical tradition and more widely.

## The Ladder at Bethel

When we read of Jacob's experience at Bethel (28.10–22) we both enter and subvert a world of the ancient Middle East in which temples provided a meeting point for humanity and divinity. The heavenly and the earthly dwelling was symbolically connected in as visible a form as was possible. Perhaps the temple was on the highest hill in an area, perhaps it was designed in the form of a *ziggurat* as a man-made ramp between earth and heaven.

Jacob's experience at Bethel reflects this understanding. The ladder links the heavenly and earthly dwelling place of YHWH. Significantly the place is actually called Bethel, i.e. 'House of God', the very name suggesting that it is the archetype of a temple. The presence of YHWH standing by Jacob fulfils the purpose for which temples were built: so that worshippers could 'see' their deity and sense his protection. It is notable that the Hebrew word *maqom*, which has the basic meaning of 'place' and often refers specifically to a 'holy place', occurs six times in this section, though it is not fully apparent in the REB translation (28.11 (3 times), 16, 17, 19).

Yet at the same time the words spoken by YHWH challenge the *raison d'être* of a holy place. YHWH promises to be with Jacob *wherever you go*. Normally worshippers had to come to a specific holy building, a temple, to find their god: but this God assures Jacob that he can find him anywhere. This is a God who is not confined by a building or even a holy land. He will not be a god who is carried along in a caravan like a household idol. He will be Jacob's travelling companion – but on his own terms. Even here in this holy place YHWH has come to Jacob before he is invoked.

Centuries later, resonances of Jacob's vision are found in the Gospel of John. In John 1.51, after meeting Nathanael, whom he describes as *an Israelite worthy of the name* (probably an oblique allusion to Jacob) Jesus speaks of seeing *heaven wide open and God's angels ascending and descending upon the Son of Man*. As elsewhere in this Gospel (e.g. John 2.12–22) a holy place is apparently being declared redundant, because Jesus Christ fulfils in his own person the reason for its original existence, to be a meeting-place for God and human beings. It is on the Son of Man, rather than on the ground of Bethel that the ladder is to be set up. Yet the subversiveness of the author of John's Gospel may have been anticipated by those who composed Gen. 28, for even as the story of Jacob's ladder provides us with an aetiology for the well-known temple at Bethel, at the same moment it inspires us to leave that temple behind.

Though we may be able to discern this, it is doubtful that Jacob could, at least if we go by his actions on awakening. He behaves rather like the disciples who witnessed the transfiguration of Jesus. After seeing Jesus in this new light, their response was to seek to build three shelters on the mountain (Mark 9.5). They had failed to comprehend that the divine light could not be held captive in a place – however awesome – but could only be refracted via a person. Similarly Jacob after his dream seems unaware that the key to unlock the *gateway to heaven* that suddenly opened last night, may be found in himself rather than at the portals of Bethel's temple. But to become the gateway to heaven for others, their means of access to the divine, is a fearful vocation. It is more comfortable to tuck such a challenge safely away in a place that you will hope one day to come back to: to consecrate a shrine at Bethel (28.18), rather than yourself. There will come a day when Jacob will be ready to become the Israel of God, but that will only happen when another human person, his brother Esau, can become in turn for him a gateway to God (33.10).

It is interesting how Jacob's experience at Bethel accords with that of Moses in Exod. 33—34. A similar anxiety is expressed about the need for God to accompany his people on their travels: indeed, it is actually spelt out by Moses that unless God goes with them they cannot fully be his people (Exod. 33.16). And startlingly, Moses himself provides a dramatic illustration of what it might mean for a human being to become a gateway to heaven. He so loses himself in his concern for his people that he becomes the answer to his own prayer; his shining face as he comes down the mountain reflecting the glory of God to them. Perhaps it is not surprising that there should be this thematic link between the story of Jacob and the narrative of Exodus, for both probably assumed their basic shape in response to exilic anxieties about the possibility of presence in a strange land.

## The Wrestler at Penuel

Perhaps however the story of Jacob's divine encounter at Penuel is the one that speaks more directly to people today. Martin Buber perceived the episode of wrestling Jacob as a metaphor for a wrestling with life's existential questions by all of humanity. Our age has had to struggle with questions of God's goodness and the problem of evil on a massive scale, none more so than Jacob's spiritual heirs, adherents of the Jewish faith, as they have tried to respond to the challenge to faith thrown up by the Holocaust. What does it mean for Israel, God's people, to be honoured with the name Israel – the one that strives with God, and will not let God go in spite of the wounds inflicted by the lengthy struggle? Elie Wiesel, the great interpreter of his people's suffering during the Nazi era, puts it like this:

> Both were wounded: Jacob at the hip, the angel in his vanity. Yet they parted friends, or was it accomplices? Jacob accepted his aggressor's departure willingly; the latter, as if to thank him, made him a gift: a new name which for generations to come would symbolise eternal struggle and endurance, in more than one land, during more than one night.[13]

The episode by the river has had a profound effect also on Christian spirituality. The tradition of mystical theology expressed by the phrase 'the dark night of the soul' draws on this biblical episode for one of its roots. So too does the willingness of spiritual writers to recognise that when we engage in prayer we are entering into dangerous territory. Prayer is not always an entering into stillness, it can involve us in arguing with God, as Job did, or even, like Jacob, in wrestling with God and suffering life-changing wounds. Gerard Manley Hopkins summed it up by saying, 'battling with God is now my prayer,' while John Donne asked God to 'Batter my heart, three-person'd God'.

The story has also been viewed as a statement of our ambivalent attitude towards the presence of God: terrifying yet life-giving. This is expressed in the great Charles Wesley hymn: 'Come, O Thou Traveller unknown' which exults in the moment when Jacob is blessed by his adversary and is left to discover his new self:

> 'Tis Love! 'Tis Love! Thou diedst for me!
> I hear thy whisper in my heart;
> The morning breaks, the shadows flee,
> Pure universal love thou art;
> To me, to all, thy mercies move:
> Thy nature and thy name is Love.

Alluding to this hymn the Methodist writer J. Neville Ward concluded his classic book *The Use of Praying* as follows:

> Sometimes faith confidently and easily interprets experience as from God; sometimes only slowly and after much argument with itself and life. And sometimes it simply has to hold on, like the troubled wrestler by the dark river, trusting that when the light breaks it will appear that the imagined enemy was Love all the time.[14]

When we meet Aslan in C. S. Lewis's *The Lion, the Witch and the Wardrobe* we discover that he is definitely not a tame lion. 'Who said anything about safe? 'Course he isn't safe. But he's good. He's the King.'[15] Jacob makes a similar discovery about his divine opponent, as the story draws our attention to the untameability and elusiveness of God. That is a motif that permeates the Old Testament, and this episode is one of its foundation stones.

In looking for a theological centre to the Old Testament, Walther Zimmerli has drawn attention to the importance of the name of God, YHWH; both in terms of its meaning, and a reticence to disclose and use it at all. Zimmerli suggests that these two features help to emphasise the sovereign freedom of God, who refuses to be the puppet or plaything of humanity. In the culture of the Ancient Middle East the knowledge of someone's name granted power over them. It is notable that though Jacob is forced to reveal his name, and is rewarded with a new one, his opponent deflects Jacob's request for a similar revelation with the question *Why do you ask my name?* Though the antagonist may be held by Jacob he still refuses to surrender himself into Jacob's power. When the day finally arrives that YHWH will disclose his name, to Moses during the Exodus, the explanation associated with it, *I AM that I am* (Exod. 3.14) , will confer upon this God a quality of hiddenness, one who is known as unknown, and who chooses to be what he will be.

So ironically though Jacob was not granted knowledge of the name, he did indeed experience the reality of YHWH, as the elusive one, through this night encounter. By his refusal to be controlled, the divine opponent is giving expression to what his name actually signifies. It is interesting, how, from this point in Genesis the actual name YHWH is used only rarely in the text, yet at the same time the 'hidden' quality of God and his activity will become more apparent, particularly in the story of Joseph and his brothers. It seems that in this episode with Jacob God has been made known as YHWH in a fashion that is even more profound than his name.

Conversely, Jacob is granted a privilege that will be withheld from Moses. The literary tradition which emphasised how God's name was revealed to Moses, also suggests that Moses could not see God's face (Exod. 33.20). By contrast Gen. 32 suggests that Jacob did so (Gen. 32.30). Perhaps the dual grace of sight and name is too extravagant, and dangerous, to confer upon any one human being. It is dangerous for God as well as human beings. For the God who Jacob meets on that dark night is not only elusive but one who risks intimacy. Trevor Dennis has commented:

> It gives us a picture of an extraordinarily intimate God. This God has his hands on Jacob! The two of them are locked in struggle for hours on end! We have not seen God at such close quarters with a human being since the creation of the man and the woman in Eden. We will not see God at such very close quarters again in scripture. It tells of a God incarnate, for he meets with Jacob in the form of a 'man'.[16]

Speaking from within the Christian tradition one can suggest that this intimate God of Jacob foreshadows the intimate relationship which God will have with his prophets and his people, par excellence in Jeremiah. But as Jeremiah knows only too well (Jer. 8.21), intimacy leads to vulnerability and perhaps ultimately to suffering. For God to be with us costs God. There is a path that can be traced from Penuel to Golgotha. It is not only a Christian insight. Once again Elie Wiesel has dug deep into the meaning of this story:

> Jacob has just understood a fundamental truth: God is in man, even in suffering, even in misfortune, even in evil. God is everywhere. In every being, not only in the victim. God does not wait for man at the end of the road, the termination of exile; he accompanies him there. More than that: He is the road, He is the exile. God holds both ends of the rope, He is present in every extremity, He is every limit. He is part of Jacob as He is part of Esau.[17]

## 4. A vision of brotherhood

From the time that human beings left Eden what it is to be a brother is a topic that Genesis has revisited again and again. It is almost as if the writers are aware that if this could be got right, then the primal relationship between human beings and God can become what it was always intended to be. The theme has been explored through the stories of Cain and Abel, Ham and his brothers, Isaac and Ishmael. It also surfaces in the dealings between Abraham and Lot or Jacob and Laban, for the Hebrew word *'ah* which is normally translated as 'brother', is often used, as with Lot and Abraham, to define a looser relationship than that of siblings. It will, of course, be a motif that will dominate the story of Joseph and his brothers, and the briefer account of the sons of Judah. But nowhere in Genesis does 'brotherhood' get explored as seriously as in the story of Jacob. In part this is a reflection of the intimacy of the relationship between Jacob and Esau, not merely even full brothers, but actually twins sharing the same womb. The intensity of their relationship is what makes it particularly dangerous – as well as offering unparalleled opportunity. That this topic is a dominant motif in Gen. 25—36 is stressed by the way chapters 29—30 focus on the relationship of the two sisters, Rachel and Leah, almost as a counter-point to that of Jacob and Esau.

The topic attains its zenith in Gen. 32—33 in the interplay between Jacob's encounter with a divine antagonist, and his meeting the next morning with Esau, the brother whom he expects to meet as an antagonist, but whose graciousness surprises him. The wordplays make the connection crystal clear. 'Truly to see your face is like seeing the face of God – since you have received me with such favour' (33.10 NRSV translation). It is only if we are prepared to continue our struggle with God that we can see our 'brothers' in their true light, as God sees them. Conversely it is when we wrestle for a more authentic relationship with our brothers and sisters we discover that we are given God's blessing. Our relationship with God and that with our brothers belong together and woe betide us if we try to separate them. If we do our faith has ceased to be biblical. The author of 1 John expresses this in a vivid passage that may actually be alluding to the story of Jacob and Esau: *If [someone] does not love a fellow-Christian* [Note: 'fellow Christian' translates *adelphos*, i.e. brother] *whom he has seen, he is incapable of loving God whom he has not seen. We have this command from Christ: whoever loves God must love his fellow-Christian too* (1 John 4.20–21). Does not Jesus' Parable of the Elder and Younger Brother (Luke 15.10–32) which has probably been coloured by the Old Testament traditions of Jacob and Esau express something of this in pictorial form? There is a wonderful tale from Jewish tradition that exemplifies this:

Two brothers worked together on a family farm. One was

unmarried and the other married with children. They shared what
they grew equally as they always did, produce and profit. But one
day the single brother said to himself, 'You know, it's not right that
we should share the produce equally, and the profit too. After all
I'm all alone, just by myself and my needs are simple. But there is
my poor brother with a wife and all those children.'

So in the middle of the night he took a sack of grain from his
bin, crept over the field between their houses and dumped it in his
brother's bin. Meanwhile, unknown to him, his brother had the
same thought. He said to himself, 'It is not right that we should
share produce and profit equally. After all, I am married and I have
my wife to look after me and my children for years to come. But
my brother has no one to take care of his future.' So he too, in the
middle of the night, took to taking a sack of grain from his bin and
sneaking across the field to deposit it in his brother's. And both
were puzzled for years as to why their supply did not dwindle.

Well, one night it just so happened that they both set out for each
other's house at the same time. In the dark they bumped into each
other carrying their sacks. Each was startled, but then it slowly
dawned on them what was happening. They dropped their sacks
and embraced one another. Suddenly the dark sky lit up and a voice
from heaven spoke, 'Here at last is the place where I will build my
Temple. For where brothers meet in love, there my Presence shall
dwell.'[18]

But Jacob's dealings with Esau also impinge on relationships other
than those of blood kin, or even (as with 1 John) of members of the
same close knit religious community. Genesis itself encourages us to
realise this by the clear link made between Esau and the nation of
Edom.

The triangle of relationships between Jacob/Israel, the divine
wrestler and Esau/Edom appears to suggest that the vocation of Israel
is to wrestle both with God and with the world of national and political reality in which God's people found themselves. If Israel turns its
back on either a relationship with God or a relationship with the 'foreign nations' (symbolised by Esau/Edom) then it becomes less than
Israel. It is both a challenge to a glib secularism, and a statement that
biblical faith must be worked out in the world, rather than become a
flight from it. It is, and will be, a struggle. But only in the struggle will
be the blessing. That is the mystery of Israel.

Rabbinic tradition suggested that the divine figure with whom

Jacob wrestled was the guardian angel of the Edomite nation. It states an important truth. Our enemies, such as Edom historically became in the history of Israel, have their place in God's scheme, and their divine protectors: and we cannot deal with God without also dealing with them.

The question Jesus asked in Mark 3.33, 'Who is my brother?' was explored centuries earlier in Gen. 32—33, and a radical, almost shocking, answer was given to it.

It may well be that these reflections have some relevance to the current world of Middle Eastern politics and religion, and complement the earlier observations on Isaac and Ishmael (see p. 155). But if Christians choose to refer to themselves as 'a New Israel' (see Gal. 6.16) then the vocation of struggling both with God and God's world belongs no less to them. The story of struggling Jacob then stands in theological continuity with the great Parable of the Sheep and the Goats (Matthew 25.31–46), which makes it clear that the face of God's Christ is to be seen in the hungry and the alien. Genesis' great themes of human beings as the image (icon) of God and the struggle for brotherhood also come together in the moving words of the Arab Christian Palestinian writer Elias Chacour:

> The true icon is your neighbour, the human being who has been created in the image and with the likeness of God. How beautiful it is when our eyes are transfigured and we see that our neighbour is the icon of God, and that you, and you, and I – we are all the icons of God. How serious it is when we hate the image of God, whoever that may be, whether a Jew or a Palestinian. How serious it is when we cannot go and say, 'I am sorry about the icon of God who was hurt by my behaviour.' We all need to be transfigured so we can recognise the glory of God in one another.[19]

The Old Testament will never again wrestle quite so powerfully with this topic of brotherhood. It is as though it is too painful to do so. Human beings cannot bear so much reality. It is easier for Jacob to travel to Canaan and Esau to Edom, rather than live together face to face. But once on a dark night and a sunlit morning we were given a glimpse that we cannot ignore. This blessing will not be taken from us.

# The Story of Joseph and his Brothers
## 37.1—50.26

If people know only one story from the Old Testament it is likely to
be either Noah's flood or the tale of Joseph and his brothers, which is
going to unfold between chapters 37 and 50. This tale catches up and
reworks into a larger canvas the topic of family conflict and fraternal
strife that was first introduced in the primeval account of Cain and
Abel, and has been revisited several times since. In the story there
are woven together several of the perspectives that have appeared in
previous sagas: brotherly jealousy, fatherly favouritism, the elevation
of the younger, the almost-lost beloved son.

And yet this section of Genesis also has a character distinct from
any other in the book. It is a more cohesive and sustained narrative,
punctured only by a few episodes (e.g. Judah and Tamar, 38.1–30; the
vision of Jacob and the list of his descendants, 46.1–27; the Blessing
of Jacob, 49.1–27) that feel as though they have stepped out of chapters 12—36. The bulk of the material in Gen. 37—50 has an urbanity,
and an urban perspective, that marks it out from the earlier narrative
of Genesis. Its writer was a consummate storyteller, who employed
subtle literary and psychological techniques. The description of it as
a 'novella' is apt. The chapters are certainly composed in an awareness of what has gone before, and detailed cross-references are made
to earlier stories, vocabulary and themes. But there is substantial involvement of different, and probably later, hands from those responsible for 12—36. It may be that those episodes (examples given above),
which currently 'jar' in 37—50, were part of an original ending which
has now been displaced by the lengthy tale we now have which so
overtly focuses on Joseph.

Although Joseph is a name known in pre-exilic Israel as a designation for a group of the northern tribes, 'the house of Joseph', including
Manasseh and Ephraim, there is little evidence (Ps. 105.16–22 is an
exception) in the rest of the Old Testament outside Genesis that a story
of Joseph's rise to power in Egypt was well known. In fact the interest

in Joseph seems often to have centred on his bones! It raises the question as to whether the development of the story of Joseph in the form in which we now have it in Genesis happened after most of the rest of Genesis was already composed – perhaps in the period when the Ptolemies of Egypt ruled Palestine (323–200 BC). It is interesting that there was an infamous Jewish tax-gatherer called 'Joseph the Tobiad' who rose high in the administration in Egypt during this period and it is tempting to wonder if there could be some link. The main body of the 'Praise of the Ancestors' given in Sir. 44.1—49.13 does not include Joseph, and moves straight from Jacob to Moses (Sir. 45.1). Joseph does appear in Ben Sira's final summary (Sir. 49.15) but the Hebrew version of this verse significantly omits the words *the ruler of his brothers and the support of the people*, which were added in the Greek translation, and therefore merely states of Joseph, *over his bones watch was kept*. There was of course a large Jewish community in Egypt in the third century BC who would have known of Egyptian court 'wisdom' traditions which play a part in the Joseph saga, as well as traditional Egyptian folk tales ('The Tale of the Two Brothers'), which may also have influenced its development. Is the story of Joseph therefore constructed out of an amalgam of Egyptian practices and folklore married with long standing Israelite traditions (particularly concerning 'those dem bones'!) about Joseph, one of the eponymous ancestors of the Israelites? Its purpose would be to explain how the family of Jacob had come to live in Egypt, and to help provide an appropriate prologue for the Exodus. It thus acts as a bridge between the traditions about the ancestors and those about the deliverance from Egypt, which had originally been distinct and separate.

That is of course necessarily speculation – and other suggestions would include relating the story of Joseph to incidents during the early period of the monarchy when northern Israelite leaders such as Jeroboam 1 had close links with the Egyptian court (see 1 Kgs.11.40). Certainly there are interesting issues implicit in the narrative about the relationship of the northern tribes (linked to Joseph) with their southern counterparts (linked to Judah).

Our view of the date of the Joseph saga is probably affected by our perception of Joseph himself. Is he a 'hero' – or the opposite? The fact that it is so difficult to decide the answer to that question is perhaps a reflection of the subtlety with which the authors of this saga have told their tale.

The structure of this section reflects its role within the wider book of Genesis. Like the Abraham and Jacob sagas it has a broadly chiastic structure, with elements at the end of the story responding to those highlighted at its outset. (For example, the 17 years that Jacob resides in Egypt corresponds to the fact that Joseph is 17 years old when the story begins; Joseph's dreams in chapter 37 are fulfilled – or not – by his brothers' clear subservience in chapter 50.) The centre of the narrative seems to be chapters 45 and 46 which describe the reconciliation of the family and their descent into Egypt. However, it has been plausibly suggested that chapters 37—50 may also act as a foil to the opening chapters of Genesis itself. The preservation of life with which God is so concerned (50.20) is an appropriate ending for a book which has begun with life's very explosion into being (see further on p. 10).

## *Going down . . . and up*
### 37.1—41.57

The coming chapters will be marked by a series of sharp reversals of fortune, particularly for Joseph, but also for the other players in the drama that is to unfold. Although chapter 38 appears at first sight to be very different from the surrounding story, there are verbal and thematic links which connect it to the chapters which precede and follow it.

Taking these chapters as a whole one of the fascinating issues that they raise is the varied modes of God's presence, or lack of it, in the story. This ranges from a total absence of God in chapter 37, to 'direct action' from Yнwн in chapter 38, to the 'frame' which Yнwн provides for chapter 39, and eventually to a link between God and the dream interpretation of chapters 40—41.

37.1–2a  *Jacob settled in Canaan*: The opening phrases suggest a permanence, of finally belonging in a place, after the wandering and alienation that had marked most of Jacob's life in chapters 25—35. But, as so often, appearances can be deceptive, and Jacob will end his life not settled in Canaan, but in the foreign land of Egypt.

*This is an account of Jacob's descendants.* For the last time the *toledot* formula appears in Genesis. It is paired with the example in 36.1. There it was used to introduce a genealogy, now it introduces a story. A similar pairing occurred in 25.12 and 25.19 where the expression was first used to introduce the genealogy of Ishmael, and then the lengthy story of Isaac and his sons. What follows is the story of Jacob's descendants, not specifically Joseph, although that is how the following chapters are often read. But the story which unfolds will have roles for Reuben, Judah, Simeon and Benjamin as well as Joseph himself, and it is arguable that it is Judah rather than Joseph who is the real hero of the tale.

**37.2b–11** *When Joseph was a youth of seventeen*: The introduction is innocent; but much can be read into it. He was shepherding – apparently a pastoral idyll. But rulers in the ancient world were often called shepherds (Ezek. 34; Jer. 23.1–6), and both Moses and David began their rise to leadership while working as shepherds. Yet his role is to assist *the sons of Bilhah and Zilpah*. These were the two slave wives of Jacob, so Joseph, son of beloved and freeborn Rachel, begins in the lowliest of all positions. It is clearly not a position he relished; *he told tales about them* – straight away he is presented as impossibly tactless. Already we sense that Joseph needs to be refined and tested before he can meet his destiny.

*Israel loved him best of all his sons*: Love, as we have already discovered in Genesis, can be a dangerous emotion. The last time a younger son had been loved, it had almost resulted in his death (22.2). The last person that Jacob himself loved (29.18), Rachel, had met an early death. Our expectation is heightened: what will happen to this beloved one?

The use of Jacob's 'new' name, Israel, at this point hints poignantly that the story that will unfold is part of the greater story of the people of God, of Israel, the people that is God's own beloved son (Hos. 11.1–3), so often lost and with so far to travel.

*A long robe with sleeves*: It is a 'royal' garment, suggesting great status: Tamar, daughter of David, wears one described in the same terms (2 Sam. 13.18). Hardly a 'tactful' present, since it makes transparently visible Jacob's favouritism for Joseph.

Clothing will be a powerful symbolic motif throughout the following chapters: its introduction here reminds us of the first gift of clothing, by Yhwh to man and woman as they left the garden (3.21). Does this hint at good or ill lying ahead?

*Joseph had a dream*: Both dreams clearly reflect Joseph's vision – hope? – boast? – of his future lordship. The symbols they employ are not haphazard – the sheaves of grain link to the later famine. We have met dreams before in Genesis, but then it was made explicitly clear that God was using them as a reliable medium of communication (see e.g. 20.3). That is not so now, there is no mention of God – indeed Gen. 37 is one of the very few chapters of Genesis from which God appears entirely absent. Joseph's universe seems at the moment to be entirely centred upon himself. Are these 'real' dreams, that will predict Joseph's future? Or is he simply engaging in wish-fulfilment? It is notable that it is not actually Joseph himself who interprets the dreams here. For the first dream it is his brothers (37.8), and for the second his father (37.10). Does this mean that the dreams are more – or less – likely to be authentic? We are left in carefully crafted suspense.

*Their hatred of him became still greater*: Both here and in the expression *still more* in v. 8 the Hebrew contains the root *yasap* (= 'add') – from which Joseph's own name is also derived (30.24). It emphasises how visceral is the brothers' hatred for Joseph; it is bound up with the very essence of his being.

*Your mother*: The implication is that Rachel is still alive, which conflicts with 35.19. Does this however hint that Joseph's dreams may not be entirely fulfilled, since Rachel will clearly not be around at the denouement of the story?

*His father did not forget the incident*: But his response was hardly wise. Jacob bears considerable responsibility for what will happen to Joseph, as he also bore much of the responsibility for the disaster which surrounded his daughter Dinah. Apart from exacerbating his elder sons' jealousy, his action in sending Joseph to *see if all was well with his brothers* (especially wearing *that* robe!) was naïve in the extreme. The Hebrew text makes it crystal clear: In 37.4 *The brothers . . . had harsh words for him* (lit. they were not able to speak to him with *shalom*). So is it likely that they will welcome Joseph when he now goes to 'see the *shalom* of his brothers and the *shalom* of the flock' (a literal translation of 37.14)?

37.12–30 *Israel said to him, 'Your brothers are herding the flocks at Shechem'*: Once again the use of the name 'Israel' alerts us to the father's role and responsibility for the destiny of his descendants. He sends Joseph on the long journey from Hebron to Shechem because this is the place where Israel will become Israel (see e.g. Josh. 24). However, given what happened when the family of Jacob were last located at Shechem (34.1–31), when the brothers' potential for violence was all too apparent, it is perhaps also a dangerous place to be sending Joseph.

*Joseph answered, 'I am ready to go'.* Two previous protagonists in the story of Genesis have indicated their willingness to hear a command with this expression – in Hebrew *hinneni*. The first one was Abraham (22.1), and it led to him being summoned to sacrifice his son; the next was Esau (27.1) and it resulted in him being deprived of his blessing. What will this response mean for Joseph?

*A man met him wandering in the open country*: Who is this mysterious man who directs Joseph to his brothers at Dothan? In doing so he leads him still further away from Jacob and presumable safety. The previous anonymous 'man' we met in Genesis was the apparently divine figure with whom Jacob wrestled at Penuel (32.24). Is this a similarly perilous – and divine – encounter? And for the careful reader the expression *in the open country* is reminiscent of the time that Cain led Abel out into the field – with sinister intent.

*They saw him in the distance*: Did the long robe with sleeves make him particularly distinctive – and somehow seal his fate? Even to wear such a costume on the journey hinted at Joseph's dreams of lordliness, which would have infuriated his brothers. It was not a working man's garment. This robe will have further important roles to play in the story.

In the brothers' scornful words, *Here comes that dreamer*, the Hebrew expression underlying the word *dreamer* means literally 'master of dreams'. The phrase emphasises Joseph's egocentrism and the brothers' anger and fear that his dreams might actually come true. It also prefaces, with a nice touch of irony, their determination to try and frustrate Joseph's ideas of grandeur through a deed which will turn him into the opposite of a 'master'.

*They plotted to kill him*: The text seems confused. Two different versions may have been conflated. The basic version appears to be one in which Reuben acts as the responsible eldest brother, preventing the murder of Joseph by suggesting that he is taught a lesson by a cooling-off period in an empty cistern (37.28a, 29–30). But while Reuben is absent Midianite traders come upon Joseph and kidnap him (with or without the other brothers' knowledge). Into this first scenario has been inserted a variant in which Judah comes up with an alternative plan – to sell Joseph to Ishmaelite traders who arrive on the scene (25b–27, 28b).

Although the interweaving of the two versions creates confusion, it also heightens Judah's culpability. For as the text now stands it means that, in spite of his fine words, Judah's suggestion to sell his brother to slavers cannot be understood primarily as a means of at least preserving Joseph's life. Reuben had already resolved that issue. Instead he is presented as sickeningly specious: *Let us do him no harm, for after all, he is our brother*. Although it meant that they were absolved of blood-guilt (compare Gen. 9.6), the earliest readers of Genesis would have been well aware that selling a person into slavery in Egypt was, in normal circumstances, condemning him to a lingering death. Did Judah have a particular animus against Joseph? After all Reuben, Simeon and Levi had all, in various ways, incurred their father's displeasure. Judah was now the oldest of the remaining sons of Leah, who might feel more acutely than any other the competition that Joseph posed in their father's affections.

Two actions heighten the awfulness of what the brothers do to Joseph. *They stripped him* and *They . . . sat down to eat*. The first is deliberately humiliating, but understandable in view of the symbolic weight Joseph's robe carried in their family. It was a focus for their anger. The second is a cruel inversion of the way that meals often provide the setting for reconciliation or covenant making.

*They sold him. . . to the Ishmaelites*: So the family of Ishmael has not entirely departed the story of Abraham's descendants. We had heard of their Egyptian connection (21.21; 25.18), now we see that it facilitates the role they are to have in working out a larger providence. It is ironically appropriate that the offspring of Ishmael, a less favoured son, should work together with another generation of less favoured brothers, to despatch the favoured one to the kind of fate that had once seemed to be Ishmael's own.

37.31–36   The robe itself now takes centre-stage. It is dipped in the *blood of a goat*. Goats have played a significant role in Jacob's life up till now: it was by the skin of a goat that he had deceived his own father (27.16), as his sons will now deceive him. They ask him: *do you recognize it?* Again a word that resonates with Jacob's own deception (27.23): Isaac had not recognised him, but now he, Jacob, recognises the robe – yet is deceived as to its meaning.

Tellingly, as the brothers present the garment to Jacob they asked: *Is this your son's robe or not?* For Joseph may be Jacob's son, but he is in no way their brother, nor are they his keeper. Jacob's extravagant, possibly even over-extravagant, grief alienates them from proper family relationships still more: Joseph, he says, is *my son* – so what place remains for the others?

*Jacob tore his clothes; he put on sackcloth*: The importance of the motif of clothing is further accentuated by Jacob's own change of garment.

*All tried to comfort him, he refused to be comforted*: The repetition of the Hebrew root *naham* (= 'comfort') emphasises the grief that Jacob wallows in. But the appearance of the root at key moments within Genesis (5.29; 6.6; 50.21) may suggest that it reflects more than personal grief. A very similar expression is used in Jer. 31.15 to describe Rachel's grief for her lost children (including, presumably, Joseph). There it relates to the historical fate of the tribes associated with the 'house of Joseph'.

*No, I shall go to Sheol mourning for my son*: Sheol is the underworld, the place of the dead. Jacob actually speaks of 'going down' to Sheol, a phrase that parallels the verb used when Joseph goes down first into the cistern, and later into Egypt. Several psalms (e.g. Ps. 30.3; 88.3–4) speak of going down to Sheol in terms of going down into a pit or cistern. For us who know of Joseph's near death in the cistern there is a hidden appropriateness to Jacob's choice of words: the near death of Joseph in the cistern, creating 'death' for his father. Jacob's life is bound up – too bound up? – with the life of his son (compare 44.30).

38.1–26   The chapter that follows has puzzled, and irritated, generations of commentators on Genesis. It seems to interrupt the flow of chapters 37 and 39: 39.1 reiterates and resumes where 37.36 left off. At first sight the story it tells has little to do with the major focus of chapters 37—50, and seems to ignore the chronology of the surrounding chapters. The events it describes must elapse over a period of 20 years or so, and can barely have been completed before the brothers travel to Egypt in search of food – but 39.1 reverts to the point in time of Joseph's kidnapping. So Gen. 38 is a jarring insertion of a possibly already existing story about Judah. Yet the insertion is there for a purpose. The chapter has significant verbal and thematic links with Gen. 37 and 39. It not only counterbalances the focus on the 'northern' ancestor Joseph in the rest of 37—50 by providing a narrative about the 'southern' ancestor Judah, but also offers an interlude that helps us to understand the development of the character of Judah between chapter 37 (when he is the 'bad guy'!) and 44.18–34 when his offer of self-sacrifice facilitates the reconciliation of Joseph and the other brothers.

*Judah parted from his brothers*: The parting is not simply a geographical one. Judah's subsequent actions, becoming close friends with an Adullamite, and marrying a Canaanite woman, distance him emotionally and perhaps religiously from his family (compare 28.8) as well. Is it his bad conscience over his leading role in Joseph's disappearance that is driving him away?

*Heading south*: This means he is appropriately travelling into the later territory of the tribe of Judah. Both the barrage of actions and the names that follow are ominous. Judah *saw . . . married . . . lay with . . . .* It is a swift and brutal mating, with no sense of tenderness about it. Their eldest son is called Er: *he was wicked in the LORD's sight.* He was at least named appropriately – the letters Er spell 'wicked' backwards in Hebrew! The name of Onan, the second son, signified 'vigorous', even though his vigour was to be inappropriately applied. The place where the third son, Shelah, was born was called Kezib, which means falsehood! An unsavoury family. By contrast Tamar, Judah's presumably Canaanite daughter-in-law, bears a name that speaks of both beauty and fertility – 'a palm tree'.

*The LORD took away his life*: The evil that Er did is not specified. But it is notable that the only two points where YHWH is involved in direct action during this chapter is in a retributive taking away the life of Judah's two sons. In Gen. 37 we might have thought that YHWH was now 'out of the picture' and the brothers' violence towards Joseph would go unpunished. The present verse is a sharp reminder to us that this is not the case. YHWH is still active in the history of this family. And what about Judah – did he see any connection between what happened to his own sons, and his leading role in depriving his father of Joseph, his beloved son?

*Then Judah told Onan . . . to do his duty as the husband's brother*: Onan was being required to fulfil the law of the Levirate (Deut. 25.5–10). This stated that if a man died without leaving a son, the next eldest brother was required to marry the widow, and the first son to be born of that union would be counted as the offspring of the deceased brother, so that his name *may not be blotted out from Israel.* In view of biblical laws of inheritance making such a marriage could often be to the financial disadvantage of the second brother. Clearly that was Onan's view, and his deliberate practice of *coitus interruptus* was intended to frustrate any possibility of a son being produced for the deceased Er. The law of the Levirate is a major theme of the Book of Ruth (which is aware of the parallel with this story of Tamar, see Ruth 4.12).

Judah's efforts to dominate the lives of his sons (*Then Judah told Onan*) seem to be highlighted, and contrast with his own freedom to choose his own wife. But ultimately his efforts at control are all in vain – we quickly discover that it is YHWH, not Judah, who runs events.

After the death of both Er and Onan Judah clearly regarded his daughter-in-law as 'unlucky'. His efforts to prevent the death of his youngest son Shelah may be understandable, but they are unfair to Tamar: to return her as a widow to her father's house is anomalous, such an action consigns her to social limbo – and deprives her of any status at all.

*Time passed*: A reminder that Tamar's purdah had gone on a long time and that Judah had no real intention of fulfilling the requirement to give her in marriage to Shelah, his youngest son.

*Judah's wife Bathshua died*: The death of Bathshua bestowed a special preciousness on Shelah, the one remaining son. There would be no more after him, so risking his life becomes even more unthinkable. It also 'explains' Judah's desire to use a prostitute. *When he had finished mourning*. The same root, *naham*, as described the grief of Jacob in the previous chapter (37.35) is used again. The contrasting speedy 'consolation' of Judah gives us the impression of someone who is infinitely more hard-headed than his father.

She *sat where the road forks on the way to Timnath*: The NRSV (and other translations) understand the expression translated as *where the road forks* as referring to a proper place name, 'Enaim'. In turn this name has an apparent connection to the Hebrew word for 'eye'. Sight is clearly a key motif in this story (note that the name is repeated in v. 21).

*When Judah saw her he thought she was a prostitute, for she had veiled her face*: A veil was probably part of the traditional dress of a prostitute. But there is an irony about this 'veiling' for it actually conceals Tamar's true identity. As in the previous chapter (37.32) and in 27.15–16 clothing becomes a means of deception.

*What will you give to lie with me?*: Tamar's question echoes the brusqueness of Judah's demand. *Lie with me* accurately conveys the impersonality of the words used in Hebrew. It is significant that the normal Hebrew idiom for sexual intercourse – know – is not used here. Transparently Judah does not know Tamar in any meaningful sense.

*A young goat*: Tamar's wages for her services again echo Judah's own deception of Jacob – by dipping Joseph's robe in *the blood of a goat*. This parallel was noticed even in rabbinic times: 'The Holy One, praised be he, said to Judah, "You deceived your father with a kid. By your life, Tamar will deceive you with a kid" ' (*Bereshit Rabba* 84).

*Give me a pledge until you send it*: Tamar is 'savvy' enough not simply to trust the word of this man. The tokens of pledge she demands

*your seal and its cord, and the staff which you are holding* amount to the
ancient Middle Eastern equivalent of Judah's identity document and
are unique to him: without them Judah could not properly function in
society. But Tamar may also be using a double entendre at Judah's ex-
pense. The word translated 'staff' (*matteh*) also means 'tribe', and can
refer to the 'tribes' of Israel. Is Tamar effectively telling Judah (though
he doesn't realise it!), 'Give me a tribe of descendants, which will establish us as part of Israel'?

*Judah sent the goat*: Judah's next actions suggest that he was embarrassed by what he had done. He uses Hirah the Adullamite as an emis-
sary to try to recover his tokens of pledge, rather than seeking Tamar
out again himself. He also suggests to Hirah that he had visited a
*temple prostitute*, which is one notch up the social ladder from a common whore.

*Tamar had . . . got herself pregnant*: The double standards are apparent. What is acceptable behaviour for Judah is prohibited for his
daughter-in-law. The double standard operates in another dimension as well. Having neglected to take any responsibility for Tamar in
the past, sending her back to her father's house, he now assumes the
role of paterfamilias and insists on his rights over Tamar's life – and
death.

Tamar's moment of triumph is all the greater – coming in the nick
of time to save her. As she shows the signs of 'pledge' which she had
obtained from Judah, the expression she uses is identical (in Hebrew)
to that with which the brothers had confronted their father with the
deceptive robe after the disappearance of Joseph: *See if you recognize
whose they are.* Once again *Bereshit Rabba* notes the parallel: 'The Holy
One, praise be he, said to Judah, "You said to your father 'Recognize'.
By your life Tamar will say to you, 'Recognize'."'

*She is more in the right than I am*: Finally Judah acknowledges Tamar's
'rights' under the religious code of the time, and that she has taken
steps to ensure them, for the well-being of the community. The last
person to be called *tsaddiq* (= *in the right*) in Genesis was the Gentile
Abimelech. Once again, an outsider, Tamar (probably a Canaanite)
has been a teacher of righteousness to members of Abraham's family.

38.27–30  The birth of Tamar's twins echoes the birth of their grandfather Jacob and his twin Esau (25.24–26), particularly in view of the
mention of *scarlet thread* (compare 25.25) and the fact that the name
Zerah (38.30) is also given to one of Esau's grandsons (36.13). The link
is a hint that this unorthodox birth to an unorthodox woman is go-

ing to be particularly significant in the fulfilment of God's promises to Abraham and his family – even though it is beyond the scope of Genesis to spell this out in full.

The focus of the birth story is clearly on Perez, named after his 'Break Out'. It is Perez who will become the ancestor of the great King David, and who will appear in the genealogy at the end of the Book of Ruth (Ruth 4.12, 18) and at the beginning of the Gospel of Matthew (Matt. 1.3). Once again a younger son (though this time ambiguously so) will have the major role to play. And the mention of the birth of Perez at just this point in the story, before we hear about the 'bondage' of Joseph in Egypt, is probably a hint that there will be a future for Jacob's family beyond Egyptian slavery – but it may not be associated with Joseph.

**39.1–39**    We move back to focus on Joseph, and pick up exactly where we left off in 37.36. And now, for the first time, God and YHWH seem to make their mark in the life of Joseph. In fact the six times the name YHWH comes in this chapter, framing it at the beginning and the end, are almost the only times that it appears in the entire Joseph saga (see comment on 49.18, p. 270). The name seems to be used by the narrator of the story to highlight his own theological convictions: that YHWH was working through the ups and downs of Joseph's life to fulfil his purposes and promises to the ancestors. So we are told four times that the LORD was with him (39.2, 3, 21, 23), a reflection of YHWH's promise first to Isaac (26.3) and later to Joseph's father, Jacob (28.15), and twice that YHWH blessed the household of Potiphar because of Joseph (39.5–6) , recalling YHWH's commitment to Abraham (12.3). In the previous chapter the activity of YHWH had been jarringly brutal, suddenly terminating the lives of Judah's wicked sons. What we have now provides a contrast: YHWH's activity can be beneficient, and part of an ongoing and almost imperceptible process. The comments on YHWH's activity set the scene for the whole of Joseph's experiences in Egypt – even though YHWH will not appear by name, he is apparently there in the background bringing about a providential outcome.

*Potiphar, one of Pharaoh's court officials*: The word translated 'court official' can elsewhere mean 'eunuch'. A number of interpreters of this passage in antiquity understood this to be Potiphar's situation. In ancient cultures eunuchs were often preferred for leading political roles. If Potiphar was a eunuch it might mean that the behaviour of his wife towards Joseph was more understandable!

*The LORD blessed the household through Joseph*: As elsewhere in the ancestral stories (e.g. 26.28) a descendant of Abraham becomes a means of blessing for others.

*Potiphar left it all in Joseph's care*: Several times in this chapter it is stated that first Potiphar, and later the prison governor give everything into Joseph's capable charge – or literally 'into his hand' (39.4, 6, 8, 22, 23). Even in situations of apparent weakness, as a slave or a prisoner, his controlling power quickly becomes apparent. This accentuates the contrast with the situation Joseph will find himself in when he rebuffs Potiphar's wife: he is forced to leave his intimate garment and his fate behind – in her hand (39.13). The powerful one is made powerless in the hand of another.

*Now Joseph was handsome in both face and figure*: When an episode is introduced with a line like this we can be sure that trouble lies ahead! What is more, the identical description, in its feminine form, had been used of his mother Rachel (29.17) and that had provoked the bitter love triangle of Jacob, Leah and Rachel. Indeed one could say that it was Rachel's beauty that had landed Joseph in this predicament in Egypt. It was because of Jacob's love for his mother that Joseph had become the spoilt son, disliked by his half-brothers.

*His master's wife became infatuated with him*: The Book of Proverbs knows of women like Potiphar's wife, the wily foreign woman out to seduce innocent young men, and warns them to beware (Prov. 7.1–27). Joseph's response is the 'wise' one that Proverbs enjoins on its readers – even though, for the moment, it appears to lead him to disaster. Is a contrast being drawn between Potiphar's wife, who by attempting to lead Joseph astray threatens the existence of his people, and Tamar, another foreign woman, whose actions in the previous chapter had helped to ensure their future?

*But Joseph refused*: In the Hebrew Bible over the word translated *refused* there is the rare *shalshelet* sign (see comment on 19.16 p. 109). Here it suggests that Joseph may have considerably wavered before making up his mind.

*'How can I do such a wicked thing? It is a sin against God'*: This is the first time the word 'God' has passed Joseph's lips. He is no longer the centre of his own universe. God (rather than YHWH) is appropriate here since Joseph is speaking to an Egyptian (see also 40.8; 41.16; etc.). The moral code by which Joseph is operating would have been accepted by both Israelites and Egyptians, for both of whom adultery was a serious offence. The Egyptian 'Story of the Two Brothers' provides a close parallel to this incident. But Joseph also refuses the advances of the woman because it would have betrayed his master's

trust. The inference of the passage is that the tenets of prudence and human decency are a good guide to the will of God: such a view is characteristic of the wisdom tradition in both Israel and Egypt.

*My husband has brought in a Hebrew to bring insult on us*: Hell hath no fury like a woman scorned. She tries to get the rest of the household on her side and distance Joseph from them by choosing to describe him as a *Hebrew*. The word takes us 'fast forward' to the time of Israel's slavery in Egypt when it will be used frequently in Exod. 1—3. Joseph's descent into Egypt may save his family's life, but it will also ultimately lead to their servitude.

*She kept it [the loincloth] by her until his master came home*: This is the second time in the life of Joseph that an article of his clothing has been used by others as an instrument of deception. The reference to Potiphar as *his master* instead of by his name reinforces the precariousness of Joseph's situation.

*Joseph's master was furious when he heard his wife's account*: But with whom? Did he have a shrewd idea of his wife's complicity? If he had really been convinced of Joseph's guilt it is likely that he would have fed him to the Nile crocodiles! Slaves were executed for less. Instead he seeks to solve the conundrum by ridding himself of Joseph in a way that may be unpleasant but is at least not inevitably terminal.

*The LORD was with Joseph*: Not only does the writer remind us again of YHWH's presence with Joseph in the guardhouse, but his comment that YHWH *kept faith with him* draws on the word *hesed* from covenant vocabulary. Joseph is the great-grandson of Abraham. Joseph has gone down into the pit, down into Egypt, down into slavery, and now down even further into prison, and apparently is forgotten. But YHWH will not forget his promises – or Joseph.

40.1–23 *Some time after these events . . . the king's cupbearer and the royal baker gave offence.* We are not told how these royal officials had erred or whether their imprisonment was justified. But the arbitrary nature of their eventual contrasting fates perhaps hints that their initial imprisonment was itself due simply to the capriciousness of Pharaoh – an implicit reminder that others, as well as Joseph, could experience a miscarriage of justice.

*Both had dreams*: The story of Joseph – and his descent into the 'pit' – had begun with a pair of dreams – does this next pair of dreams now indicate that we have reached another point of transition in Joseph's life?

*All interpretation belongs to God. Why not tell me your dreams?*: Joseph's remarks are ambiguous – probably deliberately so. Is he contrasting an 'Israelite' view with the traditional Egyptian one, which held that dream interpretation was a science that could be mastered by study? On the surface he sounds like a very different figure to the arrogant 'master of dreams' (37.19) whose own dreams placed himself at the centre and allowed no space at all for God. Yet read carefully the juxtaposition of the two sentences results in Joseph making a significant claim for himself – interpretation may belong to God, but he, Joseph, is implicitly setting himself up as God's interpreter. He may be appearing to efface himself, yet at the same time he is claiming special access to divine wisdom. From this point on Joseph will appear increasingly 'god-like'; possessing a hidden knowledge about events and people that is concealed from other participants in the story.

*When things go well with you, remember me*: After assuring the cupbearer that he will be restored to favour and 'raised up' once again, Joseph asks for a favour in return – that of being remembered. *Bringing my case to Pharaoh's notice*. Underlying this phrase is a verb (*zakar*) that comes from the same verbal root as 'remember': 'remembering' will become increasingly important in the following chapters as Joseph encounters his brothers once again.

*I was carried off by force . . . I have done nothing to deserve being put into this dungeon*: This is actually the first time since his troubles started that Joseph has been allowed to express his feelings about the injustice of his situation. Stripped of his garments (twice), he is now also metaphorically unmasked. Soon he will be reclothed in glory – once again with a mask to hide his emotions behind. The passion of these words is accentuated by Joseph's choice of vocabulary. The word he has used for 'dungeon' was that previously used for the 'cistern' into which his brothers had thrown him. He has sunk down – and down again. The betrayal by his brothers has resonated in his mind with the treachery he experienced in Potiphar's house.

*When the chief baker*: Rabbinic comments on the differing fates of the two officials tried to maintain that the arrangement of the loaves and baskets in the baker's dream suggested that he was less conscientious than his cupbearing contemporary and thus deserved his punishment. Joseph's interpretative skills are employed here with at least a hint of sadism. He uses the identical expression 'raise your head' as had previously depicted the cupbearer's restoration to favour – but then shatters the baker's hopes. In this case the head will be up – and off!

*The cupbearer . . . did not bear Joseph in mind; he forgot him*: These verbs of remembering and forgetting here accentuate this moment as the nadir of Joseph's life. He has, quite literally, reached the pits! The previous chapter, although it moved Joseph from being house slave to prisoner, at least ended with a positive note that recapitulated the chapter's introduction. Not so here. We had hoped that the dreams might indeed indicate a change of fortune for Joseph, but it is not to be. He is not only imprisoned, he is also now totally alone.

41.1–57 *Two years later Pharaoh had a dream*: This third set of dreams, again a pair, finally fulfil our hopes – and ultimately the hopes of Joseph's own dreams – while the dreams of the previous chapter had only tantalised us. The Hebrew idiom translated by *Two years later* emphasises the passing of time – Joseph remained forgotten in the dungeon for a long time, for 'two whole years'.

*He was standing by the Nile*: The story begins to take on particular local colour – as well as using a number of words borrowed from the Egyptian language, for example 'reeds' (41.2). Since the prosperity of Egypt always depended on the annual flood of the Nile, the fact that in his dream Pharaoh is standing on the river bank is appropriate and symbolic. And once again the number seven plays a key role, acting as a clear link between both of Pharaoh's dreams.

*Shrivelled by the east wind*: This too is a note of geographical realism. The 'khamsin' wind that blows from the eastern desert in Palestine and Egypt as winter moves into summer is notorious for its fierceness and ability to shrivel vegetation overnight.

*Now I must mention my offences*: An ambiguous comment. Is the cupbearer referring to his earlier 'offence' against Pharaoh, or his omission in forgetting to mention Joseph's name to him earlier? The ambiguity probably hints at the embarrassment the cupbearer felt at 'reminding' (the Hebrew root *zakar*, normally translated 'remember', is used here) Pharaoh of how he had once fallen so catastrophically out of favour. Memories are not always pleasant – and can be difficult to acknowledge.

*After he had shaved and changed his clothes*: Once again leaving his clothes behind marks a change of status for Joseph – only this time for the better.

*Not I, but God, can give an answer which will reassure Pharaoh*: Joseph seems to have learned humility and 'erases' himself to allow God to take centre-stage. But as with 40.8 we might question how real this self-effacement actually is, since he immediately assumes for himself the role of God's mouthpiece. Indeed, since on the surface the dreams

245

seem to presage disaster – rather than prosperity – it is a strange assurance that Joseph feels able to offer. Perhaps indeed that is why
Pharaoh's own wise men had felt it wiser not to interpret the dreams!
Joseph's assurance is one that cannot be fulfilled simply by his interpretation of the dreams, but only by the advice he himself then goes
on to offer.

*That Pharaoh has dreamed this twice*: Repetition is often used in the
biblical tradition to underscore the importance of an event. But, if
Pharaoh's dreams are more sure because of their repetition, is not this
also a hint that Joseph's own doubled dreams, experienced all those
years ago, will very shortly – and surely – be fulfilled?

*Let Pharaoh now look for a man of vision and wisdom*: Joseph now takes
the opportunity to extend his advice beyond bare dream interpretation, making practical suggestions as to how Pharaoh should respond
to the events predicted by the dreams.

The word 'wise' only appears in Genesis in chapter 41. In 41.8 it
describes the 'wise men' of Pharaoh's court, whose wisdom had
failed them when they had been asked to interpret Pharaoh's dream.
Is Joseph's remark a pointed one – pointing in his own direction?
Certainly Pharaoh picks up this hint when he repeats the expression
in 41.39. The suggestion that Pharaoh should *put [someone] in charge*
echoes the situation Joseph had found himself in, in both Potiphar's
house (39.4) and the prison (39.22).

*Could we find another man like this, one so endowed with the spirit of
God?*: Back at humanity's beginning, there had been a close connection between God's spirit, creativity and planning, and the task and
boundaries assigned to humanity (e.g. 1.2; 6.3). Are we to see Joseph
as fulfilling at last the role that was intended for human beings – finding through God the wisdom that the man and woman had sought
for illicitly (3.6)? And will Joseph's viceregency in Egypt correspond
in some ways to the position of viceroy of creation which God had
hoped to bestow on humanity? Joseph is virtually portrayed here as
a royal figure: wearing a royal ring, with royal garments (note the
change of attire once more!) and ornaments (41.42). The connection
with the *spirit of God* observed by Pharaoh further confirms this royal
status: for the *spirit of wisdom* was par excellence a gift bestowed on
kings (Isa. 11.2). Joseph's own past dreams of grandeur are now well
on the way to being fulfilled.

*Pharaoh named him Zaphenath-paneah*: Joseph is being thoroughly
Egyptianised. He is given an Egyptian name: which seems to mean
'God speaks and he lives'. It is worth remembering that Joseph's

father Jacob had also been renamed: by his divine assailant at Penuel (32.28). It was then that Israel had become Israel. What therefore does it imply when Israel's son is renamed by a foreign ruler, especially one who claimed to be a god? The ambiguity in this name change is reinforced by its meaning. The connection with 'life' is of course appropriate for the story of Joseph, but the name could be interpreted to mean that either Pharaoh, or even Joseph himself, was the giver of this life. He is also given an Egyptian wife, who seems to have an intriguing possible connection with the family of Potiphar, the household where Joseph was a slave. Both Abraham and Isaac had been concerned to ensure that their sons should marry within the family, preserving the purity of their lineage. Joseph's situation provides a sharp contrast: accentuated even more since his wife has important links with Egyptian religion. 'On' (modern Heliopolis) was the major sanctuary of the Egyptian sun-god, Ra.

*Joseph's authority extended over the whole of Egypt*: Walter Brueggemann points out how many times the word 'all' (variously translated into English) occurs in 41.45–57. The effect is to emphasise the total control that Joseph exercises – not only over the Egyptians, but ultimately over the destiny of the world. 'Either he [Joseph] acts for God or he usurps the life-giving function of God. Either way, he is the immediate source of life and well-being.'[1] Perhaps this apparent ambiguity with which the narrator presents us is deliberate. How far does this 'new Adam' avoid Adam's mistakes, even while fulfilling Adam's destiny?

*Two sons . . . He named the elder Manasseh*: By naming his first son 'Causing to forget' Joseph seems to be turning his back on his past, and committing himself and his family to a totally Egyptian future. To forget all his troubles – his past servitude and imprisonment – he needs also to forget his father's family whose antipathy to him had been their cause. But in a narrative in which remembrance has such a pivotal role to play can forgetfulness be a solution? Will not memories, both good and bad, be forced upon him?

*He named the second Ephraim*: If the name of the elder boy marked an attempt to reject the past, the name of the younger clearly points to a fruitful future. It is not a fruitfulness that is to be restricted to Joseph alone – it is what he was also offering to the Egyptians. It was moreover what God had commanded human beings to do at the point of their creation (1.28) and a promise that he had reiterated when he made a covenant with Abraham (17.6) and pledged to Joseph's own father Jacob when he had travelled to a foreign land (28.14). Despite all his attempts at 'forgetting' it seems that Joseph is a descendant of Abraham in spite of himself.

## Lives bound together
### 42.1—45.28

Chapters 42—45 form a parallel to 37, 39—41. In the earlier chapters we experienced the passion and resurrection of Joseph, now we are going to share in a passion and resurrection of Jacob and his other sons. A number of verbal hints make this connection clear. Both sequences are recounted in detail, with no attempt at an economy of words. And in both cases there are one, or possibly more, false climaxes – when we expect a denouement or resolution but we are forced to wait for it. There is however one important difference: in the earlier chapters Joseph is one participant among several in the story, and sometimes its victim. Now the 'voices' of Joseph and the narrator of the story seem to coalesce, and the direction of the story is quite clearly controlled by Joseph, who is privileged to have information concealed from the other characters in the plot.

42.1–38 *'Why do you stand staring at each other?'*: The hesitation of the brothers is pointed up by the harsh words Jacob uses to them. In spite of the gap of space and time (20 years!) provided by chapters 39—41 we seem to be back to the old story of intra-family hostility. *Staring* actually translates a form of the verb 'see'. The last occasions on which this verb was used with Jacob's sons as its subject it described how they saw with envy that Joseph was their father's favourite (37.4) – and how they saw an Ishmaelite caravan of slave traders bound for Egypt (37.25) to which they then had consigned Joseph. No wonder that they are now paralysed by inaction. Is it their guilty consciences, or an innate Israelite hostility to Egypt that deters them from making a move in the direction of the one country which could offer food to its neighbours in times of shortage?

*Jacob did not let Joseph's brother Benjamin go with them*: Once again the old cycle of 'favouritism', which has plagued family relationships since Cain and Abel, begins again. This time can there be a more positive outcome?

*The sons of Israel went . . . to buy grain.* Imperceptibly Joseph's brothers (42.3) have become the sons of Israel – not merely the sons

248

of Jacob. It is as the sons of Israel that they will grow to the size of a nation in Egypt, and under that name that their descendants will experience the Exodus.

*Joseph's brothers came and bowed to the ground before him*: The old dream in which Joseph saw his brothers prostrating before him is now being fulfilled – even if Joseph's brothers are oblivious of this.

*When he saw his brothers he recognized them but, pretending not to know them*: A sort of schizophrenia runs through these chapters – and the story will not be able to come to its end until this has been healed. It is a division that reaches back into earlier sections of Genesis. The word 'recognise' (Hebrew: *nakar*) has a key function in helping to create this 'splitness'. It has been used at several significant moments in the past when people have tried to deceive each other. Isaac did not *recognize* Jacob because of his deceptive garb (27.23); Jacob invites Laban to *identify* (same verb) his household gods – a task that is made impossible because of Rachel's deceptive actions (31.32); Joseph's brothers invite Jacob to *recognize* their brother's robe deceptively dipped in the blood of a goat (37.32); and Tamar also uses the word (38.25) when she invites Judah to reclaim the objects that she had previously taken from him while playing her assumed role of harlot. Here, by contrast, the fact that Joseph recognises his brother is a statement of truth: they really are his brothers, and he really does recognise them. The falsity is not now in the recognition, but what comes afterwards. For instead of acting as one might when recognising long-lost relatives Joseph pretended not to know them. Ironically, and punningly, the phrase *pretending not to know* comes from the same Hebrew verb as does the verb 'recognise' – even though its meaning in translation is so very different. It is the writer's way of suggesting to us that Joseph is for the moment internally 'split'. He cannot bring himself to be 'whole' and so the truth cannot yet be visible.

The point is underscored by the laboured repetition in the next verse: *Although Joseph had recognized his brothers, they did not recognize him*. Full and mutual recognition cannot take place until the brothers are capable of recognising their own guilt.

*He remembered the dreams he had had about them*: Recognition (Hebrew: *nakar*) and remembrance (Hebrew: *zakar*) belong together, and indeed in Hebrew the verbs have a similarity of sound. For Joseph who had called his first son 'Causing to forget' remembering is a painful process, and provokes him to anger. Memories have still much healing to go through. It is interesting to note precisely what Joseph remembers – the dreams in which his family lay prostrate before him – a memory triggered by the fact that this is what his brothers have just done. But as the dreams led ultimately to his servitude, his memories lead him swiftly to recall his brothers' treachery. The narrator encourages us to enter Joseph's thought processes without precisely spelling them out. *You are spies* might sound like an illogical accusation, but it makes sense in view of Joseph's sense of betrayal.

*We are all sons of one man*: The brothers say more than they realise, as they unwittingly seem to include Joseph among their number.

*There were twelve of us*: This could equally be translated 'There are twelve of us'. Once again the brothers inadvertantly group Joseph with themselves. The REB translation *and one is lost* weakens the irony at the conclusion of the brothers' remarks. Literally they state, 'and one is not', precisely as they are talking to that very 'one'. Throughout these verses the emphasis on unity as *sons of one man* adds to the pathos of the fractured family.

*This is how you will be put to the test*: The test that Joseph proposes would not check whether or not the brothers are 'spies' – indeed if they had been it would have facilitated the successful completion of their spying mission. It does however begin to put them to the real test Joseph is setting before them – to uncover their attitude to Benjamin, Joseph's full brother, currently kept safe by his father's side, who had apparently replaced Joseph as family favourite.

*I swear by the life of Pharaoh*: This is the only instance in the Old Testament when an 'Israelite' takes an oath by a foreign god or royal figure. Joseph's apparent assimilation is very thoroughgoing! It also begs the question when, in his next sentence, he offers the reassurance *I am a godfearing man*, as to which God or god he fears.

*If you are honest men*: The mitigation of Joseph's original command that all except one should remain prisoner, into the alternative suggestion that all except one might return, is still for the moment conditional. How will Joseph decide if they are honest men? Is it as a result of the conversation between the brothers which Joseph then overhears?

For the first time we hear of Joseph's distress in the pit. *He pleaded with us.* That agony of Joseph had not been mentioned previously. Fittingly the brothers themselves have just had to plead for their own lives – even though they did not realise to whom they were doing so. This beginning of the brothers' repentance seems to convince Joseph that they are honest men, and leads him to ameliorate his sentence even though the brothers themselves must have been puzzled as to why this has happened – especially since they do not know that

Joseph can listen to them. As in 37.22 Reuben seems to act as the conscience of the brothers.

*His blood is on our heads*: Judah had implied (37.26–27) that a reason for the selling of Joseph had been to avoid blood-guilt. Are the brothers' guilty consciences now prompting them to admit to themselves that they had effectively been consigning their brother to a death sentence?

*They did not know that Joseph understood*: If they had refused to listen when Joseph had pleaded with them in the past, it is a fine touch that Joseph should now be listening to them with an unnecessary interpreter acting as a decoy. Joseph had never really heard his brothers in his past life either – being all too full of his own importance. Is there also a significance that it should be Simeon – with 'hearing' in his name (see 29.33) whom he selects as his hostage?

*Joseph turned away from them and wept*: The three times that Joseph weeps as his reconciliation with his brothers progresses mount towards an emotional crescendo. Little by little Joseph himself seems to change to match the alteration in his brothers.

*He gave orders . . . to put each man's silver back into his sack*: Once before the sons of Jacob had returned to their father with silver instead of one of their number (37.28). This action on Joseph's part seems intended to 'spook' the brothers into remembering more deeply that earlier 'trade' of a brother for silver.

*What is this that God has done to us?*: Here and in 44.16 where the brothers see God's hand in their predicament they ironically speak more than they know. Corresponding to the 'split' within Joseph, the brothers too find themselves operating, albeit unwillingly, on two levels. On the one hand they are involved in and punished for a series of incidents for which they are genuinely innocent, which lead however to the uncovering of their long suppressed guilt relating to Joseph. We, the readers, know that the brothers' cry of anguish here relates, even if unconsciously, to God's retribution for their earlier apparent fratricide. But perhaps even we do not yet know the whole story: if we accept Joseph's 'reading' of events as will be suggested in 45.5 and 50.20 'what God has done to them' is ultimately to preserve the family of Jacob at a time of famine. Over the next two chapters these two sets of 'splits', in Joseph and the brothers, will gradually collide together. Will integration or fragmentation be the result?

*The man who is lord of the country*: The description of Joseph as lord of the country is repeated in 42.33. Even in their self-selected turn of speech the brothers find themselves putting into effect Joseph's earlier dreams of grandeur.

*You can move around the country freely*: The brothers subtly 'edit' their conversation with Joseph when they report it to their father. Not surprisingly they omit the discussion they had concerning their involvement in Joseph's disappearance. But they add this comment – which was not in Joseph's original words. 'Move around' can also be translated 'trade' and is closely related to the word 'merchant' (37.28). Are their guilty consciences prompting them to remember aloud the previous occasion when they 'traded' with Egypt – their own brother? And although Joseph had never mentioned 'trading' with the sons of Jacob, another 'foreigner' had once done so – Hamor, the prince of Shechem (34.10), and he had been treated with a duplicity that had disgusted even Jacob. Might not this mention of 'trading' start to trigger memories in Jacob's mind of just how violent and deceitful his sons could be?

*Each of them found his silver inside . . . they were afraid*: It is far from clear that the brothers had yet mentioned to their father the one lot of silver that they had discovered on the journey. Now they are in no position to conceal from him this far greater quantity. Who are they afraid of? At this distance it is surely not Joseph. Is it God? Or their father? The last thing they wanted to do was to remind him of a former occasion when they had returned home minus one of their brothers, and with a mysterious quantity of silver.

*You have robbed me of my children*: This apparent accusation is the closest Jacob gets to suggesting that the brothers had complicity in the loss of Joseph. Is it simply an extravagant figure of speech? Or has Jacob really suspected the true story all these years?

*Reuben said to his father*: In these verses the characters of both Reuben and Jacob are delineated. Reuben makes a suggestion which is well-meaning but feels as ineffectual as when he had once tried to assist Joseph. Just as then he had not succeeded in restoring Joseph to his father (37.22), so now his extravagant offer does not give Jacob the confidence that he will be able to 'restore' Benjamin. Similarly Jacob remains self-centred in his grief, in a way that parallels the end of chapter 37.

*My son must not go with you*: The comment illustrates the sharp disparity between the comparative worth of Benjamin and Simeon in Jacob's eyes. To state that Benjamin *alone is left* in front of nine of his other sons is a sharp reminder of the favouritism that had caused the problem in the first place.

43.1–34   The pace of the story now seems to slow down – at times almost unbearably so. How long will Joseph be able to maintain his charade, or will his feelings at last overwhelm him?

The language of the story shifts as well: it takes on both a new formality and a pathos. Throughout this chapter the brothers' father is referred to consistently as 'Israel' rather than Jacob. The brothers refer to Joseph as *the man* (43.3, 5), and in turn are called by him *these men* (43.16). Yet we also meet for the first time in Genesis expressions such as *kindly disposed* and *overcome by his feelings* both of which contain the Hebrew root *raham*, that is connected with the word for 'womb' and is often used when powerful emotions are at stake. It is used to describe God's parental feelings for Israel in Jer. 31.20. Indeed the exquisite passage Jer. 31.15–22 has a number of interesting links with Gen. 43. Both are concerned with Rachel's children; in both weeping is prominent. Is it possible that in Gen. 43 we have in story form something of the grief and pain experienced by the nation 'Israel' and its lost tribes (see e.g. Jer. 31.7–8) throughout its history? The note in 43.32 is possible confirmation of this. It reads not simply as a comment about social behaviour on a particular occasion, but reflects on the ongoing relationship with Egypt throughout centuries of history.

*If you let our brother go with us*: Jacob may have refused to 'trade' Benjamin to save the life of one of his other brothers, but with the continuation of the famine it is Benjamin's own life, as well as that of the rest of the family, which is at stake and this forces a change of mind on Jacob's part. His complaint to his sons that they had admitted that they had another brother is somewhat incongruous. Was he asking his sons to be deceptive? It is as incongruous as the brothers' protestation, both directly to Joseph (42.11), and repeated in their report to their father (42.31), that *We are honest men*. A strange twist coming from men who have lived a lie for a whole generation, and who even now slightly 'doctor' the report they present to their father of the conversation they had in Egypt (43.7).

*Judah said . . . 'I shall go surety for him'*: The interplay between the 'effective' Judah and the 'ineffective' Reuben (42.37) parallels their roles in chapter 37. But the word *surety* also recapitulates Judah's experiences in chapter 38, when he had offered a *pledge* (a word that comes from the same Hebrew root), to Tamar. The inner growth of Judah through that experience will become obvious in the course of the next two chapters.

*Take, as a gift for the man*: Once before Jacob/Israel had sought to propitiate a wrong by offering an expensive gift (to his brother Esau). Now even though the 'wrong' is not his own he seems to try the same tack. Inadvertently he suggests a gift that links us back to the moment when Joseph was abducted to Egypt – via a camel caravan carrying many of the same items (37.25).

*Take double the amount of silver*: Suddenly a sense of 'doubling' pervades the narratives: the money, and the journey that could have been made twice (43.10). Perhaps it reinforces the hint that in some senses Benjamin is the 'double' of Joseph. Certainly Jacob's comments about the grave or Sheol (42.38) as he expresses his potential grief for Benjamin recall the similar words he used when he actually grieved for Joseph (37.35). So are the brothers going to commit the 'double' of their first crime: it will not be difficult to 'lose' Benjamin on this hazardous journey?

*May God Almighty make him kindly disposed to you*: God Almighty is a title reserved for use at significant moments in the ancestral story (17.1; 28.3; 35.11). Its association with blessing and fruitfulness makes it appropriate at this time of famine, and its link with the patriarchal promise of descendants means that it is telling that Israel should use it as he fears for the loss of further sons. *Kindly disposed* is echoed in the way that Joseph responds to Benjamin (see above and notes on 43.30 below). Jacob is hoping, of course, that the powerful Egyptian will not maltreat a group of defenceless strangers. However we, the readers are wondering at the same time if Joseph is eventually going to be merciful to his brothers.

*They are to eat with me at midday*: Is it significant that it is noted twice that this meal is at midday? Presumably the meal that the brothers ate while Joseph was in the pit (37.25) was also a midday meal. The fear that the invitation to share in this meal engendered in the brothers (43.18) suggests that if the invitation was a deliberate attempt to prod guilty consciences, it was succeeding.

*Your God, the God of your father, who hid treasure for you*: The steward's comment verbalises many of the ironies of this narrative. Although he must have known that it was people acting at Joseph's behest who had replaced the silver in the sacks, he is in one sense telling the truth: for the implied premise is that God's will is activated via the deeds of the human protagonists in this story. And although the silver in the sacks might have seemed a threat to the brothers it was in reality treasure – a symbol of God's efforts to fulfil his promises to Abraham and his family. The phrase *God of your father* further hints at the patriarchal promises (e.g. 26.24).

There is however perhaps another irony: Are we meant to think that Joseph is acting as though he believes he is God?

*They presented him with the gifts. . . bowing to the ground before him*: The story is 'closing in' on its protagonists with the presentation of the gifts that would have reminded Joseph of his brothers' treachery, accompanied by a gesture of subservience which again recalled his own dreams.

*Yes, my lord, our father is still alive and well*: By their turn of phrase the brothers now further fulfil Joseph's dreams, this time including their father (at least by proxy) in their language of subservience. The word *well* translates the Hebrew *shalom* which appears three times in 43.27–28. We are swiftly rewound to the opening verses of the entire story when we had been explicitly told that Joseph had been sent by his father to Shechem to enquire about the *shalom* of his brothers (37.14, compare 37.4).

*His own mother's son*: As well as helping us to identify Benjamin, the only full brother of Joseph, this phrase accentuates the pathos. The Rachel who wept for her children (Jer. 31.15) and died tragically young in childbirth echoes through this phrase. Joseph's yearning for Benjamin verbally parallels the grief that Rachel and even God feel for their children: it is symptomatic that Joseph's first words to his brother are *God be gracious to you, my son!* Surely concealed behind this familial phrase seems to be Joseph's desire to recognise Benjamin as his brother – and his agony that this is a step he is still psychologically unable to take.

*Joseph . . . was almost in tears*: The emotional pressure is building up. But wise men were proud of being able to control their emotions. So Joseph ensures that his weeping is done privately.

*He was served by himself*: Just as he had been kept separate when his brothers ate that other meal years before (37.24–25).

*For to Egyptians it is abhorrent to eat with Hebrews*: We suddenly stand outside the story for a moment, and hear of centuries of alienation. The term 'Hebrews' immediately identifies the brothers as outsiders, part of a group distrusted by 'settled society' whether in Egypt or elsewhere. But the complicated eating arrangements also highlight the fact that even Joseph himself was not fully accepted by the Egyptians (43.32). For all his apparent power he too still remained a 'Hebrew' outsider.

*The eldest first and so on down to the youngest*: The mysterious knowledge that is being indicated about the family age order might well cause the brothers to look *at one another in astonishment*. It was accentuated by the special honour shown to Benjamin, since normally the eldest in a family would receive this position. In several ways this meal functions like a 'rerun' of the day when the brothers had sold the 'favourite', Joseph.

*So they feasted and drank with him*: So often in stories recognition takes place while people are eating and drinking together – remember the road to Emmaus? – that we are primed to expect Joseph's revelation of himself to his brothers to take place – now. The further delay is almost painful for the reader.

44.1–34 The story now progresses to its denouement, catching up not only events in the earlier history of Joseph and the brothers – but even incidents that date back to the adventures of Jacob himself.

*Put my goblet, the silver one, at the top of the youngest brother's pack*: Benjamin is the deliberate target for Joseph's actions – it is only by framing him that Joseph will be able to measure how far his other brothers have changed.

*The one . . . he uses for divination*: That the cup is ostensibly used for divination is clearly a significant feature of the narrative. The link is reiterated in 44.15. The reference to the divining cup helps to preserve Joseph's cover as an Egyptian: divination was a popular skill in Egypt. At the same time it would have uncomfortably reminded the brothers that Joseph was likely to be able to 'see through' them, even their previous misdeeds that they hoped were safely buried deep in the past. The use of the Hebrew root *nahash* to refer both to the divining cup and to Joseph himself as diviner suggests a further possibility. There seems to be a connection intended between this incident and Jacob and Rachel's earlier dealings with Laban. Laban (30.27) uses the identical Hebrew root when he speaks of his situation vis-à-vis Jacob. The REB translation of 30.27, *I have become prosperous* is questionable. The NRSVs, 'I have learned by divination' better preserves the likely connection with the present passage (see comments on 30.27 on p. 190). And what is the connection between this ability of Laban to 'divine', and the household gods that Rachel then stole from her father? Were they Laban's divining tools, the equivalent of Joseph's cup? (See below on 44.9.)

*If any one of us is found with the goblet, he shall die*: Once before similar rash words had been uttered. That time it had been Jacob who pronounced a death sentence on the one who had 'stolen' Laban's household gods, without realising that it was his beloved Rachel who had done so (31.32). When later Rachel died in childbirth it seemed in effect the working out of Jacob's curse. Now a similar death sentence is being uttered over the one who has stolen this religious object. It will soon turn out that Benjamin is the thief, albeit unwittingly. Will he have a similar penalty to pay to that exacted from Rachel? The association becomes sharper because it was the very act of giving birth to Benjamin himself that had been the immediate cause of Rachel's death. Are all the lies and trickery that have plagued this family for generations now going to land on Benjamin's innocent head – for him to pay the penalty?

*The goblet was found in Benjamin's pack*: By the time the discovery is made the penalty that is to be exacted has been lightened. It is agreed that the culprit will be enslaved, not killed, and that he alone will be liable. Of course this would allow the brothers, if they chose, to abandon Benjamin to his fate with a reasonable conscience – only slavery, not death – exactly as they had once abandoned Joseph decades previously. The fact that they all choose to return to the city is an indication that they have radically changed.

*God has uncovered our crime*: Which crime is Judah talking about? The 'innocent' theft of the cup of which they are publicly being charged, or the long hidden guilty 'theft' of their brother whom they had allowed to be stolen (40.15, REB *carried off*) from his native land? It is as though the two events are coalescing in Judah's mind. The divining cup, hidden in a sack of grain, has almost become a visible symbol for Joseph the diviner, 'hidden' for so many years in Egypt, land of grain.

*Only the one . . . shall become my slave*: Joseph gives them yet another opportunity to abandon Benjamin. After all, by now, the brothers must have got quite used to explaining to Jacob how they had come to return home with one of their number missing!

*Then Judah*: What follows is the longest speech by a human being in the whole of Genesis. In it the book seems to come full circle, at least in some measure 'healing' the hurts that have plagued human beings since Cain's jealousy of his brother Abel erupted into violence. Judah can finally accept the unfair and arbitrary nature of parental love, however personally painful to him it is. *His father loves him*. What has brought about this sea change in Judah – the brother who in chapter 37 took the lead in seeking to be rid of a favoured brother (37.26) by selling him as a slave? Perhaps it is his experiences with his own sons, the loss of two and the desire to keep hold of the remaining one, about which we heard so much in chapter 38, that has led him to be more understanding of the passion of parental love.

*His life is bound up with the boy's*: The way that one human life interweaves with and affects the lives of others is a key theme of the saga of Joseph, and the whole of Genesis.

It is debatable whether the REB translation of the word *na'ar* as *boy* is most appropriate here. Perhaps 'young man' would be better. The same word *na'ar* also described Ishmael (21.17) and Isaac (22.5). Its use here reminds us of the preciousness of Benjamin: is he to be lost to his father, like those earlier two boys/young men almost were to theirs?

*Let me remain in place of the boy*: With this offer to act as a substitute Judah atones for the crime of 37 in which he played a leading role. His acceptance of servitude for himself, *let me remain . . . as my lord's slave*, is appropriate retribution for his involvement in the enslavement of another. The expression *I went surety*, which is in origin a legal term, helps to underline the formal seriousness of what Judah is offering, as well as the links back to Judah's experiences in chapter 38 (see also comments on 43.9, above). Jon Levenson comments:

> The enormous power behind Judah's offer derives from the complicated set of substitutions that it articulates. Judah will be the substitute for Benjamin, accepting upon himself the slavery to which Joseph has sentenced his younger brother. But Benjamin is himself a substitute, standing in for that other beloved son and child of Rachel and Jacob's old age, Joseph. And Joseph and Benjamin are both, in some deeper sense, substitutes for their father and thus paradigms for the people Israel.[2]

45.1–28 *Joseph was no longer able to control his feelings*: As a result of the words of Judah the impasse is finally broken and the convoluted layers of mutual deceit fall away.

*Joseph made himself known to his brothers*: Finally too, knowledge, sight, recognition and hearing all coincide and all are true – instead of as previously, so often playing off against each other as instruments of deceit.

*He wept so loudly*: The motif of Joseph's weeping also reaches its climax. He has now become almost the antithesis of the traditional picture of a 'wise man', who prized themselves on their composure. Weeping is a stage on the road to healing and reconciliation, as elsewhere in the Bible it sows the seeds of transformation and resurrection. A Jewish midrash on this passage aptly puts it, 'Tears extinguish the coals of the heart' (Midrash Lekah Tov, Genesis 43.30).

*I am Joseph. Can my father be still alive?*: The words of Joseph are even simpler in the Hebrew than English. It is significant that Joseph's first thought after his self-disclosure is for his father. In view of his brothers' earlier remarks (e.g. 43.28; 44.20) it was not a question he really needed to ask. That he does so now further hints at the way that the lives of Joseph and his father are bound so closely together. Just as the apparent death of Joseph had provoked Jacob to speak of going down to Sheol (37.35), so the 'resurrection' of Joseph will bring new life to his father.

*They could not answer*: Though the brothers are formally *face to face* with Joseph they cannot yet emotionally 'face' him or speak to him. Echoes of humanity's discomfiture before Yʜwʜ in Gen. 3, and perhaps the reconciliation of Jacob and Esau, are present.

*It was to save lives that God sent me ahead of you . . . It is clear that it was not you who sent me here, but God*: Joseph is very sure of himself. Certainly the God of Genesis is a God who grants and seeks life, in spite of the flood. But just as we might remember that Joseph's dreams of greatness in chapter 37 were Joseph's own and God did not feature in them, so we might also wonder whether, now that they have been apparently fulfilled, God was quite so involved in the process that led to this as Joseph might like to believe. Are human beings quite such passive pawns in a grand schema as Joseph implies? The stories of his father (Gen. 27.1—33.17) suggest that human beings need to bear responsibility for their actions, even if they are also part of a greater providence. And by letting his brothers off the hook, Joseph is conveniently also sidestepping the fact that his own behaviour may have contributed to their hostility.

*To preserve for you a host of survivors*: The language used echoes the motif of the 'remnant' which is a significant theme in prophetic literature, particularly in relation to the exile (see e.g. Isa. 10.21–22). It is also a term used in Sir. 44.17 to describe the role of Noah. There are subtle hints that link this famine in the *whole world* (41.57) to the flood. Joseph's brothers are being told that they are fortunate to escape such a calamity.

*God has made me lord of all Egypt*: In 41.41 we were explicitly told that it was Pharaoh who established Joseph in this position. What does this imply for the relationship between God, Pharaoh and Joseph? One reading would be that Joseph was somehow 'identifying' God's will with Pharaoh's: a dubious proposition in a country such as Egypt notorious for regarding its ruler as divine.

The *land of Goshen* was a fertile area near the Nile delta, close to Sinai. Historically nomads were often allowed to settle there by the rulers of Egypt.

*Tell my father of all the honour which I enjoy in Egypt*: It is difficult to like Joseph even at this moment of apparent reconciliation. He still remains the 'spoilt' son who wants his father to realise how much he has 'made good'. And he seems very much determined to stay in control of his brothers' and his father's lives.

*He then kissed each of his brothers*: They are only able to *talk with* Joseph when they have been individually greeted by him. They, no less than Joseph himself, need to be treated as unique individuals.

*I shall give you the best region there is in Egypt*: Pharaoh is almost excessively generous. But the relationship between the Egyptians and Joseph's family will go through an almost imperceptible shift even before the end of Genesis.

Joseph's provisions and instructions for his brothers' journey are telling. There is still the same favouritism for Benjamin. The *new clothes* recall Joseph's own special robe and stripping (37.23). The *pieces of silver* remind us, and presumably the brothers too, of the silver for which they sold him. And the command not *to quarrel among themselves on the journey* offers a nice sense of pragmatic realism.

Jacob *was stunned . . . his spirit revived*: Jacob's heart literally missed a beat when they told him Joseph was alive – ironic in view of his earlier protestations. The vivid language of his spirit reviving again emphasises the interweaving of the lives of father and son.

## Hints of the future
46.1—50.26

In these chapters Jacob and Joseph seem to jostle for control of the narrative. Unlike chapters 42—45 where events are largely orchestrated by Joseph, here Jacob (or perhaps rather 'Israel') seeks the opportunity to offer a different perspective which may at times conflict with Joseph's priorities. Some of these chapters (e.g. 46.1–27; 47.27—48.22) remind us of earlier sections of Genesis. Their style, and particularly their view of God's way of working with human beings, contrast with perceptions in other parts of chapters 37—50. Perhaps they originally provided a conclusion to an earlier edition of Genesis which did not include the story of Joseph in its present form.

46.1–27 *Israel . . . came to Beersheba*: It is an appropriate location for Israel to offer these sacrifices to *the God of his father* (46.1, 3) both because Beersheba was important in the life of Isaac, his father, (26.1–33) and because it marked a traditional boundary of the land of Canaan. Israel needs divine reassurance as he leaves the land once again, particularly as he is going down to Egypt, a place which Isaac had been specifically prohibited from travelling to (26.2). But it is intriguing that the first mention of Beersheba in Genesis (21.14) is associated with Hagar. It was the place to which she and her son had been sent out to die. Perhaps the interweaving of Abraham's story with that of Hagar and her descendants is still continuing (see comments on 15.13; 16.1–15, p. 94).

This is the first time since 35.11–12 that God has spoken directly to anyone. It takes place *in a vision by night*. The phrase reminds us of two of Jacob/Israel's earlier numinous experiences which had taken place at night (28.11; 32.22). Appropriately for this time of famine the promise does not focus on land (that was mentioned previously in 35.12) but on the fact that Israel's descendants will become a *great nation*. The doubled *Jacob! Jacob!* reflects the solemnity of the occasion, and recalls the previous time the angel of God had repeated the name of a patriarch in such a way (22.11). Jacob's response also echoes that of Abraham in the earlier story. *I am here* (Hebrew: *hinneni*). That willingness to be at a deity's or a father's beck and call has led the ancestors on some uncomfortable pathways in the past – what will it lead to on this occasion and in the future?

Israel goes down into Egypt. The person, the ancestor, now begins imperceptibly to shade into the nation, his descendants. The genealogy given at this point hints at this. The promise is made by God, *I myself shall bring you back again without fail* (46.4). Perhaps this refers in part to the return of Jacob's body, after his death, to Canaan. But the writer's eyes are already set on a greater return, at the time of the Exodus, when the whole nation of Israel is brought out of Egypt.

The genealogical list of Jacob's descendants numbering 70 (46.27) echoes the list of the 'Table of the Nations' (10.1–32), which also seems to be intended to include 70 names. Israel had not been named among the other nations in that earlier list – and a key theme of the rest of Genesis has been about how that omission is to be rectified.

It is fascinating that the two sons for whom grandchildren are listed are Judah (46.12) and Benjamin (46.21). Judah is perhaps understandable in view of the interest in his family in 38.1–30 but it seems strange that Benjamin, whom we met as apparently a boy or young man in 42—45 is now himself a grandfather!

It is also intriguing that the Canaanite woman who bore a son to

Simeon should be specifically mentioned (46.10), particularly in view of Simeon's violent objection to his sister's involvement with a Canaanite (34.25).

Other than Dinah (46.15), the only female descendant of Jacob mentioned is Serah, the daughter of Asher (46.17). She will also be one of the few female figures listed in the census in the wilderness in Num. 26.46, where a literal reading might suggest that she was still alive. Rabbinic writers wove fascinating legends around Serah – suggesting that she was the one individual who spanned the period between the entry into Egypt and the Exodus, and as a result she was able to tell Moses where Joseph's bones were buried. The tradition further developed that Serah, like Enoch and Elijah, escaped death and was granted immortality. It is intriguing to wonder whether even in the biblical text there could be the foreshadowing of such later developments: is Serah mentioned here as a sign of hope – a pledge being offered at this moment of uncertainty that there is a future for Jacob and his descendants.

**46.28–30** Judah's role (46.28) in organising the reunion between Joseph and their father balances the roles he plays earlier in the story (37.26; 44.18–34) and foreshadows the fact that he will not be forgotten when the time for final blessings arrives (49.8–12).

Although this reunion itself is clearly a defining moment in the lives of both Jacob and Joseph, there is an imbalance in the emotion expressed by the two participants. Rabbinic tradition suggested that Jacob/Israel's comparative restraint was due to his belated realisation that his unhealthy favouritism for Joseph was a form of idolatry. If he was to fulfil his role as the father of the entire nation he needed to embody all, not simply one son, within himself.

**46.31—47.12** Still Joseph has not lost his astuteness. He wanted his family to settle in the land of Goshen, the eastern part of the delta, nearest to Canaan – and renowned for its fertility. But this might have been regarded as a security risk by the Egyptians. So Joseph advises his family to admit that they were shepherds, people who (according to the story) were held in horror by the Egyptians. Then Pharaoh would insist that they should settle in Goshen – as far away from the cities as possible. Joseph's ploy works – even though the brothers nearly spoil it by blurting out too much – their desire to settle in Goshen! Yet we have already quietly shifted from the situation that applied in 45.18–20 when Pharaoh's words were almost embarrassingly welcoming. The precise expression *allotted land* (*'ahuzzah*) recalls the previous times the same word was used – as property in Canaan (23.4, 9, 20) and as fulfilment of God's promise to give land there as a *possession* (17.8). Is there something jarring about the fact that this land has been given in Egypt? The mention of the *district of Rameses*, a name which is anachronistic to the period, seems like a hint of the slave labour that awaits the Israelites as they are set to build the city of that name (Exod. 1.11). All in all the episode is a quiet reminder that however powerful Joseph may be, or think he is, he (like everyone else) lives precariously in Egypt at the whim of the Pharaoh.

*Jacob blessed Pharaoh*: In the course of this negotiation there is an unexpected – at least from the perspective of Pharaoh – inversion of the normal social order. In fact Jacob is the first of the ancestors to utter a blessing on anyone other than a member of his family. In embryo the promise that Abraham's family would be a means of blessing for others is now being fulfilled.

*The years of my life on earth are one hundred and thirty*: Underlying the expression my life *on earth* is the Hebrew root that appeared first in 15.13 as *ger* (= alien) (see comments on p. 90). It also appeared in the brothers' request *to stay* (47.4) in Egypt. As Genesis is drawing to its close we are being reminded that this is a family who up till now has had 'no abiding city'. They will not ultimately find it in Egypt either: threats as well as promises are beginning to come to fulfilment, including YHWH's covenantal comment (15.13) of the 400 years to be spent as aliens and slaves in Egypt.

47.13–26   Most modern readers feel a sense of distaste as they come across these verses. Are we really meant to approve of Joseph's cleverness as Pharaoh's administrator – a cleverness that finally results in virtually all of Egypt belonging to Pharaoh? Is the famine relief operation really only a gigantic manoeuvre enabling Pharaoh to reduce people to the status of landless serfs? Only the priests remain owners of their lands. In spite of various attempts to justify Joseph's behaviour (i.e. 'at least the people survived') it is highly questionable whether the author of Genesis viewed these actions of Joseph in a positive light.

*Joseph moved the people into the towns*: Intriguingly the Septuagint and the Samaritan version of Genesis imply that this was not what was originally written here. The text of both suggest something even more sinister, 'Joseph enslaved the people as slaves'. (It only requires the amendment of a few Hebrew letters to move from one alternative to the other.) It seems likely that this reference to enslaving may have been the original reading – but that it was just too much to stomach for the revisers of the Masoretic text (the Hebrew version on which our English translations are based). And if Joseph did indeed 'enslave the Egyptians as slaves' his callous ruthlessness provided ample reasons, both practically and theologically, for the later enslavement by the Egyptians of Joseph's own descendants.

The comment that priests alone remain owners of their lands contrasts with the Israelite tradition that the priests were the one group who did not own land. In a few short verses the writer of Genesis has drawn a picture that reverses the Old Testament ideal, with its sabbatical and Jubilee traditions of freeing slaves, remitting debts and serving God, in whom perfect freedom can be found, alone.

The language with which Joseph is addressed *If it please your lordship* (47.25) echoes the kind of language used for a god. Aaron Wildavksy's comment is justified, 'If Joseph does have a moral blind spot it is that from beginning to end he does not recognize the potential of abuse of power without limits. Joseph's Egyptianisation reflects his identification with power.'[3] The next book of the Pentateuch will introduce another 'Hebrew', Moses, who will also have close connections with Pharaoh's court (Exod. 2.10). Moses however will break free of Pharaoh's control in order to free others who are slaves. Joseph was 'freed' from prison and slavery into Pharaoh's power in order to enslave those previously free. It is hard to avoid the suspicion that the two figures are being deliberately contrasted. The readers of Genesis are being invited to reflect on alternative models of leadership. Choose this day which path you will take!

47.27–31 *Israel settled in Egypt . . . and were fruitful*: Note how here for the first time in Genesis we have the name 'Israel' (not simply 'sons of Israel') used with a plural verb. Israel has now become a nation, at least in essence. We have heard the language of fruitfulness in Genesis several times before, but up till now it has usually been spoken as a promise or blessing (Joseph's words after the birth of his son Ephraim in 41.52 provide the exception). A strange place and a strange time therefore for the blessing of creation and the promise to Abraham to receive its fulfilment: a foreign land and a time of scarcity and famine. It does however also beg the question as to how far Joseph's own kin suffered the same economic hardships that the Egyptians experienced, or whether perhaps they even indirectly benefited from their plight. Is this, along with Abraham and Sarah's treatment of Hagar (see p. 92), possibly the reason that Jacob and Joseph's descendants must become slaves in Egypt (15.13)?

*Jacob lived in Egypt for seventeen years and died at the age of a hundred and forty-seven*: The mathematics of the patriarchs' ages is fascinating: Abraham lived 175 years, i.e. $5 \times 5 \times 7$; Isaac 180 years i.e. $6 \times 6 \times 5$ and Jacob 147 years i.e. $7 \times 7 \times 3$. In each case the squared number increases by one, and the other number decreases by 2. Furthermore the sum of the three numbers in each case adds up to 17, which is also the number of years that Jacob lived in Egypt (as well as being the number of years that Joseph spent in Canaan in his youth). The effect is to suggest that events in the ancestral story did not happen at random: their lives have been lived under God's precise and providential care, and form part of a greater design.

*Give me your solemn oath*: As the REB marginal note implies this process involved Joseph in putting his hand under his father's thigh, presumably therefore touching his genital organs (compare 24.2). There is an obvious connection with the covenant (of circumcision) offered to Abraham, as well, perhaps, with Jacob/Israel's own experience of wounding at Penuel (32.25). The covenant connections are reinforced by the idiom *loyally and faithfully*, vocabulary which is used elsewhere to express fidelity to a covenant (see Exod. 34.6; compare 32.10). It may be that Joseph, because of his sale into slavery, was legally no longer Jacob's son, and this ceremony was a form of reintegration into the family and covenant community. It is associated with the request *Do not bury me in Egypt* since it was important for Jacob, as for his ancestors Abraham and Sarah, (see 23.4), that God's covenant promise of land should become a personal reality, even if only to provide the grave for his burial.

*Israel bowed in worship*: Is it a gesture towards Joseph, the fulfilment of Joseph's dream of grandeur (37.9), or of thanksgiving towards God?

48.1–22  The account of the adoption and then blessing by Jacob of Ephraim and Manasseh seems to weave together threads from both the family saga and the story of the nation. If it was indeed the case that Joseph, through his sale into slavery, had, at least temporarily, legally lost his position within the family this might put any sons born to him during this period in an anomalous position which Jacob feels a need to rectify. But it is also interesting to note that 1 Chron. 9.2–3 could be read as suggesting that in the post-exilic period the core of Israel was constituted by Judah, Benjamin, Ephraim and Manasseh. It

265

is possible that some of the storyline of Gen. 37—50 (perhaps particularly this chapter) reflects this development.

*Jacob said to Joseph, 'God Almighty appeared to me . . .'*: Jacob's speech seems to recapitulate the words he had directly heard from God Almighty (Gen. 35.11–12). Once again *God Almighty* is linked with fertility and fruitfulness. It is only those who themselves have been direct recipients of God's blessing who can legitimately impart it to others: Joseph, for all his greatness, has never received a direct revelation, and so if his sons are to be included within the community of promise the words will need to be uttered by Jacob his father. The vision at Luz (identified with Bethel in 35.6) is recalled as Jacob's authority for what he is about to do.

*I shall give this land . . . as a possession for all time*: The significant word *'ahuzzah* which first appeared in 17.8 (see p. 132), reappears, here translated as *possession*. It had, however, been used in 47.11 to describe Joseph's – or Pharaoh's – allocation of land to Jacob's family. Its use here is perhaps pointed: God's promise of land in Canaan is *for all time* over against the temporary 'loan' of territory in Egypt.

*Ephraim and Manasseh will be mine as Reuben and Simeon are*: It is not quite clear whether this comparison with the two oldest sons of Jacob by Leah means that Ephraim and Manasseh will supersede Reuben and Simeon by holding the privilege of the birthright due to the first-born. 1 Chron. 5.1 seems to suggest this was the case.

The sudden and slightly surprising mention of Rachel (48.7) may be due to the fact that in chapter 35 (on which the present chapter seems to depend) her death is recorded just after the divine appearance to Jacob at Bethel/Luz. Yet it is also a reminder that that early dream of Joseph (37.10) in which (apparently) he saw his mother bowing down to him, along with the rest of his family, can never completely be fulfilled. On the emotional level Rachel's early death (after only producing two sons) helps to explain Jacob's desire to adopt *Ephraim and Manasseh* (notice the order).

*Now Israel's eyes were dim with age*: Once before an aged patriarch with failing eyesight had had to bless male heirs (27.7). Then Isaac had been deceived and had (at least from his own perspective) blessed the wrong/younger son. We remember that story as we read of how the original deceiver will now choose deliberately to bestow a special blessing on a younger son.

*Now God has let me see your sons as well*: Literally the Hebrew speaks of 'seeing your seed'. Though obscured by the variety of ways it has been translated (e.g. 'descendants', 'sons'), the word has appeared throughout Genesis. Here it suggests that Joseph's sons, as 'seed' will stand in a line which will link back to the promises made to Abraham (12.7), yet also reach into the future.

*Joseph removed them from his father's knees*: Placing a child between the knees of a person was a formal gesture that signified an act of adoption (compare 30.3).

*And bowed to the ground*: At the last it is Joseph who bows before his father – in spite of the message of his dreams which suggested the reverse.

Though introduced by the comment *he blessed Joseph* this oracle of blessing is focused more on Joseph's sons. It recapitulates the past in order to point towards the future. It echoes phrases and incidents that come from the life of Jacob/Israel and from the lives of his own forefathers. *The God in whose presence my forefathers lived* recalls the demand made of Abram in 17.1; the image of shepherd has featured at key moments in Jacob's story (29.1–10) and will be alluded to again in Jacob's blessing of Joseph (49.24); the *angel who rescued me* alludes to episodes such as 28.12; 32.1 and 32.22–32. However the choice of the word translated *rescued* (Hebrew: *ga'al*) which can also be translated as 'redeem' surely also points forward towards and hints at the Exodus, with which it is characteristically associated (Exod. 6.6). As God has redeemed in Israel's own past, so he will also redeem in Israel's future. Finally the repeated reference to *name* takes us right back to the initial call of Abram, and the pledge then, 12.2 to make his name great. Yet the very act of calling the two boys by Israel's name, is an indication that Israel himself has now become more than a person. He is being transformed into a *great people*.

*This is the firstborn; lay your right hand on his head*. Although (unlike the time when Jacob himself had seized Esau's blessing) both brothers will be blessed, a blessing bestowed by their grandfather's right hand would indicate Manasseh's pre-eminence. But that is not how it is going to be – indeed it never has been throughout the whole book of Genesis. Instead Ephraim will receive the greater blessing

*I know, my son, I know*: The emphatic repetition of *know* suggests that more may be meant than simply an old man insisting that he is in full possession of his faculties. Is Jacob claiming for himself the knowledge and wisdom that has been sought by humanity throughout Genesis – part of which seems to be focused in God's mysterious preference for a younger son?

His descendants will be a whole nation in themselves. Although Manasseh's name was given to one of the clans (e.g. Num. 26.29–34)

Ephraim was to become a synonym used frequently for the whole people of Israel (e.g. Hos. 11.1–3; Jer. 31.8). Significantly it is often employed in passages which speak of God's tender, paternal love.

*I assign you one ridge of land more than your brothers*: The old favouritism still comes to the fore. As the REB notes, underlying *ridge* is the word *shechem*, which can mean a 'shoulder' of land, but is also likely to be an oblique allusion to the city of Shechem, which has played a significant part in both the ancestral story (12.6) and that of Joseph himself (37.13). It will become part of the territory allotted to the house of Joseph in the division made in Josh. 16—17 and it will be where Joseph is eventually buried after the Exodus from Egypt (Josh. 24.32).

*I took it from the Amorites with sword and bow*: Is this an ironic reference to the pillage of Shechem in Gen. 34 (in which Jacob actually plays a passive role), or does it relate to another story circulating about Jacob which has not been incorporated in Genesis?

49.1–28  The range of blessings that Jacob offers at the end of his story (to Pharaoh, to Ephraim and Manasseh and now to his 12 sons) seem to parallel his hunger to be blessed (by his father and YHWH) near his story's beginning. And just as earlier there was considerable ambiguity about the blessings Jacob received – so now his own blessings have a questionable character. As one recent writer puts it, 'If these are Jacob's blessings, what would his curses be like.'[4] This will be the final occasion that the verb 'bless' and the noun 'blessing' is used – the motif that has dominated the entire book of Genesis and especially the story of the ancestors. Re-reading the original blessing and promise given to Abraham (12.2–3) alongside this chapter is instructive: it suggests that there is still some way to go, both now, or even in the kind of future presupposed by Jacob's words, before the divine words to Abraham can be said to have come to fruition. We are being pointed into a future beyond Genesis itself, and perhaps even beyond the present of the writer. The explicit words *I shall tell you what is to happen to you in days to come* with which the 'blessings' are introduced are a reminder that Genesis is ultimately a book of promise rather than fulfilment.

It used to be thought that the 'Blessings of Jacob' might have been an originally separate and archaic poem inserted at this point into the story of Jacob's family. That seems unlikely, at least in its present form. Several of the blessings allude with verbal puns to incidents that are recounted earlier in Genesis. Perhaps rather we should think of this as an earlier poem that has been edited and adapted to fit its present context. It is interesting to compare this passage with the corresponding Blessing of Moses in Deut. 33.1–29.

The six sons of Jacob by Leah are listed first.

*Reuben*: Though given prime position, as the first-born, Jacob's words remind us of the incident (35.22) in which Reuben committed incest with his father's concubine, and suggest that as a result of this Reuben lost the 'primacy'.

*Simeon and Levi*: Similarly harsh words are addressed to Simeon and Levi, in their case probably recalling the murderous attack on Shechem which they led (34.25–31). Unlike the 'Blessing of Moses' (Deut. 33.8–11), there is no particular awareness here of Levi as a 'priestly' tribe. However Levi's 'fervency for YHWH' expressed in the Shechem incident, may also be reflected in the violent enthusiasm Levi elsewhere shows for his priestly role (Deut. 33.9; Exod. 32.28). The text reflects the fact that in later history none of the tribes of Simeon, Levi or Reuben were significant politically or numerically.

*Judah*: With his three older brothers disposed of, the text then concentrates on Judah, reflecting both his significant position within the story of 37—50, and the importance of the tribe of Judah. It opens with a ringing pun on Judah's name, *your brothers will praise [yodu] you*. Then the terms *sceptre* and *staff* are used to highlight Judah's later strength – and to remind us that David's family sprang from this tribe. Not surprisingly this passage has been interpreted both in Judaism and Christianity as a messianic prophecy. Matt. 21.7 seems to allude to it as he describes Jesus' triumphal entry into Jerusalem. The text also probably hints at the story of Judah and Tamar in Gen. 38. Some of the words in 49.10–12 could be explained as (fairly obscure) puns on the vocabulary and incidents in this story, for example, *his eyes* which may be a reference to Enaim, where Judah met Tamar in her prostitute's garb (see p. 239).

The mysterious reference to *Shiloh,* relegated by the REB to a footnote because it was considered too difficult to translate, may refer to the fact that the town of Shiloh seems to have had at one point an important role as a religious and political centre of Israel (Josh. 18.10; Judg. 21.19; 1 Sam. 1.3). The town's own history is also something of a mystery. Although we assume from the narrative of 1 Sam. 1—4 and references in Ps. 78.60 and Jer. 7.12–15 that the sanctuary at Shiloh, in Ephraimite territory north of Jerusalem, was destroyed in the pre-monarchic period, figures associated with Shiloh (e.g. Ahijah, 1 Kgs 11.29–39) seem to play an ongoing part in the nation's history, in Ahijah's case associated with the split between northern and southern kingdoms. In fact this reference to Shiloh in Gen. 49.10 may be intended as a promise of the time when the division between south and north, which the brothers Judah and Joseph personify, is healed. Additionally several Jewish targums (Aramaic paraphrases of the Hebrew text) identify Shiloh directly as a reference to the Messiah, and this interpretation has also been adopted in some Christian circles. Joanna Southcott, an eighteenth and nineteenth century English prophetess, believed that she was going to give birth to 'the Shiloh'.

Whatever the interpretation of the precise details of the oracle about Judah it is certainly striking that it is Judah, rather than Joseph who is promised *your father's sons will bow down to you in homage* (49.8).

With *Zebulun* and *Issachar* the references in the 'blessings' are largely geographical, loosely alluding to the regions elsewhere associated with these tribes. The pun linking Issachar's name to 'hire' (*sakar*) which was made at his birth (30.16–18), is also apparent here.

The next four sons are born from the slave wives:

A pun on Dan's name introduces the words about him. The Hebrew root *din* normally meaning 'to execute judgement', underlies the REB translation *be strong*. His description as a 'viper' who 'brings down' a stronger foe have led some to see in this passage an allusion to the violent story of Samson the judge, from the tribe of Dan, and his victory in death over the Philistines, pulling down the temple of Dagon upon himself and a crowd of Philistines.

This is followed by the enigmatic outburst *I wait in hope for salvation from you, O Lord*. This is the first time that YHWH has been named since 39.23. And it is the first time that Jacob himself has called upon YHWH since 32.9–11 when he prayed *Save me*. Perhaps this utterance suggests that Jacob is still waiting for YHWH's full deliverance, promised in those encounters in his earlier life, which in 28.13–15 had included an assurance of return to the land of Canaan.

The words about the following three sons again seem to allude to the geographical location of the tribes linked to their names. The punning on Gad's name is powerful: *Gad is raided by raiders, and he will raid* [*gad gedud yegudenu, wehu' yagud*]. There is probably a connection between the prosperity predicted for Asher and the fact that the word *'ashrey* means 'fortunate'.

Then come the two sons of Rachel – first Joseph, whose blessing is as long as that assigned to Judah. The fertile territory of the area linked with the 'house of Joseph', around Shechem and Samaria, is clearly alluded to (as also in the corresponding passage in the Blessing of Moses, Deut. 33.13–17, on which the present verses may be based). The word *blessing*, which actually had not been used by Jacob in his words to his sons up till this point, now appears five times, and along with the hint about Joseph's fruitfulness (49.22) perhaps reminds us of the beginning of Genesis – as do the references to heaven (49.25, compare 1.1) and the deep (49.25, compare 1.2). But there are apparent links to other biblical texts as well, Ps. 80.1, 12 for example, and possible intricate intertextual allusions to earlier parts of the story of the ancestors. Nahum Sarna notes how the Hebrew of 49.22 may conceal a cryptic reference to *the spring on the road to Shur* (16.7) where Hagar saw the angel.[5] In fact 49.22–26 is very obscure – what REB translates as *fruitful tree* is in some other biblical versions rendered as 'wild ass'. Sarna sees here an allusion to Ishmael who is described as a *wild ass* (16.12) and an *archer* (21.20, compare 49.23). Remembering the role of the Ishmaelites in the sale of Joseph into slavery (37.25), the oracle may be reminding us how the destinies of the actions of the ancestors, for good or ill, influence the lives of their descendants. It is only when the suffering has been spent that the blessing can be gained.

And finally Benjamin – what a contrast with the way Benjamin has been portrayed in Gen. 42—44! There are tales in Judges that associate the tribe of Benjamin with acts of ferocity (Judg. 19—21), which perhaps lie behind this description of Benjamin as a tribe of particular savagery.

*These are the tribes of Israel*: At last Israel has moved from being a family to being a nation. The implication of the entry of the 70 names into Egypt is actualised – even if only as a promise for the future.

49.29–33   Jacob reaches his final moments. He has taken a long time getting there, having in effect been 'dying' since he reached Egypt. (47.9, 29–31). The importance that Jacob attaches to being buried in Canaan is emphasised by the repetition here of his earlier demand to Joseph (47.29–30). It is now spelt out in more detail: he is to be taken to the tomb at Machpelah where his ancestors were also buried. In death Leah will have to herself the husband she had to share in life, since Rachel is buried elsewhere (see 48.7), though it is also notable that, unlike Sarah and Rebecca whom he describes as the wives of their respective husbands, Jacob does not call Leah 'my wife'. That title is reserved for Rachel, and Rachel alone (see 44.27).

**50.1–14**  The aftermath of Jacob's death highlights the many ambiguities that Joseph and his family are now facing in Egypt, and in Canaan. All may not be quite as it seems. The post-death rituals offered to Jacob, including embalming, seemingly emphasise the honour in which Joseph's father is held by the Egyptians, as does the mourning period of 110 days (40 + 70) – since this was probably a significant number (see notes on 50.22). Yet when Joseph comes to fulfil his pledge to bury his father in Canaan the care with which he has to tread suggests the vulnerability of his family. Joseph requests members of Pharaoh's household, *May I ask a favour – please speak for me to Pharaoh.* Is this the same Joseph who once proudly boasted to his brothers *God . . . has made me Pharaoh's chief counsellor, lord over his whole household* (45.8)? And his choice of words sanitise his father's instructions to him. Admittedly it might not be tactful to mention that Jacob had bluntly stated *do not bury me in Egypt* (47.29), but Joseph's comment that Jacob wished to be buried *in the grave that he had bought for himself in Canaan* is a subtle distortion of the truth (it wasn't Jacob who bought that grave!) – but one made presumably to put emotional pressure on Pharaoh. The pledge with which the permission is sought *Ask Pharaoh to let me go up . . . and afterwards I shall return* suggests that Joseph and his family may rapidly be becoming not so much guests as prisoners, albeit in a gilded cage.

That impression is reinforced by the description of those who accompany Jacob's funeral cortège in Canaan – and those who do not. Do *Pharaoh's officials . . . and all the elders of Egypt* (50.7) participate as a guard of honour, or simply as a guard? And though it might have been realistic to leave behind the flocks and herds while on this journey, the children who remained in Goshen acted conveniently as hostages ensuring the family's return.

Yet ironically when the funeral cortège reaches the boundary of Canaan, the Canaanites mistake the family for Egyptians (50.11). What an unfortunate fate for a grandson of Abraham, even though he is eventually buried in his grandfather's tomb. The ancestral promise of the land seems further away from being fulfilled than it has ever been. Neither in Egypt nor in Canaan can Jacob and his family be comfortably at home.

**50.15–26**  A different set of ambiguities then arise. The brothers fear that the day of reckoning has at last arrived for their original act of betrayal, and that Joseph's earlier reconciliation with them had been feigned – due to his desire to see his father again. The deception that has played such a large part in this family's story makes its reappearance: the purported message from their father to Joseph is highly suspicious. Did Jacob really say that, or is it not more likely the brothers' own fabrication? Truth breaks through however when the brothers address Joseph directly in their own right. *We beg you: forgive our crime, for we are servants of your father's God.* In the 'false' message from their father to Joseph they described themselves as your brothers, but now speaking directly they recognise that they forfeited the right to call and be called 'brother', that day when they did their brother *no harm* (37.27) by selling him as a slave. They can only plead the bonds of shared familial faith. Their desperation is made more transparent as they finally acknowledge *We are your slaves*, accompanying their words with a grovelling gesture that fulfils the old dream that had originally angered them so bitterly (37.6–10). By selling Joseph as a slave they had set in train a process that had both led to his dream's fulfilment, and had resulted in this metaphorical 'slavery' for themselves.

In turn Joseph's reaction and response can be understood in a number of different ways. The uncertainty is probably deliberate. It reminds us that forgiveness and healing is complex. Why did Joseph weep when confronted with his brothers' devious words? Was it sorrow that he was still misunderstood? Or is it relief that the unexpressed bitterness of the years is now out in the open? It was notable that when the apparent reconciliation with his brothers had taken place in chapter 45 the initiative had been totally Joseph's own. His brothers had found it difficult to talk to him then. Now it is their turn to do the talking.

But there are then two comments Joseph makes in return, alongside insisting that his brothers have no reason to fear him. The first is a question *Am I in the place of God?* The second is a longer comment in which the 'meaning' of what has happened over the last 14 chapters of Genesis is explained. Yet both remarks may be more equivocal than is apparent at first sight. Our immediate reaction to Joseph's enigmatic question *Am I in the place of God?* is to dismiss it as merely rhetorical. We are relieved that at last the self-centred youth of chapter 37 has learned enough to place God rather than himself at the centre. But does this question also mean he is not qualified to judge his brothers – or not qualified to forgive them? And if we reflect a bit more deeply we might even begin to wonder whether our immediate instinct was right after all. Once before the identical phrase was used – by Joseph's own father to Joseph's mother as she demanded a child from him

(30.2). As we suggested there, Jacob did in some senses 'take the place of God' – at least until Joseph himself was born. There is indeed a sense that Joseph has been 'playing God' in the last few chapters, with the cat-and-mouse game he played with his family, with the oppression that he has meted out to the Egyptians, with his absolute certainty that he knows the mind of God (41.16, 25; 45.8). That perhaps makes us a little suspicious as to how we should interpret Joseph's next words in which he offers his explanation for the events he and his family have experienced. It is comforting to think of what has happened as the work of an overarching providence. Joseph's comment about *good* (50.20) also provides appropriate closure for a book which had begun with God's pronouncement of creation as *very good* (1.31) and his view about the working of providence was, broadly speaking, characteristic of Israel's wisdom tradition. Joseph was, as we know, a 'wise' man (41.33). Ps. 33.10–11 provides another example of such theology – of how the evil plans of human beings can be enfolded in the ultimate purposes of God. There are pointers in earlier parts of the saga of Joseph that this is how it is here too. In chapter 39, for example, we have been told at both the beginning and end of the chapter how YHWH was operating, there in the background nudging the human actors along even when they didn't always realise it.

But we last met that deity when Joseph was in the prison, and he seems to have disappeared from the picture since Joseph rose to glory and control of the destinies of others. So is it through Joseph's eyes alone that we should seek to read and understand the story? If Joseph is right God has, in withdrawing from the scene, succeeded in controlling it more absolutely. Karen Armstrong has commented that Genesis as a whole does not accept Joseph's 'theological view of a wholly omnipotent and irresistible God, in whose grand designs human beings are mere pawns'.[6] Should not the brothers be allowed to own their own guilt, however painful it might be? (See further in theological reflections on p. 282.)

*Thus he comforted them and set their minds at rest*: Perhaps these words of the narrator hint at an alternative theological explanation which we are being reminded of. 'Comfort' and 'set the mind at rest' (literally 'speak to the heart') are expressions that appear together in Isa. 40.1–2 to introduce chapters 40—55, a part of the Bible that contains, in passages like Isa. 52.13—53.12, some of the most profound reflections on guilt and suffering in the entire Bible. Are we meant to hold the exquisite struggle of Isa. 40—55 to *our* hearts to help us balance Joseph's perhaps too easy theodicy?

'Comfort' is a word that has appeared at key moments in Genesis. It was what Noah was born for (5.29) and what Jacob refused (37.35) after Joseph's own disappearance. In the apparent rapprochement of this divided family have we finally reached what humanity has yearned for through so many generations?

*He lived to be a hundred and ten years old*: The repetition of Joseph's age at his death (50.22, 26) suggests that it is important. There is some evidence that 110 years was considered the 'perfect' age in Egypt. It also has a mathematical relationship to the ages of his ancestors, Abraham, Isaac and Jacob. Each of their ages contains a square number (see comments on p. 265), in Abraham's case $5^2$ in Isaac's $6^2$, and in Jacob's $7^2$. Joseph's age is the sum of these squares (i.e. 25 + 36 + 49. It provides a way of suggesting that he is the 'completion' of the patriarchs, as well as once again indicating God's oversight of history. Joseph's descendant Joshua, from the tribe of Ephraim (Josh. 24.29), also lived 110 years. There are various links between the two figures – one of whom 'oversaw' the entry of the Israelites into Egypt, and the other their return to Canaan. They both also have connections with Shechem (Josh. 24.1–32).

So the age of Joseph at the end of Genesis symbolically looks both back to the ancestors, but also forward to Moses, Joshua and an Exodus from the land to which Joseph had brought his family.

The future Exodus and return to the place from where Joseph came is also the subject of Joseph's last words, *God will not fail to come to your aid*. It is fascinating however that the theological view this statement implies, of a God acting directly in history, does not exactly equate with Joseph's understanding of the workings of God as it has been expressed by him up to this point. Nor does the fragility of this paragraph quite tally with the picture of the man who has, for the last few chapters, been omnipotent in relation to his own family. Joseph's bones and his future will be in the hands of his brothers and their descendants: he will depend upon them to return him to the land from which they had banished him (Exod. 13.19). Joseph will finally get to Shechem again (Josh. 24.32), the place where he had gone to meet his brothers all those years ago (37.14), due only to the co-operation of those self-same brothers.

The final sentence of Genesis is extraordinarily 'low key' given the vast scope of this book. Read against the first verse of the story of Joseph and his brothers, which had emphasised how Jacob had *made his home* (37.1) in Canaan, the comment that Joseph was placed in a coffin *in Egypt* suggests that God's promises to this family are now no nearer to – and possibly even further away from – being realised than they were almost 100 years ago. But there is in this sentence one tanta-lising pointer to the future. The word translated *coffin* (Hebrew: *'aron*) is the identical word that will appear elsewhere (e.g. Exod. 25.10) to describe the Ark (of the covenant). When the sons of Israel eventually return to Canaan they will be carrying both Joseph's coffin and this Ark. Two boxes, one with the 'bones' of the past, the other with tab-lets containing guidance for the future. Yet perhaps the vitality of the future will depend on the remembering of the past. In his eulogy of the ancestors Ben Sira comments about the judges, *Blessings be on their memory! May their bones send forth new life from the grave! May the fame of the honoured dead be matched by their sons!* (Sir. 46.11–12). Might a similar epitaph be applied to Joseph, certainly in his own eyes? In this book of Genesis or 'beginnings' which has, from its start to its finish, focused on the importance of life, does this box of bones constitute not an end, but the 'seed' for the future?

# Theological reflections

## 1. Joseph, caution and paragon

The wealth of traces of the story of Joseph in extra-biblical religious texts and world literature offers a startling contrast to the compara-tive absence of the story in the rest of the Old Testament.

As regards the Old Testament, the relatively late date of Gen. 37—50 may partly explain the absence. So too may be the association of Joseph with the northern tribes, in view of the southern ('Judaean') bias of most of the Old Testament. But these factors are unlikely to be the whole picture. The ambiguities that we can discover by a careful reading of the story might prompt us to ask the question whether the ultimate purpose of the story of Joseph in Genesis is as a cautionary tale: that it ought to be the path *less* travelled by his descendants. It is a false trail, a dead end, which is only righted when Joseph's descend-ants eventually leave Egypt, and can pick up the story of Abraham, Isaac and Jacob again (Exod. 3.6, 15). Joseph goes wrong through his overwillingness to assimilate to the life and mores of Egypt. Remem-ber how he named his first son 'Making to forget my father's family' (41.51). But it is not simply his understandable desire to forget the painful memories associated with his family that is the problem, it is rather the very nature of the society to which he has nailed his colours. He has bought into a world where royal power is absolute, reinforced by being equated with divinity. He has become part of that ideology. He suggests as much in his words to his brothers during their apparent reconciliation. His elevation to power, previously explicitly stated as being due to Pharaoh (41.41) is now credited by Joseph to God (45.8). Implicitly Pharaoh is God. And this in turn, of course, has implications for how Joseph feels that he can behave towards those for whom he is responsible, the citizens of Egypt. He represents 'God' to them. His absolute power over their lives deprives them of their human dignity (47.18–25). It is a totalitarian vision of the state.

It is interesting to note that the story of the Tower of Babel has been interpreted as the first totalitarianism.[7] It may be significant therefore that just as the primeval story ended with the failed attempt to build Babel, so the ancestral story ends with this other, not dissimilar, failure linked to Joseph. Not that it seemed like failure at the time, at least to Joseph himself: but perhaps the reason that Joseph was so easily forgotten (Exod. 1.8) was that the memories associated with his name were not pleasant. Joseph's vision fostered an idolatry of unity. It did not allow for 'the dignity of difference', that phrase made famous by Rabbi Jonathan Sacks. Rabbi Sacks suggests that the concept of covenant, fundamental to the biblical tradition, is marked specifically by a respect for the difference and dignity of the partners involved. As Exodus will follow Genesis, the covenant at Sinai with its model for organisation of community will follow the autocracy of Egypt.

Comparisons and contrasts have often been drawn between Joseph and various other personalities who appear in the biblical literature. He has been compared with both Solomon and Ezra, and contrasted with Moses and Daniel. None of these comparisons are explicit within the biblical text but they are not unreasonable. Like Joseph they are all portrayed as figures of state who are confronted with 'real politik', and in particular with the need to define the relationship between 'Israel' and the powerful empires that dominated the ancient Middle East, such as Egypt, Babylon and Persia. The story of Joseph may well have been incorporated into Genesis at a point in history when Jewish identity vis-à-vis the Hellenistic world, particularly in Egypt, was a live issue on the theological agenda. How far is assimilation possible, or desirable? How far does it need to be resisted, and at what potential cost to an individual or the community? Should Judaism be following the path of Joseph, or of Moses, or even Joseph's own brother Judah whose story in Gen. 38 and 44 may be designed to provide another counterpoint to him? Joseph may indeed be cast into a pit and a dungeon, but unlike Daniel it is not one that is full of lions, and he does not get thrown into it for refusing to participate in idolatry.

Yet in spite of his absence from other Old Testament books, there are few other biblical characters who have featured so extensively in extra-biblical religious writings and world literature as has Joseph. It starts already in the Apocrypha; although Joseph is only briefly referred to in Ben Sira he is clearly a hero to the author of the Wisdom of Solomon. Wisdom *preserved him from sin and went down into the dungeon with him, nor did she leave him when he was in chains until she had brought him a kingdom's sceptre with authority over his persecutors; she gave the lie to his accusers, and bestowed on him undying fame* (Wisd. 10.13–14). It is interesting that Joseph's 'preservation from sin' seems to be linked to his refusal of the charms of Potiphar's wife. His self-control in this incident becomes an increasingly important dimension in the retellings of his story, and he is seen as an ethical model, keeping *God's commandment* (1 Macc. 2.53).

Not surprisingly Joseph was a popular figure among the Hellenistic Jewish community living in Egypt. As well as the Wisdom of Solomon, he appears in several of the writings of Philo, who is ambiguous about him – on the one hand admiring his chastity and temperance, but on the other suggesting that he was not oblivious to some of the temptations of power. One of the best known extra-biblical retellings linked to the name of Joseph is the romance of *Joseph and Aseneth*, probably dating from slightly before the New Testament period and written in Egypt, in which Joseph is responsible for the conversion to Judaism of Aseneth, the daughter of the Egyptian priest of Heliopolis, before he marries her (compare Gen. 41.50).

Joseph, as the ancestor of the northern tribes, was also an obvious hero for the Samaritan community, although it is difficult to date precisely the Samaritan sources in which he features. It is interesting, however, in this connection, to note Joseph's appearance, along with Abraham and Moses, in Stephen's speech (Acts 7.9–16). His story becomes an example of God's ability to be present with people away from the Temple, and outside the Holy Land. A number of New Testament scholars have seen 'Samaritan influence' on the traditions expressed in this speech, for example the fact that, according to Acts 7.16, all the patriarchs, rather than simply Joseph, are buried at Shechem rather than Hebron.

But it is in the Qur'an and Muslim sources that the figure of Joseph receives some of its most extensive development. Joseph is the one biblical patriarch who has a lengthy connected narrative and complete *sūra* of the Qur'an devoted to him, Sūra 12, titled *Yusuf* ('Of Joseph'), which refers to his adventures as 'the finest of stories' (Sūra 12.3). The outline of the tale of Joseph in Genesis is retold up to the point where Joseph's family come to settle in Egypt, though particular attention is paid to the episode with Potiphar's wife, which is considerably developed, with an 'assembly of ladies' involved all of whom vouch for Joseph's extraordinary beauty. The key to the Qur'an's interest in Joseph is given early in the Sūra, There are, 'many significant things in the story of Joseph and his brothers for those who are of enquiring mind'.[8] Perhaps part of the reason for this interest in Joseph is precisely the theological viewpoint that is implied in Genesis itself by Joseph's comments in 45.7–8 and 50.20, namely the sense of an overarching providence, and of God's sure guidance in human affairs. Joseph's final words in the Qur'anic version of his story include this comment, 'My Lord deals graciously according to His will: for He is ever wise and knowing . . . My Lord, you have brought me to power and made me learned in interpretation of storied things.'[9]

And what of the Christian tradition, and its reflection on the figure of Joseph? Early on in Christian history Joseph became viewed not simply as a model of right behaviour to follow, but also a 'type' of Christ. In the second century AD Melito of Sardis in the hymn *On Pascha* spoke of how Christ was prefigured 'in Joseph sold'. The fact that both Jesus and Joseph were traded for silver facilitated this comparison, as did the way Joseph spent time in the 'pit', particularly in view of the number of psalms which use the 'pit' as a metaphor of death.

In modern times the most extended comparison between Joseph and Christ was that made by Thomas Mann in his novel *Joseph and His Brothers*. This great novel, which covers the life of Jacob as well as Joseph himself, was produced in several parts between 1934 and 1945, a period when Mann was exiled from Germany and when Germany itself was undergoing a sort of passion. One of the features of the novel is that the association between Joseph and Christ broadens out to encompass the entirety of human suffering. In the process resonances of the ancient and archetypal myth of a dying and rising god are incorporated into the story. A mysterious figure (the man whom Joseph meets near Dothan) speaks to Reuben over the empty pit from which Joseph has disappeared and puts it as follows:

I know not what thou understandest by dead and what by living.

*Theological reflections*

Thou hast laughed at the childish elements of things, but yet I may remind thee of the grain of corn when it lieth in the grave, and ask thee how thou thinkest of it in reference to life and death . . . For it is so that the corn falling into the earth and dying bringeth forth much fruit. . . . I saw a youth descend into the grave in garland and festal garment, and above him they slaughtered a beast of the flock, whose blood they let run down, so that it ran all over him and he received it with all his limbs and senses. So that when he ascended again he was divine and had won life – at least for some time to come.[10]

Of course Mann is here reading far more into the story than the bare narrative of Genesis seems to allow, but he has tapped into themes that are embedded deep in the human psyche, and which are hinted at by the biblical writer. The recurrent motif of weeping, for example, that accompanies the gradual reconciliation between Joseph and his brothers (Gen. 42.24; 43.30; 45.2), is a reminder of how often, and how powerfully, tears can be the seed of transformation – and even resurrection. In a book that suggests that life is all-important (50.20) weeping is an essential part. *Those who sow in tears will reap with songs of joy* (Ps. 126.5). We are being told that laughter demands weeping, reaping requires sowing, fertility seems often to be prefaced with sterility, and death is part of the cycle of life.

## 2. A technicolor dreamcoat

Thomas Mann is not the only modern writer to draw creatively on the story of Joseph. In a completely different vein is the musical *Joseph and the Amazing Technicolor Dreamcoat* by Tim Rice and Andrew Lloyd Webber. Its very lightheartedness offers some unexpectedly helpful insights. The delightful cynicism of the brothers' chorus to Jacob after their sale of Joseph, 'There's one more angel in heaven, there's one more star in the sky, Joseph we'll never forget you, it's tough but we're gonna get by!'[11] enables us to cut through the over-familiarity of the biblical text to an appreciation of the outrageous way in which they seek to deceive their father at this point.

Nor is it an accident that the musical has a reference to the 'dreamcoat' in its title. 'This coat', as the brothers say, 'has got our goat.' For the story of the family of Jacob could be said to be dominated by the motif of clothing. It 'carries' the tale, and in this respect Gen. 37—50 is simply making more explicit a motif that has been in evidence since the man and the woman encountered each other in the garden, first naked (2.25), then with loincloths stitched from fig leaves (3.7), and finally with coverings of skins given as a gift by Yʜᴡʜ (3.21). Clothing is a symbol of status (24.53; 37.3; 41.42; 45.22), of transformation (35.2; 37.23; 38.19; 41.14), of deception (27.15; 37.32–33; 38.14; 39.12, 15, 18). Deprived of our clothing we are made vulnerable, and yet our clothing is curse as well as blessing, because it facilitates duplicity. It protects us from a too painful integrity, from our real selves. A few years ago I designed creative worship for Holy Week that focused around the theme of clothing. It was a powerful experience, and given the traditional linkage made between the story of Joseph and the passion of Christ (see above), could also be said to act as commentary on this part of Genesis. Think about the wealth of images: the garments strewed on Palm Sunday, the robe divested and the towel on Maundy Thursday, the purple cloak and crown of thorns at the trial on Good Friday, the discarded grave clothes on Easter Sunday. But think too about what happened later on Good Friday – how the soldiers took the clothes of Jesus, divided them among themselves – and left him to hang on the cross completely naked. Our sanitised representations of the crucifixion (even according to Mel Gibson!) do not allow us to see this. Yet there is deep meaning in that aweful nakedness. The God whom the psalmist celebrated as *clothed with majesty and splendour and enfolded in a robe of light* (Ps. 104.1–2) had first of all divested himself of his heavenly mantle to make it safe for humanity to see him once again (compare Gen. 3.10). But that was not enough. We humans next sought to clothe him with our desires and passions, and veil him again from our sight. The naked power of the cross was God's response. It is then that we are able to see God face to face in all his terrible glory – and live.

Read against this parallel we can see that as the story of Joseph draws to its conclusion we are being told about a *modus vivendi* for humanity rather than an ideal. Nakedness has to be concealed, whether it is physical or emotional or spiritual. Even Jacob's and Joseph's dead bodies have to be protected by embalming and their coffins. In words written for a Good Friday litany, God laments:

> I abandoned my power like a garment,
> choosing your unprotected flesh:
> but you have robed yourselves in privilege,
> and chosen to despise the abandoned.[12]

Do these words read as a judgement on the power and prestige of Joseph?

## 3. The ambiguity remains

In the comments on 45.7–8 and 50.20 (see p. 259 and p. 274) we raised the question as to whether Joseph's 'reading' of his and his brothers' experience was the correct one, whether it was true that God was making use of his brothers' malice towards him for a 'higher purpose'? It is of course a dangerous assumption: think only of some of the more grotesque evils of the twentieth century. To suggest that they somehow happened as a working out of a divine 'greater plan' feels like a mocking blasphemy.

Yet it is also a strangely comforting viewpoint. 'Everything works together for good' is a thought that has given meaning to many human lives. It is not an accident that Islamic tradition has viewed the story of Joseph so favourably: Joseph's own view, taken at face value about what happened and why, resonates strongly with a Muslim theology of history. Certainly one of the developmental threads we have seen running through Genesis has been a sense of trial and error as God experiments with ways of relating to humanity, and Joseph's comments seem to reflect a particular stage on that journey – perhaps not the ultimate stage, but at least the last word as far as the writer of Genesis was concerned. Robert Cohn puts it like this: 'In stages, the divine director retreats from the scene permitting the actors to shape their own world. Finally, equilibrium is achieved as Joseph and his brothers, acting on their own initiative, unwittingly and ironically become the agents of providence.'[13]

Possibly we can allow that thought to stand, but with one caveat. Joseph thinks that he understands God's way of working, and he is keen to tell his brothers so. Perhaps he does, but the problem may be that even if his vision is larger than theirs it is still not large enough. Joseph's god is too small. The God who is YHWH is marked by a refusal to be confined by the boxes that human beings seek to make for him, whether physical, spiritual or intellectual. The particular box that Joseph has constructed for him was too focused on Joseph's own family and his own immediate situation. The ultimate irony of Joseph's remark may be that even while he is right about God's ability to accomplish his purposes, he has failed to realise quite how generous and broad those purposes are. Perhaps Thomas Mann caught something of this, when on the last page of his novel his 'Joseph' admits:

'One can easily be in a story and not understand it. Perhaps that is the way it ought to be and I am to blame myself for always knowing far too well what was being played.'[14]

# NOTES

## Introduction

1 R. N. Whybray, *The Making of the Pentateuch: A Methodological Study*, JSOTSS 53, Sheffield: JSOT Press, 1987.
2 Gerhard Larsson, 'Ancient Calendars Indicated in the OT', *Journal for the Study of the Old Testament* Issue 54 (1992), pp. 61–76, 68.
3 Jeremy Hughes, *Secrets of the Times: Myth and History in Biblical Chronology*, JSOTSS 66, Sheffield: JSOT Press, 1990, p. 234.

## The Story of Beginnings   1.1—6.8

1 Ellen Van Wolde, *Stories of the Beginning: Genesis 1–11 and other Creation Stories*, London: SCM Press, 1996, pp. 132–6.
2 Robert Alter, *Genesis*, New York: W. W. Norton & Company, 1996, p. 8.
3 Carol Ochs, *Song of the Self: Biblical Spirituality and Human Holiness*, Valley Forge, PA: Trinity Press International, 1994, p. 8.
4 Emmanuel Levinas, *Nine Talmudic Readings*, Bloomington, IN: Indiana University Press, 1990, p. 85.
5 Karl Barth, *Church Dogmatics*, English translation, Edinburgh: T. & T. Clark, 1936–1981, III.4, p. 117.
6 Angela Tilby, *Let there be Light: Praying with Genesis*, London: Darton, Longman and Todd, 1989, p. 91.

## The Story of the Flood – and its Aftermath   6.9—11.26

1 Bernhard W. Anderson, *From Creation to New Creation: Old Testament Perspectives* (Overtures to Biblical Theology), Minneapolis: Fortress Press, 1994, p. 72.
2 Ellen Van Wolde, *Stories of the Beginning*, pp. 158–62.
3 Michael Fishbane, *Biblical Text and Texture: A literary Reading of Selected Texts*, Oxford: One World, 1998 p. 38 (originally published by Schocken Books, 1979).

4 Ralph W. Klein, *Israel in Exile* (Overtures to Biblical Theology), Philadelphia: Fortress Press, 1979. See especially pp. 149–54.

5 Trevor Dennis, *Looking God in the Eye*, London: SPCK, 1998, p. 25.

6 Walter Brueggemann, *Genesis*, Atlanta: John Knox Press, 1982, p. 77.

7 Walter Brueggemann, *Genesis*, p. 81.

8 Anonymous poem, quoted in Mark Link, *These Stones will Shout: A New Voice for the Old Testament*, Niles, IL: Argus Communications, 1975, pp. 28–9.

9 Frank Moore Cross, *From Epic to Canon: History and Literature in Ancient Israel*, Baltimore: Johns Hopkins University Press, 2000, p. 1.

10 Frank Moore Cross, *From Epic to Canon*, p. 7.

11 Jacques Ellul, *The Meaning of the City*, Grand Rapids: Eerdmans, 1970.

12 Jonathan Sacks, *The Dignity of Difference: How to Avoid the Clash of Civilizations*, London and New York: Continuum, 2003 (revised edition), p. 53.

*The Story of Abraham    11.27—25.18*

1 T. L. Thompson, *The Historicity of the Patriarchal Narratives: The Quest for the Historical Abraham*. Berlin: W. de Gruyter, 1974.

2 J. Van Seters, *Abraham in History and Tradition*, New Haven: Yale University Press, 1975.

3 Jonathan Magonet, *Bible Lives*, London: SCM Press, 1992, p. 25.

4 David J. A. Clines, *The Theme of the Pentateuch*, Sheffield: Sheffield Academic Press, 1997 (2nd edition), p. 30.

5 Elsa Tamez, quoted in John Goldingay, 'The Place of Ishmael', in Philip R. Davies and David J. A. Clines (editors), *The World of Genesis: Persons, Places, Perspectives*, Sheffield: Sheffield Academic Press, 1998, p. 148.

6 See e.g. Carole R. Fontaine, 'Forgotten Voices of Earth: The Blessing Subjects in Genesis 49', in Normal C. Habel and Shirley Wurst (editors), *The Earth Story in Genesis* (The Earth Bible 2), Sheffield: Sheffield Academic Press, 2000, p. 207.

7 W. Gross, *Glaubensgehorsam als Wagnis der Freiheit. Wir sind Abraham*, Mainz, 1980, p. 6, translated and quoted in Karl-Josef Kuschel, *Laughter: A Theological Reflection*, London: SCM Press, 1994, p. 51.

8 Elie Wiesel, *Messengers of God*, New York: Summit, 1976; Touchstone, 1994, p. 71 (Touchstone edition).

9 Edwin Good, *Irony in the Old Testament*, second edition, Sheffield: The Almond Press, 1981, p. 95.

10 Trevor Dennis, *Sarah Laughed; Women's Voices in the Old Testament*, London: SPCK, 1994, pp. 58–9.

11 Judah Goldin, 'Introduction', in Shalom Spiegel, *The Last Trial: On the Legends and Lore of the Command to Abraham to Offer Isaac as a Sacrifice: The Akedah*, paperback edition, Vermont: Woodstock, 1993, p. xxi.

12 Eric Auerbach, *Mimesis*, Princeton: Princeton University Press, 1953, p. 12.

13 Edwin Good, *Irony in the Old Testament*, p. 96.

14 Gerhard von Rad, *Genesis* (Old Testament Library), London: SCM Press, 1961, revised edition 1972, p. 240 (page references are to the 1972 edition).

15 J. P. Fokkelmann, 'Genesis', in Robert Alter and Frank Kermode, *The Literary Guide to the Bible*, London: Fontana Press, 1989, p. 50.

16 Michael E. W. Thompson, *I Have Heard Your Prayer: The Old Testament and Prayer*, Peterborough: Epworth Press, 1996, p. 17.

17 Robert Alter, *The Art of Biblical Narrative*, New York: Basic Books, 1981, pp. 52–3.

18 Claus Westermann, *Genesis 12-36*, Minneapolis: Augsburg Publishing House, 1985, p. 392.

19 David J. A. Clines, *The Theme of the Pentateuch*, e.g. pp. 114–19.

20 W. Zimmerli, *Man and His Hope in the Old Testament*, London: SCM Press, 1971, p. 68.

21 David Clines, *The Theme of the Pentateuch*, p. 124.

22 Jürgen Moltmann, *Theology of Hope. On the Ground and the Implications of a Christian Eschatology*, London: SCM Press, 1967.

23 W. Zimmerli, 'Promise and Fulfilment', in *Essays on Old Testament Interpretation*, C. Westermann (editor), London: SCM Press, 1963, p. 97.

24 Gabriel Josipovici, *The Book of God: A Response to the Bible*, New Haven: Yale University Press, 1988, pp. 269–70.

25 Karl-Josef Kuschel, *Abraham: A Symbol of Hope for Jews, Christians and Muslims*. London: SCM Press, 1995. pp. 26–7.

26 M. J. Bin-Gorion, *Die Sagen der Juden, Mythen, Legenden, Auslegungen*, Berlin, 1935, p. 268. Quoted and translated in Karl-Josef Kuschel, *Abraham*, p. xi.

27 Harvey Cox, *The Feast of Fools: A Theological Essay on Festivity and*

*Fantasy*, Cambridge, MA: Harvard University Press, 1969, p. 157.

28 Bernard Mandelbaum (editor), *Pesikta de-Rav Kahana*, New York: Jewish Theological Seminary, 1962, 2.451.

29 Elie Wiesel, *Messengers of God*, pp. 95–7 (Touchstone edition).

30 Steven Saltzman, *A Small Glimmer of Light*, Hoboken, NJ: KTAV Publishing House, 1996, p. 56.

31 Carol Delaney, 'Abraham and the Seeds of Patriachy' in *Genesis: A Feminist Companion to the Bible*, Athalya Brenner (editor), Sheffield: Sheffield Academic Press, 1998, p. 149.

32 Phyllis Trible, 'Genesis 22: The Sacrifice of Sarah', in Jason P. Rosenblatt and Joseph C. Sitterson Jr. (editors), *Not in Heaven: Coherence and Complexity in Biblical Narrative* , Bloomington and Indianapolis: Indiana University Press, 1991, pp. 189–91.

33 Trevor Dennis, *Imagining God: Stories from Creation to Heaven*, London: SPCK, 1997, pp. 78–9.

34 Naim S. Ateek, 'Biblical Perspectives on the Land', in *Faith and the Intifada*, ed. Naim Ateek, Marc H. Ellis, Rosemary Radford Ruether, Maryknoll, NY: Orbis, 1992, p. 108.

35 David J. A. Clines, *The Theme of the Pentateuch*, pp. 99–126.

36 Norman C. Habel, *The Land is Mine: Six Biblical Land Ideologies* (Overtures to Biblical Theology), Minneapolis: Fortress Press, 1995. See especially pp. 115–33.

37 Patricia Crone and Michael Cook, *Hagarism: The Making of the Islamic World*, Cambridge: Cambridge University Press, 1977, pp. 8–9.

38 See Pamela Tamarkin Reis, 'Hagar Requited', *Journal for the Study of the Old Testament*, Issue 87, March 2000, pp. 75–109.

39 Shin Shalom (Joseph Shapira Shalom) as translated in *Forms of Prayer for Jewish Worship*, The Assembly of Rabbis of the Reform Synagogues of Great Britain, Vol. III (Prayers for the High Holy Days), London, 1985, p. 891.

*The Story of Jacob     25.19—36.43*

1 David M. Gunn and Danna Nolan Fewell, *Narrative in the Hebrew Bible*, Oxford: Oxford University Press, 1993, p. 109.

2 Robert Alter, *The Art of Biblical Narrative*, p. 53.

3 Karen Armstrong, *In the Beginning: A New Reading of the Book of Genesis*, London: HarperCollins Publishers, 1996, p. 77.

4 Robert Alter, *Genesis*, New York and London: W. W. Norton & Company, 1996, p. 158.

5 Heather A. McKay, 'Jacob Makes It Across the Jabbok. An Attempt to Solve the Success/Failure Ambivalence in Israel's Self-consciousness', *Journal for the Study of the Old Testament*, Issue 38, June 1987, pp. 3–13.
6 J. P. Fokkelman, *Narrative Art in Genesis*, Amsterdam: Van Gorcum, Assen, 1975, p. 188.
7 Gerhard von Rad, *Genesis*, p. 325.
8 Roland Barthes, 'The Struggle with the Angel: Textual Analysis of Genesis 32:23–33', in Barthes et al. (editors), *Structural Analysis and Biblical Exegesis: Interpretational Essays*, Pittsburgh: Pickwick, 1974, pp. 21–33.
9 J. P. Fokkelmann, 'Genesis', in Robert Alter and Frank Kermode, *The Literary Guide to the Bible*, p. 51.
10 Carl Gustav Jung, *Answer to Job* (English translation), London and New York: Routledge, Routledge Classics, 2002, p. 115.
11 Robert Alter, *Genesis*, p. 187.
12 Lyn M. Bechtel, 'What if Dinah is not Raped? (Genesis 34), in John W. Rogerson (editor), *The Pentateuch: A Sheffield Reader*, Sheffield: Sheffield Academic Press, 1996, pp. 263–80.
13 Elie Wiesel, *Messengers of God*, pp. 106–7.
14 J. Neville Ward, *The Use of Praying*, Epworth Press, 1967, p. 158.
15 C. S. Lewis, *The Lion, the Witch and the Wardrobe*, London: Geoffrey Bles, 1950, Lions, 1980, p. 75.
16 Trevor Dennis, *Looking God in the Eye*, pp. 81–2.
17 Elie Wiesel, *Messengers of God* p. 132.
18 This story is generally ascribed to 'Jewish tradition', although it is impossible to link definitively to any rabbinic source. However Professor Alexander Scheiber of Budapest devoted a number of special studies to the history of the legend. According to Scheiber's researches, the earliest attestation of the story appears in the writings of Alphonse de Lamartine, a French author who claims to have heard it from the mouth of an Arab peasant during a journey through the Holy Land in 1832. It may therefore in fact originate in Muslim or Christian circles. See comments by Eliezer Segal http://www.acs.ucalgary.ca/~elsegal/Shokel/940505_Pal_Midrash.html
19 Elias Chacour, *We Belong to the Land*, Collegeville: University of Notre Dame Press, 2001, pp. 46–7.

*The Story of Joseph and his Brothers   37.1—50.26*

1  Walter Bruggemann, *Genesis*, pp. 328–9.
2  Jon Levenson, *The Death and Resurrection of the Beloved Son: The Transformation of Child Sacrifice in Judaism and Christianity*, New Haven and London: Yale University Press, 1993, p. 163.
3  Aaron Wildavsky, *Assimilation versus Separation*, New Brunswick and London: Transaction Publishers, 1993, p. 159.
4  Aaron Wildavsky, *Assimilation versus Separation*, p. 163.
5  Nahum M. Sarna, *Genesis* (JPS Torah commentary), Philadelphia: Jewish Publication Society, 1989, p. 343.
6  Karen Armstrong, *In the Beginning: A New Reading of the Book of Genesis*, p. 113.
7  Rabbi Naftali Zvi Yehudah Berlin, quoted in Jonathan Sacks, *The Dignity of Difference*, p. 52.
8  Kenneth Cragg, *Readings in the Qur'an*, London: Collins, 1988, p. 130.
9  Kenneth Cragg, *Readings in the Qur'an*, pp. 136–7.
10  Thomas Mann, *Joseph and His Brothers*, London: Vintage, 1999, pp. 415–16.
11  Tim Rice (words), Andrew Lloyd Webber (music), *Joseph and the Amazing Technicolor Dreamcoat*, London: The Really Useful Group Ltd, 1991, pp. 31–42.
12  Janet Morley, in *Bread of Tomorrow: Praying with the World's Poor*, edited by Janet Morley, London: SPCK/Christian Aid, 1992, p. 101.
13  Robert L. Cohn, 'Narrative Structure and Canonical Perspective in Genesis', in John W. Rogerson (editor), *The Pentateuch: A Sheffield Reader*, Sheffield: Sheffield Academic Press, 1996, p. 102.
14  Thomas Mann, *Joseph and His Brothers*, p. 1207.